Q & A SERIES

JURISPRUDENCE

THIRD EDITION

LB Curzon

Cavendish
Publishing
Limited

London • Sydney

Third edition first published in Great Britain 2001 by Cavendish Publishing Limited, The Glass House, Wharton Street, London WC1X 9PX, United Kingdom

Telephone: +44 (0)20 7278 8000

Facsimile: +44 (0)20 7278 8080

Email: info@cavendishpublishing.com

Website: www.cavendishpublishing.com

© Curzon, LB   2001
First edition   1992
Second edition   1995
Third edition   2001

British Library Cataloguing in Publication Data

Curzon, LB (Leslie Basil), 1921–
Jurisprudence – 3rd ed – (Q&A series)
1 Jurisprudence
I Title
340

ISBN 1 85941 623 3

Printed and bound in Great Britain

PREFACE

This collection of Questions and Answers has as its objective the provision of structured material designed to assist students preparing for first examinations in Jurisprudence. The mode of presentation adopted involves the setting of a question of the type often asked in examinations of this nature, and the providing of an appropriate answer. The answers are not to be considered as 'model answers'; they are intended specifically as illustrations of the type of answer required, with particular reference to content and structure.

The format is as follows:

Introduction to chapter. This indicates the subject matter to be covered by the questions.

Checklist. The relevant jurisprudential concepts to be tested are noted. They should be learned or revised carefully before the answer presented is considered.

Question. The rubric and its specific demands should be studied carefully. 'Comment', 'Critically examine', 'Outline', are not interchangeable terms; each requires its own pattern of answering.

Answer plan. This indicates the approach which is taken to the question and suggests a skeleton plan which is followed. Students should consider the advisability of planning an answer in this form; the production of a skeleton plan is a useful method of arranging content.

Answer. Content and structure are of major significance and ought to be noted carefully.

Notes. Details of suggested reading are given under this heading. Students who require guidance in the choice of reading material might consider the following texts: Harris' *Legal Philosophies*; Freeman's *Introduction to Jurisprudence*; Hart's *The Concept of Law*; Dworkin's *Law's Empire*; Davies and Holdcroft's *Jurisprudence – Texts and Commentary*. Useful adjunctive material may be found in Kelly's *A Short History of Western Legal Theory*; *The Western Idea of Law*, edited by Smith and Weisstrub; *Philosophy of Law*, edited by Feinberg and Gross; *The Nature and Process of Law*, edited by Smith. (Only the most up-to-date editions should be used.)

In this third edition, material used in the previous edition has been revised and new questions appear relating to the jurisprudential thought of Cardozo, Cicero, Dworkin, Fuller, Posner, Radbruch, Stephen and Unger.

LB Curzon
January 2001

CONTENTS

TABLE OF CASES

TABLE OF STATUTES

GENERAL ASPECTS OF JURISPRUDENCE

Introduction

Questions in this chapter deal with some typical introductory topics which are related to the general framework of jurisprudence. The nature of the subject area is of particular significance. Questions of the place of logic in our law are touched on. The 'open-ended' type of question is often considered appropriate to this area of the syllabus.

Checklist

Ensure that you are acquainted with the following topics:
- definitions of jurisprudence
- general scope of the study
- induction and deduction
- jurimetrics

- analogies
- the problem of 'definition'
- definition of 'logic'
- the syllogism

Question 1

'For those who study jurisprudence today, it is nothing but a troubling mass of conflicting ideas': Arnold.

Why, then, study the subject?

Answer plan

The question is an invitation to argue on the positive features of jurisprudence in reply to Arnold's dismissive comment. A discussion of those features is required, together with comment on reasons for the contemporary (but not unwelcome) conflict of ideas. A skeleton plan might take the following form:

Introduction – acknowledgement of conflict of ideas in jurisprudence – positive features of a study of the subject – why criticisms have arisen – conclusion on the role jurisprudence has to play.

Answer

It is necessary, initially, to comment briefly on Arnold's statement by noting what seems to be a highly subjective and not uncommon reaction to the undoubted ferment of opinions, principles and ideologies characterising contemporary jurisprudence. It may be that the emergence of a jurisprudential tradition of questioning everything, of accepting no 'self-evident' principles, of 'debunking' ideas which have held sway for decades, and 'deconstructing' hallowed theories, creates an impression of a nihilism triumphant. Arnold's use of pejorative terms, such as 'troubling', 'conflicting', may indicate a lack of awareness of the value of a continuous probing of 'received knowledge'. So it is in other contemporary disciplines: consider physics (in which the recent appearance of 'string theory' demands a rethinking of traditional concepts), economics (in which not only traditional theories but the very reasoning processes that produced them are under attack) and linguistics (in which the works of the 'founding fathers', such as Chomsky, are under intensive criticism). And so it is in jurisprudence where, for example, the American Critical Legal Studies movement is engaged in a radical reappraisal of the objectives and methodology of legal studies, and the 'Law-Economics' movement perceives some aspects of economic theory as of direct relevance to jurisprudential analysis. The continuous flux in the evolution and enunciation of legal theories must, by its nature, give rise to conflict, which observers, such as Arnold, find 'troubling'. The alternative to a conflict of ideas can be a lack of vitality or a sterility which vitiates intellectual progress in jurisprudence.

One must be aware, however, that a study of jurisprudence is not considered an essential component of the education and training programmes of large numbers of lawyers. Concentration by some jurists on highly abstract theorising, to the exclusion of the severely practical concerns of the law, may have contributed to suspicion of the subject and a rejection of its pretensions. Posner's condemnation of much recent jurisprudence as 'much too solemn and self-important' and of its votaries as writing 'too marmoreal, hieratic, and censorious a prose' is worthy of note.

Much of the true value of jurisprudence resides elsewhere than in the day-to-day practical applications of the law. It is claimed that its study provides a discipline of thought which seeks not to ignore the realities of legal practice, but rather to give added dimension to an understanding of those realities. Jurisprudence offers an overall view of the law, a unified and systematic picture, in which the nature of legal institutions and theories becomes more comprehensible. Austin viewed jurisprudence as providing a 'map' of the law which presents it as 'a system or organic whole'.

Some legal scholars and students have found a major attraction of jurisprudence to be its intrinsic interest, which emerges from the importance of the perennial questions with which it deals. 'What are human rights?', 'Are there any absolute values in the law?', 'What is justice?' These problems exemplify matters which have been raised over the centuries by philosophers and jurists. Not only the content of legislation and the administration of legal institutions, but the basis of society itself, have been affected by attempts to answer questions of this nature. They are of abiding human interest.

The intellectual discipline required for a study of this area of thought must be of a high order. Intensive, systematic analysis, the ability to exercise one's critical faculties, and to engage in a continuous questioning of one's own basic assumptions – all can be heightened by a study of jurisprudence. The intellectual skills required to see into the essence of current arguments which turn, for example, on 'the right to silence', 'the value of the jury', 'the presumption of innocence', can be sharpened by a consideration of legal theorising.

The study of jurisprudence should enlarge one's perception of the patterns of fact and thought from which today's legal structures have emerged. Specifically, awareness of the evolution of legal thought provides a key to an understanding of *change* as a basic phenomenon of the law. It is the continuous shifting of views and the transformation of social institutions which tend to be reflected in jurisprudence – and which give rise to the deep conflicts which trouble many observers, such as Arnold. The ability to perceive a process of change beneath the apparently static processes of the law can be intensified by jurisprudential analysis. It is of interest to note the recognition of change which emerged in the decision of the House of Lords in *Page v Smith* (1995) and in which could be discerned a modification of views concerning nervous shock and tort – an area in which there has been much jurisprudential speculation and debate. The War Crimes Act 1991 was preceded by wide-ranging debates which turned on important aspects of legal theory, involving changing social attitudes towards crime, punishment, and retribution. A shift of emphasis in the role of forseeability and intent in assault, which has formed the basis of much recent jurisprudential debate was evident in the decision of the House of Lords in *R v Savage* (1991). Perception of the law as an aspect of a changing social environment and attitudes characterises much contemporary juristic thinking, particularly evident in cases involving 'the right to life': see, for example, the decision of the Court of Appeal in *Re A (Children)* (2000), in which the court was asked to pronounce on the lawfulness of the surgical separation of conjoined twins.

Additionally, awareness of change and its reflection in legal theory, may enable jurists to note, and perhaps warn against, the invisible, unacknowledged, yet extremely potent influence of 'defunct scribblers' who continue to affect the thoughts and the activities of those 'practical persons' who have 'no time for theorising'. Jurists and philosophers have pointed out the significance of the paradox that those who affect to reject theory are, effectively, embracing it. The statement, 'I don't need any legal theory to tell me that violence can be met effectively only by a law which sanctions counter-violence', is, in fact, the expression of a basic, complex theory. The belief, 'You haven't to be a theoretician to know that the law has no place in family relationships', implies acceptance, consciously or unconsciously, of a profound analysis of functions of law. A study of the growth and social context of legal theory makes clear the relationship of theory and practice, the one modifying the other.

The very wide range of contemporary jurisprudence has enlarged its relevance and interest. The days when legal theory was equated with an implied rejection of the significance of 'problems of the real world' have gone. The figure of the jurist as a recluse, uninterested in law in action, is now seen as mere caricature. Modern jurists include many who demonstrate a profound concern for social justice and communal harmony – this is obvious in the writings of contemporary American legal theoreticians. Dworkin, for example, argues cogently that the real purpose of the law can be found in the aim of ensuring that a community acts towards *all* its members in a 'coherent, principled fashion'. Rawls proposes acceptance of a public conception of justice which must constitute the fundamental character of any well-ordered human association. Nozick lays stress on the importance of using principles of justice so as to clarify problems inherent in the holding and transferring of society's resources. It may be that a pattern of concern has now emerged in which the responsibilities of the law, its theoreticians and practitioners, are clearly emphasised, a pattern which is in clear contrast to the implications of Arnold's perception of a 'chaotic' jurisprudence.

Where jurists survey the established socio-legal order, their jurisprudential analysis is often of significance for students of the law who are a part of that order, and whose perceptions of law as an instrument of social policy are thereby challenged. One type of perception relates generally to the relationship between jurisprudence and other disciplines. Because modern jurisprudence ranges very widely over society and because it builds some of its theoretical framework on material derived from contact with other disciplines, students are brought to an awareness of the interdependence of *all* social studies and to acceptance of the complex nature of their own place within the social framework – a positive step which belies the negative nature of Arnold's comment.

The role of the lawyer within our society – and it is that to which many law students aspire – is the subject of continuing analysis by jurists, with the result that the very rationale of the legal profession in the Western world has become a matter of debate and can no longer be taken for granted – a valuable event in itself. Thus, Luban has investigated facets of the role of the lawyer as 'partisan advocate' – a creature of the common law adversarial system. He believes that the standard view of the role of the lawyer, based on principles of 'partnership and non-accountability' in some respects, may no longer be acceptable to society save in a highly qualified form. He calls for a more intensive debate on professional ethics as they relate to the individual conscience and socio-legal institutions and suggests that the lawyer acts as a 'broker of the conspiracy at the centre of the legal system' – a conspiracy between citizens and legal institutions, each acting within defined areas so as to maximise power. Jurisprudential analysis of this nature is thought-provoking and valuable.

Perhaps the most important product of a study of jurisprudence emerges in an enhanced ability to discern the shape of legal things to come, albeit in shadowy and inchoate form. The attitudes of today's legal theoreticians in relation to matters such as *mens rea*, causation, the concept of economic loss in tort, the basis of property rights, and the nature of parental responsibility, might mark tomorrow's ideologies and legal structures. A study of the modes of thought of contemporary jurists contemplating 'the destination of the law' cannot but be advantageous to those who have an interest in the future of society and the law.

None of these comments should be taken, however, as denying the existence of trivial, often worthless, theorising in the name of jurisprudence. Feinberg's objections to 'portentous and hoary figures from the past' being paraded, each with an odd vocabulary, and a host of dogmatic assertions, to the confusion of students, are not to be ignored. These objections may add weight to Arnold's complaint. But interest in the past for its own sake has little appeal to lawyers or students. *'Jurisprudence for its own sake'* is now almost a meaningless slogan. Jurisprudence has changed its objectives and its methodology. The search for justice in human relationships, the search for certainty in the law and the continuous probing of the role of the State in the recognition, promulgation, and enforcement of human rights are rarely absent from legal theorising. The result is a challenging of entrenched positions and narrow certainties, and a questioning of the hitherto unquestionable. This is, indeed, a sign of 'conflict'; but it is also a sign of vitality.

When Stone wrote of the science of jurisprudence as 'the lawyer's extraversion ... the light derived from present knowledge in disciplines other than the law', he acknowledged the structures of legal theory as being linked totally with other studies, thus proclaiming the relevance of jurisprudence to life in general and everyday law in particular.

In that sense, a study of jurisprudence can be valuable in that it ensures perceptions of the law in the setting of a comprehensible, changing world. At times, these perceptions will appear, in Arnold's words, as 'a troubling mass of conflicting ideas', chaotic and often contradictory. But this is not necessarily a negative or undesirable state of affairs, for it is in the attempted resolution of apparent contradictions that the study of jurisprudence can be advanced.

Notes

Valuable material concerning this question may be found in Freeman's edition of Lloyd, *Introduction to Jurisprudence*, Chapter 1; Dias, *Jurisprudence*, Chapter 1; and Posner, *The Problems of Jurisprudence*. Luban's *Lawyers and Justice* is stimulating; D'Amato's *Jurisprudence, a Descriptive and Normative Analysis of Law* contains introductory chapters of unusual interest. Lord Goff's 'The search for principle', in *Proceedings of the British Academy* (1983), contains interesting critical observations concerning jurisprudence.

Question 2

Is there any value to be derived from attempts to define 'jurisprudence'?

Answer plan

The general difficulties involved in definition, as outlined by Popper, should be mentioned. The specific problem, related to jurisprudence, arises from the difficulty of attempting a precise, inclusive and formal definition. The process of defining a term should be mentioned and attention drawn to the advantages emerging from the effort to define. It is of importance to refer to some of the many 'authoritative' definitions. A skeleton plan on the following lines is suggested.

Introduction – note the essence of the problem and indicate the value of a search for a definition – basic difficulty of defining 'by characteristics' – consideration of some definitions – advantages of pursuing a search – objections to the process – conclusion on the positive nature of attempting to define.

Answer

Attempts to define jurisprudence are made by jurists for whom the delineation of its proper subject matter is seen as a fundamental task, and by teachers and students anxious to recognise, even in imprecise terms, the general range and boundaries of their subject area. Linguists and jurists are aware of the problems inherent in the technique of defining terms; students may be confronted, at an early stage of their quest, by warnings as to the 'misguided and misleading' nature of the search for definitions. Our comments concerning the value of attempts to define will note the difficulties of the process, but will stress the importance of the arguments of those who assume that the nature of jurisprudence *is* knowable and amenable to precise description, or definition. We shall emphasise the value to be derived from exploring those paths which might lead to an acceptable definition.

By 'definition', we have in mind a precise enunciation of the principal characteristics of the defined object which will allow it to be distinguished from other objects. It will mark out boundaries, or other limits, thus enabling us to state with a high degree of accuracy that, for example, 'a tort is ...', 'possession means ...', 'a contract comes into existence when ...'. There are, however, basic problems involved in the process of defining 'by characteristics'. Popper, the philosopher of scientific method, rejects in their entirety arguments for the 'value' of definitions; he sees these arguments as involving no more than 'infinite regressions', so that controversies concerning the 'correctness' of a definition can lead only to empty discussions about words. Consider, for example, the definition of 'alienation' as 'an exercise of the power of disposing of or transferring property'. Popper would dismiss this as, at best, mere tautology, or, at worst, a collection of words which demand further elucidation. What is the meaning of 'exercise', 'power', 'transferring'? Consider, next, Holland's apparently simple definition of 'jurisprudence' as 'the formal science of positive law'. The terms which make up the defining formula ('formal', 'positive', etc) require, according to Popper, further specific definition, with the result that an infinite regression seems likely to follow on any definition based on a collection of terms.

Hart, in that section of *The Concept of Law* (1961) entitled 'Definition', raises a general predicament facing those who seek to define any terms in law. He follows the philosopher, Wittgenstein, who states that 'the meaning of a word is its *use* in the language'. We will understand the meaning of terms such as 'jurisprudence', 'motive', 'duty', by considering the ways in which these terms are put to use in the language. Hart suggests that the content of legal vocabulary can be clarified only by a consideration of the conditions under which statements in which particular terms have their 'characteristic use' are true. Consider, for example, the word 'duty', defined by some jurists as 'an obligation under the law, related to recognition of another's rights'. Hart would ask that the usage of the term be examined in statements, such as: 'Employers have a duty to carry out the provisions of the National Minimum Wage Act 1998'; 'We have a duty to pay income tax'; 'Society has a duty to help those who are unable to help themselves.' It becomes necessary, Hart argues, to examine the standard uses of the relevant expressions and the way in which these depend on a social context, itself often left unstated. Hence, statements such as 'Jurisprudence is an examination of the interface of legislation and communal activities' or 'Jurisprudence seeks to lay bare the class nature of law and its practices', require a careful examination of the *precise usage of the separate terms* which make up these sentences.

Other problems must be taken into account by those seeking to define legal terms. The shifting nature of words, changes in their meanings and in perception of their 'significance', make verbal analysis a difficult matter. Hence, it is argued, the precision required in order to define becomes virtually impossible. Thus, attempts to define 'dishonesty', following the decision in *R v Ghosh* (1982), have become very difficult. Doubts as to the meaning of the word 'natural' in expressions such as 'natural justice' remain even after frequent and complex attempts at definition. Further, given advances in epistemology – the theory of knowledge and its methods and validation – how ought we to interpret the vital word 'knowledge' in Wortley's definition of jurisprudence as 'the knowledge of law in its various forms and manifestations'? When Cross defines jurisprudence as 'the study of a lawyer's fundamental assumptions', what weight is to be placed on the ambiguous adjective, 'fundamental'?

Notwithstanding these and other problems arising from verbal analysis and an expanding subject area, 'useful' definitions are plentiful. Their usefulness rests, for the student, in their power to point an inquirer in certain directions, and to adumbrate, even in a rough manner only, the essential features of the field of study. Such definitions range from the prosaic ('the skill or knowledge of law': Cotgrave) to the lapidary ('the knowledge of things divine and human, the knowledge of the just and unjust': Ulpian); from the terse ('the scientific analysis of the law's essential principles': Allen) to the verbose ('any careful and sustained thinking about any phase of things legal, if the thinking seeks to reach beyond the practical solution of an immediate problem in hand': Llewellyn). Definitions of this type represent the continuing, valuable attempts of jurists to determine the essential qualities and characteristics of a subject area.

An attempt to define jurisprudence may be of particular value if the processes involved are *systematic*, that is, if they are related to an identifiable objective and necessitate a search for unique and characteristic qualities. This demands awareness of the vast area of knowledge subsumed under the general heading of 'jurisprudence'. There is no other area of legal studies which is so extensive. Indeed, with the possible exception of 'philosophy' itself, there can be few divisions of knowledge with such a wide-ranging content as that of jurisprudence. A glance at a bibliography of jurisprudence can be a sobering experience, for few areas of knowledge seem at first sight to be outside the scope of the jurist's studies. Politics, sociology, economics, ethics, semantics, psychology – all impinge on the literature of jurisprudential thought. The search for a definition of jurisprudence must, therefore, take into account a wide variety of human experience and must attempt to exclude the totally irrelevant. The search for relevant characteristics and qualities cannot but be valuable in itself for those seeking to comprehend the overall basis of the subject.

The search for a base upon which a definition might be erected ought to produce a growing awareness of disciplinary inter-relationships. At first sight, it would seem, for example, that the connections between recent advances in the study of the neuronic basis of motor activity in the human body, and the concepts of 'motivation' and 'intention' in the criminal law, are very slight. Research has suggested, however, the existence of connecting links between our physical nature as reflected in brain activity, and our subjective goals – the very stuff of some areas of jurisprudential speculation. The changing concepts of the nature of property, in relation to issues of social responsibility, as reflected in the work of Reich, Glendon and Gray, the mounting dissatisfaction with the M'Naghten Rules when considered in the context of current research into mental trauma, exemplify the bonds between seemingly disparate disciplines, the significance of which will emerge swiftly in any methodical attempt to study the dimensions of the 'concept field' of today's jurisprudence prior to attempting a precise definition. The essential unity of all knowledge is mirrored in the contributory sources of legal theory, so that those who seek for a comprehensive definition would reject as facile a definition of jurisprudence as 'a study of the workings of a legal system'.

The attempt to construct an adequate definition of jurisprudence will necessitate an examination of some of the better-known examples. This activity can provide a profound insight into the significance of historical context for an understanding of some aspects of legal theory. Consider the celebrated definition attributed to Ulpian ('the knowledge of things divine and human ...'). Here is language used in a fashion which represents clearly the manner in which a third-century Roman jurist and imperial official conceptualised his world. Pound, writing in 20th century America, and defining jurisprudence as 'a consideration of the ethical and social merits of legal rules', reflects the mores and aspirations of an important social and intellectual group within that country. Legal theories and definitions are not produced *in vacuo*: hence, the search for a definition can lead to a valuable consideration of the historical circumstances which have attended the growth of those theories.

A further valuable product of the quest for definition may emerge in deepened understanding of the long *pattern of development* which has produced modern jurisprudence. Each generation of legal thinkers stands on the shoulders of its predecessors. ('In a sense, we are all Epigones': Wundt.) The definitions favoured by one generation do not appear spontaneously, but are often rooted in the legal and social complexities of previous eras. Thus, attempts by the American positivists of the early 20th century to define jurisprudence in instrumental terms indicate the *evolution* of legal thought as part of a continuing line of theoretical analysis. Awareness of this aspect of legal thought is deepened by an examination of comparative definitions.

Reference was made above to objections raised against the very process of definition as applied to jurisprudence, in particular to the difficulties held to be insuperable in relation to 'infinite regressions'. Allied to these objections, and arising from the difficulties of the process, is the condemnation of the search for definition as a *diversion* from the more important task of discovering 'the rational interdependence and ultimate significance' of legal thought. Definitions of jurisprudence, it is suggested, can be no more than highly subjective reactions to phenomena, which add little, if anything, to our understanding of the 'true' objective nature of those phenomena. Concentration upon description or definition is seen as removing attention from the coherence of theory. (It is not made clear, however, in what sense description vitiates coherence of thought.)

In 1913, Vinogradoff, who was then Professor of Jurisprudence at Oxford, voiced his objections to the use – or place – of definition in the process of studying jurisprudence. His arguments continue to be in use today. Vinogradoff argues that definitions given at the outset of a course of study may impose on students, who have only vague ideas at this stage, patterns of thought which they tend to accept passively, largely because of the dogmatic mode of assertion common to definitions. Definitions ought to emerge towards the *end* of a course of study as a natural reaction to the conflict of ideas which characterises jurisprudence. In our day, Olivecrona has stated that it is impossible to start *from* a definition, since that would involve a *petitio principii* (the logical fallacy of 'begging the question'). Before a definition can be reached, he states, the constituents of a body of knowledge must be analysed.

One may reply in terms which, in themselves, constitute arguments for the value to be derived from attempting to define jurisprudence. Vinogradoff's argument seems to be directed essentially against the manner in which definitions are utilised in the teaching of the subject. The point at which definitions ought to be introduced into a course of study depends on pedagogical principles – it cannot be determined solely by the nature of the object of study. It has been found possible in many cases to attempt a preliminary definition at a very early stage of one's studies and to modify it repeatedly, where that is necessary, so as to reflect one's increasing awareness of the complexities of the subject area. This will involve attention to content, links between concepts and the unique nature of some of those concepts – an important activity in juristic investigation.

We summarise the value of a methodical attempt to define jurisprudence in the following terms: it involves a useful examination of the wide area of the subject matter; it necessitates investigations of the interconnections of content; it reinforces the significance of the historical context of legal theories; it deepens appreciation of the continuing, evolutionary pattern of legal thought; it necessitates a rigorous testing and amendment of formulations. If the search for a definition of jurisprudence be considered as a 'journey' for the legal student, it may be better, perhaps, to 'travel rather than to arrive'. If the ultimate destination be comprehension of the major areas of jurisprudence, then the journey towards a definition can be considered not as leading to a terminus, but rather to a milestone marking a point from which further travel will be necessary. It is the *continuing processes* involved in definition which are valuable as tools for analytical investigation.

Notes

Popper's classic essay, 'Two kinds of definitions', is reprinted in Miller's selection, *A Pocket Popper*. Dias, Chapter 1, deals with definition in jurisprudence, as does Hart's essay 'Definition and theory in jurisprudence'. Moles comments on Hart's analysis in

Definition and Rule in Legal Theory: A Reassessment of HLA Hart.
Vinogradoff's arguments are set out in his *Common Sense in Law*,
Chapter 1. An interesting exposition of problems related to the
analysis of legal terminology is given by Shuman in *Jurisprudence
and the Analysis of Fundamental Legal Terms.*

Question 3

Comment on the role of formal logic in English law.

Answer plan

It is important to differentiate 'formal logic' and 'legal reasoning'.
The former involves a scientific approach to problems of induction
and deduction; the latter is an imprecise description of a common
attitude to the determination of a legal dispute. The answer ought
to show how far formal logic is used in a judgment, and attention
should be directed to some of the problems involved in attempts
to apply a rigid system of rules to legal procedure. The following
skeleton plan is used as a framework for the answer:

> Introduction – definition of logic – its restricted use in law –
> the Aristotelian *syllogism* – inflexibility of formal logic –
> reasoning in adjudication – references in judgments to logic
> – argument by analogy – logic and prevention of
> inconsistency – arguments concerning logic and control –
> Dewey's warning on logic and law – the danger of
> abandoning logic in the law – conclusion referring to the
> 'Hand formula' and jurimetrics.

Answer

We define logic, for the purposes of this answer, as a science that is
concerned with the canons and criteria of validity in thought and
demonstration. It is a methodology, a technique, enabling
conclusions to be drawn from information presented in a specific,
prescribed manner. In English law, it plays a restricted role and is
never used as the sole rationale of a legal decision, so that it is

unlikely for a judgment to rest on the belief that the 'plaintiff has demonstrated the logical superiority of his case'. Almost invariably, its use is qualified, as will be illustrated below. Reference will be made to those who believe that an extended use of logic, as the basis of a scientific approach to the law, is desirable.

There are several different types of logic; in Europe, Aristotelian logic is dominant. Aristotle taught that logic was 'the science of sciences', that is, a methodological introduction to the other sciences. It necessitated 'thinking about thinking' and involved a system of rules by which deductive thought might be represented and analysed. The essence of deduction involves the derivation of a conclusion from a set of statements ('premises'). Aristotle advocated the use of the syllogism – a formal scheme of demonstration. A simple example is as follows: (1) All A is B; (2) Some C is A; (3) Therefore, some C is B. There are here three 'categorical propositions', containing only three terms (A, B and C), with each of the terms appearing in two statements. (By comparison, 'inductive logic' involves reasoning from particular statements to a general truth.)

The rules of logic are precise, inflexible and systematic. They are, therefore, incapable of modification to suit particular circumstances. 'Logic with a changing content' is a contradiction in terms. To seek to modify the rigid rules of logic is as unproductive as an attempt to solve a problem in terms of Euclidean geometry by 'changing' Euclid's fundamental propositions. Hence, syllogistic reasoning is not always adequate for the representation or solution of a problem in English law, and, save for some trivial matters, it is rarely possible to compress the essence of a complex legal problem within the unyielding framework of a formal syllogism. Indeed, if the schemes of formal logic *were* applicable to the analysis and resolution of disputes, then settlement would be possible in a mechanical way without the intervention of legal procedures. X's dispute with Y arising from Y's alleged invasion of X's property rights might be resolved swiftly and correctly by reference to an exact, immutable system of logical propositions. It is precisely because this *cannot* be done that the process of adjudication becomes necessary.

This is not to say that the use of 'reasoning' has merely a minor role in the legal process. But 'reasoning' and the application of formal logic must be differentiated. Thus, a judicial decision which is clearly 'unreasonable', that is, irrational, will not stand – a principle enunciated in *Associated Provincial Picture Houses Ltd v Wednesbury Corp* (1948); a finding which 'flies in the face of the facts' would be difficult to sustain. This is far removed, however, from situations in which purely formal logic is used in the solution of a problem. Strict logical rules cannot be utilised to 'make' decisions in English law, if only because the disputed facts are often imprecise and 'untidy' and cannot be presented in the exact form required for the exercise of those rules. Thus, in a decision of the House of Lords (*Hammersmith and Fulham LBC v Monk* (1991)), the question was whether a periodic tenancy held by two or more joint tenants was determinable by a valid notice to quit given by one joint tenant without the knowledge or consent of the other(s). The facts were not always precise and the House did attempt to reason from ordinary contractual principles. But the train of logic which had led from consideration of one precedent to another and which did suggest that one joint tenant *could* validly end a tenancy, was halted when reference was made to a statement to the contrary in *Howson v Buxton* (1928). This was considered and rejected as having 'insufficient weight'. Other matters than purely logical principles have to be taken into account.

References are made occasionally within a judgment to the significance of logic, but generally within a wider context, for example, public policy, social concerns. In *R v Gotts* (1992), the House of Lords decided that duress was *not* available as a defence to a charge of attempted murder. Lord Jauncey asked: 'Is there logic in affording the defence of duress to one who intends to kill but fails, and denying it to one who mistakenly kills intending only to injure? ... I can see no justification in logic, morality or law in affording to an attempted murderer the defence which is withheld from a murderer.' It is of significance, however, that these remarks were preceded by reference to 'the pervading climate of violence and terrorism'. Lord Jauncey was placing his reference to logic within a setting of social facts and desirable policies. Similarly, in *R v R* (1991), in which the House of Lords decided that a husband could be criminally liable for raping his wife, the matter was approached by means of a logical interpretation of the word 'unlawful' as used in s 1 of the Sexual

Offences Act 1956, and s 1 of the Sexual Offences (Amendment) Act 1974. But it was preceded by an important observation on historical and social change: the status of women had changed in recent years out of all recognition, so that marriage is to be regarded now as a partnership of equals. Again, purely logical reasoning is taken into account *together with* interpretations of social realities.

The use of 'reasoning by analogy' which is prevalent in English law and which, if it is to be in accord with the rules of formal logic, demands the application of rules in exact style, illustrates a general departure from the strictness of those rules. Analogy arises from a process of arguing from similarity in known respects to similarity in other respects. 'Running a country is like running a ship – the crew must obey the captain' – here is an analogy involving perceived similarities. Cast in formal terms, argument by analogy may be stated thus: 'X has certain elements, P, Q and R. Y also has elements P, Q and R. But X also has S. Therefore, Y has S.' The analogy may be utilised so as to promote the understanding of a legal concept by indicating similarities between that concept and others that may be more familiar or more readily grasped. Argument by analogy has been used in English law to support, for example, the concept of the right of the State to interfere so as to prevent breaks in 'the seamless web of the law' in relation to breaches of conventional morality. The statement of Lord Simonds in *Shaw v DPP* (1962), suggesting the existence of a residual power in the courts of law which can be used to guard the State against attacks 'which may be the more insidious because they are novel and unprepared for', stems from an analogy between the defence of the state by its 'guardians' and the defence of morality by the 'guardians of the law'. Specific criteria of formal rules relating to analogy (for example, 'the greater the number of elements shared by X and Y, the stronger the conclusion', or 'as the dissimilar elements between X and Y increase, so the conclusion is weakened') tend to be neglected in legal arguments based on analogy. Critics have pointed to some of the decisions in 'causation cases' (in particular, *R v Jordan* (1956) and *R v Blaue* (1975)) as having resulted from false analogies between the laws of physical causation and the type of causation perceived in the facts of these cases.

17

Some jurists have suggested that the unwillingness of English lawyers to follow rigidly the principles of formal logic may be a sure guarantee of continuing inconsistencies in the law. They point, for example, to the continuous 'lease or licence' saga in land law, exemplified by *Facchini v Bryson* (1952), *Somma v Hazelhurst* (1978), and *Street v Mountford* (1985), and argue that, had the concept of a lease been applied in strictly logical fashion to a consideration of the facts in these and similar cases, uncertainty and inconsistency might have been avoided. (The continuing inconsistencies may be perceived in *Mehta v Royal Bank of Scotland* (2000) and *Bruton v Quadrant Housing Trust* (1999).) Holmes' comments on the question of consistency in law are pertinent: the law, he declares, is always approaching and never reaching consistency. 'It will become consistent only when it ceases to grow.' Pound reminds jurists that so called 'scientific legal systems', dominated by strictly logical reasoning, will result in the 'petrifaction' of law and the stifling of independent consideration of new problems and of 'new phases of old problems'. Jurists who support the stance of Holmes and Pound have noted that the principles of formal logic were *not* responsible, for example, for the vital changes in the law of torts effected by the enunciation of the 'neighbour principle' in *Donoghue v Stevenson* (1932), or the important development of the 'proximity test' in *Alcock and Others v Chief Constable of S Yorks Police* (1991), or the articulation of the so called '*Bolam* test' in relation to standards of skill to be expected from professional persons (*Bolam v Friern Hospital* (1957)).

Others argue that law based on systematic logical principles will enlarge control over the increasing diversity of legal situations. 'It is like fishing with large nets rather than single lines.' Cohen, in an examination of the place of logic in the law, suggests that this argument ignores the important differences between the natural sciences, in which logic is essential, and the legal order, which involves matters which are neither as definite nor as rigid as those of the physical order. The facts of the physical order allow highly exact description (for example, in quantitative terms); the facts of the legal order can almost always be disputed and disregarded as wrong in principle. 'The specific gravity of mercury is 13.6' is a statement which, in terms of its logical derivation, is on a different level from that occupied by the statement, 'The court finds for defendant'. Cohen warns that, like some other useful instruments, logic can be 'very dangerous and it requires great wisdom to use it properly ... A logical science of law can help us digest our legal material, but we must get good food before we can digest it'.

Dewey, jurist and logician, urges caution in the face of arguments advocating a more intensive application of syllogistic logic to legal questions. He notes that the syllogism implies that thought or reason has fixed forms of its own, 'anterior to and independent of concrete subject matters and to which the latter have to be adapted whether or no'. This is to put the activity of rigid demonstration *before* that of search and discovery and to fall into the trap of accepting that for every possible case which might arise in the legal system, there is a fixed antecedent rule 'already at hand'. The result is to produce what Pound terms 'a mechanical jurisprudence'; it flatters the human longing for certainty. Thinking derived from a consideration of premises is, in itself, not to be condemned; the problem for the jurist is to *find* statements of general principle and particular fact which are worthy to serve as premises. Hence, Dewey concludes, *either* logic in legal thinking must be abandoned, *or* it must be a logic relative to consequences rather than to antecedents – 'a logic of prediction of probabilities rather than one of deduction of certainties'.

The difficulties of relying *solely* on formal logic in a search for solutions to problems of jurisprudence and to cases arising within the legal system are obvious. The danger may be, however, in the *total rejection* of logic as a tool in legal reasoning. In Cohen's phrase, law without concepts or rational ideas, law that is not logical, is like pre-scientific medicine. Lord Devlin, too, warns: 'The Common Law is tolerant of much illogicality especially on the surface; but no system of law can be workable if it has not got logic at the root of it' (*Hedley Byrne v Heller* (1964)).

It is of interest to note, however, that attempts have been made to cast some aspects of legal thought and practice into patterns of strict logical (and algebraic) terminology. Kolm has presented his arguments for 'pure distributive justice', in the form of mathematical and formal logic. D'Amato has sought to convey the essence of Austin's thought through the medium of cybernetic models reflecting the logical interconnections of Austin's command theory of law. Judge Learned Hand (1872–1961) has summarised, in his 'Hand formula', a logical expression of the results of many American cases involving matters of basic negligence standards. He expresses his logical argument in algebraic terms. Let the standard of care be considered in terms of three variables: P (the probability of harm resulting to the claimant from any act or omission by the defendant); L (the gravity of the resulting harm or loss); B (the cost or burden of preventing the harm or loss). Then consider the expression $B < PL$, that is, in the words of Judge Posner, 'If the burden to the injurer of avoiding the accident was less than the loss if the accident occurred, multiplied by the probability that it could occur, then the injurer is negligent'. (The formula is explained and illustrated in *Conway v O'Brien* (1940).)

The school of *jurimetrics*, which seeks to apply to legal problems the techniques of logic, an elementary calculus of legal probability and the utilisation of computer techniques, in the name of its slogan, 'A scientific jurisprudence for a scientific age', has had very limited success, particularly in handling the problems of the qualitative judgments which figure large in our law. In Posner's words: 'We have in law the blueprint or shadow of scientific reasoning, but no edifice.' A jurisprudence in which scientific formal logic replaces legal reasoning would appear, at the moment, to lie, in Celan's phrase, 'well north of the future'.

Notes

The rules of formal logic may be found in *Fundamentals of Logic*, by Carney and Scheer. Bodenheimer considers law and scientific method in Chapter 17. Dewey examines the problem in 'Logical method and law' (1924) 10 Cornell LQR. Cohen's article, 'The place of logic in the law', appears in *Law and the Social Order*. A lucid account of basic problems related to logic and the law is given by Levi in his essay, 'The nature of judicial reasoning', in *Law and Philosophy*, edited by Hook, and by Posner in 'Law as logic, rules and science', in *The Problems of Jurisprudence*.

CHAPTER 2

PRECURSORS OF MODERN JURISPRUDENCE

Introduction

The precursors of modern jurisprudence selected as the basis of the questions in this chapter are Plato (c 427–c 347 BC), Aristotle (384–312 BC), Cicero (106–43 BC), Grotius (1583–1645), Hobbes (1588–1679), Locke (1632–1704) and Rousseau (1712–1778). Plato, Aristotle and Cicero were concerned with fundamental problems such as the nature of justice and the functions of law. Hobbes, Locke and Rousseau sought, through their theories of 'the social contract', to explain the place of government and law within society. Grotius was concerned with questions of liberty and order. The theories produced by these philosophers formed the basis of many problems which continue to be posed in modern jurisprudence. Questions of the type forming this chapter call for an understanding of the *basic* teachings related to justice, law, state and government. Answers must concentrate on *fundamentals*.

Checklist

The following topics should be revised carefully:

- Plato's theory of the state
- Plato's view of justice
- Plato's 'ideal state'
- the 'good' according to Aristotle
- man as a 'political animal'
- distributive and corrective justice
- 'natural rights' according to Locke

- the social contract viewed by Hobbes
- Hobbes' 'natural laws'
- Hobbes' 'sovereign'
- Locke's 'state of nature'
- the social contract viewed by Locke and Rousseau
- Aristotle's view of the state
- *pacta sunt servanda*

Question 4

Give an account of the fundamental features of Plato's theory of justice.

Answer plan

The problem here is how to compress the fundamentals of this complicated theory into a relatively small space. It is possible to deal in this way with the theory in *outline only*. Particular attention should be given to Plato's views on 'harmony' and the state, and reference should be made to his ideal state. A skeleton plan is suggested as follows:

Introduction – emergence of the state from the very nature of man – justice as a 'general virtue' – justice and the degeneration of the state – the ideal state of Magnesia – necessity for a code of laws – the modern approach to Plato's theory of justice.

Answer

Plato (c 427–c 347 BC), together with Aristotle, laid and shaped a large part of the foundations of the entire intellectual and cultural traditions of the West. His theory of justice was expounded in *The Republic* (c 370 BC); a development of that theory and its application to an ideal state are embodied in *The Laws* (c 340 BC). Neither the theory nor its application is found attractive to modern jurists in general, save for a group who favour an authoritarian approach to the law and who claim to find support for their views in *The Republic*. Critical studies of *The Republic* and *The Laws* (which, in a sense, are complementary) have been responsible for much of the theorising which burgeoned into early European jurisprudence.

The Republic is, in a number of respects, the crowning work of Plato's philosophical writings: it brings into sharp focus many of his basic beliefs regarding the nature of man and the essence of good government and law. It takes the form of a discussion between Socrates and his friends and is, essentially, an application of Plato's ethical theory to the delineation of the features of an ideal State. Socrates is used as a mouthpiece for Plato's own thoughts. The dialogue moves swiftly towards the central question of *the nature of justice*. Socrates' friends attempt definitions which collapse under his scrutiny. The concept of justice as 'paying one's debts and giving each his due' is rejected swiftly. The argument that justice is 'nothing but the interests of the strong' is exposed as a contradiction. Answers to the question, 'Why should one be just?' constitute the central part of Socrates' vision of justice. He suggests that, because it is easier to perceive things in the large than in the small, it might be better to look for justice 'writ large' in the state. Hence it would be valuable to seek to establish what makes a 'just state' rather than to concentrate on a 'just individual'. Because justice will figure large in the attributes of an ideal state, it is necessary to outline such a state with particular reference to its constitution and its attitudes to justice.

It is important to note that Plato uses the Greek word *'dikaiosune'* for 'justice'. In its true sense, it means 'righteousness', and bears no overtones of 'equality'. Plato's view of 'justice' does not take in egalitarianism: this is evident, for example, in his dismissal of democracy as 'distributing an odd kind of equality to equals and unequals'.

The state must be considered as emerging from the very nature of man and as reflecting the structure of human nature. Individuals are not self-sufficing, hence, a division of labour is essential, allowing each person to perform, at the right time, 'the one thing for which he is naturally fitted'. A multitude of crafts and craftsmen will emerge. Exhaustion of the community's resources may result and wars with other communities will take place, necessitating the creation of an army of warriors. From the ranks of the warriors will emerge the guardians of the state, and from the most highly trained guardians will come an elite which will rule the state. The three classes – craftsmen, guardians, and rulers – epitomise, according to Plato, the 'three parts of the soul', that is, the appetitive, the spirited and the rational. The virtues associated with the three classes are temperance (among the craftsmen), courage (characterising the guardians), and wisdom (to be found among the rulers). Members of the three classes would have to be taught (on the basis of what Plato refers to as 'a convenient fiction ... a single bold flight of invention') that nature approves a perfectly stratified society and that it had mixed gold in the composition of those who were to be the rulers, silver in the guardians, and brass and iron in the craftsmen.

The achievement of justice in a state depends on whether the elements of wisdom and philosophy could achieve dominance. Evils within society will continue until the philosophers acquire political authority, or until those in authority become philosophers.

Justice is a general virtue; it necessitates all parts of the state fulfilling their special functions and thereby achieving their respective virtues. It will be attained within the state only when and if each class fulfils its functions. When every individual stays in his place, and does the special task for which his aptitudes equip him, then will justice emerge. *Justice is, indeed, harmony,* reflected in a 'correct balance of the soul'. It involves a harmony of the fundamental virtues of temperance, courage and wisdom. Therefore, each person within the state must attain his own individual harmony based upon these virtues. Hence, in the 'just state' the craftsman must pursue the appropriate virtues which will teach him to accept his position within society and to obey the rules made by the elite.

'Balanced uniformity' within the state, which mirrors the desirable healthy, harmonious unity within individuals, will produce the settled community within which justice will flourish. Plato recognises, however, that not all states can achieve and maintain an appropriate degree of harmony, nor can individuals attain their own internal harmony because of variations in human character. Even the state in which justice predominates may contain the seeds of its eventual decline. Plato notes five forms of government, each one of which reflects appropriate kinds of 'mental constitutions' within individuals. The ideal state, characterised by a high degree of justice in its constitution, and in which the philosopher-rulers are supreme and each person's appetites are controlled by individual reason, is termed by Plato an *aristocracy.* The essence of the aristocratic state is the proper subordination of classes. Justice emerges naturally from this arrangement. But this type of state tends to degenerate into a *timocracy,* epitomising ambition and love of honour, and mirroring the individual in whom irrational characteristics are assuming a significant role. Further degeneration takes place and culminates in the rise of a *plutocracy* in which power is in the hands of those who are concerned mainly with wealth. This degenerate form of state is a reflection of those individuals whose principal characteristic is greed. Hence, 'the rich rise and the virtuous sink'; self-gratification produces antagonistic groups of rich and poor, and justice is weakened.

The legitimising of all appetites under a plutocracy produces an insatiable craving for wealth, equality and unrestricted freedom. The stage is set for *democracy* – a further degeneration. Modern jurists emphasise that Plato probably could not have had in mind a style of democracy other than that which he had experienced in the small city state of Athens. Direct popular government, as practised in Athens, seemed to him a total violation of the concept of a state ruled by those with special, trained aptitudes. Within a democracy, justice will be incomplete and inadequate. The final degeneration takes the form of *despotism*, a reflection of the 'enlargement of the unjust soul'. The absolute despot who enslaves a community mirrors the single 'master-passion' which has enslaved the individual soul. The harmony which is necessary if justice is to prevail has been shattered totally, so that justice disappears completely under despotism.

Some years after *The Republic* was written, Plato produced a detailed, practical plan for his ideal 'just state'. *The Laws* is an account of the structure and organisation appropriate for this 'Utopia'. The significance of law is emphasised: law is viewed by Plato in this work as essential for the moral salvation of the community and the maintenance of an appropriate standard of justice. The ideal state involves government based on a minutely-detailed code of laws which points the way to achievement of 'the true good'. The resulting picture of an ideal state has few attractions for contemporary jurists who find its picture of a regimented community to be repulsive. The ideal state emerges as an authoritarian regime based on laws which are almost unalterable and which seek to control every aspect of individual life.

The state will be named 'Magnesia'. Its guiding principles are: the existence of certain absolute standards of morality and their embodiment in a code of laws; the total obedience of the population to the rules and regulations made for them; the total prohibition of any attempt by citizens to modify the prevailing moral ideas or the code of law which expresses those ideals. Magnesia will be 10 miles from the sea, with a population of 5,040 citizens, plus some resident aliens. Justice will necessitate the encouragement of modest living standards, so that 'excess', which can destroy harmony, is discouraged. Each family will own a farm and most of the manual labour will be performed by slaves (who enjoy none of the rights of citizens). Trade will be carried out by the resident aliens. All persons will be educated in a manner which will prevent their subversion by undesirable ideas, which will fit them for their destined occupations and allow them to defend the state. (A constant state of undeclared war between Magnesia and other states is taken for granted: peace is 'only a name'.) In the interests of the social harmony upon which justice will rest, there will be a state religion and adherence will be enforced rigidly.

The government of Magnesia will include officials elected by the citizens. It will, however, observe the general policies laid down by the 'Guardians of the Laws'. The imposition of standards so that harmony and justice might prevail is the direct responsibility of this governing elite. Members of the elite will pursue a programme of philosophical studies, designed to enable them to comprehend the 'true reasons' behind the laws of the state and their significance for the maintenance of justice.

Justice will reflect harmony, and that harmony will require an all-embracing, detailed and systematically-arranged code of laws. It is the criminal code of Magnesia which has attracted considerable attention from generations of political scientists and jurists. Its range of penalties is very wide; the nature of the penalties is often, in our eyes, bizarre. Apart from basic crimes, such as theft, assault and homicide, there is a long list of offences, trivial and serious, attracting severe penalties. Thus, it is an offence under this code to attend weddings when forbidden to do so, to fail to marry, or to arrange for extravagant wedding feasts. There are penalties for the pursuit of an unsuitable occupation, for the carrying on of retailing (except in the case of resident aliens or temporary visitors), or for the staging of unauthorised comic plays. Meddling in law or education, the inconsiderate planting of trees, and truancy from school, also attract penalties. The code of laws will assist in the establishment and maintenance of that *unity of purpose* from which justice will flow.

Some aspects of Plato's penology are based on his belief in reform rather than vengeance – in the interests of justice for all citizens. He perceives crime as involuntary, in the sense that the 'true nature' of the offender has been conquered against his own fundamental wishes. Hence, he should be 'cured' rather than punished. Yet, in contrast, Plato's code prescribed the death penalty for the 'incurable' criminal in a large number of cases, particularly where the security of the state is endangered. The punishment to be meted out to slaves is often of an abhorrent nature.

The modern approach to Plato's theory of justice acknowledges that he was a remarkable 'child of his time', that his attitudes were conditioned by beliefs which are not easily comprehended in our day, and that to condemn him, say, for his acceptance of slavery, is to condemn an entire era. His lasting contribution to legal theory is in the basis of early jurisprudential thought founded on concepts of harmony, virtue and balance as desirable ends to be reflected in the law. Our own society, its laws and institutions, have changed since Plato's time, and our conceptions of justice are far-removed from his. But, in Friedmann's words, the fundamental issues for jurisprudence have *not* changed: the problems and conflicts which are discussed in *The Republic* continue to exercise us today.

Notes

The Republic has been translated by Lee, Jowett, and many other scholars; a large number of editions exists. *The Laws* has been translated by Saunders. Friedmann's *Legal Theory*, Chapter 2, contains an account of the essence of Plato's theory of justice. The theory is analysed in Calhoun's *Introduction to Greek Legal Science*, and in Jones' *The Law and Legal Theory of the Greeks*.

Question 5

'Man when perfected is the best of animals, but if he be isolated from law and justice he is the worst of all': Aristotle (*The Politics*).

Discuss.

Answer plan

The question calls for comment on Aristotle's view of man as seeking to achieve 'the good' and fulfilling his role within society. Aristotle's legacy to jurisprudence is his concept of law as a means to an end. His classification of justice as 'distributive' and 'corrective' is of particular significance. No more than an outline answer should be attempted. The following skeleton plan is used for this answer:

> Introduction – concept of 'the good life' – man's dual aspect – law as the community's sovereign guide – educational element in law – essence of equity – distributive and corrective justice – social framework for the just society – conclusion, noting the significance of Aristotle's theories in relation to modern jurisprudence.

Answer

One of the most celebrated polymaths of all time (his writings have been described as 'of unparalleled scope and dimensions'), Aristotle (384–312 BC) was educated at Plato's Academy in Athens and was influenced deeply by Platonic rationalism. In his writings on law and justice (set out in the 10 books of the *Nicomachean Ethics*), he seems to advance well beyond Plato's general idealism. Aristotle was concerned, in particular, with how man might achieve 'the good'; indeed, for him the 'science of the good' was politics. The 'good life' involved the exercise of reason, so that it became an activity of the soul aimed at perfect virtue. The highest of the moral virtues was justice: general justice, which requires strict observance of the law by all, is 'complete virtue'. 'In justice all virtue is summed up.' Man must be involved closely with law and justice if he is to perform his 'true functions'; to separate him from the exercise of those functions is to separate him from law and justice, thus taking from him the possibility of self-development and the attainment of ultimate happiness, and removing him from reaching that perfection which marks him as 'the best of animals'.

Aristotle views the world as a unity, a 'totality of nature'. Man is a part of nature, but in a 'dual sense': he is a constituent element of the natural order, but his active reason, which differentiates him from everything else, allows him to *control* nature. He has a will which, when it acts on the basis of an insight into reason, gives him a power denied to all other animals – the power to distinguish good from evil so that he is able to dominate nature by his spirit. Man's nature requires the powers and qualities separating him from other creatures to be developed to the full. Man is essentially moral, social and rational, and the natural law will embody the obligations which will be apparent to him if his reason is 'perfected'. Man's laws may be judged by the extent to which they assist in that perfection. *Laws are to be considered 'just' only if they permit the full development of human innate powers.*

Laws that are 'rightly constituted' should be the community's 'sovereign guide' Their sovereignty should embrace *all* issues, with the exception that rules formulated by the community's executive should prevail in those areas in which general pronouncements are impossible. The rule of law is preferable to a system emanating from a single citizen, even though he is of outstanding quality. Aristotle sees clearly the disadvantages inherent in personal rule and personal promulgation of laws. One who commands that *law* should rule is commanding, in effect, that 'God and reason' alone ought to rule; but he who commands that *one man* should rule 'adds the character of the beast'. 'Appetite and high spirit' pervert those who hold high office, even when they are the best of men. Law must be seen, therefore, as based upon 'reason free from passion'. Aristotle stresses that it is the office of the law to *direct the magistrate* in the 'execution of his office and the punishment of offenders'. Friedmann points out that it is to this statement that some modern jurists turn for support in their opposition to the power of unfettered administrative discretion.

The law has an educational element too. Because its aim is the attainment of the good life, the life characterised by the exercise of those faculties separating man from beast, the lawgiver must assist the citizen to become 'good' by habituating him, through the law, to an understanding of 'the good'. Indeed, law will derive its validity among citizens from the very *habits* upon which obedience is founded. Where citizens understand that the law is to be viewed as a pledge that members of the community will do justice to one another, and where they understand that 'good law' means 'good order', they will respond appropriately with good behaviour. Because of the educational nature of the law, and because of the habits it inculcates over long periods, Aristotle warned of the evils arising from changes in the law made without careful consideration. Law has no power to command obedience except through habit which can result *in time*; readiness to change from old to new laws, without full preparation, may enfeeble the power of the law.

Circumstances may arise, as Aristotle noted, when the application of universal, rigid rules will result in hardship in some individual cases. It is not always possible, he said, to make universal statements about some things. When a lawmaker promulgates a universal rule and a case emerges which is not covered by it, there arises a necessity to 'correct' that rule. 'It is the nature of the equitable to correct the law where, because of its universality, it is defective.' In his *Rhetoric*, he expresses a fundamental notion of equity in Western law: 'It is equity to pardon the human failing, to look to the lawgiver and not to the law, to the spirit and not the letter, to the intention and not the action ... to prefer the arbitrator to the judge, for the arbitrator observes what is equitable, whereas the judge sees only the law.' Aristotle suggests that a defect arising from the absoluteness of the law be rectified by the judge deciding as the lawgiver would *himself* have decided had he been present on the occasion in question and would have enacted if he had been cognisant of the case in question.

Aristotle makes a clear distinction between 'positive law' and 'natural law'. *Natural law* must be seen as having everywhere the same force; it 'does not exist by people thinking this or that'. Its force resides in its derivation from human nature everywhere and at all times. *Positive law* derives its special force from the fact that it is set down as law, whether it be considered just or unjust. Both types of law make a contribution to the good of the community.

One of the best known contributions of Aristotle to jurisprudence is his perception of 'distributive' and 'corrective' (or 'remedial') justice. An essential feature of justice is its concern with *relationships among individuals*, reflecting good judgment and a fundamental sense of fairness. 'Justice alone is the good of others because it does what is for the advantage of others.' The unjust man is the man who breaks the law and the man who takes more than his due. Hence, distributive justice involves 'some sort of equality' among individuals in accordance with what they deserve. It demands the equitable distribution or allotment to members of the community of 'the things of this world' in accordance with the principle of *proportionate equality*, which necessitates a measuring standard of 'merit and civil excellence'. Equal things should be distributed to equal persons; unequal things should be given to unequal persons, in proportion to their merits. Should A be 'twice as deserving' as B, A's share will be twice as large as B's.

Corrective justice relates to the administration of the law within a community. The importance of redressing the undesirable consequences of encroachment upon the property and other rights of an individual stands high in the tasks of those who administer the law. The violation of a norm of distributive justice, which leads to X depriving Y of his rights so that X makes an unjustified gain, must produce the consequences of X returning Y's property to him, or compensating Y for the loss incurred. It is the task of the judge to be 'a sort of animate justice' and to repair the situation resulting from a breach of the community's rules. Failure to achieve high standards of corrective justice results in man's isolation from those forces which make for his good.

Although laws and justice prevent the degeneration of man into a selfish, uncaring person, in that he is subjected to rules which are based on 'doing good' to others, a social framework is required so that good and justice might flourish. The definition and study of the state occupy places of much importance in Aristotle's scheme of justice and 'the good'. He classifies the main forms of government known to him under the headings of 'monarchy', 'aristocracy', and 'polity'. The aim of government is to fit the man for the good life, and the state is to be seen as a union of families enjoying a 'perfect and self-sufficing life, a happy, honourable and just existence'. Aristotle rejects monarchy as 'obsolete' and 'objectionable' because it subjects those who are equal to the rule of an equal. In an aristocracy (generally favoured by Aristotle), only the 'best' are citizens. 'Best' means for Aristotle those who are the most capable through natural endowment and education. They will comprise a small, intellectual and wise elite. 'Polity' refers to constitutional government and may involve rule by the masses under law and a system of justice protected by a constitution.

These types of government tend to degenerate, and the degeneration makes it difficult to attain and sustain the just society. Monarchy degenerates to its corrupt form, known as 'tyranny', in which the selfish ends of the ruler predominate over the need for justice and law. Aristocracy is transformed into its corrupt form of 'oligarchy', characterised by rulers who are interested in their personal advancement and not in the general good. Polity is degraded into 'democracy' in which selfishness predominates and the common good is not perceived as an important objective. Democracy, said Aristotle, arises when men think that if they are equal in any respect, they are equal in all respects. These corrupt forms of government are characterised by a lack of moderation and a corresponding absence of justice.

Friedmann argues that Aristotle's work 'anticipates all the major themes and conflicts of modern Western legal thought'. Certainly, many of the vital questions discussed in contemporary jurisprudence may be traced to his study of law and justice. The purpose of justice, its nature, the significance of distributive and corrective justice, the need for a system of equity which will temper the rigours of the law by allowing for individual cases – all appear in his writings. His emphasis on the 'dual character' of man may be found at the basis of much discussion in our own time. Because man is, by his very nature, a 'political animal', he is destined to fulfil himself only within society – 'he who is unable or unwilling to live in society is a beast or a god'. Such a society is established with a view to 'the good', of which justice is among its highest manifestations. It is through law and justice that man will achieve his goals; without them he degenerates, inevitably and totally. Law and justice are, therefore, means to an end. That end is the full development of man. In his 'perfected form' he is, indeed, 'the best of animals'. Justice has given him a vision of 'the good', the law has provided the means of realising the vision. The good life for human beings should be an ideal rooted firmly in human nature.

Notes

Aristotle's theories concerning law and justice may be found in his *Nichomachean Ethics*, translated by Rackham. There are interesting expositions of his contributions to jurisprudence in Bodenheimer, Chapters 1, 3 and 11; Lloyd, Chapter 3; and Dias, Chapter 4. Friedmann analyses his theories in Chapter 2. An interesting background to Aristotle is given in Grene's *A Portrait of Aristotle*.

Question 6

Describe the teachings of Cicero in relation to the basis of the state and the nature of law.

Answer plan

Cicero (106–43 BC), Roman politician and lawyer, was able, through his teachings, to transmit to his contemporaries, and to posterity, important aspects of Greek (Stoic) philosophy which might otherwise have disappeared. His main interests were in legal and political philosophy and he sought to propagate the virtues of the brotherhood of mankind and a universal law. Cicero's writings have been studied by philosophers, historians and lawyers for many generations; the questions he sought to answer remain on the agenda of our jurisprudence. The following skeleton plan is presented; it should place emphasis on the significance of the natural law, which Cicero saw as of supreme importance for the development of civilisation:

Introduction – Cicero's life as statesman and jurist – the essence of the state – forms of government – their strengths and weaknesses – importance of a mixed constitution – essence of law – law, God and the nature of man – justice, good and bad law – natural law – conclusion, Cicero as a founder of western jurisprudence.

Answer

Marcus Tullius Cicero (106–43 BC), statesman, lawyer, scholar, writer, and, reputedly, Rome's greatest legal orator, was declared by the legal historian, Maitland, to have left his ideas 'on every page of western jurisprudence'. As a jurist, he sought to bring the lessons of Greek philosophy into a consideration of law as the highest reason, implanted in man and providing a universal standard by which justice and injustice might be measured. Born in Arpino, he studied with Philo in Rome and Antiochus in Athens. He became one of Rome's consuls in 63 BC, and participated as a principal figure in the crushing of the insurrection by Catiline. Following exile in 58 BC, he returned to Rome, became an augur in 53 BC, and was promoted to govern Cilicia. He opposed Mark Antony's seizure of power after Caesar's assassination. Antony gave personal orders for the murder of Cicero, which took place in brutal fashion in 43 BC. Cicero's major political and legal tracts were completed between 54–44 BC; all have been studied extensively by generations of scholars, and reflect his view of the significance of the basis of the state and the essence of law in a manner which gives them relevance for our day.

'If the man lives', he stated, 'who would belittle the study of philosophy, I quite fail to see what in the world he would see fit to praise'. By 'philosophy', Cicero had in mind what we now refer to as 'moral philosophy'. A study of what is meant by 'right' and 'wrong', a search for the essence of justice and an investigation of virtue, were fundamental to his view of the place of the law in human affairs. In this investigation, he kept in mind the Stoic belief that virtue is the only good and that the virtuous man is the one who has reached happiness through knowledge. Allied to his acceptance of the primacy of philosophy was a belief that virtue linked man to a divine Providence. All men counted for something; all have an inherent value in themselves; all were linked by a bond of kinship derived from their place in divine Providence; all had the right (which the law must recognise and declare) to be treated well by one another. The Stoic conception of the universe and all creatures therein as sharing a common destiny found expression in Cicero's belief in the essential brotherhood of man. These themes found expression in his legal and political doctrines.

Cicero's views on the nature of the state are set out in *De Republica* (54–52 BC). Human beings should engage in political activity, in the widest sense of the term. Nature has given to mankind a compulsion to do good and a desire to defend the well-being of the community, so that there is a common drive to work for the community's benefit, and this drive will prevail over temptations presented by a life of pleasure and ease. The desire to increase the wealth of the community, to enrich men's life, acts as the spur to unite and work in a common endeavour, to engage in those types of activity which demand the formal framework which only the state can provide.

The state framework can exist in a variety of forms. Cicero chooses, in *De Republica*, to examine three forms of government which can give expression to man's inherent impulse to create societies. Where the supreme authority is vested in one man – a king – the government, known as a 'monarchy', is entrusted with the duty to govern virtuously. When the government is entrusted to a select group, we speak of an 'aristocracy'. When the state is so organised that 'everything depends on the people', we have in mind a 'democracy'. Cicero observes that any of the three types of state may be tolerable, though not perfect, but one may, in certain circumstances, be preferable to the others.

The monarchical state can ensure a reasonably stable and secure government, always provided that wickedness and greed are excluded from the work of those who assist the the monarch. The problem is that the personal rule of the monarch means that the rest of the population play only a limited role in state affairs, legislation and debate. Government by an aristocracy, where 'the best' are chosen, has the advantage that nature has decreed that those possessing superiority of ability and character ought to be in charge of those with lesser endowments. Rule by an aristocracy frees the mass of the people from many troubles and anxieties, since grave matters of state are the responsibility of others. The problem of the aristocratic form of government is its tendency to slip into unrestrained rule by a minority, and there is an abandonment, gradually but surely, of the place of reason within the procedures of government.

Democracy is a recognition of equality – all share in the process of government, and all accept a law which recognises and supports systems of duties and rights. Harmony, it is said, can be maintained with relative ease in a state where all have the same basic interests. But Cicero is emphatic in his rejection of the theory of the state based upon the concept of 'so called equality'. Equality of this nature proves in the event to be highly inequitable. 'For when the same respect is given to the highest and lowest in the community, equity is most unequal ... this cannot happen where the state is ruled by "the best".' Where no degrees of merit are recognised and acknowledged, equality becomes unequal and degenerates rapidly.

Moderation in all things, including government, must be sought, and Cicero declares himself in favour of a fourth type of government, characterised by a carefully-proportioned amalgam of the best features of monarchy, aristocracy and democracy. (He acknowledges, however, that he is personally most attracted to the state ruled by a monarch.) The state should possess 'elements of regal supremacy', 'the best' in the state should be recognised and given tasks and a place in society which acknowledges their talents, and certain affairs ought to be reserved 'for the judgment and wishes of the masses'. A constitution of this nature, in which law will play a role of extreme importance, will confer on citizens a high degree of equality, 'without which free men will not endure for long', and provide much stability, 'for there will be little reason to demand change in a society in which all are established firmly in their own places'. The good state will express the virtue and sense of purpose, the harmony and unity under the law, which, for Cicero, represent the 'the ruling power in the human mind', namely, reason ('for that is the best part of the mind').

De Legibus (52–51 BC) is, essentially, an exposition of the far-reaching doctrine of natural law, in which Cicero perceived the plan of divine Providence, which could be realised only when mankind places itself resolutely under the law. *Omnes legum servi sumus ut liberi esse possimus* – 'We must all serve the law if we are to be free'. Law is viewed by Cicero in very wide terms. Its nature must be sought in the very nature of man; all men share in the divine reason and all are brought and bound together by the partnership which characterises justice. To seek to understand law is to learn the nature of justice and the essence of 'good' and 'bad' law.

The science of law – that which we now speak of as jurisprudence – is derived, not from the written law ('not from the Praetor's Edict nor from the Twelve Tables'), but from the very deepest recesses of philosophy. Philosophy teaches us to investigate fearlessly, so that we may speak of law as 'the highest reason, inherent in nature, which tells us what should be done and forbids us to act in contrary fashion.' Indeed, 'law, the function of which is to command right actions and to forbid wrong doing, is wisdom'. But there is a much more profound matter to be recognised: reason is present in God and man so that some kind of partnership exists between them. Those who share reason also share correct reason, and since that is law, men may be perceived as partners with God through the law. Law is, therefore, very much more than 'the Praetor speaking in Rome'. It is an aspect of divine Providence, which 'has placed in our ears a power of judging right and wrong'.

In more precise terms, Cicero teaches that law is not the invention of the intelligence of human beings, nor does it come from resolutions passed by communities. Rather it is 'an eternal force' which rules the entire world by the excellence of its wisdom in relation to commands and prohibitions. Law is, in truth, an aspect of God's intelligence, for it is God who commands or forbids everything through reason. We may think of the law as representing the intelligence and profound reason of a wise person from whom commands and prohibitions issue forth. Further, reason does not become law when persons have reduced it to writing; it was law when it came into being at the same time as the Supreme Mind. The true, authentic and original law is 'the right reason of Jupiter, the Lord of All'.

The functioning of law demands that man exercise his rational power of choice and learn from nature how to distinguish a 'good law' from a 'bad law'. That which promotes honourable outcomes is good, and is in accordance with nature's teachings; that which is dishonourable is an expression of the rejection of what nature has commanded. Indeed, 'goodness itself is good not because of the opinions of people, but because of nature, the ultimate arbiter'. Every virtue will disappear if nature is ignored so that injustice triumphs. In essence, therefore, justice is necessary if we care to attain the highest good. Cicero describes the concept of 'the highest good' as living by a code of moral excellence, which necessitates following nature, working to her law and not omitting to do those things which nature requires to be done.

Duty is an essential aspect of the law of nature, but how ought citizens to react in the presence of a tyranny? Ought they to obey rules which are clearly contrary to the natural law? In an interesting passage in *De Officiis* (44 BC), Cicero insists that no duties are owed to tyrants. 'Just as certain limbs are amputated if they show signs themselves of jeopardising the health of the other parts of the body, so those fierce and savage monsters in human form [the tyrants] ought to be cut off from what may be called humanity's common body.' This passage has been cited repeatedly as a justification of the removal of tyrants who seek to destroy the common bonds uniting society. Others have interpreted it as a metaphor by which Cicero seeks to proclaim that no man has a right to rule in a fashion which will destroy the unity of the community without being challenged by first being exposed as a destroyer of the social harmony demanded by Providence.

In a style which hints at Cicero's legendary power as a rhetorician, he sums up, in *De Legibus*, the essence of natural law. 'There is in fact a true law – namely right reason – which is in accordance with nature, applies to all men, and is unchangeable and eternal ... To invalidate this law by human legislation is never morally right, nor is it permissible ever to restrict its operation ... There will be one law, eternal and unchangeable, binding at all times upon all peoples, and there will be, as it were, one common master and ruler of men, namely God, who is the author of this law, its interpreter and sponsor ...' It is the spirit of this formulation which remains central to the theory of natural law, which continues in our time as a potent factor in the jurisprudential thinking of the West.

Stammler, writing of the excellence of the Roman jurists, and their universal significance, praises them in terms which apply, in particular, to Cicero. 'They had the courage to raise their glance from the ordinary questions of the day to the whole. And in reflecting on the narrow status of the particular case, they directed their thoughts to the guiding star of all law, namely, the realisation of justice in life.'

Notes

De Republica and *De Legibus* are translated and discussed by Rudd in a recent edition which provides useful notes on the background to Cicero's work. 'Some reflections on Cicero's naturalism', by Arkes, in *Natural Law Theory*, edited by George, is a valuable commentary on Cicero's interpretation of the theory of law. *Cicero's Social and Political Thought*, by Wood, and *Cicero, the Senior Statesman*, by Mitchell, furnish material relating to Cicero's times and his general theories concerning society. *Law and the Life of Rome*, by Dorey describes the place of legal theory and procedures in Cicero's day.

Question 7

What did Grotius contribute to the jurisprudential thought of his day?

Answer plan

Grotius (1583–1645) was a significant figure in jurisprudence not only in his own day, but in the centuries which followed. He sought to apply the 'God-given faculty' of reasoning to fundamental problems arising from natural law rooted in religious dogma. His most important contribution was in the field of the law of nations – international law. Horrified by the unrestrained barbarities of the Thirty Years War, he attempted to lay the foundations for a civilised approach to armed conflict, which he accepted as an inevitable aspect of international life. He called for a humane approach to problems involving war prisoners and hostages and sought to interest nation states in applying the principles of law to their relationships. The following skeleton plan is suggested:

Introduction – significance of reason – man as a sociable creature, rules of social living – social contract – natural law – the law of nations – conclusion, significance of Grotius' work.

Answer

Grotius, known also as Hugh de Groot, was a jurist, theologian and statesman who spent a considerable proportion of his life in imprisonment or exile. He was affected deeply by the dreadfulness of the Thirty Years War and published his great work *De jure Belli ac Pacis* (On the Law of War and Peace) in 1625 in an attempt to lay the foundations of a law which might govern relationships of independent states. 'Such a work is all the more necessary because in our day ... there is no lack of men who view this branch of the law with contempt as having no reality outside of an empty name.' *De Jure Belli* provided some of the jurisprudential foundations of a pattern of thought which can be found in today's developed international law. Grotius' treatment of natural law suggested that such a law would exist *even if God did not exist* – a significant shift of natural law theory away from reliance upon God's providence and towards an emphasis upon human reason. Grotius is indeed a precursor of many of our views on international law and the place of reason in the concept of natural law.

Reason – God's great gift to mankind – occupies a vital place in Grotius' general jurisprudential analysis of phenomena. Nature is purposive, and natural law is imposed by Divine order upon all men, and they can discover and comprehend it solely by the light of the processes of reasoning. In the final analysis, Grotius believes that the gift of reason is man's sole asset in his struggle to attain a condition of happiness. This is reflected in the methodology which he adopted in an attempt to 'unhook' the young science of law from the rigidities of dogmatic theology: he prefers to argue in a manner which is in 'the spirit of geometry', in that it involves deductions from self-evident axioms, an approach which was similar to that of his celebrated compatriot, Spinoza (1632–77), who would seek to deduce the existence of God, and the essence of law, from axioms in the style of 'the spirit of geometry'. Grotius was suggesting to his contemporaries a new method of interpreting reality.

Fundamental to Grotius' system of jurisprudential thought is his concept of man as an 'inherently sociable being' – a novel idea for many jurists of his day:

> Man is, to be sure, an animal, but an animal of a superior kind, much farther removed from all other animals than the different kinds of animals are from one another ... But among the traits characteristic of man is an impelling desire for society, that is, for the social life – not of any and every sort, but peaceful, and organised according to the measure of his intelligence, with those who are of his own kind; this social trend the Stoics called 'sociableness' ... For the very nature of man, which even if we had no lack of anything would lead us into the mutual relations of society, is the mother of the law of nature.

Man is *not* made so as to seek only his own profit and advantage. His rationality teaches him to aim at the creation of social harmony, and that is right and just; but any event which disturbs the social harmony is wrong and unjust. The maintenance of social order, which is consonant with human understanding, 'is the source of the law properly so called'.

In the task of maintaining social order, Grotius suggests certain essential attitudes which ought to be widely accepted and acted upon. These include: '... the abstaining from that which is another's, the restoration to another of anything of his which we may have, together with any gain which we may have received from it; the obligation to fulfil promises, the reparation of a loss incurred through our fault, and the infliction of penalties on men according to their deserts.' Grotius is asking his contemporaries to consider a new approach to the basic requirements of social living.

The 'social contract' is accepted by Grotius as a series of events which did occur in history – it is not for him a hypothetical construct. At an early stage in man's development when states had emerged, each state had chosen the type of government which seemed suitable at that time. When the people of a state entered the contract under which they transferred to their ruler their own rights of government, they gave up, of their own volition, their right to control that ruler, even though his government proved to be weak. The state is defined by Grotius as 'a complete association of free men, joined together for the enjoyment of rights and for their common interest'. The ruler must observe, in the common interest, the principles of the natural law. Grotius does suggest that free men may have the right to resist the ruler if he transgresses against the law, or reveals himself as an enemy of the entire people. This was not an interpretation of citizens' rights which commended itself to Grotius' contemporaries.

Entry into the social contract has the effect of intensifying the freedom and rights of citizens; one of these rights affects the ownership of property. Grotius suggests that originally all things were in the class of *res nullius* and, with the coming into force of the contract there is introduced a general agreement for the division of material goods among individuals. The processes by which property is divided appear, and are refined, at a relatively later stage in man's social development. They include: division by individual participation in the agreement by which a specific division is made; by discovery or acquisition: by lawful acquisition from persons who have exercised their natural rights of disposition.

It is in the area of the theory of natural law that Grotius made a distinctive contribution to the thought of his time. He defines natural law thus:

> The law of nature is a dictate of right reason, which points out that an act, according as it is or is not in conformity with rational nature, has in it a quality of moral baseness or moral necessity; and that, in consequence, such an act is either forbidden or enjoined by the author of nature, God.

Grotius is implying in the so called 'impious hypothesis' that the law of nature will obtain 'even if we should concede that which cannot be conceded without the utmost wickedness, that there is no God, or that the affairs of men are of no concern to Him'. Further, the law of nature cannot be changed even by the will of God: 'Just as even God, then, cannot cause that two times two should not make four, so He cannot cause that which is intrinsically evil to be not evil.'

This constitutes an important step in the journey to establish 'the true significance of the natural law'. Grotius has, in the words of Bodenheimer (*Jurisprudence* (1974)), 'grounded the natural law on *an eternal reason* pervading the cosmos, although he admitted the alternative possibility of a theist foundation'. Natural law is *not* merely divine law; it is produced by *reason* directed towards man's social objectives which God has ordained. Grotius had, indeed, 'unhooked' natural law from the general theological doctrines accepted by his country's jurists and scholars of religion.

Grotius suggests two measures which will prove whether or not some event is or is not in accordance with the essence of natural law. The first method is *'proof a priori'*: it involves demonstrating 'the necessary agreement or disagreement of anything with a rational or social nature.' The second method involves *'proof a posteriori'* in concluding, 'if not with absolute assurance, at least with every probability, that this is according to the law of nature which is believed to be such among all nations, or among all those that are more advanced in civilisation'.

The view that Grotius 'secularised the natural law' by detaching it from dogmatic theology (and rehabiliating it in the non-Catholic world) is not accepted by all jurists. The contemporary neo-Thomist, Finnis, in his *Natural Law and Natural Rights* (1980), suggests that Grotius did not remove God from his concept of the natural law: he argues that Grotius was merely shifting the emphasis on the significance of reason in natural law towards man's own natural reason. It is not possible within Grotius' system, suggests Finnis, to discard the importance of that which has been commanded or prohibited by God. Rose, in his *Law of Nature* (1952), notes that Grotius was seeking to emphasise 'the reason of God' as distinguished from his will, as the source of law, 'and as a reliance upon reason as the means for discovering God's will in the absence of revelation'.

In his writings on international law, Grotius sought to express to his contemporaries his alarm at what was being done in the name of conflict between nations:

I observed [throughout the Christian world] a lack of restraint in relation to war, such as even barbarous races should be ashamed of; I observed that men rush to arms for slight causes, or no cause at all, and that when arms have once been taken up there is no longer any respect for law, divine or human; it is as if, in accordance with a general decree, frenzy had been openly let loose for the committing of all crimes.

He notes that, just as there are laws in each state aiming at securing advantages for that state, so between most states, 'some laws could be and indeed have been established by common consent which look to the advantage not of single communities but of the whole great concurrence of states'. This is, he avers, 'the law of nations'. There can be no valid argument raised against the need for international law: 'If no community can subsist without law ... surely the community that embraces the whole human race, or at least a great many nations, needs law.'

In answer to the argument raised by his contemporaries that laws lose their authority in time of war, Grotius replies that this is not true. A declaration of war except where the object is the enforcement of justice should be considered wrong; to continue a war already begun, unless conflict is kept 'within the bounds of justice and good faith', is wrong. Wars should be conducted only against those 'who cannot be restrained by courts of law'. War is a resort against those who are strong enough to resist judgments, or imagine that they are. But in order that wars may be considered right, they must be conducted 'as scrupulously as judicial proceedings habitually are'. Teachings of this nature were, in their time, a remarkable development of the growing concern for a semblance of international law and order. Grotius was attempting to draw attention to the implications of the *bellum justum* (the 'just war') as involving reference to reason and natural order. (He does not oppose the right of a nation to wage war: 'The end and aim of war being the preservation of life and limb, and the keeping or acquiring of things useful to life, war is in perfect accord with those first principles of nature.') He urges moderation in warfare (unusual in his age), examines the problem of the status of hostages, the destruction of property and problems arising from the religious beliefs of defeated peoples. He seeks – very unusually – to analyse matters arising from the concept of neutrality in terms of the status, rights and duties of a neutral state.

An investigation of the law of nations, such as it was in his day, revealed to Grotius two types of law which existed together. The first was the law of nature. The second was a type of general law, the rules of which could not be made clear by deduction, but which appeared to originate in the will of mankind. The natural principles of man's social life, in particular the desire to live peacefully, could be found in some aspects of the *jus gentium* – the law of peoples which had begun in the time of the Romans as a private law for foreigners, based on custom and acquiring, later, the status of widely-accepted rules. (These rules involved: abstaining from that which is another's and restoring to another anything of his which we may have; fulfilling promises; making good losses incurred through our fault; inflicting penalties according to an offender's deserts.) Grotius called for the existing law of nature and the concept of consent (as implied in the *jus gentium*) to be combined so as to create a foundation for an acceptable 'law of nations'. Specifically, such a law would emphasise the significance of the principle – *pacta sunt servanda* (promises and treaties must be obeyed); pacts link the positive law to the demands of the natural law.

Grotius sought to answer a perennial question raised repeatedly by his contemporaries: Why should states bother to observe international law? He argued, in reply:

> Just as the national who violates the law of his country so as to obtain some immediate advantage [for himself] destroys that by which the advantages of himself and his posterity are for all time assured, so the state which transgresses the laws of nature and of nations removes the bulwarks which safeguard its own peace for the future.

(War can be perceived as essentially a 'law suit' involving an offender and armed forces which operate in the absence of a court able to deal with the matter.) Although the law of nations had no sanctions through which it might be enforced, Grotius argues (with an optimism which had disappeared from most European states by the end of the 17th century) that obedience to the law of nations would be rewarded by 'a good conscience' and Divine protection.

Grotius asked searching questions of his contemporaries, through the medium of his writings on law and politics, which called for answers based upon a fundamental reappraisal of much that had been taken for granted – the inevitability of war, the expectation of brutality as an aspect of armed conflict, the law of nature as an expression of the theology of an earlier age. Novel thinking was needed, but it had to be based on rational concepts, and an acceptance of the view that society *as a whole* needs to be analysed on the basis of natural law. The answers given by Grotius now form a part of our own jurisprudence. McAinsh, writing on the contemporary significance of Grotius, states:

> By insisting upon the sanctity of treaties and upon limiting both the occasions for war and the ways in which war should be waged, Grotius had a profound impact on the direction of Western thought about the relations between states. Indeed, such achievements as ... the League of Nations ... and the United Nations owe much to the thought of Grotius.

Notes

Sabine's *A History of Political Theory* contains an analysis of the thought of Grotius. *De Jure Belli ac Pacis* has appeared in a large number of translations, of which Kelsey's is the best known. An important article on Grotius may be found in Hearnshaw's *Social and Political Ideas of Some Great Thinkers of the Sixteenth and Seventeenth Centuries*. Westerman, in *The Disintegration of Natural Law Theory*, examines the significance of Grotius' shift from natural law to natural rights. Lauterpacht's essay, 'The Grotian tradition in international law', in *The British Yearbook of International Law* (1946), sets out the measure of Grotius' influence on contemporary jurisprudence.

Question 8

What are the essential features of Hobbes' theory of the Social Contract?

Answer plan

The Social Contract (or 'Covenant') theory can be traced back to the ancient Greeks. It enjoyed wide currency in the 17th and 18th centuries through the writings of Hobbes, Locke and Rousseau and affected theories of the law concerned with the rights and duties of governments and citizens. The theory involves the fiction of a 'state of nature', in which, according to Hobbes (1588–1679), there were no enforceable criteria of right and wrong; it was a state of perpetual struggle which could be ended only by the surrender of individual liberties into the hands of a sovereign. The question asks for 'essential features'. Attention should be given, therefore, to the 'state of nature', the 'natural laws' and Hobbes' basic remedy for social conflict. A skeleton plan is proposed along the following lines:

Introduction – Hobbes' 'laws of motion' – *Leviathan* – analysis of the state of nature – natural laws – the Social Contract – indivisibility of the sovereign power – law as command of the sovereign – problem of 'bad law' – conclusion, Hobbes' theories in our time.

Answer

Hobbes' legal and political theories are derived from his natural philosophy which is based on his 'law of motion'. All human behaviour, according to this law, mimics the activities of 'bodies in motion'. Just as the natural tendency of moving bodies to follow a line of their original direction will result in their colliding with other moving bodies, so the assertion by some individuals of their rights and freedoms will bring them into conflict with other individuals asserting the same type of rights and freedoms. The result is a continuous collision of wills, and perpetual struggle. In his *Leviathan* (published in 1651, the year in which the future Charles II fled to France after being defeated by Cromwell), Hobbes outlined his views on law, the individual and the state. It pleased no faction: Anglicans and Catholics resented his ideas concerning the role of the church; Royalists objected to his analysis of sovereignty; Cromwellians resented his advocacy of absolute monarchy. The doctrine embodying the fiction of a Social Covenant struck a chord in legal theory which echoes even today.

The condition of men before the emergence of states or civil societies, referred to by Hobbes as 'the state of nature', is analysed closely. In such a state, all men are equal and all have a right to act so as to survive. The 'right of all to all' involves a freedom to possess, use and enjoy, all that an individual could obtain for himself. Man was driven by the will to survive and by the fear of violent death. The continuous clash of wills and 'bodies in motion' produced anarchy and a resulting 'war of all against all'. Neither 'good' nor 'evil' was recognised in this conflict: 'good' tended to be equated with 'survival', while 'evil' was associated with 'threats to survival'. In this state, individuals possess no capacity to build an ordered community.

Certain 'natural laws' emerge in the state of nature and attract some support because they are considered as involving concern for individual safety. They are essentially rules of behaviour, the observation of which might assist personal survival. Hobbes considers the first of these laws to be fundamental: 'peace is to be sought after'. This law is 'natural' because it is an obvious extension of concern for individual survival. An individual will have a better chance of survival if he assists in the creation and maintenance of overall conditions of peace. A person will be impelled, naturally, to seek a peaceful environment because of his desire to survive.

From the first law, Hobbes derives a second. Although men have rights to *all* things, these rights ought not to be retained to their full extent; certain rights ought to be 'relinquished or transferred'. A man should be willing, when others are similarly minded, to relinquish his rights to all things 'and be contented with so much liberty against other men as he would allow other men against himself'. To refuse to part with one's rights to all things is to act against the law of nature and 'the reason of peace'. A third law concerns the duty of a man to carry out a contract to which he is a party.

These laws are considered by Hobbes to be immutable and eternal; they have application to all societies and are supplemented by precepts, such as the need to avoid ingratitude, and the using of things in common that cannot be divided.

Without observance of the laws of nature there will be continuous struggle arising from the conflict of individual judgments as to how best to survive. The result will be 'no arts, letters or society ... continual fear and danger of death, and the life of man will be solitary, poor, nasty, brutish and short'. To avoid this necessitates a Social Contract which will bring about a commonwealth or state, and which will create laws distinguishing good and evil (that is, what is contrary to and what is not contrary to the statutes of the realm).

Men will create a civil society only by virtue of a covenant between individuals. (Some jurists have suggested that Hobbes' use of the Biblical term 'covenant' may reflect his acquaintance with the remarks of the Biblical translator, Tyndale: 'Faith according to the covenants is our salvation ... Where thou findest a promise, there must thou understand a covenant.' The term is used in the famous declaration of the Pilgrim Fathers in 1620, on the *Mayflower*, where reference is made to a solemn, mutual covenant for combination into a 'civil body politic'.) In Hobbes' words, it is as if men should say to one another, 'I authorise and surrender my right of governing myself to this person or this assembly of persons, but on the vital condition that you, too, will surrender your right to him and authorise all his actions in like manner'. In essence, the Social Contract (or covenant) is absolute and irrevocable. The parties to the Contract are individuals, making promises to transfer their rights to govern themselves to some sovereign. The Contract is *not* made between the individuals and that sovereign. Indeed, the sovereign has an absolute power to govern; there is no point at which he may be considered as subject to those who made the Contract among themselves. Further, it is important to note that Hobbes has in mind, when referring to the sovereign, a 'person' or 'an assembly of persons'. The theory of the Social Covenant does not necessarily demand an absolute monarch (although that would reflect Hobbes' preference); it could have application to an elected assembly.

'Indivisibility of the sovereign power' is an important aspect of the contract theory. The citizens have agreed, in effect, that the totality of their individual wills and judgments will be represented henceforth by the single will and judgment of the sovereign. He acts on behalf of the citizens, and his actions are taken as an affirmation of the identity of their wills with his will. His will is their will; his actions reflect this unity. From this principle follows an extremely important political and legal concept – it is illogical and wrong, according to Hobbes, for a citizen to engage in resisting the sovereign. In doing so, he would be resisting himself, and, further, resistance would be a manifestation of the type of independent judgment which characterised the 'state of nature' and is, therefore, undesirable. The sovereign's power must be total and, in effect, absolute.

Without a sovereign, civil law and social contract are not possible. For Hobbes, a law is the command of the sovereign 'to do or to forebear'. Law requires a legal order and a central power of enforcement. In the absence of power to enforce a law, a covenant is mere words. Hobbes suggests, too, that there can be no 'unjust law'. To the care of the sovereign belongs the making of good laws. But 'good law' does not mean 'just law', because a law made by the sovereign cannot be unjust. Justice means, in practice, obedience to the law, and this is why, according to Hobbes, justice comes into existence only *after* a law has been made by the sovereign. Justice cannot itself be the appropriate standard for the law. Further, when the sovereign makes a law, he does so as though the citizens were making it collectively. That upon which they have agreed cannot be 'unjust'. Keeping the contract under which individuals have agreed to obey the sovereign is vital to justice. Because law is the command of the sovereign, and because justice involves obeying that law, an 'unjust law' is impossible.

Hobbes does make clear, however, that there can be 'bad law'. If the sovereign, in making a law, fails to ensure the safety of the people who have entrusted him with appropriate powers, then the law may be considered 'bad'. (Indeed, human sovereigns may command legitimately only those activities that do not constitute contraventions of the law of nature.) Yet this is not a matter for the people to judge lightly, nor should it be used as a justification for disobedience and rebellion. Given that the sovereign alone has the power to judge what has to be done in the interests of the security of the people, he must proceed on the basis of the exercise of that power. To question his judgment, to voice disagreement, is to revert to the anarchy which characterised the undesirable state of nature. This is a part of the price to be paid for the peace which is intended to flow from the surrender of one's individual will. Where a sovereign makes 'bad law' or performs acts which seem contrary to the general interests of the community, it is, says Hobbes, a matter between him and his God, not between him and the citizens. (Hobbes declares that the sovereign is 'obliged by the law of nature, and must render an account thereof to God, the author of that law, and to none but Him'.) But where it is quite clear that the sovereign has lost the capacity to maintain the peace and protect the safety of the citizens, *or* where he has acted in an obvious attempt to destroy the individual's right of self-preservation, citizens may be absolved from their duty of loyalty. There is, therefore, always a check upon the exercise of absolute power exercised by a sovereign who opposes his own interest to the common good.

The fear of anarchy and social violence is ever-present in Hobbes' writings – a sure reflection of the conflicts of his day. Total obedience to an absolute sovereign, to the protector of the community's peace, seemed essential to Hobbes. Indeed, he insisted, in terms which offended the church deeply, on the subordination of church and religion to the state. If circumstances arose in which a Christian were to interpret the actions of his sovereign as a violation of Divine law, then he must continue to give obedience to that sovereign, failing which he may decide 'to go to Christ in martyrdom'. The church itself has the same type of legal status as that enjoyed by any other corporation. As with all corporations, the true head is, according to Hobbes, the sovereign.

Hobbes represents, in Friedmann's words, a jurist who has shaken himself free from medieval society and its ideas and, in so doing, has completed the revolution of the Renaissance. He has removed the authority of Divine law from the church, and has challenged its pretensions. The protection of the individual within the community has become a matter of great importance. Law is seen as a means of preventing anarchy and assuring survival in peace. There can be no society distinct from the state. Legal authority is to be vested in a sovereign whose laws will depend upon appropriate sanctions. Hobbes insists that 'governments without the sword are mere words, and of no strength to secure a man at all'. Real law is civil law and that is constituted by the law commanded by the sovereign and enforced by his will.

Almost every aspect of Hobbes' Social Contract theory was reflected in the works of jurists and political theoreticians who were prominent in the 18th and 19th centuries. Locke built upon Hobbes' individualism, although he opposed his theory of absolutism. Hobbes' utilitarianism, which led him to view the sovereign as 'a utilitarian creature' of individuals who had empowered him to act on their behalf so as to prevent mutual destruction, was linked to Bentham's later view of the law as serving the totality of individuals within a community. The concept of laws espoused by Austin – 'laws properly so called are a species of command ... all positive law is deduced from a clearly determinable lawgiver as sovereign' – may be likened to Hobbes' view. In our century, the 'enlightened absolutism' favoured by Hobbes has been utilised by some jurists in order to buttress concepts of law at the basis of theories of the collectivist, totalitarian system of government. Others view his analysis of law as a call for the state to concern itself with ensuring the security of citizens' well-being, and for a jurisprudence which will recognise the welfare of individual members of the community as one of the supreme objectives of the law and the legal system.

Notes

Hobbes' *Leviathan*, edited by Oakeshott, contains an exposition of his views on government, society and law. Friedmann, Chapter 11 and Bodenheimer Chapter 3, outline the significance of Hobbes in legal theory. *The Logic of Leviathan*, by Gautier, is a critical account of Hobbes' theories. Peters gives a useful picture of the man and his work in *Hobbes*. Hampton's *Hobbes and the Social Contract Tradition* examines aspects of social contract theories.

Question 9

'Locke's theory admirably expressed certain ideas which were in the ascendant at his time and about to develop continuously throughout the 18th century and most of the 19th century': Friedmann (*Legal Theory*).

Give an account of this theory.

Answer plan

Locke's theory concerning the state and the individual differs radically from that of his predecessor, Hobbes. The 'state of nature' as envisaged by Locke is not that envisaged by Hobbes. This should be emphasised in the answer. Locke's concern for the dangers which could arise from an absolute monarchy should be noted. In particular, the essence of the Social Contract as reflecting the rights of citizens and their power to remove a government in certain extreme circumstances can be seen as a harbinger of the jurisprudential theories which emerged in Europe and America after Locke's day. The following skeleton plan is suggested:

Introduction – the *Treatises of Government*, with an emphasis on liberty – man's 'natural state' – essence of the Social Contract – preservation of property – division of powers – right of a people to reject tyranny – continuing significance of Locke's views – conclusion, noting the importance of his awareness that tyrannies begin where law ends.

Answer

Locke's jurisprudential thought has been characterised as reflecting the doctrines underlying the 'Glorious Revolution' of 1688. His *Treatises of Civil Government* (1699) presented law as a shield against the pretensions of autocracy and despotism and as an instrument for realising and protecting the natural rights of human beings. Where Hobbes had stressed *security*, Locke (1632–1704) placed an emphasis on *liberty*. His writings indicate a reaction against absolutism, a concern for the significance of powers delegated by a people to its government (which prepared the way for later theories of political democracy), an awareness of the importance of the concept of inalienability of individual rights and a sanctioning of the rights of property in particular. These ideas were to flower later in the doctrines which supported the Founding Fathers and the rise of democracy in America.

The 'natural state' of man, was according to Locke, in contrast to that postulated by Hobbes, a situation of total, perfect freedom. Men were able to decide on their activities and to dispose of their persons and possessions as they thought fit, 'within the bounds of

53

the law of nature, without asking leave, or depending upon the will of any other man'. It was a state characterised by 'equality', wherein power and jurisdiction were reciprocal. The law of nature allowed men to live together according to reason 'without a common superior on earth with authority to judge between them'. Liberty, not licence, prevailed and, according to the dictates of the law of nature, no one was encouraged to harm another in his life, health, liberty or possessions.

But dangers and inconveniences arose. First, the individual's enjoyment of the natural rights of life, liberty and possessions was uncertain and was exposed to the hostile activities of others. Secondly, there was a lack of impartial judges with authority to determine disputes according to any form of established law. Each man was both judge and executioner in his own cause and each tended to avenge transgressions in intemperate fashion. Thirdly, there was a lack of a commonly-accepted power to back up and support sentences where wrongdoing had occurred. So as to end this disorder and insecurity, men found it necessary to enter into a Social Contract. Its object was the preservation of life, liberty and estate against the injuries inflicted by others. Fundamental to the Contract is a *pactum unionis,* whereby men agree 'to unite in one political society', and a *pactum subjectionis,* whereby a majority gives power to a government which will protect the individual. This is a contrast to Hobbes' advocacy of total subjection of the individual to the sovereign. The 'law of nature' stood, for Locke, as an eternal rule made for all men, 'legislators as well as others'. An anticipation of the doctrines of popular democracy, with legislatures accountable to the people, may be discerned here.

It is the *right to enforce* the law of nature which, by virtue of the Social Contract is given into the hands of the 'body politic', thus creating a 'political, or civil society'. Nothing more is surrendered. Hence Locke rejects the concept of absolute monarchy as a desirable type of government. A government with limited powers is preferable. (This ideal was to be pursued after Locke's day by jurists and others striving for the 'rule of law' within societies.) Those who have given their 'natural power' of deciding disputes among themselves into the hands of the community are conferring upon that community the role of 'umpire', whereby government is given an authorisation to set up 'a judge on earth' with power to determine controversies and redress injuries'. Indeed, without an authorisation of this kind, without a right to enforce the law, men will remain in 'the state of nature' with all its difficulties and perils.

In words which have been echoed in a variety of forms in centuries after Locke (as in the English case of *Entick v Carrington* (1765) and the American case of *Savings and Loan Association v Topeka* (1875)), he emphasised that God had given the earth 'to the use of the industrious and rational ... not to the fancy or covetousness of the quarrelsome and the contentious', and he enunciated 'the great and chief end of men's uniting into commonwealth and putting themselves under government' as 'the preservation of their property'. The term 'property' is used in a wide sense so as to include 'life, liberty and estate'. Friedmann and other jurists have noted that Locke's views in relation to property ('a combination of noble ideals and acquisitiveness, and the protection of vested interests') underpinned later struggles within democratic societies for a sanctioning of the right to own and dispose freely of the fruits of one's labours.

Locke finds that the institution of private property existed in nature and, therefore, preceded the establishment of civil society. God gave the land to persons in common, commanding them to labour and to use the fruits of the earth. Where men remove parts of the land from the common supply and mix it with their own labour, they are entitled to the objects resulting from their toil. There is a 'natural right', therefore, to appropriate to one's own use land and its produce (the so called 'theory of unilateral acquisition'). Indeed, says Locke, land values arise largely from the labour expended on the land. Private ownership is enlarged, as a result of the use of money as a means of exchange, well beyond those boundaries authorised by a simple act of appropriation. The call for extended rights of private ownership of the land and other types of property became important in moves in the 18th and 19th centuries towards an extension of general political rights, when it was realised that the ownership of land conferred economic and political power. Locke's influence on this area of thought remains powerful. Gray, writing in 1991, speaks of the 'brooding omnipresence of Locke' as a pervasive influence on all philosophical thinking on property, even today.

Because of the significance of property rights in Locke's pattern of liberty, he was obliged to maintain that no part of a person's property ought to be taken from him by the government without his consent. Such an improper exercise of government power should be considered as a violation of the Social Contract by virtue of which power is exercised. The community as a whole must ensure that its governing body does not move beyond the powers bestowed on it. The legislative authority may not assume to itself any power to rule 'by extemporary arbitrary decrees; it is bound to dispense justice and decide the rights of citizens by promulgating laws'. Nor should these laws be varied so as to have 'one rule for the rich and poor, for the favourite at Court, and the countryman at plough'. Locke is enunciating an ideal which was to be advocated repeatedly in the writings of later jurists who called for equality of all before the law.

The supreme power within a community has no other end, according to Locke, but 'preservation'; it can never have a right to 'destroy, enslave or designedly to impoverish subjects'. This necessitates a 'division of powers' within the state: a legislative power to create rules, an executive power to enforce them, and a 'federative power' to control the state's external relations. Where the legislative and executive powers are concentrated in the same hands, a breach of the desired ends of the Social Contract is likely. But this danger was not viewed by Locke as an argument for removing the prerogative of the executive to use its general discretion for the good of the community. Where appropriate laws have not been promulgated by the legislature, where no general directions have been given to the executive, where unusual stress and emergency demand swift action, the executive may act for the public advantage. But separation of powers (a concept which Montesquieu (1689–1755), and jurists in our day, see as essential to the rule of law) remains for Locke an important guarantee of the preservation of a commonwealth and its individual members.

Even where powers are separated, abuse and violation of individual rights may occur. There is needed, therefore, a final guarantor of the law of nature. Fundamentally, Locke rejects the 'rights' of a 'tyrant'. The people as a whole, acting in the name of the liberties which have been entrusted to the supreme power under the Social Contract, may remove a legislature which, deliberately or otherwise, forgets the purpose and nature of its trust. Locke, who had experienced the practice of absolute government under the Stuarts, urged that the power of the state must 'never be supposed to extend further than the common good', so that where a legislature moves beyond its powers, as understood by the community, the people may apply appropriate checks. He argues that nobody can transfer to another more power than he has in himself, and nobody has an arbitrary power over himself or over any other person to destroy his own life or take away the life or property of another. The final resort by the people to an 'appeal to Heaven' which, in practice, may take the form of resistance or revolution, is seen by Locke as necessary if the law of nature is to be upheld against oppressive laws which seem to deny its validity.

Locke's appeal to 'natural rights' as the true guarantee against a regime which seems to abuse its powers, so that the community has the right to resume a trust which is in danger of betrayal, is yet another theme which came to dominate advances in the eighteenth and nineteenth centuries towards the rule of law and the extension of democracy. The American Declaration of Independence (1776) embodies the essence of Locke's doctrine relating to the fundamental right of a people to 'alter or abolish' a form of government which becomes destructive of the ends perceived by the people as constituting the very purpose of the state. The Declaration suggests the concept which Locke had stressed, but in a novel manner – the idea of a government resting upon trust, upon a *fiduciary relationship* of government and governed, rather than upon the mere duties flowing from a Social Contract. But Locke must not be considered as advocating rebellion in all cases of an abuse of governmental powers. The justification of popular resistance must be sought in a long series of abuses and a very clear threat to the 'lives, liberties and estates' of citizens. Nor does resistance imply revenge; it is an activity aimed at the restoration of an order violated by an oppressor.

The political and legal ferment within societies of the 18th and 19th centuries was often within the context of circumstances envisaged by Locke. His warnings that *whenever laws end, tyrannies will begin*, and that 'what duty is, cannot be understood without a law' were utilised by jurists who sought to express theories resting on the need for a widening of the basis of law. His cautions concerning the consequences of unbridled governmental powers were remembered in calls for the creation of popular power and an extension of the franchise. Although doubt was cast, in increasing measure, upon the veracity of Locke's 'state of nature' (thus, Hamilton, writing in this century, speaks of this 'state' as being, 'a curious affair, peopled with Indians of North America and run by the scientific principles of [Locke's] friend, Sir Isaac Newton'), his contribution to political and legal theory is profound. Keeton reminds us that it is from Locke that we derive, today, 'the principle of democratic government, resting upon the consent of the governed' – an extraordinarily valuable legacy of the *Treatises of Civil Government* and the subsequent jurisprudential and political thinking which they engendered.

Notes

Locke's *Two Treatises of Civil Government* are available in an edition by Laslett. His theories are discussed in Lloyd, Chapter 3; Dias, Chapter 4; and Bodenheimer, Chapter 3. Comments on Locke's theory of property may be found in 'Property according to Locke', by Hamilton, in (1932) 41 Yale LJ and 'Property in thin air', by Gray, in [1991] CLJ 293. *John Locke: a Biography*, by Cranston, explains the nature of the society in which Locke lived.

Question 10

'Man is born free and everywhere he is in chains.'

Outline the nature of the social doctrine associated with the author of these words, referring, in particular, to his views on law.

Answer plan

Rousseau, the author of this quotation from *The Social Contract*, sought the fundamental norm of man's life in society in the omnipotence of 'the general will. This concept became a basic feature of his social and legal philosophy. Each member of the community must surrender himself, without reservation, to the general will from which he will ultimately derive his freedom. Respect for the community's laws becomes vitally important where law mirrors the general will. In spite of Rousseau's expressed concern for liberty, it is no accident that some totalitarian jurists and politicians have sought to derive justification of their views from his work. 'Paradox is everywhere in Rousseau.' The following skeleton plan is suggested:

> Introduction – the general will – respect for the law – essence of the social contract – why man is 'in chains' – sovereignty is lodged in the people – Rousseau and totalitarian ideology – conclusion, Rousseau and freedom.

Answer

'Man is born free and everywhere he is in chains.' These words are to be found in the opening section of *Du Contrat Social* (On the Social Contract), published in 1762 by the leading philosopher of the French Enlightenment, Rousseau (1712–88), philosopher, musician and literary scholar. Born in Geneva, Rousseau moved to France where he became very critical of contemporary European political regimes and, in particular, the prevalent attitude of governments in relation to the governed. In 1753, he began a detailed examination of the origins of inequality among men and asked whether the condition was authorised by natural law. He studied the basis of the institution of private property and considered the role of law in relation to property in general. In 1762, he published a highly influential treatise on education, *Emile* (in which he argued that education should 'follow nature') and *The Social Contract*, which outlined a concept of sovereignty as residing solely in the people. Exile to Switzerland and England followed. Rousseau died in France in 1788.

Rousseau's work has been characterised as 'brilliant paradox', which enlarged natural law thinking through the formulation of a theory of association 'which may defend and protect with the whole force of the community the person and property of every associate, and by means of which, coalescing with all, may nevertheless obey only himself, and remain as free as before'. Critics, such as the French legal theorist, Duguit (1859–1918), censure Rousseau as 'the source of all the doctrines of dictatorship and tyranny'. Few would deny, however, the formative influence of Rousseau's teachings upon those who made the French

Revolution, in the name of liberty, and those who fashioned American independence and the doctrine of the rights of man.

The general philosophical and political views advanced by Rousseau are based upon his concept of 'the greatest good' as 'not authority, but liberty'. To study man correctly is to study his relationship, not with things (for that is a programme of childhood) but with his fellow men (for 'this is the programme of his entire life'). The freedom and the equality of men must be guaranteed, for they will not emerge automatically within any community; that guarantee will be given by a state which takes into account men's 'inalienable rights' and their undoubted power of self-determination. Rousseau draws attention to the paradigm presented by nature in the form, structure and aims of the family – the fundamental unit within society; in such a unit there is no inequality, no servitude, no oppression of one member by another. Let the state consider this example and construct frameworks of organisation based upon the aim of liberty for all. Appropriate laws must be passed to assist in this endeavour.

Respect for the law, argues Rousseau, is essential if the law mirrors the 'general will' of members of the community. Should an individual express disagreement with the proclaimed law, should he act in a manner which indicates clearly that he is refusing, in deliberate fashion, to accept and obey the general will, then 'he must be constrained by the whole body of his fellow-citizens to do so'. This means that 'it may be necessary to compel a man to be free'. 'Freedom' is defined by Rousseau in precise terms: it is 'that condition which, by giving each citizen to his country, guarantees him from all personal dependence and is the foundation upon which the whole political machine rests, and supplies the power which works it'. It involves the recognition by the individual citizen of the community's rights which provide legal force to undertakings entered into by citizens; in the absence of such recognition, those undertakings 'would become absurd, tyrannical and exposed to vast abuses'. To use force to compel obedience to the law is to enlarge freedom for all. The function of law in these circumstances is to guard the community against those whose activities undermine wide communal interests.

Rousseau insists upon the untrammelled right of the community – the sovereign, omnipotent people – to change its laws as and when it wishes to do so. Unlike Locke, Rousseau places no constitutional limitation on the people's powers and no barriers to their exercise. Law serves, but does not dominate, the sovereign people. Indeed, laws are, properly speaking, only the conditions of civil association. 'The people, being subject to the laws, ought to be their author: the conditions of a society ought to be regulated solely by those who unite to form it.'

The Social Contract (1762) should be considered in the context of Rousseau's other writings, particularly the *Discourse on the Origins of Inequality Among Men* (1755). In the *Discourse*, he described, in purely hypothetical terms, mankind's so called 'natural state'. In that state, men enjoyed a kind of equality; they lived in relative isolation from one another; they did not live in subordination to any individual. Because of natural disasters men decided to come together in groups based upon primitive norms of social interaction; this resulted in 'a golden age' in humanity's evolution which taught mankind to differentiate good from evil. A further stage followed when iron and wheat were discovered: these commodities 'civilised mankind and ruined the human race' because of the disputes and violence resulting from the division of land which followed on intensified cultivation. Wars resulted in the making of laws which were used to protect the institution of private property owned by those who possessed the land.

In his *Discourse on Political Economy* (1755), Rousseau noted that the social inequality which had stemmed from land ownership could not be abolished, but the injustice which it caused could be reduced in its impact on the community. The private will of wealthy property owners must give way to respect for the general will. The morals of the community must reflect austerity and patriotism. Resources in publicly-owned property must be buttressed by taxes on luxuries and inherited wealth.

The Social Contract is a detailed version of Rousseau's concepts of society, its basis, structures and laws. Why is man everywhere in chains? How can the natural freedom which belongs to man be preserved and widened within communities? It was these and allied questions which *The Social Contract* attempted to explore and answer. Rousseau emphasises the need for the foundation of a form of association which will allow the community's strength to be used so as to protect the person and property of individual

61

citizens (that is, members of the association) so that each 'when united to his fellows renders obedience to his own will and remains as free as he was before'. The social contract must be such that, in the event of the violation of the basic compact, each associated individual would immediately resume 'all the rights which once were his, and regain his natural liberty, by the mere fact of losing the liberty for which he had renounced it'. Fundamentally, each member of the community 'makes surrender of himself without reservation' to the supreme direction of the general will. Rousseau argues:

> Who gives himself to all gives himself to none. And since there is no member of the social group over whom we do not acquire precisely the same rights as those over ourselves which we have surrendered to him, it follows that we gain the exact equivalent of what we lose, as well as an added power to conserve what we already have.

Rousseau summarises his doctrine in these words: 'Each of us contributes to the group his person and the powers which he wields as a person under the supreme direction of the general will, and we receive into the body politic each individual as forming an indivisible part of the whole.'

Where men associate, and the act of association becomes a reality, each of the contracting parties 'disappears' and is replaced and represented by a collective assembly which is given a unity, a 'collective self' and 'a will'. The 'Sovereign People' is born, composed of citizens who are subject to the laws and legal institutions of the state. Each member of the association of people owes a duty to each of his neighbours; as an individual citizen, he has obligations to the entity of the Sovereign People. The contracting parties (to the act of association) are obliged by virtue of the contract to render one another mutual assistance as and when it is required.

The result of the compact embodied in the act of association is that, in the case of the individual citizen, 'justice is substituted for instinct in his behaviour' and his actions take on a new, moral basis. Duty replaces mere physical impulse, ennobling his sentiments and elevating his soul. He has become 'an intelligent being and a man'. He has ceased to be a 'slave' subject to his gross appetites; in obeying the laws which have been promulgated in the name of society, he has become 'free'.

The gains and losses to be attributed to the social contract are, says Rousseau, clear and obvious A citizen loses his natural liberty 'and his unqualified right to lay hands on all that tempts him, provided only that he can compass its possession'. His gain is civil liberty, to be realised as a citizen within the community, and the right to ownership of that which apparently belongs to him. (Rousseau differentiates 'natural liberty' which a person enjoys only as long as he is strong enough to maintain it, and 'civil liberty' which is dependent for its exercise upon the general will.)

The 'general will' must not be confused with 'the will of all members of society'. By 'general will', Rousseau has in mind the 'general will' as *the corporate will*, that is, the will of the corporate community. It is as if the body politic, which has come into existence as the result of a compact of citizens, has taken on the character of 'a moral person', possessed of a will which makes laws directed to the preservation and welfare of citizens, individually and collectively.

Why, then, is man to be found everywhere in chains? Rousseau argues in *The Social Contract* that 'since man is born free and is his own master, no one can govern him without his consent'. He notes, too, that since the exercise of the general will ensures equality of treatment among citizens of the community, it should not by its very nature be subject to abuse. The abuse of power arise, and man is fettered, because exercise of the general will requires the enforcement of laws and this process is entrusted to the government which is subordinate to the sovereign. The body known as 'the government' has a tendency to put its own corporate requirements before the interests of the citizens, thus – paradoxically – diminishing the power of the sovereign. In the interests of freedom and democracy, therefore, the government must be confined strictly within the limits of its powers and duties; it must not be allowed to take over the sovereignty which belongs solely to the people. It is the ignoring of the general will by governments which results in the loss of individual liberty and the enslavement of mankind.

Rousseau detects the possibility of a contradiction between man as citizen and man as an individual being: the demands on man within a community are such that the general will of citizens may often differ dramatically from the specific wills of persons as 'individuals'. If the general will is to conquer the individual's mind and heart, man must be transformed in his nature, and this involves tasks for the legislator. The community's laws must reflect the spirits, aims and objectives of the general will so that the individual is given a new *persona* as citizen, allowing (and, indeed, encouraging) him to identify himself closely and permanently with the community. *The general will cannot be realised in practice unless the human mind is transformed,* and a 'new man' – a citizen is created, partly as a result of the educative function of legislative enactments. Here is a concept of 'law in the service of the community', educating and transforming persons in the interests of the creation of a 'general will'.

The basis of man's rights is to be found, according to *The Social Contract*, in the social order itself: that order constitutes a 'sacred right' from which true liberty flows. It is civil liberty which is fundamental to the existence of rights such as equality, ownership of property. Rights of this kind are bestowed on citizens, as such, and not on men as men, as postulated in natural law theory. But always, according to Rousseau's vision of the common good, which derives from the general will, rights of individuals, say, to their own estates, are to be subordinated in all circumstances to the rights possessed by the community over all persons and things. *The social compact into which man has entered gives the community an absolute power which can be exercised within limits specified by general conventions.*

Because sovereignty resides collectively in the citizens of a community, decisions of the people should emerge in democratic fashion from the exercise of a free vote. Citizens should refuse to cast votes for their selfish advantage; rather should they indicate their preferences for courses of action which will lead to an extension of the common good, in the form of benefits to be enjoyed by the community as a whole. Altruism must replace greed and self-interest. Rousseau teaches that people are 'naturally good'. They will vote for 'good measures'; they will recognise the significance of what is demanded in the name of the general will. On some occasions the people may be deceived, but they will never be corrupted. Democracy can thrive only as an expression of the people's sovereign power. The inalienable will of the people allows them to confer powers upon elected officials, but they cannot voluntarily surrender their right of sovereignty.

In sum, sovereignty is lodged in the people as a whole; it cannot be 'divided and portioned out'. The law within a community merely expresses the common will of the people in relation to matters of common interest. Government by the sovereign people involves the existence of gatherings which legislate directly in pursuance of the general will. Where a community is so large as to make gatherings of this nature impossible, forms of government may be established, but such government *rests upon the consent of the governed*; its authority will decline when it is seen to be legislating solely for its own circumstances.

It is easy to see why the doctrines of Rousseau have had, and continue to have, some kind of appeal for libertarians of all shades and for jurists who see the sole *raison d'être* of law as in the service of the people. The stress on the innate virtues of the people, the calls for a democratic form of government, the demands for curbs on governmental powers, and the insistence on general welfare taking priority over private rights, constitute a brew which has sustained democratic reformers over the generations. *The Social Contract* is seen by many as a 'handbook for freedom'.

Paradoxically, but, perhaps, not surprisingly, Rousseau's theories have supplied grist to the mill of some ideologists of totalitarian politics and jurisprudence. Friedmann, in *Legal Theory* (1967), notes that Rousseau's glorification of the collective will as embodying 'the good and the reasonable' fabricated a line of thought which Hegel was to develop later into 'a dangerous climax'. Russell's *History of Western Philosophy* (1954), suggests that, in practice, the first fruits of *The Social Contract* were the revolutionary terror and cruelties of Robespierre, and that the jurisprudential writings which favoured the dictatorships of Russia and Germany were in part an outcome of Rousseau's teachings.

In a number of cases, the ideologists of Fascism and the Corporate state, who wrote in the 1920s and 1930s, sketched theories which appeared to owe much to the doctrines of *The Social Contract*. Rocco, an Italian jurist who was a prominent advocate of dictatorship, advanced as a slogan: 'Everything for the state; nothing against the state; nothing outside the state.' Gentile, writing of the need to create a strong centralised apparatus of law and government, argued that maximum liberty coincides with maximum state force. 'Every force is a moral force, for it is always an expression of will.' The Italian fascist state was to be perceived as 'an organism having ends, life, and means of action superior to those of the separate individuals or groups of individuals which compose it'. The distorted shadow of Rousseau hangs over an ideology of this nature.

Whether Rousseau would have welcomed an extension of his theories in these directions is very doubtful. For him, liberty was mankind's most important possession. It was a gift of nature, and to deprive a man of his liberty could never be a 'right action'. Man's fundamental characteristics are such that he craves for freedom, and the apparent surrender of rights inherent in his social compact is illusory since men receive more than they surrender in the making of that compact. The ends envisioned by Rousseau in *The Social Contract* are in no sense compatible with those proclaimed by 20th century apologists for state tyranny. He would have argued that the task of politics, jurisprudence and the law is to remove men's chains, not to tighten them. In his *Letters from the Mountains* (1764), he is unambiguous: 'Liberty without justice is a veritable contradiction ... there is no liberty without laws, or where any man is above the laws ... A free people obeys, but it does not serve; it has magistrates but no masters; it obeys nothing but the laws, and thanks to the force of the laws it does not obey man.'

Notes

The political works of Rousseau, including *The Social Contract*, have been translated by Cole. Broome's *Rousseau: A Study of His Thought*, and Chapman's *Rousseau: Totalitarian or Liberal?* are of considerable interest. Wright's *The Meaning of Rousseau* is a valuable interpretation of the paradoxical nature of the theories set out in *The Social Contract*. Cobban's *Rousseau and the Modern State* is an exploration of the relevance of Rousseau's thought for our times.

CHAPTER 3

NATURAL LAW

Introduction

Natural law, which is the subject of the questions in this chapter, is an enduring concept in European jurisprudence, ranging from Aristotle, who held that there is a natural law which 'everywhere possesses the same authority and is no mere matter of opinion', through Cicero, who taught that 'Nature herself has placed in our ears a power of judging', and Aquinas, for whom the natural law was 'the participation of the eternal law in the rational creature', to today's neo-Scholastics, who seek to establish new values based on fundamental criteria often related directly to the social teachings of the Roman Catholic Church. Natural law is often contrasted with the 'positive law', namely, the legal rules promulgated in formal fashion by the state and enforced through defined sanctions. A problem for students is to decide which 'type' of natural law is being referred to, since the term has been used in so many different senses. It is essential, therefore, to *check the precise historical and juristic context* of the term, particularly when answering questions on this topic.

Checklist

Ensure that you understand the following topics:

- natural and positive law contrasted
- natural law with a changing content
- derivation of 'ought' from 'is'
- Aquinas' divisions of law
- *lex injusta*
- Radbruch's 'free law'
- Finnis' 'human goods'
- neo-Scholasticism

Question 11

What is Aquinas' theory of law?

Answer plan

Thomas Aquinas (1225–74) was concerned with systematising knowledge, on the basis of Catholic doctrine, so that the cosmos might understood be as a vast unit in which everything had a place and a meaning. Within this system of knowledge, God's plans for mankind occupied a special place, and the law was to be comprehended as a part of those plans. Aquinas propounded a theory of law based on his conception of 'reason'; this resulted in a fourfold division of law in which so called 'natural law' is of much significance. The answer given below is based on the following skeleton plan:

> Introduction – background of Aquinas – influence of Aristotelian thought – fourfold division of law – problem of morality – violation of the natural law and its consequences – conclusion, stressing the work of Aquinas as a synthesiser of philosophy and religious thought in his interpretation of law.

Answer

St Thomas Aquinas occupies an important place in the history of the development of natural law doctrine. He had studied as a Dominican monk under Albertus Magnus, and, in later years, produced works of lasting significance in which he effected a synthesis of the logic of Aristotle, the religious thought of the early Christian Fathers, and some of the patterns of classical Roman law. In his celebrated *Summa Theologica* (c 1266), he set out a fully systematised approach to law which, even today, dominates the thinking of many Catholic jurists, as evidenced by the growing neo-Scholastic school of jurisprudence. Law is to be understood as part of God's plan for mankind – this is the belief which is central to the concepts mentioned below.

It is important to remember the context within which Aquinas worked. The authority of the Catholic Church was expanding, and those whose task it was to explain doctrine were guided by a strict pattern of thought. Interpretation of the Scriptures had produced two principles which were of direct relation to attempts at explaining the nature of law. First, the principle of *unity* (based on 'one God, one Church') was reflected in the wish for 'one Church believing in one law'. Secondly, the principle of *supremacy of law*, which was seen as an aspect of the unity of the world, taught that all persons, including rulers, were under the law's dominion. Aquinas' general approach to law was fashioned with these principles in mind.

At this time, a study of the works of Aristotle was not always welcomed by the dominant church hierarchy, which viewed his 'scientific rationalism' as a potential threat to church dogma. Aquinas did not share this attitude. He was deeply impressed by Aristotle's emphasis on reason and the primacy of intelligence. He made a deep study of Aristotle's works, lectured publicly on their significance, and was affected profoundly by their elucidation of the part which could be played by reason in the understanding of phenomena such as law.

In the *Summa Theologica*, Aquinas seeks to establish the framework of a systematised 'science of theology'. He employs the highly formalised style of argument which was common in his day (and which was to be found in the procedures of the civil courts in those parts of Europe where the inquisitorial style of trial was common). Questions are posed, sub-questions emerge and are answered, further argument leads to attempted refutation until an outline of proof and a final enunciation of an answer to the original question appear. The exposition of law associated with Aquinas is derived from his answers to Questions 90–97 in the *Summa*. Law is perceived always as God's instrument for assisting man in the lifelong process leading to the perfection of his nature.

Aquinas begins his examination and interpretation of law by considering 'morality'. The very basis of moral obligation is to be discovered within man's nature. Built into his nature is a group of God-given 'inclinations'. They include self-preservation, propagation of the species and (reflecting man's rationality) an inclination towards a search for truth. Man is guided by a simple and basic moral truth – *to do good and to avoid evil*. Because man is rational, he is under a natural obligation to protect himself and to live peacefully within society. A peaceful, ordered society demands human laws, fashioned for the direction of social behaviour. These human laws will arise from man's rational capacity to discern correct patterns of 'good conduct'. The rules underlying human laws will derive from a moral system which ought to be taken into account by *all* mankind – a sort of 'natural law'.

Law must be thought of, according to Aquinas, as linked essentially with reason. A law may be considered as a 'rule' and also as 'a measure' of the nature of human activities. He reminds us that the word *lex* is derived from *ligare* (to bind) and that law 'binds us' to act in particular ways. The rules and measures of human acts are to be thought of in terms of law and also in terms of our reason. Reason directs us to the fulfilment of 'our ends' (an Aristotelian concept). Man's laws should go hand in hand with reason. Indeed, man's laws may be thought of as *'ordinances of reason for the common good, made by those who have care of the community, and are promulgated'*. The natural law is 'promulgated' by the very fact that God has instilled it into man's mind so that it can be known 'naturally'. The natural law is the product of God's wisdom. We can better comprehend that wisdom by studying human nature and the natural law. Theology *and* philosophy together will help in this quest for comprehension of the truth. Aquinas is suggesting that a synthetic approach to a study of the law, in which Christian dogma and Aristotelian philosophy will assist, will produce a clear understanding of the nature and power of God's law.

A *fourfold division of law* is put forward by Aquinas. The first type of law is *lex aeterna* – 'eternal law'; all laws, in so far as they participate in 'right reason', are derived from the eternal law. This is the Divine Intellect and Will of God directing *all things*. God's rational guidance is not subject to constraints of time – it is eternal. Not to know eternal law – God's plan for his creatures – is to be without direction, so that one's true ends can never be achieved; but awareness of the eternal law is imprinted on us. God alone knows the eternal law in its totality, but those few 'blessed persons' who have been able to know God in His essence may perceive its truth.

'Divine law' – *lex divina* – is the eternal law governing man and may be known by him through direct revelation, as in the Scriptures, for example, The Ten Commandments. Man requires a type of law that can direct him to his end, namely, eternal happiness; such law contains no errors, and forbids all sins, allowing no evil to go unpunished. Aristotle had argued that man had a natural purpose and an end, so that natural law, known through human reason, could provide an adequate guide. Aquinas distances himself from Aristotle at this point. Because man's eternal happiness is related to God's plans, man needs direction from God's law, in addition to human law and natural law. Natural law comes from man's rational knowledge of 'the good', but that knowledge is, by its nature, limited. Divine law comes, through revelation, directly from God. Revelation is the guide for man's reason, allowing his highest nature to be perfected by Divine grace. Here is an interesting example of Aquinas giving a 'Christian gloss' to the views of the 'pagan Greeks' and achieving an imaginative synthesis.

The third type of law is 'natural law' – *lex naturalis*, which is man's participation in the eternal cosmic law, as it is known through reason. Because of man's possession of God-given reason, he may enjoy a share in Divine reason itself and may derive from it 'a natural inclination to such actions and ends as are fitting', such as the search for good and the avoidance of evil. Where man exercises his reason correctly he will understand the fundamental principles of God's plan. Basic principles for human guidance will emerge, such as that 'good' ('that which all things seek after') is to be done and evil is to be shunned. But because of bad customs and habits, some humans will ignore the natural laws; the result is a division of their energies from those tasks of a life-fulfilling kind.

The fourth type of law is 'human law' – *lex humana*, involving the particular application of the natural law and resulting in legislation by governments. Just as men draw conclusions in the various sciences from naturally known, but indemonstrable, principles, so, declares Aquinas, human beings must draw from the precepts of the natural law answers to problems which emerge when they live together in society. Where human law conforms to the law of reason, it conforms to the law of God and advances human development.

A significant aspect of Aquinas' concept of human law, which has overtones of relevance for the present day, is the relationship he perceives between human law and its moral dimensions. He repudiates the thesis that a law is a law merely because it has been decreed by a sovereign. He suggests that a rule takes on the character of 'a law' only where it has appropriate moral dimensions. Certain questions must be asked: does the rule exist in conformity to the precepts of the natural law, and does it suggest agreement with the basis of the moral law? 'That which is not just seems no law at all', he declares. Where a human law diverges from the law of nature, it is no longer a law, but a mere perversion of the law. *Such a law cannot bind in conscience.* This is not to say, however, that it must not, therefore, be obeyed; obedience to it might be essential so as to prevent an even greater evil, such as the spread of lawlessness, scandal or great harm.

Aquinas takes a further step forward. Laws which are opposed to the Divine plan, such as the laws of tyrants inducing to 'idolatry', must not be observed: our duty is to obey God rather than man. *A law which is a violation of the natural law should not, in general, be obeyed.*

There are many jurists, inside and outside the Catholic Church, who see Aquinas as a divinely-inspired genius, able to synthesise a variety of approaches and capable of bringing system into an unwieldy group of theories. In moving beyond his predecessors and contemporaries, he was able to produce a unified set of principles in relation to the law. Natural law is envisaged as a source of *general principles* rather than detailed jurisprudential rules. Above all, perhaps, is *the elevation of human reason* in the service of comprehension of the law. God's law is the 'reason of Divine wisdom'; Christianity is reason; human institutions, including those related to law, required the exercise of reason if they are to be built in enduring fashion. The Thomist view of law is, fundamentally, that of Cicero, writing in *De Republica* (52 BC): '... true law is right reason in agreement with Nature ... God is the author of this law, its promulgator and its enforcing judge.' In essence: 'The proper effect of the law is to make men good ... it should lead men to their proper virtue.'

Notes

The theory of law expounded by Aquinas is discussed in Lloyd, Chapter 3; Harris, Chapter 2; Riddall, Chapter 5; and Davies and Holdcroft, Chapter 6. A classic account of the work of Aquinas is given by D'Arcy in *Thomas Aquinas*. Gilson's *The Philosophy of Aquinas* gives the setting of Aquinas' legal thought. Bloch relates the theory of Aquinas to contemporary problems in 'The relative natural law of Aquinas' in his book, *Natural Law and Human Dignity*. Lisska's *Aquinas' Theory of Natural Law* contains an account of the principles of the *Summa*.

Question 12

Elaborate Stammler's concept of 'natural law with a variable content'.

Answer plan

Stammler (1856–1936), a German jurist and disciple of the philosopher, Kant, considered the advantages to be gained from a system of law based on fundamental natural law principles which allowed for interpretation, and even modification, in the light of social requirements. The question necessitates an examination of this seemingly-paradoxical viewpoint, given the 'eternal character' of natural law. Some detailed examination of Stammler's argument is needed together with reference to the social principles he advocated in relation to the law. The following skeleton plan is used:

Introduction – the paradox within the concept – essence of Stammler's views – the 'concept' and the 'idea' of law – Stammler's views on reason – principles of 'respect' and 'participation' – the principles in practice – conclusion, summary of Stammler's views.

Answer

The concept of 'natural law with a variable content' appears somewhat paradoxical. The essence of natural law, as that term is generally understood, is its unchanging, everlasting nature. For some jurists, natural law emanates from Divine revelation and reflects the immutable, eternal aspects of God's plan for mankind. Stammler, with whom the variable concept is linked, believed that *every era should have its own 'law of nature', its 'right law', which would co-exist with its positive law*. The rules of the positive law would have to 'justify' their existence and continued use by an evaluation according to standards posed by the relevant, dominant philosophical and ethical doctrines of the era. Should a law be found wanting as a result of this evaluation, it would be corrected by further legislation or by the practice of the courts. Stammler was suggesting that in a progressive society, positive law needs to be tested *regularly* by the light of the community's prevailing *moral* ideals, in particular.

The ideal of the classical natural law which was to be found in a perfect code with an unchangeable, unconditionally valid legal content, seemed to Stammler to reflect the impossible. The jurist's task was to discover a valid formal method by means of which the changing material of 'empirically-conditioned legal rules' could be so worked out and judged that the law may have *the quality of objective justice*. For this, a new approach to an understanding of the law was required.

It is essential, says Stammler, to distinguish the *concept of law* from the *idea of law*. Confusion of the two is common. The 'concept of law' is little more than a merely formal definition. Its underlying meaning is 'the inviolable and autocratic will'. The law is an aspect of man's *social existence*; it relates to individuals living together and constituting a community. It embodies the collective will of that community and is 'autocratic' in the sense that the laws bind all members. Law is, therefore, the result of 'binding volition' (a phrase used in some earlier versions of natural law) and members of the community are not free to accept or reject it as they please. The 'concept of law' is a reflection of 'inviolable volition'; it binds its adherents in a unity of purpose. 'Unity of purpose', 'will of the community', echo the classical natural law doctrines.

Stammler, having acknowledged the need for a 'binding together of the community in a unity of purpose', proceeds to discuss the 'idea of the law' – a much more complex phenomenon than the 'concept of law'. The 'idea of the law' will mirror the need for *justice within the community*. But justice is not to be viewed as a mere abstraction. For Stammler, justice arises from *necessity* – the necessity for all 'legal efforts' to be aimed at the attainment of the most perfect natural harmony of social life that is possible *in a given place at a given time*. Here is a meeting-point of the absolutism of the natural law ('perfect harmony') and the awareness of the need to view legal principle in a context of place and time.

As a disciple of Kant, Stammler accepts the Kantian principle of *man as an end in himself*. The recognising of members of a community as ends in themselves, and not as mere objects of an arbitrary will, is a necessary objective of the 'right law' which Stammler sees as the true 'idea of law'. His own social ideal, which, again, has overtones of some earlier views of classical natural law, is of a 'community of free-willing men', bound by a law which is derived from their common interests but reflecting the fundamental recognition of that community as an end in itself. Kant's 'categorical imperative' is given expression by Stammler in his advocacy of man as an end, directed by laws inspired by natural principles of justice, manifesting the community's 'pure will'.

In the tradition of the natural law, Stammler emphasises the role of 'reason in the law'. One's social responsibilities may be determined by the use of reason, and the realising of the community's social ideals demands 'a rational curbing of one's own singular desires' based on respect for the community in general, and other individuals in particular. The exercise of reason is vital for the individual if the community, of which he is a part, is to move towards the standards of reciprocity which are essential where people are treated as ends in themselves. Essentially, Stammler is following the pattern of those of his predecessors in the natural law who elevated reason to a supreme position in the determination of the law. But Stammler does not make clear the precise meaning he attaches to 'reason'. Ginsberg, for example, has criticised Stammler's theory as based on too abstract a view of 'reason'. He pays lip service to some remote concept of reason, says Ginsberg, but makes virtually impossible the relating of 'particular aims' of action to the 'universal'. In practice, argues Ginsberg, the actual law would be placed 'at the mercy of empiricism and the blind forces of tradition'.

Within a social framework dominated by a desire for justice, as an expression of the community's collective will (and reminiscent of many structures suggested by the earlier natural law), is a group of principles which must be kept in mind if individuals are to attain freedom under the law. The 'principles of respect' and the 'principles of participation' must be translated into practical law by the community's legislators; they should be embedded within enactments and other social rules. The community's needs will find a place in the overall framework of fundamental principle.

The 'principles of respect' demand that the content of an individual's volition be not rendered subject to the arbitrary power of another. This will mean, in practice, that no act of an individual's will is to be subjected to the mere caprice of another. Each member of the community is an end in himself and is to be treated accordingly. Respect for him as a person demands that he be safe from the whims of another. Further, every legal demand on an individual must be made in such a manner that the person obligated may retain, in the terminology of the natural law, his 'self-respecting personality'. A juristic claim has validity, therefore, only if this principle is respected, that is, only on the condition that the individual of whom it is made be allowed to preserve his dignity as a member of a united, free community of individuals. Stammler is calling, in effect, for the preservation of human dignity – an essential feature of the classical natural law.

The 'principles of participation' are as important as those of 'respect'. A member of the community may not be excluded from it in arbitrary fashion. This means in practice that power may not be exercised with the result that some person is deprived of his social status and reputation. The concept of 'man as an end in himself' demands from those who live by it that, because dignity involves the recognition of the right to participate in a community, that right shall not be invaded by others. Further, a power of control conferred by the community through the law may be justified only to the extent that the person affected thereby is enabled to retain his self-respect. Stammler's principles seem directed to a recognition of Kantian fundamentals concerning the 'imperatives' for social behaviour. The place accorded to man by the natural law is recognised; the rules relating to his treatment within the community are to be designed accordingly and, in practice, will recognise the needs and morals of that community.

Stammler insists on an application of the principles of respect and participation with an understanding of the specific, variable sets of circumstances arising in different types of society. Valid, basic rules are required if the 'idea of law' is to be realised – a concept acceptable to natural law doctrine. But a society in transition, in flux, will require, not a modification of the 'idea of the law', but rather *an adaptation of rules to the realities of that society*. Here is 'natural law with a variable content'. Tradition gives way to real needs, not at the expense of the fundamental rule, but so that the essence of the rule shall be recognised translated, or transformed, according to time, place and other circumstances.

Stammler seeks to demonstrate the significance of his principles of respect of participation by applying them to a variety of actual problems derived from the German civil law of his day. The phenomena of the cartel and the trust received particular attention. Cartels and trusts are based on associations of firms formed so as to restrict, or exercise a monopolistic influence on, the production or sale of commodities. Prices and output are regulated, markets are divided up. Stammler argues that these economic organisations do achieve an important social purpose: they oppose 'the anarchy of production and sale' and can give some kind of protection and defence to individuals who, under conditions of unrestricted freedom in the market, will be unable to realise their 'proper activities as human beings' within the social economy. On the other hand, cartels and trusts may be viewed as representing combinations made for personal ends. They can easily become the means of abuse of the community. The principles of respect and participation must be applied to an examination of the problem. Is a cartel, by its policies and activities, invading the rights of producers outside its ranks? Are they being deprived of the right to participate in the community? Is the cartel exploiting members of the community by arbitrary demands? Is it ignoring the necessity for co-operation within the community? These questions illustrate the kinds of criteria Stammler would keep in mind in deciding a practical question, with the fundamental duties of traders and producers in mind. The reality is to be viewed in the light of natural law principle, not merely on the basis of the desire to make a swift decision.

We may summarise Stammler's purely formal view of natural law by emphasising his concern for its traditional concepts which, he believes, assist in providing a correct understanding of what has to be done if man is to be treated with respect. He wishes, however, to mould some of those concepts into a jurisprudential structure which rests upon the axiom that it is not possible to view a principle in terms of a content which will *always* stand up to the demanding test of time. It is not the law of nature, but the nature of law which is common to all countries and communities in all ages. The nature of law may be comprehended only when perceived (as through the eyes of the advocates of the classical natural law) as a harmonious whole. Rules must be 'right' for a community, and the criterion for the testing of their 'rightness' must be of a formal nature – mere relativism will not suffice. A community of free-willing individuals, each an end in himself, each contributing to a community in which he may realise his potential, is Stammler's ideal. The law, attuned to the needs of such a community, and reflecting the harmony of which the natural law speaks, results in 'the right law' and assists in the journey to the realisation of that ideal.

Notes

Stammler's *Theory of Justice* explains his attitude to natural law. Friedmann, Chapter 16, and Jones, in his *Historical Introduction to the Theory of Law*, Chapter 4, consider the implications of Stammler's views. Hussik analyses the theory in 'The legal philosophy of Stammler' (1924) 24 Col LR 373.

Question 13

Outline the circumstances of Radbruch's conversion to the principles of natural law. What are the elements of the earlier jurisprudential theories which he rejected and those which he later embraced?

Answer plan

The celebrated German jurist, Radbruch (1878–1949), is best known today for his move away from the relativist-positivist jurisprudence of his earlier years and his conversion to a natural law doctrine which became of much relevance in the reconstruction of German law and legal institutions in the post-war era. An appropriate answer will explain the effect on his thinking of the perversion of law under the Nazi dictatorship. An outline of the 'free law' movement and its philosophy should be given, together with his later teachings based on the need for acceptance of a transcendent law resting solely on justice. The encapsulation of his thinking in 'Five Minutes of Legal Philosophy' should be set out. The following skeleton plan is used:

> Introduction – Radbruch's background and involvement in activism – fundamentals of the 'free law' movement in relation to jurisprudential positivism and relativism – circumstances of Radbruch's conversion – revulsion against earlier beliefs – the principles of natural law as given in 'Five Minutes of Legal Philosophy' – conclusion, significance of Radbruch today.

Answer

Radbruch, who occupied the chair of law at Kiel, was concerned in his early years as an academic with questions of philosophy which were of particular importance to his work in jurisprudence. The fundamental question of the possibility of a derivation of 'ought' from 'is' was bound up with his strong faith as a Lutheran Pietist and his interest in socialism and justice. As a very reluctant political activist, he spoke out against militarism in politics and was imprisoned in 1920, following the Kapp military attempt at a *coup d'état*, narrowly escaping a death sentence. In the Weimar Government, he served as Minister for Justice, but returned to academic work. He played a leading role among a group of colleagues – lawyers and politicians – who sought to harmonise their left wing political theory with the need for working out new jurisprudential principles.

In the 1920s and early 1930s, Radbruch occupied a dominant role in the 'free law' movement. The jurisprudential theories which he and the movement advocated were based on a perception of law as a means to the creation of a democratic, socialist and humanist society. Law and justice required re-interpreting within the context of desired social ends. Law was to be analysed as 'the sum of the general rules for man's common life'. The totality of the facts and relations involved in the realisation of the goals of justice would provide the working data for the discipline of jurisprudence. An appropriate analysis would require three inter-related tasks: clarification of the nature of possible legal systems, paying particular attention to their inherent contradictions; clarification of appropriate methods of attaining desired legal objectives; and clarification of legal values in terms of their philosophical foundations. From such an analysis, which would reflect positivist and relativist methodologies, there would emerge a new sociological and functional 'jurisprudence of interests' which would replace the dominant 'jurisprudence of concepts', which, in the context of Germany's prevailing legal system, was concerned with a generalised law, to be applicable in all cases, no matter what specific social problems might be involved.

Radbruch wrote of three 'pillars of law' which ought to support a new, humanistic jurisprudence: justice, expediency and certainty. Difficult problems would arise inevitably within a legal system, and their resolution demanded the recognition of 'tension-creating antinomies'. *Justice* necessitated that those who are equal should be treated by the law as equals, and those who are unequal should be treated in a manner which kept in mind their significant differences. The law and its institutions must reflect, therefore, the fundamental moral values of justice and equality. A second pillar was *expediency*. It is necessary to individualise judicial decisions (while retaining a sense of principle) and this demanded a recognition of the principle of relativity, resulting in the judicial interpretation of 'prevailing political and social habits', so that the judge's decision in a case would not be made in a social vacuum (the expedient decision would reflect communal concerns). A third pillar, *legal certainty*, necessitated a formal acknowledgment of the nature and purpose of the positive law and existing judicial decisions.

The 'free law' jurists drew attention to a requirement for the promulgation by the state of the very essence of its legal order. Certainty in the law demanded that the law be seen as positive. (If what is just cannot be settled, then what ought to be right must be declared, and this must be done by an agency able to carry through what it lays down.) The three pillars may produce practices which contradicted one another. Legal certainty demands stability in the law, but justice and expediency would require swift adaptation of the law to meet novel circumstances in a changing society. If there be uncertainty, however, then which pillar ought to play the dominant part? Radbruch's reply was that no one pillar would be considered as dominant. But, he continued, *where a conflict seems to be irreconcilable, then legal certainty ought to be preferred*. It is more important that 'the strife of legal views be ended than that the matter be determined justly and expediently'. These words, said Radbruch, returned repeatedly to haunt him. The 'free law' movement had made the fundamental error of ignoring their own oft-repeated warning that a humanist law must be many sided.

Radbruch's jurisprudential thought was concerned also with the goals of legal systems which gave meaning to the very functions of the law. His relativist approach was clear in his enumeration of the non-absolute ends of law – individualism, collectivism and transpersonalism. *Individualism* values the human being and his integrity above communal requirements. 'Liberty for all' favours the significance of the free contract and individual freedoms. *Collectivism* underlined the importance of community life, using slogans such as 'Nation above all else'. Its typical jurisprudence favoured notions of organic communal life, as embodied in theories of corporate personality. *Transpersonalism* favoured the promotion of the virtues of civilisation, emerging from common aspirations; its slogan was 'Civilisation through communal advance' and its jurisprudence ranged widely, culminating in an emphasis on the advantages of a society of states recognising the binding nature of international law and a general reverence for what humanity has achieved.

Radbruch favoured transpersonalism, but he seemed to stress, in the name of relativism, the difficulties of choosing one 'end of law' as against others merely by reliance on scientific argument. To try to appeal to absolutes, to personal notions of right and wrong, is to invite failure. In later years, Radbruch was convinced that, at this point in its arguments, the 'free law' movement 'took the wrong turning', providing some kind of ideological sustenance for the emerging intellectual support for dictatorship which was growing swiftly and widely in the 1930s.

The totalitarian regime which emerged in Germany in 1933 had proclaimed as 'enemies of the Reich' those who questioned its fundamentals. Radbruch's opposition to the new regime was known widely and he did not hesitate to speak out against what he considered 'a new jurisprudence in which the rights of the individual counted for little against the demands of the state'. He was warned to desist from open hostility to the new legal authorities, but declined to remain silent. A visit to Oxford in 1936 was followed, surprisingly, by a return to Germany and, within months, he was deprived of his private papers, ordered to remain outside the academic field, and entered upon a period of 'intellectual exile', during which he was dismissed from his academic posts.

It was the very lawlessness of the dictatorship, the brutality of the new regime, which acted as the point of no return for Radbruch. In a lecture given to young German law students in the final years of his life, he referred to four steps along the road which led to his conversion to the need for a break with the positivism and relativism of the 'free law' movement, and the necessity to embrace a 'natural law'. The first step came with his awareness of the ease with which existing statutes passed in the pre-Nazi regime were re-interpreted by Nazi jurists and judges in order to deprive large sections of the German population of rights and remedies under the law. The very words of statutes and regulations drawn up so as to maintain liberty were perverted in a way which assisted in the creation of tyranny.

The second step in Radbruch's conversion was his growing awareness of the scale of the defection of Germany's jurists and judges to the new regime. A small group of judges decided to resign their positions, but, in the general ranks of lawyers, university teachers of law and judges at all levels (including the most senior) were found, in Radbruch's words 'the most vocal and committed supporters of the new regime', often using the very terminology of the 'free law' movement to attack those who spoke of the need to respect absolute justice, the rights of minorities and the need for fair trials of those alleged to have broken the law.

A third step was taken by Radbruch in the direction of a new approach to law when he learned of the defection of a personal friend and one of the leaders of German jurisprudence, Carl Schmitt (1889–1985), professor of public law at the University of Berlin. Radbruch said he had detected in Schmitt's writings in the early 1930s signs of a rejection of 'jurisprudence as a guarantee of freedom', and a movement towards narrow certainties which seemed to negate the very idea of freedom of discussion on fundamentals of law. Schmitt became the powerful director of the University Teachers' Group of the Nazi League of German jurists. His writings began to refer repeatedly to the need for unbreakable rules which would restore Germany's 'vanished sense of order', and Germany's need for an all-powerful leader who would prevent a descent into the abyss of decadence. Racism of an unusually virulent type characterised his essays responding to those who asked for the maintenance of minority rights, and Radbruch found that debate with Schmitt became impossible. Where Schmitt led, others followed, and the organs of jurisprudential thought became mere propaganda sheets.

Towards the end of the war and the collapse of the dictatorship, Radbruch (who had been under virtual house arrest and, therefore, deprived of news) was made aware of the intense and unremitting cruelty inflicted by legal institutions in the name of the law. His final step, leading to rejection of earlier held opinions, was taken, apparently, when he heard details of the persecution of the student resistance movement and what he termed 'the obscene role of the judges in passing sentences of death on the student leaders, and the medieval brutality of their execution'. 'Law must never again become the unprotesting slave of tyranny.' To this end, he dedicated his final years as an advocate of a new jurisprudence.

The new jurisprudence demanded unwavering analysis of what had gone before. The 'free law' movement had played, unwittingly, a role in preparing the way for the ready acceptance of Nazi jurisprudence. The espousal of an uncritical positivism had, objectively, assisted the arguments of those who sought to deny legitimacy to any criticism of the written law. Statements such as, 'The law is the law and it is not for the judges to query its letter', had twisted positivism, declared Radbruch; it must never again be used as a prop for dictatorship.

Radbruch moved to a consideration of the agenda required for discussion among European jurists. Those who were to prepare the agenda were urged by Radbruch to examine and reject firmly the relativism which had assisted in plunging Europe into barbarism. Certain human activities, such as the use of torture, deprivation of rights practised on grounds of race or religion, slavery and murder for political ends, could never be justified and were absolutely wrong in all circumstances. There were principles which stood above the positive law and which demanded respect from all persons.

The preparation of a new legal system for Germany, the writing of new legal codes, and the explanation to young students of law of the first principles of a new approach to jurisprudence, occupied Radbruch towards the end of his life. His lectures in the final years spoke of the creation of a legal theory and corresponding institutions which would stand against the threat of oppressive regimes and against their ideological underpinning. He stated repeatedly and emphatically that there were circumstances in which it would be 'wrong' for judges to obey the law. 'If laws consciously deny the will to justice, if, for example, they grant and deny human rights arbitrarily, then these laws lack validity, the people owe them no obedience, and even the jurists must find the courage to deny their legal characteristics.' His conversion was complete.

Radbruch was unable to complete a detailed statement of his new position, but he used a revised version of the outlines of a lecture which he published in 1945, four months after the German surrender, in order to plead with new audiences for an urgent consideration of a fresh approach to jurisprudence. He insisted that his arguments be heard and considered inside and outside Germany. It was for others to fill in the detail of the principles which he sketched. The lecture (and subsequent argument prepared for publication) was entitled 'Five Minutes of Legal Philosophy'. It required, he maintained, no more than five minutes for an adumbration of the few principles which ought to characterise legal thinking in the post-war world.

First minute. Suppose we maintain that a law is valid merely because it is a law and that it exists as a law *only* because it receives its backing from powers of enforcement. This is wrong. A view of the nature of law and its validity which rests on the errors of positivism has, in the past, prevented jurists and other members of the community from resisting law which is clearly arbitrary and obviously wrong. The positivist theory which seeks to equate law and power, which tells us that law can exist only because of its surrounding power is wrong. We must seek to propagate the theory that rejection of 'law=power' is essential because of what happens invariably in regimes which are based on false equations of this nature.

Second minute. Some jurists and their supporters have attempted to replace the 'law=power' tenet with another which seeks to convince us that, in reality, law is 'that which benefits the people'. Should we follow a principle of this nature and accept its implications, then it would lead to our accepting the view that any kind of illegality, any breach of a solemn agreement, has to be considered as law because persons will argue that such actions may objectively and, perhaps in the long run, benefit the people. 'I have acted in the interests of the people ... my will coincides with what is necessary for national salvation and survival', is a statement symptomatic of the capricious whim of a tyrant equating his wishes with the needs of a people. Principles of this nature call for their firm rejection. 'This tenet should not be read as: Whatever benefits the people is law. Rather it is the other way around: Only what is law benefits the people.'

Third minute. It is essential to accept that law is the will to justice, and by justice is meant: to judge without regard to the person, to treat everyone according to the same standard. There is no justice, there is no law, when applause is given following the cruel murder of one's opponents while cruel and degrading punishments are meted out to individuals who carry out the same kind of act against others who share one's own political views. There can be no support for laws which act as obstacles to the carrying out of the demands of justice.

Fourth minute. Is validity to be granted to laws which are bad, detrimental or unjust merely for the sake of legal certainty? Or is it to be denied them because they are socially detrimental or unjust? It must be 'indelibly impressed on the consciousness of the people and jurists' that there *can* be laws that are so unjust or so socially detrimental that it is necessary to deny their validity, even, indeed, their very character as law.

Fifth minute. Some principles of law are stronger than any statute. Should a law conflict with these principles, it is to be considered as having no validity. These principles constitute 'the natural law' or 'the law of reason'. Their details are often less than clear, but there exists a solid core of such principles and they now enjoy such a wide consensus in declarations of civil and human rights that the entertaining of doubts about them is a sure mark of 'the deliberate sceptic'.

Radbruch's 'Five minutes manifesto' constitutes his last testament and contains the essence of his new-found acceptance of natural law doctrine. Positive law can, and, indeed, must be subjected to intensive and continuous criticism and, where it is not in accord with those immutable criteria which define justice, it is one's duty to call for its rejection. Criteria which are based upon a view of law in relativistic terms are dangerous and have no place in a jurisprudence which seeks to build upon basic notions of right and wrong. The creation and maintenance of the democratic and humanist state, built consciously upon notions of equality and justice, demand a law and a jurisprudence which are unashamedly committed to human values. The 'free law' movement lost its way and gave misguided instructions to those who sought, often belatedly, to oppose tyranny. The new doctrines of legal thought seek to repair the damage caused in the past by the propagation of views which, in the event, separated concepts of justice from human rights and aspirations.

Some contemporary jurists maintain that it is a misnomer to speak of Radbruch's final teachings as providing evidence of a 'conversion'. Wolf, for example, has sought to demonstrate that Radbruch's final stance is the result of an *evolution* in his thought; there was no sudden change in his views, no recasting in revolutionary terms of principles which he had held throughout his life. His revulsion against the experiences of the latter part of his life merely made his denunciations more emphatic. The intensity of belief which, in his early days, led to his incarceration was always to be found in his writings and actions. His final years appear to have moved him in the direction of a species of natural law thinking; Wolf argues that this was indeed movement, but not of a qualitative nature. Friedmann points to evidence from which one may deduce that Radbruch had never abandoned the fundamentals of his earlier thought; he had restated certain principles which, unhappily, could be buttressed by the lessons of history. The natural law framework of his final thoughts is modification, not abandonment of earlier teachings. Friedmann points out, that, nevertheless, Radbruch's work remains of significance for our times.

Notes

Most of Radbruch's writings remain untranslated. His translated writings include 'Anglo-American jurisprudence through continental eyes' ((1936) 52 LQR 50); 'Jurisprudence in the criminal law' ((1936) 18 Journal of Comparative Legislation 312); *Legal Philosophies of Lask, Radbruch and Dabin*, translated by Wilk. 'Five Minutes of Legal Philosophy' may be found in Feinberg's anthology, *Philosophy of Law*. 'The legal philosophy of Radbruch', by Fuller ((1954) 6 Journal of Legal Education 481) outlines Radbruch's general approach to jurisprudence. The writings which document the Hart-Fuller debate on law and morality contain detailed expositions of the 'conversion' of Radbruch and its implications for today's jurisprudence.

Question 14

What are the main features of the Neo-Scholastic movement in jurisprudence?

Answer plan

The Neo-Scholastic movement is a 20th century development of thought based on the jurisprudential ideology associated primarily with St Thomas Aquinas. The effect of the movement on contemporary jurisprudence has been to revive interest in the application of natural law doctrine to life in our times. An answer to this question should bring out the point that not all the Neo-Scholastics accept the theology of Aquinas in its entirety. Reference should be made to a representative selection of jurists who represent this school of thought. The following skeleton plan is suggested:

Introduction – essence of Neo-Scholasticism – characteristics of Neo-Scholasticism as viewed by Adler and Cavanaugh – Dabin – Rommen – Le Fur – Renard – Maritain – Adler – Lucey – conclusion, Neo-Scholasticism and man's common good.

Answer

Neo-Scholasticism comprises several philosophies founded upon medieval Scholasticism (an endeavour to discover 'the whole of attainable truth' through Catholic doctrine). Particularly prominent within the Neo-Scholastic school is Neo-Thomism which, in relation to jurisprudence, is concerned with the development and adaptation of the teachings on natural law enunciated by St Thomas Aquinas. He had defined law as 'an ordinance of reason for the common good made by him who has the care of the community, and promulgated', and considered 'natural law' to be derived from Divine law as revealed in man's reason. The natural law provided limits for the positive law. Noted below are some representatives of the Neo-Scholastic movement in jurisprudence – European jurists such as Dabin,

Rommen, Le Fur, Renard and Maritain, and American writers, such as Adler and Lucey.

Adler, whose views are expounded below, sees Neo-Scholasticism as characterised by six widely-held doctrines concerning natural law. First: government-made laws are not the only directions of conduct which apply to persons living within society. Secondly: there are rules and principles applicable to *all* persons, not merely to one person or even one society of a given time or place. Thirdly: there are vital rules of conduct which are not man-made. Fourthly: through the exercise of his reason man may discover these principles. Fifthly: these principles are the source of all particular rules of conduct. Finally: these principles provide the standard by which all other rules are to be judged good or bad, right or wrong, just or unjust. Cavanaugh has restated the Thomist doctrine in emphasising that natural law is not an ideal but a reality. 'It is not a product of men's minds, but a product of God's will. It is as real and binding as the statutes in the United States Code.'

Dabin, a Belgian jurist, set out in *The General Theory of Law* (1929) a view of the legal order as the sum total of the rules of conduct laid down by civil society under the sanction of public compulsion so as to realise the general order postulated by the ends of civil society and the maintenance of that society as an instrument devoted to those ends. Natural law should dominate the positive law; indeed, positive law is prohibited *absolutely* from contradicting the natural law. (This is an interesting modern development of the view of Aquinas that a positive law, even though it serves the end of society, may, nevertheless, be of no moral significance.) Dabin stressed his belief that the precepts of natural law must be accepted as possessing a universal and immutable validity, 'suffering neither doubt nor discussion'. They are capable of being deduced from the very nature of man as revealed in the basic inclinations of his nature, 'under the control of reason, independently of any formal intervention by any legislator whatever'.

Dabin's theory of justice owes much to mediaeval thought. Justice takes three forms. 'Legal justice' is a merger of law and morals; it is concerned with 'ordination for the common good', that is, the determination of the duties owed by members of society to the social world – effectively, obedience to laws. It is the virtue most necessary for the public good because its objective *is* the public good. 'Distributive justice' determines the duties of the collectivity towards its members; it provides for the distribution, under the law, of rights and powers. 'Commutative justice' is embodied in the adjustment of private relationships. It is the task of legislators to work for the public good; therefore, anything contrary to 'natural morality', for example, fundamentally immoral legal rules, must be condemned as contrary to the public good.

Rommen, a German jurist, published in 1947 *The Natural Law*, in which he provided a restatement of Catholic doctrine concerning natural law. He wrote with his memories of the lawlessness of the Nazi regime in mind, and suggested that the true foundation of the natural law was to be found in the essential, immutable 'dignity of human personality'. Two self-evident propositions could be discerned within the content of natural law: 'What is just is to be done and injustice is to be avoided' and 'Give to everyone his due'. The natural law will always reflect reason, and man's duty is to act in accordance with reason so as to fulfil 'the order of being'. Immoral laws are devoid of obligation. Ultimately, the true and the just are one, and true freedom will be found in being bound by justice. Rommen envisages a variety of different social and political systems in which human dignity might find guarantees; these systems would express the diversity of peoples and changes in socio-political evolution.

Le Fur, a French writer on legal theory, set out in his *Problems of Law* (1947) a statement on rules of law as comprising duties and rights *granted* to members of a community. Problems of law arising within a community could be solved by the imposition of sanctions based on force, by the will of the majority who would act, in the words of Aquinas, with consciousness of 'the ultimate need of preserving the life of the community'. The community's laws must rest on reason, that is, the principles of the natural law. Reason will work best when basic ethical principles, reflecting the harmony of God's creation, are applied to 'social facts' and, in particular, those concerning history and economics. Fundamental principles of natural law involve: the keeping of freely-concluded contracts ('the sanctity of obligations'), respect for properly-constituted authority, and the duty to repair, or compensate for, unlawfully inflicted damage. Modern legislators should seek to provide for the building of the positive law, with its detailed rules, upon the foundation of these three principles, which reflect the natural law teachings of Aquinas.

Renard, a French professor of law, published *The Theory of the Institution* in 1930. In it, he developed a concept of the natural law as finding expression in 'the institution' – the embodiment of that social order which is a part of God's order. The 'institution' was to be viewed as 'the communion of men in an idea'. The most important institutions were the state and the nation. Renard seems to have attempted to develop aspects of the medieval theory which favoured the concept of a community as based on a 'cooperative union of guilds'. The 20th century could learn from this type of institution by developing an organic, unified society which would reflect 'self-sufficient constituent groups'. The natural law and its interpretation would be the key to the solution of society's problems. Legislation was to be interpreted as the product of the wills of those who form the legislative organs of the community's institutions. The *enacted laws* of a community are valid only if they do not enunciate ideas contrary to those proclaimed by the institutions. The *judicial acts* of the institutions are valid only if in accordance with the natural law. For Renard, the Neo-Scholastic approach to jurisprudence involves an acceptance of the necessity of subordinating individual purpose to the collective objectives of the institutions. Some loss of freedom might result, but security for the individual would increase.

Maritain, a French philosopher and a convert to Catholicism, published in 1947 his highly acclaimed *Rights of Man and Natural Law*, in which he argues for a codified system of law which will recognise 'the supreme value of every human soul'. His views are rooted in the philosophies of Aristotle and Aquinas, and he affirms natural law as 'an expression of what is natural in the world'. Man's dignity is derived from his having been created in the image of God, and his human rights are also derived from God. The natural law which is rooted in man's nature follows the eternal law which exists in the very nature of God. Man is naturally inclined towards the moral law and, by using his reason, he is able to know and implement that law. The natural law allows us to attune ourselves to the necessary ends of humanity. As our moral conscience has developed, so our knowledge of the natural law has increased. Man's very important right to freedom is derived from natural law. When the positive lawmakers decide on matters related to 'promotion of the public interest', they must keep in mind the dictates of the natural law concerning the dignity of man. Above all, says Maritain, jurists must assert with force that an 'unjust law' is not a law.

Adler, former professor of law at Chicago University, epitomises those Neo-Scholastics who do not accept the theology of Aquinas, but who are attracted to his contribution to the doctrine of natural law. *A Dialectic of Morals* (1941) called for a bulwark against legal positivism and for the mapping of a road which would bring sceptics back to those paths of reason which lead to the truth about man and his nature. Human conduct *can* be based on a knowledge of right and wrong, and moral judgments are *not* merely matters of opinion. When legislators make laws they must keep this in mind. But it must not be forgotten that positive law remains qualitatively distinct from the natural law – they do not share the same essence. Thus, positive law compels obedience by an exercise of external force; natural law does not. Positive law requires promulgation through extrinsic channels; natural law emerges from natural enquiry. The rules of positive law may be evaluated in relation to the constitution of a country; natural law is beyond such relativity.

A restatement of natural law associated with the earlier Scholastic jurists requires, according to Adler, an assertion that without principles of natural justice there can be no meaning attached to the concept of 'natural rights', and, without a meaningful concept, there can be no settlement of disputes except through power, prejudice and pressure. Natural law is, in itself, inadequate in the face of modern demands for government under the law. A place must be found for positive law within the framework of the natural law so that positive law approximates increasingly to 'a perfect embodiment of natural justice'. In this way, a jurisprudence emphasising the virtues of the medieval concept of justice as reflecting God's plan may be developed for the contemporary world and its legal institutions.

Lucey, an American jurist and priest, has called for emphasis to be given to man's dignity and to his fundamental duties and rights 'given to him by God, which no man has a right to destroy'.

'Those duties and rights make him *sui juris* as far as others are concerned.' They do not change basically, although their application and exercise will vary according to time and place. Because man is social by nature, he is impelled toward civil society and this necessitates a civil law which must be respected. In man is a God-implanted necessity for authority, and respect for it. Within society, government, as well as those who are governed, must be subject to the law. The Neo-Scholastic approach should recognise that although natural law is, in the strictest sense, immutable, the positive law must alter in accordance with our perceptions and requirements of 'the common good'.

Essentially, the Neo-Scholastic movement is able to embrace those who see the natural law as embedded within the theology associated with Aquinas, and those for whom that theology is not relevant, but who see natural law as emerging from the very special attributes of human beings. Natural law is accepted by most adherents to the movement as being immutable; but there is an acceptance of the need for recognition of changes in the quality of men's needs, Maritain sums up for many jurists within the Neo-Scholastic movement: 'Natural law is the ensemble of things to do and not to do which follow (for example, that we should do good and avoid evil) in necessary fashion from the simple fact that *man is man*, nothing else being taken into account.'

Notes

Friedmann, Chapter 19; and Bodenheimer, Chapter 19, consider the central features of Neo-Scholasticism. Hall criticises Maritain in 'Integrative jurisprudence', in *Interpretations of Modern Legal Philosophers*. Reuschlin writes on 'The Neo-Scholastics' in *Jurisprudence: Its American Prophets*.

Question 15

MacCormick, commenting on Finnis' *Natural Law and Human Rights*, states that the text necessitates our abandoning 'our caricature version of what a natural law theory is'.

Do you agree?

Answer plan

Finnis has attempted in recent years to restate the natural law in terms acceptable to contemporary society. This has involved him in an enumeration of 'human goods', that is, fundamental values of man's existence that are 'self-evident', the securing of which requires a system of law. The 'human goods' must be discussed in the answer. Consideration should be given to the claim that Finnis has restored 'meaning' to the true natural law which has been discredited because of distorted versions of its pretensions. Criticisms of Finnis ought to be mentioned. A skeleton plan is presented as follows:

> Introduction – the caricature of natural law – essence of Finnis' restatement of natural law – the seven 'human goods' – law's end as the common good – criticism of Finnis' catalogue – imprecision of his categories – problem of the 'self-evident' nature of the goods – conclusion, misgivings remain.

Answer

'Natural law' is seen here as the system of jurisprudential thought which asserts the existence in nature of a rational order from which we can derive universal and eternal value-statements, allowing us to evaluate the legal structure with objectivity. The 'caricature' version which MacCormick has in mind is, presumably, sketched from the claims of those jurists who see natural law as based rigidly upon a unique revelation of truth, as flaunting the principle that 'ought' cannot be derived from 'is', and as proclaiming a set of immutable principles, including the assertion that unjust laws cannot be law. Some of Finnis' attempts to remove distortions of the image are considered below. It will be suggested that his attempts create their own problems.

Natural Law and Human Rights (1980) is, in essence, a restatement of natural law in novel and contemporary terms. Finnis' central thesis consists of two major propositions. First: there are certain 'human goods', that is, *basic values of human existence*, that are self-evident, and that can be secured only through the law. Secondly: these goods may be achieved through 'practical reasonableness', and this, too, necessitates law. The human goods constitute a catalogue of forms of 'human flourishing', exemplifying the conditions required by individuals if they are to attain their full potential (an end which was reiterated in earlier versions of the natural law). 'Practical reasonableness' involves a use of the word 'practical' in an Aristotelian sense, as meaning 'with a view to decision and action'; it is an aspect of 'human flourishing'. Finnis is seeking, in his categorisation of human goods, to provide a rational basis for morality and a justification for law.

The forms of human goods that are 'irreducibly basic' are *seven* in number: life, knowledge, play, aesthetic experience, sociability (friendship), practical reasonableness and religion. These constitute 'human well-being', and any real understanding of law or justice must rest on a comprehension of the nature of these 'goods'. Although there may be innumerable forms of human goods, Finnis claims that those outside his list are merely ways, or combinations of ways, of attaining any of the seven enumerated. By 'life', he has in mind the drive for self-preservation. The term signifies every aspect of vitality, including anything done by mankind to further its preservation. 'Knowledge' corresponds to man's basic drive of 'curiosity'. It is knowledge for its own sake, and ranges widely from scientific and philosophical speculation to mundane questions. 'Play' involves engaging in performances which have no point beyond the performances themselves.

'Aesthetic experience', perception and enjoyment of 'dance or song or football', for example, may involve actions of one's own, or mere contemplation. 'Sociability' necessitates being in a relationship of friendship with at least one other person. 'Practical reasonableness' refers to freedom and reason, integrity and authenticity. It relates to bringing one's own intelligence to bear effectively on the problems of choosing one's actions and life-style and shaping one's character. Finnis uses the term 'religion' in an unusual sense as referring to a concern for an order of things 'beyond' each and every individual.

These human goods are, according to Finnis, 'basic' because they are are not derived from other goods and any other values will be seen as merely subordinate to them, and 'objective', which may be evidenced from a survey of anthropological research which reveals that 'all human societies show a concern for the value of human life'. Each constitutes a principle for 'practical reasoning'. They are also 'self-evident': thus, the 'good' of 'knowledge' is self-evident, in that it cannot be demonstrated, but, equally, it needs no demonstration, no further argument: it has the quality of 'ultimacy'. Finnis insists that all self-evident principles are not validated by individual feelings and that in every field of human inquiry there is, and must be at some point, an end to derivation and inference. At that point, we find ourselves 'in face of the self-evident'. The goods are also equally 'fundamental': none can be *shown* to be more fundamental than any of the others and, therefore, there is no objective priority of values among them. They possess the property of 'incommensurability'.

'Practical reasonableness', which is a human good, is also a proposition in Finnis' overall scheme: it comprises 10 principles allowing the individual to distinguish the social from the unsocial type of thinking, thereby enabling him to distinguish morally right and wrong actions. First, an individual should have a rational plan of life, reflecting a harmonious set of purposes and effective commitments. He should pay equal regard to all the human goods and should not neglect the significance of others' participation in those goods. He should have a certain detachment from the projects he undertakes and should not abandon his commitments lightly. Opportunities ought not to be wasted by using needlessly inefficient methods and there must be respect for the human good in any act performed. *One should foster the common good and act according to one's conscience.* (In a later work, Finnis added a further principle, namely, that one should not choose 'apparent goods', knowing them to be a mere simulation of real goods.)

It should be observed that Finnis, in his articulation of a scheme of common goods and values, is moving beyond any particular set of religious tenets. His view of the natural law suggests the *objective nature* of the values he enunciates; these values are not the exclusive property of Catholic believers. His emphasis on the need to reason about moral matters (and that necessitates decisions on which goods are worth pursuing) goes beyond a purely religious approach to 'the good life'.

Finnis views the law as involving rules made by 'a determinate and effective authority' for a 'complete community', strengthened by appropriate sanctions, and directed at the reasonable resolution of the community's problems of co-ordination. *Law is a means to an end*: its end is 'the community's good', and its manner and form should be adapted to that good by specificity, minimisation of arbitrariness and 'maintenance of a quality of reciprocity between the subjects of the law' among themselves and in their relations with the authorities. (The common good is defined by Finnis as 'a set of conditions which enables members of a community to attain for themselves reasonable objectives, or to realise reasonably for themselves the values for the sake of which they have reason to collaborate with each other ... in a community'.)

The maxim *lex injusta non est lex* is viewed by Finnis as pure nonsense. He denies the correctness of its attribution to Aquinas and stresses that in natural law tradition wicked laws may have legal validity where they are enacted constitutionally and where accepted by the courts as guides to judicial decisions. One may have, according to natural law tradition, a 'collateral obligation' to conform to some iniquitous laws so as to uphold respect for the legal system as a whole.

A perusal of Finnis' views suggests to many critics a number of unsolved problems. Thus, the list of 'human goods' may be no more than a subjective addition to the long list of similar catalogues, such as the ancient Chinese Six Virtues and Eight Happinesses. Such catalogues tend to reflect, in a highly subjective manner, personal preferences, class and social mores and religious principles, indicating reactions to compelling, but often temporary, crises within society. Finnis, it is argued, may be reflecting little more than attitudes held desirable by a small group. His list of human goods is value-laden and in no sense universal. There is evidence to suggest that some of the goods might be rejected as desirable ends by some sections of the community. What measure of agreement could be hoped for among nihilists, liberals and Marxists on matters of 'play' or 'aesthetic experience'?

Some of Finnis' categories are presented in wide and imprecise terms, making their significance difficult to grasp. 'Knowledge', in his words, embraces a spectrum from 'the intellectual cathedrals of science and philosophy' to 'everyday mundane gossip'. This is a very wide heading for activities of such a disparate nature. Also, it has been pointed out that the pursuit of knowledge 'for its own sake' is forbidden to some sects and religious orders for whom the very questioning of fundamentals may constitute an undesirable practice, if not a heresy. Further, Finnis' category of 'religion' has a meaning which is so wide as to rob it of any significance for wide groups of persons searching for a guide to thought and action.

The problem of the 'self-evident nature' of the 'human goods' is an obstacle for those jurists who search for a rationale behind the catalogue. The history of much endeavour in the realm of speculation is a story of a refusal to accept any statement as 'self-evident'. Indeed, according to critics, the term is an abnegation of the individual's duty to seek continuously for verification of theories. The same critics express doubts as to the 'self-evident' nature of, say, 'play' (in Finnis' sense) as a basic 'human good'. Weinreb, in a trenchant criticism of Finnis, notes that the text states, or suggests repeatedly, that those who are against the 'human goods theses' have not thought out their position carefully, or are 'blinded by bias', whereas, in fact, each of Finnis' conclusions has been contested by many thoughtful, morally committed persons.

Finnis' view of the law in terms of what it achieves, rather than what it is, has been considered less than helpful. It suggests a mere instrumental view of law and fails to examine the question – vital for advocates of the natural law – of the fundamental significance of law in our society. His argument concerning *lex injusta* has been criticised as resting on casuistry and as providing no guide for action to individuals within a community in which the law is perceived as oppressive.

There is doubt as to Finnis' general attitude to 'the good' and 'the just'. It has been suggested that his exposition is far too abstract to be of use in the resolution of day-to-day problems relating to disputes and the law. Yet there is a powerful attraction in his restatement of natural law doctrine: it is a carefully argued investigation of common good, moral choice and the place of the law in the co-ordination of human activity, and it is far removed from the 'caricature version' of natural law which emphasises an authoritative view of the common good and the means of its realisation. It calls for a fundamental examination of the place of the individual within society. In the tradition of the natural law, he urges for emphasis to be placed on the human condition and on the ways in which man may fulfil himself. His greatest achievement, in the eyes of some jurists, may be, in Weinreb's words, that he has called attention to principles which he claims to possess eternal validity and to transcend mere historical discourse, and that 'he has helped us to recognise the level of agreement about human ends and how to achieve them, and he has provided a shelter from the wind of moral relativism' – an accomplishment in itself.

Notes

Extracts from Finnis, and a useful commentary are to be found in Davies and Holdcroft, pp 186–204. Dias, Chapter 22; and Lloyd, Chapter 3, comment on the 'human goods' theory. Ridall, Chapter 11, outlines the essence of the theory. A criticism of Finnis is contained in *Natural Law and Justice*, by Weinreb. MacCormick writes on 'Natural law reconsidered' in (1981) OJLS. A detailed examination of Finnis' views appears in Westerman's *The Disintegration of Natural Law Theory*.

CHAPTER 4

TRANSCENDENTAL IDEALISM

Introduction

The questions in this chapter are concerned with the doctrines of transcendental idealism as they relate to law. Transcendental idealism is a philosophy which is concerned with the attempt to view human ideas as possessing an autonomous existence. Human thought is perceived as 'the exclusive support' of the universe as known to man. In essence, Kant asked what can our understanding and reason know, apart from experience. His answer is: we do indeed possess a faculty of acquiring knowledge without appeals to our experience, namely, *a priori* knowledge. Two very important figures in the history of western philosophy are considered in this chapter, Kant (1724–1804) and Hegel (1770–1831). Neither was a lawyer; each was a philosopher concerned with an examination of the essence of human thought. Neither had in mind the investigation of any existing legal system; each sought to derive principles of jurisprudential ideology from fundamental philosophic views. Both believed that man is a rational being capable of exercising free will, and stands separated from the rest of nature (and able to dominate it) because of that fact. Jurisprudential thought has been affected profoundly by Kant and Hegel, particularly in areas of scholarship concerning the essence of duty and responsibility, rights and duties, and the functions of the state.

Checklist

Ensure that you are acquainted with the following topics:

- autonomy of the will
- categorical imperative
- *honeste vivere*
- Hegelian dialectic
- State as Mind on Earth
- unfolding of Absolute Spirit

Question 16

Give a general account of some aspects of the teachings of Kant which are of particular relevance to jurisprudence.

Answer plan

Kant, who taught at the University of Königsberg, was one of the greatest philosophers of the Enlightenment (the European movement in the 17th and 18th centuries concerned with the attempt to find knowledge through reason). He sought to establish a systematic framework of knowledge and aesthetics, and made a detailed study of the basis of rights and duties from which he deduced principles and axioms which remain highly relevant in any consideration of responsibility under the law. The required answer should set out some general comments concerning Kant's basic beliefs and the essence of his teachings. Reference must be made to the nature of the 'categorical imperative' and its fundamental significance for jurisprudential thought. The following skeleton answer is used:

> Introduction – features of transcendental idealism – man's sense of duty – the nature of the categorical imperative – Kant's definition of law – rights and duties – conclusion, criticism of Kant's views.

Answer

Kant (1724–1804), professor of logic and metaphysics at the University of Königsberg, is best known for the system of philosophical thought built upon his *Critique of Pure Reason* (1781), *Critique of Practical Reason* (1788) and *Critique of Judgment* (1790). His main interests were the theory of knowledge, ethics and aesthetics. Law *as a means to an end*, in the context of a universal law of justice, was of particular interest to him. It is perhaps symbolic that, given his interest in the concepts of moral obligations, freedom and the law, he became involved towards the end of his life in a dispute with the Prussian authorities on the right to express and publish religious opinions; this resulted in his being forbidden to lecture or publish in this area of discussion. Kant's contribution to fundamental thinking on the subjects of duty, punishment, individual rights, remains of significance in our jurisprudential thought.

Law and morality were considered by Kant as having a basis in *a priori* concepts of 'ought' which could be used in conjunction with the 'dictates of reason'. '*A priori*' refers to facts which can be known independently of scientific knowledge. *A priori* knowledge is, according to the philosopher Sahakian, 'the given contents of immediate experience in its qualitative fullness.'

Knowledge, argues Kant, is limited in its scope. Thus, it is limited to the actual world of experience: we can *know* the law, we can comprehend legal and moral values, but that knowledge reflects limited modes of perception and thinking. The *ways* in which our faculties of thought operate upon the data of our experience are decisive. The world does not constitute ultimate reality: it is transcendent in that it is 'beyond the reach or apprehension of ordinary experience'. *Phenomenal reality*, the world as we experience it, must be distinguished from *noumenal reality* (that is, non-sensual reality). When, for example, a jurist experiences events concerned with legal phenomena, his experiences come to him through the lens of his *a priori* categories of thinking. We can know only *sensed objects*: external reality exists independently of mankind and is known by us only as it appears and is organised through our perceptions. We must always take into account the limits of our knowledge and remember that what we 'know' is the result of 'co-operation between the knower and that which is known'.

Man is, in Kant's view, an inseparable part of the natural world: he is always subject to immutable physical laws, and to that extent his will and actions are determined and not entirely free. But his experience and his reasoning powers suggest to his conscience that he is a relatively free, moral individual who is capable of making conscious choices between good and evil. Indeed, morality and the law are aspects of the intelligible world in which man may live in freedom and enjoy the making of moral choices. The 'intelligible world' is, for man, the 'real world'. Man's life should be dominated by the objective of a free existence (in which the law must play its part in guaranteeing order). Kant declared that 'man's "good will" is good not because of what it accomplishes, not because of its usefulness in the attainment of some set purpose, but alone because ... it is good of itself'. Good behaviour, which is desirable in man, is that conduct which obeys the laws of moral behaviour; the positive law must, where necessary, reflect views of moral behaviour.

Man's obvious 'sense of duty' suggests to Kant that all individuals serve under an obligation which can be perceived as *an imperative*. The most significant of imperatives are those of a moral kind, requiring in every case 'an action objectively necessary *of itself* without reference to another end'. A man ought to tell the truth not in order to attain a particular end, but because his very rationality demands such an action from him. The 'moral imperative' is, in effect, *categorical* (that is, unconditional).

Kant is not concerned to enunciate 'lists' of actions which the 'good man' should or should not undertake. Rather, he is concerned to set out fundamental, overall principles which, when we comprehend them, will act in the nature of a compass directing us along a path of action in accordance with the surrounding circumstances. There are three formulations of the Kantian categorical imperative. The first states:

> *Act only on that principle whereby you can at the same time will that this maxim should become a universal law.*

Assume that X finds himself in a predicament from which he cannot escape unless he borrows money from Y. Y insists, in the event of making a loan, on repayment within one month. X knows that he will be unable to repay; but his predicament is of a very severe nature. X might secure a temporary advantage by telling an untruth to Y. Ought he to act in this opportunist fashion? No, says Kant: X must *never* act in such a way. X should ask himself: 'Is it right to act on the principle of self-advantage? What would happen if the principle involved in my acting in this way were to be the basis of a universal law?' In such a case, X realises, promises would be meaningless and all would be at a disadvantage.

A second formulation by Kant takes the following form:

*So act as to treat humanity whether in your own person or in
that of any other, in every case as an end withal, never as a means
only.*

Consider the situation of Y in the example given above. Kant
argues that Y's rationality as a person is *an end in itself,* and that Y
becomes a mere 'thing' when he is used by X as *a means* for some
other end, as when X deceives him. Y, as a person, has an absolute,
intrinsic worth, which X's deceit destroys. X's deceitful action is a
denial of the categorical imperative; it is, therefore, a wrongful
activity.

A third formulation is as follows:

*Always so act that the will could regard itself at the same time as
making universal law through its own maxim.*

Kant stresses the significance of *the autonomy of the will:* an
individual's will is relatively free and, as such, is at the basis of his
morality. Every rational person should act entirely 'under the idea
of freedom'. Rational nature exists as an end in itself, and to
recognise this freely is to obey 'the supremely practical, universal
law'. Freedom and morality are so inseparably united 'that one
might define "practical freedom" as independence of the will of
anything but the moral law alone'.

Kant's well known definition of 'law' runs thus:

Law is the totality of the conditions under which the
arbitrary will of one can coexist with the arbitrary
preference of another according to the general law of
freedom.

The definition relates to *the objective of the law,* and not its essential
features. A law which does not meet this end is, according to
jurists who accept Kant's principles, necessarily invalid; actions
which correspond to this concept of law are 'right'. Essentially,
Kant is propounding the following thesis: if a person's actions can
coexist with the freedom of all other persons according to a
general law, then whoever prevents that person taking those
actions is doing him an injustice. The removal of the circumstances
of that injustice is 'just' in the full sense of that term. Law 'carries

with it the right to coerce him who seeks to interfere with it'; we may look upon law as 'a mutual coercive obligation'. (Coercion is to be viewed as 'the hindrance of the hindrance of freedom'.) Observation of the law allows man, as a rational being, to assist in the attainment of 'a universal harmony of 'things and persons', guided by the principle of reason. The American jurist, Pound, wrote, in his *Interpretations of Legal History* (1930), that Kant's concept of law appears to be 'the final form of an ideal of the social order which governed from the 16th to the 19th century: an ideal of the maximum of *individual self-assertion* as the end for which the legal order exists.'

Rights and duties are of much importance in Kant's system of law. He wrote of 'the science of Right' which has for its object the principles of *all* the laws which it is possible to promulgate by external legislation. 'Right' should be seen as comprehending 'the whole of the conditions under which the voluntary actions of any one person can be harmonised in reality with the voluntary actions of every other person according to a universal law of freedom'. An action may be considered 'right' when, in itself, or in relation to the maxim on which it proceeds, it is such that it can co-exist with the freedom of the will of each and all in action, according to a universal law.

Kant makes a 'universal division of rights', thus: natural right and private right; innate right and acquired right. Natural right is said to rest upon pure rational principles *a priori*; positive right (for example, statutory right) results from the will of a legislator. Innate right is that which belongs to all persons by Nature and is independent of 'all juridical acts of experience'; acquired right is that which is founded upon juridical acts. There is, according to Kant, only one innate right – 'the birthright of Freedom'. Freedom is defined by Kant in this context as:

Independence of the compulsory will of another, and in so far as it can coexist with the freedom of all according to a universal law, it is the one sole original, inborn right belonging to every man in virtue of his humanity.

In sum, Kant's view of civil freedom rests, according to Rosen, on three principles: every person has the right to pursue his own happiness as he considers fit, provided that this does not interfere with the liberty of others; no one may curtail that right in the name of promoting the good of other persons; interactions of a consensual nature are just.

Kant's scheme of duties is based upon that promulgated by the Roman jurist, Ulpian (d 228), and adopted by Justinian in 533 as a summary of basic precepts relating to an individual's duties – *honeste vivere, alterum non laedere, suum cuique tributere* (to live honestly, not to harm another and to give every man his due). In Kant's commentary on this passage, he interprets *honeste vivere* as involving the proposition: Do not make yourself a mere means for the use of others, but be to them likewise an end. *Alterum non laedere* is interpreted by Kant so as to imply the proposition: Do no wrong to any person even if you are under the necessity, in observing this duty, of withdrawing from all connection with others. *Suum cuique tributere* is interpreted as meaning: Enter into a state in which every person can have what is his, secured against the action of every other.

The principle of *retributive justice* as a basis of punishment for offenders was of particular interest to Kant. The essence of his view, which continues to be cited in our own day in jurisprudential discussions relating to penal policy, was set out as follows:

> Judicial punishment can never be used merely as a means to promote some other good for the criminal himself or for civil society, but instead it must in all cases be imposed on him only on the ground that he has committed a crime; for a human being ought never to be manipulated merely as a means related to another's purposes ... First, he must be found to be deserving of punishment before consideration can be given to the utility of this particular punishment for himself or for fellow-citizens.

Punishment is imposed, in Kant's interpretation, because the offender has committed a crime and not merely to further some other goal, such as his reform. The quality of a 'just penalty' should take retaliation into account. Crimes against the state, Kant argued, might be pardoned, but not crimes against individuals. An offender must, above all, receive his 'just deserts' whenever this is possible; this must be related to what he has *done*, for justice 'has as its object only what is external in actions'.

Kant constructed a theory of the state, based in part on the concept of 'an original contract'. Individuals constitute themselves as a state as the result of a 'contract' by which they surrender a large element of their 'external freedom', which is resumed later when they become members of a 'commonwealth'. The united will of the people constitutes the sole legislative power; the 'united will' cannot, by its nature, commit injustice to individual citizens. The enactment and administration of the law is one of the state's most important functions. (Kant refers to the state as 'a union of a number of men under juridical laws'.) The state should interfere as rarely as possible with the affairs of citizens, but *must* at all times ensure protection of rights. Separation of powers within the state is considered by Kant as essential. Men's freedoms and rights are guaranteed ultimately only by the will of the legislature, and that will must not be resisted: a 'right of rebellion' is not acceptable to Kant. In his favoured state, 'the supreme will' has rights, but has few compulsory duties towards the citizens who are its subjects.

Criticism of Kant's contribution to legal philosophy has been wide-ranging. Transcendental idealism, it is contended, is too abstract to provide a firm foundation for *behaviour* which is to be evaluated as 'good'. Human action according to the categorical imperative seems, in Cairns' view, to be 'for saints, not for ordinary human beings'. Radin suggests that it is not possible to act in the light of one's activities being considered as a universal rule of conduct, for acts are conditioned by time, place, background, and other relative factors. Further, the inflexible nature of the categorical imperative could create insuperable difficulties in practice. Assume that A, acting from base motives, wishes to injure B, who is being concealed by C. Ought C to answer truthfully A's angry inquiry as to B's whereabouts? How should C react when faced with the dilemma resulting from ethical commands in the form of absolutes? Kant gives no easy answer: he speaks of a lie as the violation of an unconditional duty which must hold in *all* circumstances.

The 'directionless nature' of the categorical imperative has been criticised. If the *consequences* of an action, which Kant rejects as constituting a criterion, are to be subsidiary in significance to 'the exercise of freedom of will', how are individuals to *judge* the importance of consequences? Kant's edifice of thought has produced little guidance for the perplexed – so it has been argued. A request for bread is answered by the proffering of a stone, minutely and exquisitely chased – but a stone nonetheless.

Jurists who emphasise the positive significance of Kant's transcendental idealism note his view that moral decisions ought not to be arrived at solely on the basis of emotions: reason *must* play an important role in such decisions. Kant's plea for the importance of human worth and dignity, which can be found at the basis of the theory of the categorical imperative, remains of importance in our continuing discussions of the foundations of law. His philosophy, which emphasises the role of human will, places responsibility for actions on the *individual*, and accountability of the individual within the community assumes much importance in modern discussions on criminal and tortious liability. Kant continues to exercise an influence in jurisprudential argument which turns upon the interpretation of moral and legal duties. It is not easy for today's jurists to set aside his view of the importance of treating one's fellow-citizens as 'ends, not means', of acting so as to 'make everything the concern of all' and of perceiving 'the greatest problem of the human species, the solution of which nature compels him to seek' as that of 'attaining a civil society which can minister justice universally'.

Notes

Russell's *History of Western Philosophy* contains a valuable section on Kant. Paton's *The Categorical Imperative* explores Kant's attitude to right, wrong and the law. *Legal Philosophy from Plato to Hegel*, by Cairns, gives a general interpretation of Kant's views. Hall's *Foundations of Jurisprudence*, in which Kant is considered as a representative of the natural law tradition, examines the implications of his jurisprudential teachings. Rosen's *Kant's Theory of Justice* outlines the jurisprudential implications of Kant's thought.

Question 17

Outline some of the fundamental theories of Hegel which are of interest for an understanding of man and the law.

Answer plan

Hegel, professor of philosophy at Jena, Heidelberg, and, later, Berlin, constructed a vast scheme of philosophical analysis in which the entire universe was presented as a systematic whole. All phenomena, material or metaphysical, were viewed as interdependent and existing as part of a dialectical process of 'unfolding'. Law played an important role in man's development, but applied to him only in so far as he was 'wholly free'. Hegel was a major influence on the development of the study of philosophy and history. Given the wide range of theories for which he was responsible, the answer should be based on a *selection* of his views which are concerned with his methodology (the dialectic, which has affected jurisprudential thought in a variety of ways) , his theory of the state and his attitude to the law. The following skeleton plan is used:

> Introduction – the interdependence of all things – the dialectic – theory of the state – law in relation to man – punishment of offenders – conclusion, criticisms of Hegel.

Answer

The place of Hegel (1770–1831) in western philosophy as possibly the greatest of its systematisers of thought rests upon his principal works, *Phenomenology of Mind* (1807), *Encyclopaedia of Philosophy* (1817), and *Philosophy of Right* (1821). He occupied the chair of philosophy at the University of Berlin from 1818 and assisted in moulding the thought of an entire generation of philosophers and jurists. The Young Hegelian Movement (which included, for a short period, Marx) was composed of students and scholars who were attracted by Hegel's systematic, comprehensive philosophy which attempted to examine the nature of Absolute Idealism by searching for an 'organic theory of truth'. Law – its concepts, objectives and institutions – was to be studied in its application to man as 'a wholly free being', and in relation to its place in the state. 'Right' and 'law' were to be perceived as aspects of man's attempts to enter the transcendental realm of 'actualised freedom' without which he could not fulfil himself; they are vital matters in man's development.

Findlay, in his essay 'Hegel' (*A Critical History of Western Philosophy* (1964)), notes the difficulties inherent in any attempt to translate Hegel's work and to present the essence of his views 'in a language understandable in our own age'. Hegel uses a unique vocabulary ('a barbarous diction of his own') which is perplexing: terms such as 'will', 'absolute', 'state', are given unfamiliar meanings so that translation and comprehension are unusually troublesome. This problem must be kept in mind in seeking to understand the Hegelian system of thought.

'That which is reasonable is real, and that which is real is reasonable.' The task of vindicating the truth of this aphorism, set out in *Philosophy of Right*, is, for Hegel, the supreme duty of philosophy. He believed that only ideas had a genuine 'reality', that the intelligible and the real world could be identified absolutely, as could the forms of thought and the laws of nature. There is, for Hegel, no contradiction between 'reason' and 'reality': the philosopher must examine these categories so that their significance and interdependence become apparent and clear.

Hegel's argument for the interdependence of all things involves acceptance of the concept of Absolute Spirit 'unfolding' so as to produce sequences of interconnected reality. The principle of movement in this process of unfolding and development is known as *the dialectic*. An awareness of the structure and significance of the dialectic is essential for any understanding of phenomena: an understanding of the development of jurisprudential thought is facilitated by the use of dialectical modes of analysis. The *process of change*, which, for Hegel, is a visible aspect of reality, cannot be halted; to understand it, however, is necessary if one wishes to control it.

The dialectic can be envisaged in terms of *a triad*. Initially, in a process of development, there is a *positive thesis*, which, in time, is negated by its *antithesis*, further development produces a *synthesis* which, in turn will give rise to its antithesis ... and so on. The process continues until a synthesis is reached which appears to be identical with the first ('positive') thesis; but the quality of the process has 'deepened', making explicit that which was merely implicit. 'Reality' has been uncovered, even in a small, limited fashion. The history of general thought, the history of humanity, the history of legal thought indicate the dialectical process operating through categories of knowledge which have become more and more complex.

Hegel's dialectic must not be confused with Marx's methodology of dialectical materialism. Marx uses the dialectic within a framework of *materialist* philosophy; Hegel is concerned with the unfolding of 'Absolute Spirit'. The process of the unfolding of Spirit illustrates for Hegel the process of the dialectic: subjective Spirit (for example, in the form of thought) is the first thesis, which generates the antithesis of objective Spirit (the creation of a legal system following intensive scholarship, for example), and the synthesis is made manifest in, for example, the complex philosophy of law. For Hegel, dialectics embraces the entire sphere of reality, including 'Spirit', which was rejected by Marx as 'mere illusion'.

Hegel's theory of the state differs from that associated with Kant. The state, in Kantian terms (the so called 'political state') was little more than an institution which had the task of enacting and executing the community's laws. Hegel perceived the state in an extended sense as 'the actuality of the ethical ideal', that is, a *growing organism* which allows a people's ethical life to expand by assisting in the creation of customs, values, beliefs, patterns of law, etc. In this sense, the 'ethical state' may be said 'to absorb and synthesise all other human institutions'. It is the 'ethical state', however, which Hegel sees as allowing persons to attain *self-fulfilment* by encouraging full communion among themselves. 'The state finds in ethical customs its direct and unreflected existence, and its indirect and reflected existence in the self-consciousness of the individual in his knowledge and activity.'

In the Hegelian system, the state is very much more than a mere institution:

The state in and by itself is the ethical whole, the actualisation of freedom; and it is an absolute end of reason that freedom should be actual. The state is Mind on earth and consciously realising itself there ... the march of God in the world, that is what the state is. The basis of the state is the power of reason actualising itself as will. In considering the Idea of the state, we must not have our eyes on particular states or on particular institutions. Instead we must consider the Idea, this actual God, by itself.

In a passage which has been anthologised repeatedly as an example of an early articulation of the ideology of totalitarianism, Hegel speaks in absolutist terms:

What the state demands from us as a duty is, *eo ipso*, our right as individuals since the state is nothing but the articulation of the concept of freedom. The determinations of the individual will are given an objective embodiment through the state and thereby they attain their truth and their actualisation for the first time. The state is the one and only prerequisite of the attainment of particular ends and welfare.

In sum, Hegel affirms: 'Just as spirit is superior to nature, so is the state superior to the physical life. *We must, therefore, worship the state as the manifestation of the Divine on earth.*'

In relation to the constitution of the state, Hegel recommends the creation by the community of a constitutional monarchy and its appropriate legal institutions; In a well ordered monarchy, the law alone has objective power to which the monarch has but to affix the subjective 'I will'. Concerning international law and the individual state, Hegel argues that because there is no authority which is superior to that possessed by individual states, inter-state disputes may have to be resolved by war. His justification of war was enunciated repeatedly in the totalitarian jurisprudential philosophies prevalent in Europe of the 1930s:

There is an ethical element in war. By it the ethical health of the nations is preserved and their finite aims uprooted ... War protects the people from the corruption which an everlasting peace would bring upon it.

History, according to Hegel's interpretation, illustrates the workings of an evolutionary force (the 'unfolding of Absolute Spirit') at work in the world. Historical evolution demonstrates the realisation of the concept of freedom, a slow process in which states and nations hand on to their successors 'the flame of freedom'. Man's spirit is embodied in institutions (political-legal) which, in terms of the dialectic, are negated, allowing a subsequent struggle resulting in a new synthesis as history moves to a *'higher level'*. Thus, ethical life, which determines to a large extent the scope of legal relationships, involves three 'dialectically consecutive stages: the stage of the family, the stage of the civil society, and, finally, the stage of the state (which is always "inherently rational")'. The 'World Spirit', working through human reason, legal thought and institutions, will move humanity towards ethical and universal freedom.

In the evolutionary processes of history, the law – ideology and structures – will have the function of assisting in the realisation of freedom in its external manifestations (such as the design of appropriate legal institutions). The law will create a framework in which the rights and personality of individuals will be respected and upheld. 'The legal system is the realm of actualised freedom ... Right and law are altogether freedom as an idea.' The co-existence of right and law is an important objective for jurists and legislators.

'The Universal', writes Hegel in *Philosophy of Right*, 'is to be found in the state, in its laws, its universal and rational arrangements'. Law is 'the objectivity of Spirit; volition in its true form'. 'Only that will which obeys law is free, for it obeys itself – it is independent and so free. When the state or our country constitutes a community of existence, when the subjective will of man submits to laws, the contradiction between liberty and necessity vanishes.' Law, argues Hegel, will apply to man only in so far as he is 'a wholly free being'. The essence of law as promulgated by the institutions of the state is that each individual must be respected and treated by other individuals as a free being. *Reason demands a standard of lawful behaviour from all persons.* To violate the rights of one individual is to violate the rights of the entire community: lawful behaviour must be accepted as an indivisible concept.

114

There are circumstances in which compulsion may be applied, in the interests of the community, to a particular individual, as where, for example, he has placed unwanted constraints on another individual.

Hegel maintains that the law is concerned not with commandments, but solely with *prohibitions*. The law operates so that what is not forbidden in express terms within a community is allowed. Thus, an individual may not act so as to disturb the property rights of another. Where the law as it relates to the ownership and possession of property appears to take the form of a positive command, it is based, in reality, upon a prohibition: this emerges from a close study of the *development* of property law.

The problem of punishment, which, in Hegel's time, concerned jurists and governments, is seen by him as related to *retaliation*. An offender ought to be subjected to the same mode of treatment as that for which he has been responsible. The object is the restoration of the condition of equality which has been violated by his actions. Retaliation must not be in the hands of an injured party or his representatives. Where justice takes the form of mere revenge, yet another offence has been committed. The judge must order and supervise the execution of punishment.

Criticisms of Hegel have intensified during recent decades, largely because of the attachment of many of his disciples to the principles of totalitarianism which underpinned the aggressive world wars. His glorification of war, 'panegyrics of power', and veneration of the state have grated on the ears of modern jurists and others who view his philosophy as fundamentally anti-liberal. Bodenheimer notes, in his *Jurisprudence* (1974), in extenuation, that it is doubtful whether Hegel advocated a programme of totalitarian repression within a state. His repeated references to the value of 'freedom' and the need for man to enjoy 'liberty' are taken as evidence of his anti-authoritarian stance. This argument does not fit easily, however, into the general concept of state authority as advocated repeatedly in *Philosophy of Right*, for example. Further, the veracity of the 'process of the dialectic' has been doubted by many contemporary philosophers and other scholars: some see it as a mere 'fantasy in triads', while others argue that the processes of development of phenomena do not invariably follow patterns of synthesis reconciling thesis and antithesis.

Friedmann reminds us that few philosophers have provoked the admiration and intense condemnation applied to the writings of Hegel. Anglo-American jurisprudence has rejected his perception of the unity of law, morality and politics. Few jurists accept his unique concept of 'freedom through the state'. Yet support for the Hegelian interpretation of the world and its legal and political institutions continues. Klein, for example, suggests that there may be a positive side to Hegel's efforts to find some underlying *purpose* in world history, which involves investigation of the links between individual morality, the ethical life of the community and the pursuit of coherence in legal doctrine and practice. This, in turn, necessitates a continuous juristic examination of the state which, in Schlink's words, 'is still here, more powerful and dangerous than ever, so that the task of apprehending it as something inherently rational is more important than ever'.

Notes

Hegel's *Philosophy of Right* appears in a translation by Knox. A selection of extracts from Hegel's writings is given in Lloyd's *Introduction to Jurisprudence*, Chapter 11; Findlay's *Hegel: A Re-examination* considers criticisms of transcendental idealism. MacIntyre's edition of *Hegel: A Collection of Critical Essays* is of much interest. Avineri's *Hegel's Theory of the Modern State* considers the idea of state power as viewed by Hegel. *The Philosophical Propaedeutic*, edited by George and Vincent, sets out the content of some lectures delivered by Hegel, including material on 'The science of laws, morals and religion'. *Hegel and Legal Theory*, edited by Cornell and Carlson, is a collection of papers presented at a conference on Hegel, organised by the New York Cardozo School of Law.

CHAPTER 5

UTILITARIANISM

Introduction

This chapter is made up of questions concerning the doctrine associated with Bentham (1748–1832), JS Mill (1806–73) and Stephen (1829–94). The principles of utilitarianism which they expounded made a direct impact on jurisprudence, particularly in areas involving the criminal law. Utilitarians perceived the 'true good' as *happiness* and argued that each person always pursues what he considers to be his personal happiness. The legislator's task is to effect a balance of public and private interests. Hence, the criminal law may be viewed as a mode of producing *a coincidence of the interests of the community and of the individual*. Bentham was concerned, in particular, with influencing legislation and policy along utilitarian lines. Mill was less dogmatic. His major interest was in the liberty of the individual and the consequent need to set limits to government action. Stephen's attack on Mill's views is of particular interest. Questions in this area of jurisprudential thought require an understanding of the general principles of utilitarianism and the arguments used by Bentham, Mill and Stephen in support of the particular policies they put forward concerning reform of the law.

Checklist

Ensure that you are acquainted with the following topics:
- essence of utilitarianism
- felicific calculus
- Bentham's views on punishment
- utilitarianism and the criminal law
- Mill's fundamentals of liberty
- paternalistic legislation
- legitimate role of government

Question 18

How did Bentham apply the general principles of utilitarianism to the specific problem of punishment for criminal offences?

Answer plan

The general principles of utilitarianism should be set out, together with a brief indication of Bentham's view of the criminal law. It is in this setting that the question of punishment has to be considered. The following skeleton plan is suggested:

> Introduction – Bentham's general views – essence of utilitarianism – aim of legislation – essence of the criminal law – fundamentals of punishment and its rationale – criticism of Bentham's concepts – conclusion, positive features of Bentham's approach.

Answer

Philosopher, economist, jurist and legal reformer, Bentham (1748–1832) was able to spin from the thread of the 'principle of utility' a vast tapestry of ethics and jurisprudential doctrine, known as 'utilitarianism', which sought an answer to the question, 'What ought an individual to do?' Bentham's answer was that he should act so as to produce 'the best consequences possible'. 'Consequences' include all that is produced by an act, whether arising during or after its performance. A summary of the main principles of utilitarianism is given below, together with details concerning Bentham's application of those principles to the problem of punishment for criminals – a matter with which he was closely involved in his campaigns for a revision of the criminal law, and in which he had been influenced by the Italian jurist, Beccaria (1738–94). Central to Beccaria's theory of punishment was his belief that an act, and not an offender's intention, constituted the measure of actual harm done, and that the prevention of further offences was the sole justification for imprisonment.

The 'principle of utility' was set out by Bentham in his *Introduction to the Principles of Morals and Legislation* (1789). He defined it as 'that property in any object whereby it tends to produce pleasure, good or happiness, or to prevent the happening of mischief, pain or evil and unhappiness to the party whose interest is considered'. Nature had placed mankind 'under the governance of two sovereign masters, pain and pleasure'; they indicate what we *ought* to do and determine what we *shall* do. The principle that we desire pleasure and wish to avoid pain is utilised by Bentham so as to make the judgment that we *ought* to pursue pleasure. The principle of utility cannot be demonstrated because it is not susceptible to proof; indeed, says Bentham, it is needless even to attempt a demonstration.

Bentham attempted to give the theory some measure of mathematical precision. A thing will promote the interest of an individual when it tends to add to the *sum total* of his pleasure, or to diminish the *sum total* of his pains. It was possible, he argued, to make a *quantitative comparison* of the pleasure and pain likely to result as the consequences of alternative courses of action. A person should sum up the likely pleasures and pains so as to arrive at the 'good' or 'bad' tendency of the act in question – the 'felicific calculus'. An account of the number of persons whose interests appear to be involved should be taken, and the calculus applied to each. The result would be an estimate of the good or evil likely to be produced within the community as a whole.

The aim of the legislator, according to Bentham, should be to produce *the greatest happiness of the greatest number*. 'Community interest' was no more than the sum of the interests of those who compose a society. The art of legislation involves the discovery of the means to realise 'the good'. The legislator considering the ambit and content of the criminal law must take into account the fact that the acts he desires to prevent are 'evils' and that they are greater evils than the laws (which are infractions of liberty) to be used to prevent them. Legislation ought to aim at four goals: subsistence, abundance, security (the protection of status and property) and the diminution of inequality. The laws which a legislator should seek to promote should be seen in relation to desirable conduct to be expected from persons or classes of persons.

In considering the criminal law, Bentham applied the principle of utility in rigorous fashion. First, the mischief of an act should be measured. 'Mischief' consisted of the pain or evil inflicted by the act. If an act tended to produce evil, it must be discouraged. 'Evil' could be 'primary' or 'secondary'. If X steals from Y, this is 'primary' evil. 'Secondary' evil arises where X's theft weakens the general respect for property. Bentham stresses that secondary evils may often outweigh primary evils.

Because the legislator is concerned to increase the total happiness of the community, he must discourage acts likely to produce evil consequences. A criminal act is one which is obviously detrimental to the happiness of the community; hence, the law should be concerned solely with acts that diminish the pleasure of persons by the infliction of pain. The criminal law is intended to assist in the active promotion of the community's total happiness by punishing those who commit offences characterised as 'evil' according to the principle of utility.

Bentham would not accept a division of offences into *mala in se* (acts wrong in themselves) and *mala prohibita* (acts wrong because the law prohibits them). The principle of utility insists that an act cannot be wrong 'in itself'; whether it is right or wrong depends on *consequences*. If it is highly probable that an act will produce harm, it should be prohibited; if unlikely to produce harm, its prohibition is unjustified. We prohibit murder and theft and punish those responsible, not because the acts are wrong in themselves but because of the evil consequences for others. For precisely the same reasons, we punish also those who commit minor offences.

Punishment, said Bentham, is in itself an evil: it necessarily inflicts suffering on the offender. But the object of the criminal law is the augmentation of the community's happiness; hence, if punishment is to be administered, it must be shown that the pain to be inflicted on offenders will prevent or exclude some greater pain. The 'usefulness' of punishment emerges only if its infliction achieves a greater measure of happiness for the community. It has no value if it merely adds more units of pain to the community as a whole. Mere retribution is valueless because it only adds to the total quantum of pain caused by the offences.

Bentham insisted on an examination of *why* society ought to punish offenders. There is no value in inflicting punishment where it is 'groundless'; hence, an offence which admits of compensation, and which can be followed by such compensation, ought not to be punished. Punishment which is too expensive ought not to be inflicted. The 'proportion' between punishment and the offence must be kept in mind. Punishment should be great enough to outweigh profit derived by the criminal. The greater the offence, the greater should be the punishment.

Punishment ought to be variable and adapted to suit circumstances, but the same punishment should be given for the same type of offence. The quantum of punishment should never exceed the amount required to make it effective, so that extravagant punishment should be rejected as wasteful. The more uncertain it is that a criminal will be caught, the greater should be the punishment when he is apprehended and convicted. Punishment should act as a deterrent, should be reformatory where that is possible and should have wide popular support. Hence Bentham's acceptance of the need for capital punishment, which, he believed, did provide a deterrent. It is interesting to note the support for capital punishment shown by Bentham's disciple, John Stuart Mill. On one of the rare occasions on which Mill spoke in the House of Commons, in 1868, he advocated the retention of the death penalty (and underlined the need to preserve severe punishments, such as flogging).

Bentham's utilitarian principles as applied to the criminal law and punishment led him to prepare practical schemes for the 'rational punishment' of offenders. Among a large number of such plans, which were often worked out in considerable detail, was the design of a *Panopticon* – a prison in which the conduct of the inmates was to be controlled by total surveillance throughout the day. Bentham stated that its object was 'to grind rogues honest'. This process was to be achieved by an uninterrupted survey of behaviour, which would result in the remodelling of the offenders' attitudes. Bentham had in mind reform of the prisoners – mere punishment with no objective other than retributive detention seemed to him a wasted opportunity.

Bentham's radical approach to law and punishment was vigorously opposed in his time, although a number of penal reforms are now attributed to him. Controversy surrounds his approach to punishment even today. It is argued that the utilitarians disregarded the claims of justice in determining whether or not a punishment was 'right'. For them, the utility of the punishment was the sole consideration, but for many jurists, other matters would have to be taken into account before accepting the 'correctness' of a particular type of punishment. Objection is taken, too, to the 'pleasure-pain calculus' which is considered unreal and absurd, particularly in relation to the criminal law. Principles of punishment derived from a construct of this nature are considered flawed and, therefore, unreliable.

Opposition to Bentham's views also stems from jurists who cannot accept his reasoning concerning the general happiness of society as constituting the *summum bonum*. It is thought that Bentham's view of mankind was naive in the extreme. People are much more complex than the principle of utility suggests, and the causes of crime are much more complicated than the utilitarian model indicates. Modern investigations of criminal psychology put forward a psychological picture of anti-social motivation which is at odds with Bentham's views.

Plamenatz, the historian of the utilitarian movement, suggests that although much of Bentham's work was often superficial and crude, it was far ahead of its time in proposing new methods of analysing social and legal problems. These methods and the resulting proposals for reform of the criminal law can be accepted, Plamenatz argues, on their own terms. It is not necessary, therefore, to accept Bentham's 'felicific calculus' or his belief in 'the greatest happiness of the greatest number' in order to agree with his powerful pleas for a rethinking of the fundamental purposes and modes of punishment. There is much in his analysis which is ingenious, original and thought-provoking. It remains worthy, according to Plamenatz and others, of consideration by jurists of all persuasions. The contemporary school of penology which accepts the utilitarian (or 'reductive') justification of penalising offences, holds that penalties imposed by the law act to reduce the frequency of offences by: deterring the offender and potential imitators; reforming the offender; educating the public by incarcerating some offenders. Bentham's influence remains much in evidence here.

Notes

Bentham's *Introduction to the Principles of Morals and Legislation* is published in an edition by Burns and Hart. Ogden has edited his *Theory of Legislation*. Summaries of Bentham's views are given in Dias, Chapter 20; Harris, Chapter 4; Lloyd, Chapter 4; and Bodenheimer, Chapter 6. Extracts from Bentham's work are presented in Davies and Holdcroft, Chapter 7. Interesting background material is provided by *Utilitarianism: For and Against*, by Smart and Williams, and *Bentham: An Odyssey of Ideas*, by Mack. *The English Utilitarians*, by Plamenatz, contains a history of the movement. For the extraordinary story of the trial and execution of Bentham's servant, Franks, on a charge of 'burglarously breaking and entering the dwelling house' of his master, see Chapter 10 of *The London Hanged: Crime and Civil Society in the Eighteenth Century*, by Linebaugh. Note, also, *Bentham's Prison*, by Semple. *A Reader on Punishment*, edited by Duff and Garland, explores the concepts underpinning contemporary penology. Hart's *Punishment and Responsibility* examines Bentham's views in detail.

Question 19

To what extent might a modern legislator find JS Mill's views on the limits of toleration and government powers in relation to the individual to be of relevance to contemporary problems?

Answer plan

The eloquent plea on behalf of freedom of speech by Mill (1806–73), contained in his essay, *On Liberty* (1859), contemplates a society in which interference with individual rights is kept to a minimum. Freedom will flourish only where there is respect for citizens and where conditions prevail allowing for the recognition of points of view, no matter how unpopular they may be. An answer to this question should seek to consider some of the many ways in which Mill's conclusions on matters concerning the fundamental freedom of the individual might be relevant to problems of our own day. A skeleton plan along the following lines is suggested:

Introduction – Mill's insistence on a synthesis of justice and utility – liberty as a 'good' and as a means to an end – freedom of expression – 'paternalistic' legislation – duties towards others – principles of government interference – conclusion, relevance of Mill's analysis.

Answer

The views of Mill (1806–73), set out in his essay, *On Liberty* (1859), constitute a statement as to the fundamentals of a desirable balance of interests between the state and the individual citizen. His powerful plea for individual liberty emerges from an analysis of relationships of individual and general interests, of 'justice' and 'utility'. The philosophy of utilitarianism suffuses the essay: liberty, for Mill, rests on no 'natural law' or other metaphysical doctrine, but on a synthesis of the essential features of justice and the concept of utility. A modern legislator would be interested, for example, in Mill's warning of the dangers of the oppression of minorities by majorities, in his insistence on the need for safeguards against those forces that might deny an individual's free and full self-development, and in the intensity of his concern for the preservation of liberty by imposing limits to government action. The legislator will find no detailed instructions for legal and governmental action, but rather a basic appraisal of principles in the area of state intervention designed 'for the good of the people'.

What better can be said of any condition of human affairs, asked Mill, than that it brings human beings nearer to 'the best thing they can be'? Mill's interest in state, law and society centres on their ability to provide the circumstances in which individuals might flourish. Liberty, which in itself is 'a good', is also a means to an end: the end is man's attaining his optimum development, including his full freedom. Mill is reminding legislators and others that in arranging a social and legal framework, they have to keep in mind the long term goals of justice and human development. Further, asks Mill, when should society enact legislation which interferes with an individual's liberty of action? Our legislator might understand the import of Mill's question in relation, say, to the Regulation of Investigatory Powers Act 2000 or the Care Standards Acts 2000: what *right* (apart from its democratic mandate) has a government to enact legislation of this nature?

Mill's answers to the questions he poses form a key to an understanding of his concept of liberty as essential for the development of society. There is only one purpose, according to Mill, for which a government can rightfully exercise power over a citizen *against his will*, and that is to prevent harm to others. The citizen's own physical or moral good will not, on its own, constitute a sufficient warrant. Legislators are urged by Mill to consider the thesis that they may not *compel* a citizen against his will 'to do or forbear' because it is better for him to do so or because his happiness will be intensified as a result; they may remonstrate or reason with him, but they may not force him. The overriding exception is where harm may be caused to others. Conduct which is calculated to produce evil to some other person provides a sufficient reason for the exercise of power against the person who intends such a course of action.

Legislators contemplating current problems relating to liberty of thought and expression would find Mill's views to be highly relevant. He is emphatic in his insistence that a society in which this liberty is not respected cannot be 'free', and that such freedom must be absolute and unqualified. Indeed, he argues, if all mankind minus one individual shared one opinion, mankind would be no more justified in silencing that individual than he, if he had the power, would be justified in silencing mankind. To silence the expression of opinion is to rob the human race of the opportunity of exchanging error for truth or of the opportunity of acquiring a clearer perception of truth as produced when it collides with error.

Mill stresses this theme by stating a case for the free expression of opinion. A contemporary legislator, under pressure to support or oppose enactments relating to the suppression of a highly unpopular type of opinion, might wish to contemplate this case. First, says Mill, if an opinion is silenced, that opinion, for aught we know, may be true; if we deny this, we are assuming our infallibility. Secondly, even though the silenced opinion be erroneous, it may contain a portion of truth ('truth often comes on the scene riding on the back of error'); but since current opinion on any matter is rarely the *whole* truth, it is only through the collision of contrary opinions that the remainder of a truth might emerge. Thirdly, unless received opinion is subjected to vigorous and earnest challenge, it may be held with little comprehension and may take on the character of mere prejudice. Finally, if the opinion is unchallenged and degenerates into dogma, it prevents the growth of any real conviction from reason or personal experience.

The modern legislator will probably respond that this line of reasoning ignores practical necessity. What of the demands of the community for protection against the expression of opinion in circumstances which might inflame sentiment and lead to public disorder? Was it 'wrong' to enact, for example, s 23 of the Public Order Act 1986 (dealing with possession of racially inflammatory material)? Is freedom of expression to be allowed to overt racism or the encouragement of terrorism?

Mill would reply in measured terms. No one claims that men should be free to act upon all their opinions; no one claims that actions should be as free as opinions. Quite to the contrary, opinions should lose their immunity when the very circumstances of their expression constitute a mischievous act. Mill gives as an example of an intolerable expression of opinion a speech in which corn dealers are accused of starving the poor, delivered to a mob gathered before a corn dealer's home. The liberty of an individual must be limited to the extent that he may not make himself a nuisance to other people. However, if a person merely acts according to his opinion in matters *which concern himself,* he should be allowed to carry his opinions into practice at his own cost. In matters which do not primarily concern others, individuality may be permitted to assert itself; but where there is a chance of injury to others, a person may be restrained.

The modern legislator may respond further by questioning the relevance of this thesis in the face of a growing tendency to 'paternalistic legislation'. Mill's reply would be based on his belief that, in general, it is the privilege of an individual who has arrived 'at the maturity of his faculties' to use and interpret experience in his own way. Mill intends that his principles shall be applicable only to *mature persons* (he excludes, for example, minors). Today's legislators might consider the relevance of Mill's thesis to the contemporary theory of 'the least restrictive alternative', which suggests that if there is an alternative way of accomplishing some desired end without restricting an individual's liberty, then, although it will probably involve considerable inconvenience and expense, it should be adopted.

To an individual, says Mill, should belong that part of his life in which he is largely interested, and to society, the part which largely interests society. A modern legislator may consider this thesis relevant to today's problems only if it casts light on the basic problem – where does society's (that is, government's) authority begin? The problem might be posed thus: what are the 'rightful' limits to an individual's sovereignty over himself?

Mill's answer begins with an assertion that society is not founded on any type of 'contract' and there is no purpose in inventing one so as to deduce social obligations from it. All persons who receive the protection of society owe some return; the fact that one lives in society makes it necessary that each individual should be obliged to observe a specific mode of conduct towards others. That conduct involves not hurting the interests of others (that is, those interests which by express enactment and tacit understanding are classified as 'rights'). Further, each individual must bear a share of the efforts incurred in protecting society from injury. Wherever and whenever a person behaves in a way which affects the interests of others in a prejudicial manner, society, through its legal institutions, must have and exercise jurisdiction. But where it is obvious that the interests of no person apart from himself will be affected by an action, that person must have the freedom (legal and social) to perform the action and accept its consequences.

This is not to suggest that members of society, or its representatives in government, ought not to be concerned with individuals' conduct of their own lives. There is, Mill claims, need of 'disinterested exertion' intended to promote the good of others. But that benevolence, he insists, can and must find other methods of persuading people to their good rather than 'whips and scourges either of the literal or metaphorical sort'. Nor must it be forgotten that no individual, no group, no government has a *right* to say to an individual 'of ripe years' that he shall not do with his life for his own benefit what he chooses to do with it. In the same vein, Mill emphasises that whenever there is a definite risk of damage to an individual or to the public, the case must be removed from 'the province of liberty' and must be considered as falling within the area of morality or law.

Given that there is a legitimate role for government to play in the affairs of individuals, Mill advocates three important principles to be kept in mind by legislators. First, government interference which does not involve the infringement of liberty should be considered very carefully when that which has to be done is likely to be better done by individuals than by the government. Mill is suggesting that legislators ought to remember that there are no better persons to determine how or by whom an undertaking should be conducted than those who are personally interested in it. Secondly, although individuals may not perform some types of administrative task as competently as government officials, nevertheless, they should be allowed, as a mode of furthering their development and social education, to carry them out. Thirdly – and Mill sees this as a most cogent reason for restricting government interference – there is the 'great evil' of a government adding unnecessarily to its powers by creating a bureaucracy. Large scale ownership by the state might seriously diminish freedom. Not all the freedom of the press and the existence of a popular constitution would make a country dominated by a government bureaucracy, free, otherwise than in name.

A modern legislator may find, indeed, that the problems which Mill posed and attempted to answer are of particular relevance to him and to those who administer the law. Today's problems may be outwardly different from those which confronted Mill, but, fundamentally, many of the problems are based on precisely the same tensions which arise in any society committed to individual liberty, social order and cohesion

In our day, the coming into force (in October 2000) of the Human Rights Act 1998, and the decisions of the European Court of Human Rights, have led – as was expected – to a reconsideration by wide sections of the community, including jurists and legislators, of the problems inherent in processes of government related to areas of intervention in the lives of citizens.

Mill's thought can be interpreted as possessing a particular relevance. Some areas of human behaviour ought to be accepted, he argues, as being outside the proper sphere of communal control – they are:

> The inward domain of consciousness, demanding liberty of conscience in the most comprehensive sense; liberty of thought and feeling; absolute freedom of opinion and sentiment on all subjects, practical or speculative, scientific, moral or theological; liberty of tastes and pursuits and liberty of combination among individuals; freedom to unite for any purpose not involving harm to others.

Valuable words of guidance, indeed, for today's legislators.

Notes

Mill's *On Liberty* appears in a variety of editions. His theories are considered in Riddall, Chapter 14; Bodenheimer, Chapter 6; Friedmann, Chapter 26; Ryan's *Mill*; and Himmelfarb's *On Liberty and Liberalism*. Dworkin examines government paternalism in *Morality and the Law*, edited by Wasserstrom. Mill's background is analysed in *John Stuart Mill*, by Britton, and *John Stuart Mill: Critical Assessments*, by Wood.

Question 20

What is the basis of Stephen's critique of Mill's views?

Answer plan

Sir James Fitzjames Stephen (1829–94), a celebrated judge and legal historian, was a prominent advocate of the doctrine of Utilitarianism, which was one of the foundations of Mill's approach to legal and political questions. In his book, *Liberty, Equality, Fraternity*, he attacked Mill's 'perversion' of utilitarian teachings and sought to show that Mill had misunderstood vital matters, such as the basis of human nature, the structure of power and the place of women in society. The answer should show an acquaintance with Stephen's basic beliefs and the essence of his disagreement with Mill. The problem of Stephen's relevance for jurisprudence in our day ought to be noted. A suggested skeleton plan might take the following form:

> Introduction – fundamentals of Stephen's critique of Mill – Liberty analysed – Equality considered – Fraternity examined – the relevance of Stephen's outlook for jurisprudence in our day – conclusion, Stephen as more than a mere historical curiosity – his influence on some contemporary legal thinking.

Answer

Stephen (1829–94), judge of the Queen's Bench Division and author of the influential *Digests of the Laws of Evidence and the Criminal Law* and *History of the Criminal Law in England*, was a contemporary of John Stuart Mill and shared with him an attachment to the doctrine of Utilitarianism. Mill's essays, *On Liberty* (1859), *Utilitarianism* (1861), and *The Subjection of Women* (1869), were viewed by Stephen as based on profound error, on a complete misunderstanding of the fundamentals of human nature and contained doctrine which promised to subvert civilisation as Stephen understood it. In his polemic, *Liberty, Equality, Fraternity* (1873), Stephen sought to demolish Mill's theses by attempting to show how 'sentimental' liberalism had to be divided sharply from 'hard-headed' liberalism and how the jurisprudential features associated with Mill's views had no place in the legal thinking appropriate for a civilised society. Stephen's fundamental Christianity, which contrasted sharply with Mill's agnosticism, underpins his thinking, but is not central to his rejection of the basis of Mill's thought.

The single basic principle of Mill's *On Liberty* rests on his belief that an individual's liberty may be justifiably limited by the law only where he is likely to act so as to do harm to others; legislators and jurists must accept, therefore, that there are some areas of human activity which must remain outside their control. Stephen views this principle as dangerous and as possessing the potential for the destruction of law and order. The principle, argues

Stephen, appears to breach the utilitarian doctrine that society's behaviour is governed in the final analysis by pleasure, pain, hope and fear. Legislators should be encouraged to move society's motives and activities towards those ends which will increase the sum total of 'happiness'. This will involve the use of a variety of sanctions (social, legal, religious). To throw aside some sanctions of this nature, as seems to follow on from Mill's arguments, must blur the distinctions between good and evil, leading inevitably to breakdown in social values and structures.

Liberty, Equality, Fraternity (LEF) argues that Mill's 'single principle' is muddled, that, in practice, the principle would necessitate toleration of an absence of constraint in most human affairs, and that licence would replace liberty and the rule of law. Stephen urges the adoption of 'ordered liberty', which would involve liberty based upon law and morality. Liberty of this nature would increase human happiness in considerable measure. But conduct which offends morality is not acceptable and tends to vitiate the significance of liberty. Posner sees *LEF* as based upon a recognition of opposites: Mill's view of liberty is replaced by 'power and restraint'; his view of equality is replaced by 'natural inequality, physical and intellectual, of human beings'; 'fraternity' is replaced by an absolute necessity for 'respect and justice'.

Stephen voices his objection to Mill's views set out in *On Liberty* thus: 'There is hardly anything in the whole essay which can properly be called proof as distinguished from enunciation or assertion of the general principles quoted.' Stephen suggests that the growth of liberty, in the sense understood in a democracy, diminishes, and does not increase, originality and individuality. The hope that people will become more vigorous, and happier, merely by the removal of restrictions which surround their activities is as fallacious as hoping that a bush planted in an open field will develop naturally into a forest tree. Mill ignores 'the fact' that almost all people require some coercion and restraint to act as astringents in the full development of their powers. Further, Mill's basic assertion, using the language of Utilitarianism, that liberty is 'good in itself' is unacceptable. Stephen sees the question of whether liberty is a 'good or bad thing' as irrational. How would we answer a question as to whether fire is a good or a bad thing? Does not the answer depend upon an examination of surrounding circumstance?

131

Mill, argues Stephen, fails to recognise that the very elements of compulsion may be discerned as foundations of our way of life. Power and force *precede* the freedom by which we live: without them, we cannot hope to enjoy the happiness which demands the presence of freedom. Disguise it how you will, says Stephen, it is force in one shape or another which determines the quality of the relations among human beings. Jurisprudence recognises that law rests ultimately on the possible use of regulated force. The social progress which Mill states to be highly desirable, does not involve a lessening of the role played by force in social affairs, but merely alters its form. Liberty must not be seen as a mere absence of restraint. Power precedes liberty and derives much of its significance in jurisprudential theory from its place in the ordered society. It is only under the protection of a powerful and highly organised government that the continued existence of liberty can be assured. At the basis of our national existence is recognition of the principle of compulsion. 'It determines whether nations are to be and what they are to be ... It determines precisely, for one thing, how much and how little individual liberty is to be left to exist at any specific time or place.' Mill's view of liberty as involving minimal interference by the law of the state does not feature in Stephen's concept of liberty and social existence.

The 'single principle of liberty' which is central to Mill's *On Liberty* is rejected unhesitatingly by Stephen in *LEF*. The principle is singled out by him as devoid of merit: its adoption would subvert morality and freedom and would undermine human organisation because it misunderstands the constituents of human nature. If, says Stephen, we strenuously preach and vigorously practise the doctrine that our neighbour's private character is outside the province of our concern, will this contribute to any enlargement of liberty and the sum of human happiness? Could any person desire gross licentiousness, monstrous extravagance or the like to go unnoticed, 'or being known, to inflict no inconvenience?'. Some actions performed in public or private have to be viewed as fundamentally wrong, and it is for legislators, judges and the wider community to condemn them fearlessly and without hesitation. A person who fears to do this is, in effect, betraying the standards which are the concern of the law. Stephen then moves the argument in a direction which places Mill a long way off: moral outrage, he says, *can* provide sufficient grounds for prohibitory legislation, and legislators and judges have a duty to notice and reflect public anxieties in the face of particular types of private, immoral conduct. Mill's dichotomy of public and private codes of morality may lead to the collapse of society as a whole.

Mill, says Stephen, is advocating, in the name of liberty, a doctrine which is ambiguous and potentially destructive. Discussions concerning liberty are misleading or idle unless we know 'who wants to do what', by what restraints he is prevented from doing this, and for what reasons it is proposed that these restraints be removed. No true general assertions about liberty may be made. Mill seems to have forgotten this, and his arguments are flawed in that they misunderstand the nature of human beings and the social and legal mechanisms which make freedom possible. Without order, without the power which is there to be used in the maintenance of order, without the restraint which is to be applied if society is not to degenerate into brutish existence, freedom cannot exist. Mill's 'sole principle' ignores our duty to maintain the structures of power and to speak out against public *and* private behaviour which weaken morality.

The concept of equality, which Mill sees as a necessary condition for liberty in society, is not acceptable to Stephen. In *On Liberty*, Mill speaks thus: 'Human nature is not a machine to be built after a model ... but a tree which requires to grow and develop itself *on all sides*, according to the tendency of the inward forces which make it a living thing.' Stephen was among those who interpreted this as a call for social equality. Mill developed his views in *The Subjection of Women* (1869), described by Stephen as 'a work from which I dissent from the first sentence to the last'. In this essay, Mill asks for 'equality for women in all rights, political, civil and social, with the male citizens of the community'. The principle of the subordination of women ought to give way to a principle of 'perfect equality'. Liberty is indivisible and cannot exist where a high proportion of the community is deprived of rights. For Stephen, this would involve disaster for men and women.

Stephen opposes the concept of equality. It is impossible of attainment, given human nature, and its implications would be impossible to accommodate within the jurisprudence of his day.

Democracy, which is the political expression of equality, according to Mill, is also rejected by Stephen. Mill, he declares, has failed to realise that in a pure democracy 'the ruling men will be the wire-pullers and their friends; but they will no more be on an equality with the voters than soldiers or ministers of state are on an equality with the subjects of a monarchy'. It is the fact of wide differences in human endowment which, for Stephen, rules out the practical possibility of a political system allowing equal rights for all. No logical jurisprudence can be built on a misconception of human relationships.

The concept of equality of men and women, which Mill advocated earnestly, is, according to Stephen, almost unfit to be discussed. It impinges on matters of fundamental decency. Stephen's words reverberate strangely in our ears. 'There is something – I hardly know what to call it; indecent is too strong a word, but I may say unpleasant in the direction of indecorum – in prolonged and minute discussions about the relationships between men and women and the characteristics of women as such. I will therefore pass over what Mr Mill says on this subject with a general expression of dissent from nearly every word he says.' But Stephen does find occasion to overcome his distaste for a discussion on this topic to make the following points. The institution of marriage is, for him, a sure guarantee of safeguards for wives, given the duty of husbands to protect them. If jurisprudence, legislation and the practice of the courts were such as to interfere with the status of wives, the significance of husbands' duties, involving protection, would be downgraded. The idea of equality of status of husband and wife and its effect on the subordination of wife to husband would weaken the position of married women irretrievably if it became the foundation of any legislative provisions.

Basic to Stephen's position is his refusal to ignore what he perceives as the inferiority of women as decreed by nature and providence. All the talk in the world, he declares, can never shake the undeniable proposition that men are stronger than women *in every way*. Men have greater muscular and nervous force, greater intellectual force, greater vigour of character. This 'basic truth' must be reflected, too, in the education deemed suitable for women. In no circumstances ought women to be educated in matters more appropriate to the male character. For Mill to call for equality in all things, including education, is perverse and could be destructive of the social fabric.

Equality, like liberty is, according to Stephen, 'a big name for a small thing'. Mill's insistence on its presence in the body politic (and legal) testifies to his lack of awareness of the significance of basic and ineradicable human differences. Equality, if not like liberty, a word of negation, is a word of relation. It tells us nothing definite unless we are aware of what two things are affirmed to be equal, and what they are in themselves, 'and when we are informed upon these points we get only statements about matters of fact, true or false, important or not as it may be'. Equality is a will-o'-the-wisp, a delusive hope of the kind rejected by utilitarians in particular, who ought to have recognised its false attractions.

It is in Stephen's denunciations of the concept of fraternity that his differences with Mill rise to a climax. He savages Mill's call for 'a general love for mankind', which he perceives in *On Liberty* and *Utilitarianism*, and suggests that Mill's maudlin and muddled view of humanity blinds him to reality. Stephen enunciates his own view in uncompromising fashion. Many men are bad, the vast majority are indifferent and will be swayed this way or that according to circumstances. Between all classes of men, there will always be occasions of enmity and strife, so that even good men may be compelled to treat one another as enemies either because of real conflicts of interests or because of different ways of conceiving 'goodness'. This bleak picture leads Stephen to deny the very possibility of fraternity among persons and peoples. He notes, too, on the basis of his reading of history, the fanaticism which seems to accompany visions of fraternity and, in a passage which has been cited by many commentators as an example of his 'flawed vision', he notes: 'If in the course of my life I come across any man or body of men who treats me or mine or the people I care about as an enemy, I shall treat him as an enemy with the most absolute indifference to the question whether we can or cannot trace out a relationship either through Adam or some primeval ape.' 'Liberty, Equality, Fraternity' as a slogan has no place in an ordered society in which discipline and submission are required if freedom is to survive. Its value for those endeavours essential to achieving the greatest happiness for the greatest number is minimal.

Stephen's critique was published over a century ago, and the economic and social conditions of his day have left little mark on our society. The jurisprudence to which he contributed was predicated on the basis of attitudes towards equality and morality which no longer command universal approbation. Mill's calls for liberty and equality have not been ignored and the advent of concepts of universal human rights and legislation promoting the social and legal equality of men and women are viewed as inevitable in societies which cherish tolerance and freedom. For many jurists and legislators, Stephen's strictures are seen as a quaint survival from a jurisprudence which has little relevance for our times. It is important to note, however, that some of Stephen's views have continued to be heard in our day. The well known Hart-Devlin debate on the Wolfenden Report produced an expression of opinion which repeated some of Stephen's opinions in the very form in which they were couched by him. The division between public and private morality, the view of sexual deviants as dangers to the fabric of society, were reminiscent of the arguments set out in *LEF*. Posner, writing of Stephen's influence today, quotes a statement by Judge Robert Bork: 'No activity that society thinks immoral is victimless. Knowledge that an activity is taking place is a harm to those who find it profoundly immoral.' (Posner comments that this is the philosophy of Mill's *On Liberty* with a minus sign placed before it.)

It would be wrong to suggest that the objectives for which Mill campaigned have been attained in their entirety; the work of contemporary scholars in the field of feminist jurisprudence suggests that the principle of patriarchy which Stephen saw as a permanent aspect of our civilisation, remains acceptable in many areas. But, by and large, majority opinion in the western world is committed to Mill's general views, and sees Stephen's polemic as reflecting perceptions which are now largely of historic interest only. What is of continuing significance for our jurisprudence is the implication of Stephen's work for lawyers and others who believe that the concepts of liberty and equality are not absolute and have to be considered continuously and carefully in the light of changing circumstances.

Notes

Liberty, Equality, Fraternity has appeared in a number of editions, the most recent of which is edited by Warner, who contributes a valuable preface, commenting on the background to Stephen's work. Posner's *Overcoming Law* contains a chapter, headed 'The first Neo-Conservative' in which Stephen's views are summarised. *Stephen and the Crisis of Victorian Thought*, by Colaiaco, gives an account of Stephen's life and jurisprudential thought.

CHAPTER 6

LEGAL POSITIVISM

Introduction

The essence of legal positivism is summed up by Fuller in *The Law in Quest of Itself* (1940): all those associated with the law are called upon to choose between two competing directions of legal thought, namely natural law and legal positivism. *Natural law* denies the possibility of a rigid separation of 'is' and 'ought' and tolerates a confusion of them in legal discussion. *Legal positivism* insists on drawing a sharp distinction between the law 'that is' and the law 'that ought to be'. Questions on legal positivism often tend to concentrate on the essence of the doctrine, the criticisms it has attracted, and the work of leading proponents of positivism, such as Austin, Hart and Kelsen. Each of these jurists is represented in the questions forming this chapter.

Checklist

Ensure that you are acquainted with the following topics:

- definitions of legal positivism
- empiricism
- Austin's concept of law
- Austin's doctrine of sovereignty
- Hart's criticism of Austin
- Hart's concept of a legal system
- Hart's primary and secondary rules
- essentials of Kelsen's pure law theory
- norms and Grundnorm
- criticisms of the Grundnorm

Question 21

What do you understand by 'legal positivism'?

Answer plan

The question calls for an outline of the general doctrine associated with legal positivism and provides an opportunity for criticism. The background to the doctrine, associated with the empiricism of Hume and Comte, should be mentioned. Hart's enumeration of the various uses of the term 'positivism' ought to be explained. Account should be taken of the objection to legal positivism stemming from the belief that it downgrades the significance of 'right' and 'justice' in relation to the law. The following skeleton plan is presented:

Introduction – legal positivism as a mode of legal analysis – philosophical and logical positivism – Hume and Comte – Hart's analysis of the use of the term 'positivism' – methodology of the legal positivists – criticisms of the doctrine – conclusion, legal positivism considered as having advanced from its early preoccupations with the 'naturalistic fallacy'.

Answer

The term 'legal positivism' is used here to signify a doctrine which rejects any metaphysical speculation concerning the law and which studies a community's laws precisely as they are, without taking into account matters such as social context, political and psychological background, which are considered extraneous. The basic features of the doctrine, its methodology and claims, are noted below, together with some criticisms of positivism and its implications.

It is important, initially, to distinguish the term 'legal positivism' from 'philosophical' and 'logical positivism', although it should be noted that legal positivism has been influenced by the writings of the philosophical and logical positivists. 'Philosophical positivism' (which is mentioned below in comments on Hume and Comte) is a doctrine which holds that our knowledge of matters of fact is derived solely from the data of experience; metaphysical, so called 'transcendental' knowledge, which is not based on experience, is held to be of no worth. 'Logical positivism', which stems from the writings of Carnap, Wittgenstein, Ayer and others of the 'Vienna Circle', involves a total rejection of statements that are not based on tested and verified experience of the senses; 'meaning' is ultimately to be established solely in terms of experience, so that metaphysical assertions are dismissed as meaningless. This doctrine has influenced the writings of the legal positivist, Hart, who urges the significance of understanding the mode in which statements about the law are couched.

Fundamental to legal positivism is its attitude to the problem of 'is' and 'ought'. Positivists ask us to consider the use of 'ought' in sentences such as: 'If I release the pen I am holding, it *ought* to fall to the ground'; 'You *ought* not to steal'; 'Those who kill *ought* to be punished severely'. The term 'ought' may refer to what is likely to happen as a physical probability, or it may be used as a 'moral ought'. May one, without fallacy, deduce 'ought' from 'is'? May we infer a normative statement from a merely factual statement? The answer of the legal positivists is that if normative rules reflect no more than subjective opinions, they *cannot* be deduced from physical reality. What, then, is the value said to be derived from a search for the 'moral verities' presumed to be at the basis of the law? What is the point in basing legislation on so called 'immutable principles' which, in themselves, possess no veracity? Analysis, for legal positivists, involves concentrating on a study of the law *as it is*, that is, the law 'posited', that is, laid down, for citizens.

Bentham argued in his *A Fragment on Government* (1776) that it is possible to consider jurisprudence as comprising two modes of analysis, the expository and the censorial. *Expository jurisprudence* involved identifying the essence of law as it is: this demands purely scientific consideration of the 'true propositions' of English law which will lead, in turn, to a study of the source of legal commands which are at the heart of that law. *Censorial jurisprudence* necessitates a consideration of what our law ought to be. These two types of jurisprudence are to be accepted as logically separate and ought never to be thought of as a unified

141

jurisprudential outlook. Today's legal positivists keep in mind the fundamental separation made by Bentham: it emerges when they urge that what is to be accepted as 'law' in a given community is derived from social fact or convention (the so called 'social concept'), and that it is not possible to perceive any obvious or necessary links between law and morality (the so called 'separability concept').

Hume (1711–76), the 18th century Scottish philosopher, developed the doctrines of empiricism, which called for a detailed observation of phenomena as the basis for scientific investigation. He used this method of enquiry in an examination of 'natural law'. To Hume the natural law was 'real' only in the sense that some persons entertained feelings that it existed; there was no other sense in which its 'truth' might be asserted meaningfully. The 'truths' which some jurists saw in natural law based upon 'reasonable human conduct' could not be demonstrated. So called 'guides to human action' were mere relative *values* inspired directly by human motives; they required no 'eternal framework'. Hume's thoughts were enlarged by Comte (1798–1857) in the following century. He taught that *a priori* metaphysical speculation had no validity and that all theories should be subjected to rigorous, empirical investigation. Comte's writings were among the first to contain the term 'positivism' used in a philosophical sense.

The teachings of Hume and Comte cleared the way for the application of precise modes of reasoning to problems of jurisprudence. The law, hitherto the object of metaphysical speculation, was subjected to analysis on the basis of experience. In particular, a growing number of jurists followed Bentham and insisted on the separation of 'ought' and 'is'. It was felt that some of the methods of the natural sciences might be considered appropriate to the study of the social sciences, including legal theory.

In Hart's *The Concept of Law* (1961), five uses of the term 'positivism' in relation to Anglo-American jurisprudence are noted. First, the term is used to describe the concept of law, favoured by Bentham and Austin, in which laws are seen as the commands of human beings (the 'social concept'). Secondly, the term is used to describe the view that there is no necessary link between law and morals, as emphasised by Kelsen (the 'separability concept'). Thirdly, the term is employed to name the idea of analysis or study of meanings of legal concepts. Fourthly, the term denotes the view that a legal system is a 'closed logical system' in which logical means alone are to be used to deduce correct decisions from pre-determined legal rules. Finally, the term is used to indicate the theory that moral judgments cannot be established, as can statements of fact, by rational argument or evidence or proof. Hart himself uses the term 'legal positivism', in his chapter on 'Natural law and legal positivism', to show that it is *not a necessary truth* that laws reproduce or satisfy certain demands of morality (though they may often have done so). Raz suggests, in the same vein, that a jurisprudential theory is acceptable only if its tests for identifying the content of the law and determining its existence depend totally on those facts of human behaviour capable of description in terms which are *value-neutral*, and which are applied without using moral argument; the social sources of the law will determine its very content.

Among many legal positivists there is a shared approach to methodology of *investigation* of legal problems. This approach involves an investigation of the structure of laws within a legal system so as to reveal their real foundation. A *classification* of the functions of the legal system is undertaken. Concepts within the legal structure require *identification* and *analysis*. The legal positivist uses these techniques to answer questions such as: What is 'law'? What are 'laws'? What are the essential functions of law?

As noted above, positivists seek to *exclude value judgments and moral considerations* from their examination of the law. In Austin's words: 'The existence of law is one thing, but its merit or demerit is another.' This is not to imply that positivists are not interested in matters of morality in relation to the law, for this is demonstrably not so. Many leading positivists have contributed in great measure to debate and social movements associated with problems of social morality. It is in the *examination of legal phenomena as such* that positivists will set aside moral considerations, as will an epidemiologist investigating the incidence of a disease within the community. The positivist's data in relation to legal matters is intended to emerge from a study of social reality only. Further, legal positivists seek to confine their investigations to the law which has been enacted and promulgated by the legislative organs of the state, namely, the 'positive law', which can be equated, therefore, with the juridical norms laid down by the state.

Criticisms of legal positivism are headed by a general attack on the theoretical foundations of Humean doctrine. The basic theory, it is said, is flawed and its rejection of metaphysical speculation has resulted in attempts to remove from the attention of jurists large areas of significant, intellectual human activity. The positivists are, however, not convinced that the 'flaws' in Humean analysis have been demonstrated satisfactorily. Hume has, they say, constructed a system of investigation which *can* explain the phenomena of the world, including law and the workings of legal institutions. Further condemnation of legal positivism, stemming from dissatisfaction with its basic position, is centred on its preoccupation with a search for facts without giving any attention to the possibility of an underlying, unifying *purpose* in the law. The positivist answer declares that the search for and interpretation of facts is a necessary prelude to any search by others for 'purpose': let others investigate hypotheses concerning the likely direction of the law, but let them not confuse their speculative methodology with the spirit of scientific enterprise which characterises legal positivism.

The positivists' exclusion from an investigation of legal facts of the entire context of the law is criticised by those who maintain that law exists *only* within a social setting and that it cannot be investigated adequately if that setting is ignored. Dworkin, in his forthright rejection of legal positivism, insists that the legal positivist who refuses to engage with the philosophies and practices of political activity can never hope to contribute to the building of a liberal society in which the rule of law is central. Fuller reminds positivists that the law is a product of human effort, and that we risk absurdity if we try to describe it in disregard of the aims of those who brought it into being. The positivists' response states that the context of law is a matter for the considered judgment of the historian, the sociologist and the economist; it is not for the jurist as such.

Two specific criticisms relating to positivism, morality and justice, have been heard increasingly in recent times. First, it is said that it is an error to ignore the 'reality of absolute morality' which increasingly guides communities. Society's belief in *what ought to be* has been and continues to be a powerful stimulus to change. The positivist reaction draws attention to the 'relative nature' of much social morality (as, for example, in the decriminalisation of some sexual behaviour seen in the past as deviant and intolerable), making objective investigation of this phenomenon very difficult. A second criticism suggests that the positivist approach leads inevitably to a downgrading of concepts of 'right' and 'justice'. The positivist retorts that he does not deny the significance of these concepts; he is attempting to investigate their positive manifestations within legal systems and has no intention of downgrading their importance within the law.

Fuller takes issue with the positivists' claim that their intention is, primarily, to promote clearer thinking in the law. Is the end sought in this quest worthwhile? Would clarity in legal discussion really be advanced if positivism could attain its goal of wide acceptance of some clear distinction between law and morality? Drawing a distinction of this type surely cannot be justified as an end in itself. Additionally, says Fuller, positivism exerts a 'serious inhibitive influence' over legal scholarship by fencing in the legal writer with the question: does what you have written state the law or only your idea of what the law ought to be?

These are powerful criticisms but they have not deflected the legal positivists from their course. Early preoccupations with the 'naturalistic fallacy' (that is, the non-separation of 'ought' and 'is') have given way to a more intensive analysis of matters such as the phenomenon of language in the law and its significance in legal discourse. Positivist studies continue to analyse the legal order while, at the same time, calling attention to the difficulties of accepting as valid those ideas of law which are based on attempts to transcend the empirical reality of existing legal systems: 'justice', 'fairness', 'equality' remain vital social principles, but the investigation of their validity, which demands a consideration of their morality, for example, must remain outside the terms of reference of a jurisprudence which seeks to comprehend in rational style law and its institutions.

Notes

The essential features of legal positivism are discussed in Friedmann, Chapter 21; Bodenheimer, Chapters 7 and 8; and in Lloyd, Chapter 6. Shuman's *Legal Positivism* and Raz's *The Authority of Law* expound the problems associated with positivism. Simmonds comments on the discussion in 'Between Positivism and Idealism' [1991] CLJ 308. Hart's *The Concept of Law* and Fuller's *The Law in Quest of Itself* consider the doctrine of positivism and its implications. See, also, 'Legal positivism', by Coleman and Leiter, in *A Companion to Philosophy of Law and Legal Theory*, edited by Patterson.

Question 22

'Austin's theory is in the last analysis a psychological one': Jones (*Historical Introduction to the Theory of Law*).

Is it correct, therefore, to place Austin in the 'psychological school' of jurisprudence?

Answer plan

Austin (1790–1859), a friend of Bentham and JS Mill, was one of the earlier positivists who sought to explain law in terms of commands issued by 'a sovereign'. His best known work, *The Province of Jurisprudence Determined* (1832), attempts to clarify the distinction between law and morality and to ascertain the limits of jurisprudential investigation. Examination questions concerning Austin tend to concentrate on the detail of his theory and on criticisms of that theory. This question, somewhat unusually, calls for a consideration of Austinian doctrine in relation to psychology. The answer should deal with the main features of the theory and should note those points at which Austin seems to touch upon psychological matters. There should be comment on the problems which must arise in jurisprudence (as elsewhere) when the work of a jurist who lived in a past era is analysed in terms of a science of our times. The following skeleton plan is suggested:

Introduction – psychological overtones in Austin's theory –
Austin's description of law – commands – sanctions –
Austin's analysis of sovereignty – psychological nature of
Austin's comments on law – Allen's comments on
Manning's views concerning Austin – the psychological
school of jurisprudence – conclusion, doubtful
classification of Austin as a member of the 'psychological
school'.

Answer

'Austin's theory' is taken to mean, within the context of Jones'
statement, the concept of law as a species of command, and his
analysis of sovereignty. In *The Province of Jurisprudence Determined*
(1832), which contains the essence of his theory, Austin
(1790–1859) attempted to define the precise scope of
jurisprudence. This involved drawing a clear line between 'law'
and 'morality'. For Austin, jurisprudence was concerned *solely*
with positive laws 'as considered without regard to their goodness
or badness'. ('The existence of law is one thing; its merit or
demerit is another. Whether it be or be not is one enquiry; whether
it be or be not conformable to an assumed standard is a different
enquiry.') Law was to be viewed as a species of command issued
by a person or body of persons to whom habitual obedience is
rendered, that is, 'law set by political superiors to political
inferiors'. There are undeniable overtones within Austin's theory
of matters which are properly within the province of psychology –
command, obedience, habit – and it *can* be argued with force that a
theory based on concepts of this nature should be classified as
'psychological'. It would be wrong, however, to read into Austin's
work, produced at a time when the outlook and science of
psychology were almost unknown in England, suggestions of an
attempt by the author to view the essence of jurisprudence in
terms of percepts and intellectual constructs which were well
beyond his time.

A law, according to Austin, is a description of a rule laid down
'for the guidance of an intelligent being by an intelligent being
having power over him'. Within this description are terms rooted
in the 'mentalistic' terminology of scientific psychology.

'Intelligent being' refers clearly to sentient persons exercising their mental faculties; the term 'power' may have wider connotations than mere physical might, and can be explained in psychological terms as a perception by one person of another's ability and readiness to exercise coercion. Austin's description of law is of orders ('rules') promulgated by one person or body of persons and *perceived* by those individuals to whom they are directed as 'directions concerning conduct'. This view of law is, fundamentally, of a psychological nature in that it rests upon perceptions (that is, apprehensions within the mind) by 'the governed' within a community.

Laws, says Austin, may be categorised as 'improperly so called' and 'properly so called'. The former category is divided into laws 'by analogy', and 'laws by metaphor'. Laws by analogy are rules set out and enforced by mere opinion, such as a communal 'law of honour'. Such laws are aspects of 'positive morality': they are 'positive' in that they are man-made, and they relate to a 'morality' which has to be distinguished from the positive law. Laws by metaphor describe the natural law, for example, those describing the determination of movement of inanimate bodies.

The laws 'properly so called' are *general commands*, comprising the laws set by God to his human creatures, and laws set by men to men. The laws of God do not fall within the province of jurisprudence. The laws set by men to men may be categorised according to the nature of the relationship existing among them. If this relationship involves men who have political superiority over others, or who exercise legal rights conferred by their superiors, their 'laws' comprise 'positive law' or 'law' in its strict, simple sense. *The aggregate of such laws is, according to Austin, the essential and appropriate matter of jurisprudence.* By contrast, where laws are set by men who are not political superiors, or who do not exercise legal rights conferred by superiors, these 'laws' are mere examples of 'positive morality', as where rules relating to membership of a private club are published, and accepted by club members.

The *general commands* given to the community directly or circuitously are by their nature 'continuing commands', that is, they determine more than specific acts. Further, they are promulgated to persons 'in a state of subjection' to the author. It is possible to interpret this concept in psychological terminology. A 'state of subjection' may arise from perceived political and social status: those who are disenfranchised and who play no part in the enactment of the community's 'rules' will tend to view themselves as 'inferior', and will be aware of a 'state of subjection'. 'Subjection' is primarily a *mental state*.

Austin's analysis of the nature of a 'command' gives support to those who view his theory as 'psychological'. If, says Austin, you express or intimate a wish that I should or should not perform an act, and if I am sure that you will 'visit me with an evil' if I fail to comply with your wish, then the expression or intimation of your wish is *a command*. Further, a command is distinguished from other significations of desire not by the *style* in which the desire is signified, but by the *power and purpose* of the party commanding to inflict an evil or pain in case the desire be disregarded. The psychological basis of Austin's 'command' is clear. The command arises from the expression of a 'wish'; its 'power' depends on 'awareness' by the person to whom the wish is made known that evil will follow upon failure to conform to the wish, and upon his perception of the strength of those undesired consequences likely to emerge as the result of disobedience. 'The greater the eventual evil, and the greater the chance of incurring it, the greater is the efficacy of the command, and the greater is the strength of the obligation.' Here is 'command' viewed by Austin in terms of *perception* – the essence of psychological interpretations of the law.

Austin sees 'command' and 'duty' as 'correlative terms', the meaning denoted by each being implied or supposed by the other. Because X is 'liable to evil' from Y if he fails to comply with Y's signified wish, X is 'bound' or 'obliged' by Y's command, that is, he is under a *duty* to obey it. Again, Austin is viewing an essential feature of his theory – the concept of duty – in terms of *personal and considered responses* to the actions of others.

The enforcement of obedience, the 'sanction', is analysed by Austin as 'the evil which will probably be increased in case a command is disobeyed', that is, in the case of a duty being disregarded. Such an evil may be styled 'a punishment'. It is the sanction – the 'fear of evil' and awareness of the power of another to inflict punishment in the event of non-compliance with a wish – which transforms the expression of a mere wish into a 'command'.

Punitive sanctions are, in Austin's view, essential for valid law. In psychological terms, the motivating force behind conduct which is consciously directed to the carrying out of the wishes embodied in a law is the 'fear' of being visited with 'an evil'.

Austin's analysis of sovereignty is an important part of his teachings. He distinguishes sovereignty from other types of 'superiority'. The essence of sovereignty is to be found in the phenomenon of 'obedience to a perceived superior'. The bulk of members of society are, according to Austin, in the *habit* of obedience or submission to a *determinate and common superior* (a person or body of persons, for example, a monarch or a Parliament); that person or body is not in the habit of obedience to any determinate human superior. Hence, if a determinate human superior, not in the habit of obedience to a like superior receives habitual obedience from the majority of members of a society, *that superior is 'sovereign' in that society* (and the society is 'political and independent'). Essentially, therefore, sovereignty involves the very fact of 'obedience' – a psychological state which reflects subjection and submission, and perceptions of a 'superior-inferior' relationship. 'Habitual' obedience suggests, in psychological terms, attitudes resulting from the force of *habit*; that habit may have resulted from repeated reactions to the acts of the sovereign power. ('Habit' has been defined by some contemporary psychologists as 'a course of action resulting from the simultaneous perception of a situation and its meaning'.) In modern psychological parlance, it may be the result of deliberate 'conditioning', as where the sovereign so acts as to intend the creation of a set of desired responses to stimuli, for example, obedience induced by exposure to the trappings of majesty and power.

To deny the force of the psychological concepts at the basis of Austin's theory is to reject the essential features of *law within society* as he viewed that phenomenon. It should be remembered that Austin was a utilitarian, closely influenced by his friends, Bentham and JS Mill. For Austin, the proper purpose or end of a sovereign government is 'the greatest possible advancement of human happiness' – an objective which is not easily separated from the states of mind with which psychology is concerned in its investigations. For Austin, law rests on the perception of the nature and consequences of commands. It involves acknowledgment of a person or body as a sovereign to whom habitual obedience must be given. The force of personal attitudes is at the heart of Austin's theory, which, to a considerable extent, can be described in Jones' words, as 'a psychological one'.

It would be unproductive, however, to seek to read into Austin's theory the constructs of our current views of psychology. An attempt of this nature was made by Manning in his article on 'Austin today' (1933). Allen's reply is of particular interest. Manning had suggested that Austin had given merely 'a particular account of the relation between law and communal psychology', and that the Austinian concept of sovereignty was based on the idea of a sovereign as 'a mere abstraction, and his sovereignty just a brace of ideas'. Allen notes that one cannot extract this meaning from anything Austin wrote or meant. Manning is merely transferring ideas and arguments 'from one place to another, both in time and conception' at his will. This is, indeed, the problem raised by attempts to read into Austin's formulations a methodology of investigation of which he can have had no possible understanding. The danger is, says Allen, of taking the dogmatic and explicit doctrines of one age and attempting to paraphrase them into 'the terminology and philosophical facts of a later era'.

To employ, for example, Freudian or Jungian theories of human obedience in a modern 'interpretation' of Austin may be valid for us, since our age has at its disposal knowledge of techniques of investigation which were denied to earlier times. But to use these techniques so as to imply that Austin himself had in mind ideas which were generally beyond his time is invalid. In a very general sense, it is true to say that, because jurisprudence concerns human beings, and because all human activities have a psychological dimension, then jurists must recognise that their theories are touched, if only tangentially, by the phenomena which psychology investigates. This observation may be applied with some justification to the 'psychological' interpretations of Austinian doctrine.

To say, however, that it is possible to classify that doctrine as belonging to the 'psychological school of jurisprudence' gives rise to difficulty. A fully-fledged psychological theory of law is one predicated on the fundamental and decisive significance of mental phenomena in legal events. Thus, Petrazycki, for whom rights and duties are 'phantasmata', existing only in the mind, but creating 'imperative-attributed experiences', may be considered a supporter of the 'psychological school'. Ehrenzweig, who views the legal order as an enterprise structured in order to moderate conflicting individual views of justice, and who sees those conflicts as explicable in Freudian terms as a product of individual 'early personality development', may be considered as belonging to that school. Jurists who perceive the tensions within a legal system as reflecting Freudian categories, or as mirroring Jung's 'split in the individual between the ego and the shadow', may be classified as members of the 'psychological school'. But Austin, for whom the formal relationships of sovereign and subjects comprise the essence of the socio-legal framework, might be placed within that school only as a result of an unwarranted extension of the declared aims, framework and methodology attributed to the 'psychological jurisprudence' movement.

Notes

Austin's teachings are considered by Lloyd, Chapter 4; Dias, Chapter 16; Harris, Chapter 3; Friedmann, Chapter 22; and Riddall, Chapter 2. There is a full treatment of the Austinian theory, together with extracts from *The Province of Jurisprudence Determined*, in Davies and Holdcroft, Chapter 2. Allen, Chapter 1, examines the 'psychological interpretation' of Austin's views propounded by Manning in 'Austin today', which appears in Jennings' edition of *Modern Theories of Law*. Morrison's *John Austin*, and Rumble's *The Thought of John Austin* provide background information on Austin's concepts of the fundamentals of law.

Question 23

'Criticisms of Austin's theory of law mounted steadily in the 19th century; but it was Hart who delivered the *coup de grâce* a century later.'

Explain.

Answer plan

Austin was criticised in his lifetime for a variety of reasons, but largely because of his uncompromising positivist approach to interpretations of the law. Specifically, it was claimed that he had misunderstood the significance of the social functions of law and that he had failed to separate the concepts of legal authority and political power. Hart later subjected the 'command theory' to intensive scrutiny in *The Concept of Law* (1961). The question calls for an awareness of the criticisms faced by Austin in his lifetime and the general lines of the attack mounted by Hart. The following skeleton plan is suggested:

> Introduction – reminder of Austin's theory – narrowness of his perspective – simplistic view of the law – linguistic looseness – restricted view of sovereignty – Hart's criticisms – conclusion, noting Austin's failure to understand significance of 'rules'.

Answer

The essence of Austin's much-criticised theory is to be found in his basing the very nature of law not on ideas of 'good' or 'bad', 'just' or 'unjust', but on the concept of power exercised by a superior. Positive law, or, as he terms it, 'law properly so called', can be understood only if there is a separation of questions of law and those of morality. The law is characterised by its constituent elements of command, sanction, duty and sovereignty. It may be comprehended in terms of the command of a sovereign backed by sanctions. Legality is determined by source, not by any measure of its substantive merits, so that the very criteria of legality reflect fact rather than questions of value. The theory was published in the first half of the 19th century, in a year which witnessed the death of Bentham and the passing of the Reform Act. It bears the marks of the philosophical and jurisprudential thought associated with Austin's friends, Bentham and JS Mill, in particular, their positivism and utilitarianism. Early criticisms of Austin turned on his positivism – denounced as 'a sterile verbalism which produced a travesty of reality' – and on an apparent narrowness of perspective. By the time of his death in 1859, the theory had been condemned as a totally inadequate explanation of law based on a misunderstanding of the nature of 'command' and 'obedience'. Hart's detailed examination of Austin's theory in *The Concept of Law* (1961) underlined the essential weaknesses of 'the command theory of law'.

'Narrowness of perspective' was a criticism directed at Austin with particular force by those who saw him as a 'naive empiricist'. It was claimed that he had not understood the implications of the positivism he espoused and that his separation of questions of law from those of morality shut him off from awareness of the real complexities of law within society. This same narrowness of vision was detected by those critics who claimed that Austin's preparatory work for the exposition of his theory had been confined to an enquiry into certain aspects of English law and an investigation of Roman legal theory of the classical era. This appeared to constitute too narrow a base for the construction of a *general* theory of jurisprudence. The result, said the critics, was a selective doctrine founded upon mere abstractions with few roots in established historical fact.

Further criticism emerged from what was perceived as Austin's 'simplistic view' of law. It was argued that he had confused 'law' with the mere product of legislation. He had failed to understand that 'law' was much more than legislative enactments; it included, for example, customary law and international law, neither of which received adequate treatment in his analysis. Above all, perhaps, the analysis did not extend to an adequate examination of judge-made law. Much law results from the decisions of the courts and it is not easy to see, therefore, in what sense judge-made law may be considered as emanating solely from 'the commands of a sovereign', unless one accepts the doubtful view of judges as mere delegates of the state.

Critics noted, too, some 'linguistic looseness', or ambiguity, in Austin's exposition of his command theory. The term 'command' has its own singular connotations and overtones. Its general use suggests a person who 'issues orders in a peremptory fashion'. It is difficult to use the word accurately in referring to the content of a large proportion of legislation. The characteristics of a 'command' are often absent from many contemporary statutes.

Austin's concept of 'sovereignty' was attacked by those who considered it to be over-simplified and incapable of application to a wide range of problems arising from the legal structures of democratic societies in particular. Austin's view of the sovereign as possessing unlimited powers seemed to have no validity within a parliamentary constitution. The idea of 'indivisibility' of the sovereign power created difficulties for those who sought to apply it to the analysis of a federal state. Bryce, writing at the turn of the 19th century, suggested that Austin may have blurred the distinctions between the *de facto* sovereign (who receives the 'habitual obedience' of subjects) and the *de jure* sovereign (the law-enacting institution). Thus, our constitutional law makes a clear distinction between Her Majesty the Queen and the Queen in Parliament. Austin, it was claimed, had concentrated too readily on the *form* of the law, on its outward manifestations in relation to the sovereign, and had neglected the *functional aspects* of sovereign power within society.

It was a weakened theory of 'law as command' that Hart set out to demolish. In *The Concept of Law* (1961), he speaks of his aim in the book as having been 'to further the understanding of law, coercion, and morality as different but related social phenomena'. With this in mind he examines, initially, Austin's concept of law as being, basically, 'orders backed by threats'. Superficially, the criminal law may provide many examples of this view. Thus, s 13 of the Terrorism Act 2000 states that a person commits an offence if he wears an item of clothing in such a way as to arouse reasonable suspicion that he is a member or supporter of a proscribed organisation; a person found guilty is liable to a fine, imprisonment or both. Here is a precise 'order' backed by 'threat of application of sanction'. But, in Hart's words, 'there are other varieties of law, notably those conferring legal powers to adjudicate or legislate (public powers) or to create or vary legal relations (private powers) which cannot, without absurdity, be construed as orders backed by threats'. Thus, contract law, creating facilities for individuals to realise their wishes by conferring upon them powers to create structures of rights and duties, provides examples: see the Contracts (Rights of Third Parties) Act 1999. Hart points out, too, that many laws of a public nature (constitutional law, for example) exemplify 'power-conferring' *rules*, not 'order plus threat'. Those who argue, however, that the 'nullity' which may be a consequence of a failure to comply with the law (as illustrated by lack of compliance with the provisions of the Wills Act 1837) and which is, therefore, in effect, a 'sanction', must be met with the counter-argument that the effects of failure to comply with the statute may be to the advantage of persons involved, and will not necessarily involve the 'evil' of a sanction.

Hart points out, further, that in Austin's theory, the sovereign lawmaker is not himself bound by the orders he issues. He stands, to that extent, above and beyond the law. But, in practice, the legislator is often bound by the orders he makes and promulgates. Thus, the House of Lords – an important part of the legislature – is bound by the Parliament Acts 1911 and 1949 which effectively limit its powers. The House of Commons is bound effectively by its 'standing orders relative to public business', as published in 1989. The Austinian view of the legislature as 'subject to no rules' seems inadequate in the face of the fact of the 'self-binding force' of some parliamentary legislation.

The origin of our law cannot be understood correctly, according to Hart, by considering it merely as having emerged from 'order plus threat'. Some very important specific rules of our law (now embodied in mercantile law, for example) originated in custom. It is not possible to explain their origin merely in terms of 'enactments of the sovereign legislature'. Thus, the customs of merchants in relation to early forms of bills of exchange were recognised as possessing the force of law within groups of financiers long before the Bills of Exchange Act 1882. No 'sovereign' commanded, in the form of an 'order and threat', that the strict codes of practice binding the early 'money scriveners', which originated in the customs of Florentine and Venetian bankers, should have force among the merchants of London. Austin's command theory is of doubtful value in this context.

Hart places particular emphasis on the total inadequacy of the Austinian concept of 'habit of obedience' in relation to sovereignty. Austin, it will be recalled, explained sovereignty in terms of the obedience displayed by subjects towards their sovereign. The authoritarian ruler ensures that his people are conditioned to acceptance of orders and obedience in all circumstances; the citizens of a parliamentary democracy have the *habit* of obeying legislation promulgated on behalf of the Queen in Parliament. But, says Hart, let us suppose that within a state, one ruler is followed by another. How may we account for the continuity generally observed and the fact that laws may outlive the lawmaker? Citizens were 'in the habit' of obeying their first ruler. At what stage is their habitual obedience 'transferred' to his successor? When may it be said that the citizens become 'habituated' to the power enjoyed by the new ruler? Hart's answer involves a perusal of the *rules* which ensure that there shall be an uninterrupted movement of power from one ruler to another. The simplistic notion of mere 'habits of obedience' is an inadequate explanation of the phenomenon of the *transitional transfer* of legislative powers. Hart argues that the explanation of the seemingly paradoxical 'movement of obedience' may be discovered in the existence of accepted fundamental *rules* regarding the right to legislate; these rules have been internalised by members of the community.

Further deficiencies in Austin's analysis of sovereignty are uncovered by Hart. The concept of 'a sovereign with unlimited power' (the 'omnipotent ruler') has no application to our type of parliamentary democracy. Where may we locate 'the illimitable sovereign'? Thus, Parliament may not generally extend its life beyond the period of five years, as stated by the Parliament Act 1911. (There was an exception to this rule in the two World Wars.) The voluntary surrender by Parliament of some aspects of its sovereignty (as noted in *Factortame Ltd v Secretary of State for Transport (No 2)* (1991)) in relation to the need to give full effect to European Union law, is of significance. But in spite of limitations upon its 'omnipotence', Parliament's enactments continue to express validly its sovereign status. Nor is the Austinian dilemma in the face of Parliament's practice resolved by reference to the electorate as 'the true sovereign power'. Hart notes that the power of the electorate is undeniably limited. Its delegation of the exercise of its sovereignty to Parliamentary representatives creates in practice a situation in which large sections of the electorate may be subjected to rules and orders of which they may not approve. There is doubt, for example, as to whether Parliament's decision not to restore capital punishment for the offence of murder represents the currently held views of the majority of 'the sovereign electorate'.

Little remains of the Austinian edifice. Hart uncovered and demolished its basic structure. Austin's inability to recognise the significance of 'rules' in a system of law accounts, in Hart's view, for his failure to comprehend the nature of law. Hart points out that the Austinian theory was fashioned from elements such as orders, threats, and obedience; these elements did not include, and could not by their combination yield, the idea of 'a rule', 'without which we cannot hope to elucidate even the most elementary forms of law'. It would be left to Hart himself to construct a concept of law based on the idea of a combination of 'primary and secondary rules', which would provide a credible alternative to the Austinian theory of 'law as command'.

Notes

Austin's theory is outlined in *The Province of Jurisprudence Determined*. Hart's criticisms are contained in *The Concept of Law* (Chapters 2, 3 and 4 in particular). Appropriate extracts from Austin and his critics, including Hart, appear in Davies and Holdcroft, Chapter 2. A useful article by Tapper, 'Austin on sanctions', appears in the Cambridge Law Journal ([1965] CLJ 271). Lloyd, Chapter 4; Harris, Chapter 3; and Riddall, Chapter 2, comment on the criticisms of Austinian doctrine.

Question 24

What are the fundamentals of Hart's concept of 'a legal system'?

Answer plan

Hart (1907–92) envisages a legal system as derived from 'a union of primary and secondary rules'; his theory is expounded in *The Concept of Law* (1961). Hart's view is that a legal system can exist *only* when certain conditions are fulfilled: obedience must be given by citizens to certain *rules*, the validity of which depends on the system's basic 'rules of recognition', and the system's secondary rules must be accepted as common public standards by the community's officials. This question is straightforward and demands an exposition of the fundamentals of Hart's system of primary and secondary rules. The following skeleton plan is suggested:

> Introduction – Hart's 'characteristics of the human condition' – social habits and social rules – primary rules – secondary rules – rules of recognition, change and adjudication – essence of a 'legal system' – conclusion, meaning of 'the existence of a legal system'.

Answer

Hart (1907–92) views the concept of a legal system from the perspective of a positivist. Legal institutions and other phenomena related to the law must be studied exactly *as they are*; law is, in general, to be considered apart from morality and is to be subjected to a systematic analysis. Law as a 'social phenomenon', which is how Hart views it, involves, for those who wish to study it, reference to 'the characteristics of the human condition'. In *The Concept of Law* (1961) in which Hart articulates his concept of the essential features of a legal system, he lists those characteristics as: human vulnerability (each one of us can be subjected to undesired physical violence); approximate equality (making necessary mutual forbearance and compromise); limited altruism (tendencies to aggression which require control); limited resources (we need food, shelter, clothing, all of which are in limited supply); and limited understanding and strength of will (our understanding of long term interests cannot be taken for granted). There arises, therefore, within society, a need for *rules* to protect 'persons, property and promises'. *It is the problem of rules – their constituent features and inter-relationships – which dominates Hart's interpretation of the essence of a legal system.* We note below Hart's system of 'primary and secondary rules' and his view of the circumstances necessary for the existence of what may properly be called 'a legal system'.

Hart's view may be summarised as follows: if a legal system is to obtain within a community, two circumstances must co-exist. First, there must be a variety of 'valid obligation rules' which are generally obeyed by the bulk of members of society. Secondly, the officials within that society must accept, additionally, certain rules of 'change, adjudication and responsibility'. This terminology must now be examined.

The term 'rule' is not to be viewed in Austin's terms, namely, as 'a command'. Within a society, there are 'social habits' and 'social rules'. *Social habits* (which are not conterminous with 'rules') may be exemplified by members of a group who visit the theatre every Friday evening. Failure by some members to attend the theatre on Friday evenings will not be perceived as a 'fault' which should, in itself, attract criticism. *Social rules* are more significant: where they are broken (as in matters pertaining to morality, etc) criticism will result because a 'fault' is thought to have been committed; a breach becomes a matter of general concern. Existence of a social rule involves its acceptance by social groups as a whole. Awareness of a rule, and support for its significance and acceptance within the group, are termed by Hart 'the internal aspects of that rule'. The 'external aspects of a rule' refer to the fact that an observer outside the group could be aware of its existence because particular patterns of behaviour appear to be followed and regulations may be discerned. Social habits have an external aspect only; social rules have an external *and* an internal aspect. Hart attaches particular significance to the internalisation of rules by those who participate in a legal system: it involves a 'critical, reflective attitude to certain patterns of behaviour and a common standard', and this ought to be displayed in criticism and self-criticism, demands for conformity to standards, and an acknowledgment that such criticism and demands are justified.

Social rules are, under Hart's classification, of two kinds – mere 'social conventions' and 'rules constituting obligations'. The former phrase refers to, for example, rules of correct behaviour in a place of public worship. The latter phrase involves conformity, which is considered essential if society's life, its components and quality, are to be maintained. Hart states: 'Rules are conceived and spoken of as imposing obligations when the general demand for conformity is insistent and the social pressure brought to bear upon those who deviate or threaten to deviate is great.' An example might be the general rules forbidding violence to individuals. The 'rules' relating to obligations impinge on the idea of 'moral duties', and are *what we understand by 'law'*. 'Moral duties' constitute a significant and important portion of a society's moral code; some may have originated in ancient customs; the breach of a moral obligation does not in itself usually result in punishment of the offender, but, nevertheless, there are often intense pressures to carry out those duties.

The rules relating to obligations which we speak of as 'legal rules' are of two types. Hart refers to them as 'primary' and 'secondary' rules. Essentially, the primary rules of obligation are the fundamental prohibitions which ensure necessary regularity in a legal system and may be epitomised by the criminal law and those parts of the law of torts involving obligations. Thus, the Road Traffic Act 1988, as amended, imposes duties on those who drive motor vehicles on the roads. The rule in *Rylands v Fletcher* (1865) imposes strict obligations on those who, for their own purposes, bring on their land and collect and keep there anything likely to do damage if it escapes. Primary rules, in Hart's sense, generally concern requirements to do or abstain from certain actions.

Hart argues that a small community, closely knit by common sentiment and belief, and placed in a stable environment, might be able to live with a set of rules approximating to the 'primary rules of obligation' he has described. But this would not be possible in a large community, because of the very nature of the primary rules. Thus, doubts might arise as to what the rules are, or as to the basis on which those doubts are to be settled: the problem would be one of *uncertainty*. Further, the *static nature* of the primary rules might create a further problem: deliberate adaptation to new circumstances might be difficult. A third defect would be the *inefficiency* of the diffuse social pressures by which the rules are maintained: there would be no specialised official agency empowered to ascertain whether or not a rule had been broken. Primary rules would not, in themselves, suffice as 'building bricks' for the construction of a legal system; something more is necessary.

A supplementary system of 'secondary rules' would be needed, and these rules would be 'parasitic' on the primary rules, that is, they are 'rules about rules'. They will provide that members of the community may, by performing actions or saying things, introduce new rules of the primary sort, modify old rules, and control the operations of primary rules. The conferring of public or private powers will result from the application of the secondary rules. These rules would create or vary the obligations of members of the community. *The union of the primary and secondary rules constitutes 'the law'.*

The defect of 'uncertainty', that is, the lack of authoritative procedures for settling disputes as to the precise nature of the primary rules, would be remedied by a secondary rule which Hart terms 'the rule of recognition'. This rule will specify certain features, the existence of which will affirm conclusively that the rule in question 'is a rule of the group to be supported by the social pressure it exerts'. References to authoritative texts, to legislative enactments, to custom, to general declarations of specific purpose, or to past judicial decisions, will constitute the authoritative criteria for identification of primary rules of obligation. The rule of recognition may be, indeed, the 'ultimate rule' of a legal system since it is itself the test of legal validity within that system. Hart gives the example of the fundamental rule that what is enacted by 'the Queen in Parliament' is law; that rule provides criteria for assessing the validity of other rules within the system, but there is no rule providing criteria by which its own legal validity might be assessed. The very existence of the rule of recognition is no more than a matter of fact; that fact is shown in the various practices of loyal institutions, and the behaviour of the community.

The defect of 'static rules' within a system may be remedied by secondary 'rules of change'. Essentially, they empower specified individuals to make changes in 'legal positions'. Thus, the law of contract may be characterised as a group of secondary rules in that they serve to alter existing legal positions: the rules of consensus, of offer and acceptance, create a situation (of legally enforceable agreements) which alters a previous position in which there was no contract between the parties concerned. Section 136 of the Law of Property Act 1925, allowing the legal assignment of choses in action, makes possible new situations in relation to debts and other 'legal things in action'. The Wills Act 1837 allows a person who makes a will to alter a position in which his property rights might pass under the rules relating to an intestacy.

The defect of 'inefficiency' may be remedied by the provision of secondary rules giving authorised individuals power to determine in authoritative fashion the question as to whether some person has breached a primary rule. This type of secondary rule is known as the 'rule of adjudication'. Procedures relating to the appointment of judges, courts, and declarations in the form of judgments, will be covered by this rule. The Courts and Legal Services Act 1990 is an example of this type of secondary rule.

Primary and secondary rules (of recognition, change and adjudication) constitute the 'law' which is the essence of a legal system. Hart gives a unique answer to the question: What is meant precisely when it is said that 'a legal system exists'? Two basic conditions must be satisfied before it can be said with accuracy that 'a legal system exists'. First, rules, and, in particular, the rule of recognition, must be obeyed. Secondly, the secondary rules must be accepted by the community's officials as 'common public standards'.

The first of these conditions involves general obedience *in practice* by the mass of citizens to the community's rules which have a validity derived from the rule of recognition. The obedience required must be much more than mere 'lip service'. It must extend in practice to the community's daily life. Rules imposing obligations concerning the necessity to respect the property of others, for example, must be observed strictly if obedience is to be a reality. It is necessary, too, that obedience be given by *the bulk* of citizens (but not by all, since that is an impossibility). Obedience to the system's rule of recognition is of great importance; in our system, for example, there must be agreement on the necessity to observe as binding those rules made by the legislation enacted in Parliament.

Hart's second condition refers to the relationship of the community's officials to the secondary rules. The officials must not only obey those secondary rules, they must collectively 'accept' them. This applies in particular to acceptance of the 'rules of recognition' as providing common standards for the making and enunciation of judicial decisions. Thus, when a judge asserts that no court of justice may enquire into the manner in which Parliament made a law, he is demonstrating acceptance of the rule of recognition as it refers to the power and authority of Parliament.

Hart suggests that to assert that 'a legal system exists' is to make a 'Janus-faced statement' which looks both towards obedience by ordinary citizens (which, of course, will include an element of acceptance of rules) *and* to the acceptance by the community's officials of secondary rules as common standards of official behaviour. In accepting these common standards the officials will show a critical and reflective attitude to the appraisal of their own and one another's performance. The internalisation of the rules they profess to follow acquires unusual significance as partial indicia of the real existence of a legal system.

Notes

Hart's *The Concept of Law* is analysed in Lloyd, Chapter 6; Dias, Chapter 16; Harris, Chapter 9; and Riddall, Chapter 4. A detailed analysis is given in Davies in Holdcroft, Chapter 3. MacCormick discusses Hart's theory in *Legal Reasoning and Legal Theory*. A valuable exposition of the theory is given by Summers in 'Hart's concept of law' (1963) Duke University LJ 629. Barry's article, 'Herbert Hart: the concept of law', in *The Political Classics*, edited by Forsyth and Keens-Soper, examines Hart's analysis of law. A second edition of *The Concept of Law*, appeared in 1994; it contains an interesting postscript by Bulloch and Raz, constructed from Hart's notes in which he responds to Dworkin's criticisms.

Question 25

'A system of coercion imposing norms which are laid down by human acts in accordance with a constitution the validity of which is pre-supposed if it is on the whole efficacious.' Outline the theory from which this definition of law emerged.

Answer plan

The initial problem is the identification of the theory from which the definition emerged. It is, clearly, that associated with Kelsen, the so called 'pure theory of law'. Kelsen (1881–1973), an Austrian-American jurist, argued that an acceptable theory of law must be 'pure', that is, logically self-supporting and not dependent upon any extra-legal values. In every system of law can be found some basic assumption, some authoritative standard, accepted as such by a significant proportion of the community. From that fundamental assumption – the 'Grundnorm' – will be derived the norms which constitute 'the law'. An answer to the question will necessitate an explanation of Kelsen's analysis with particular reference to the concept of the norm. The skeleton plan for an answer is as follows:

Introduction – essence of the pure theory – norms – sanctions – the Grundnorm – illustration of norms – effectiveness and validity of norms – norms and the state – conclusion, pure theory as expression of positivism.

Answer

The quotation is, in fact, a definition of law stated in Kelsen's *General Theory of State and Law* (1945). The reasoning from which the definition stems is his celebrated 'pure theory of law', formulated first in 1911 and revised in its final form in 1964. It is, above all, a theory of *positive law*, concerned exclusively with the process of defining its subject matter with as much accuracy as is possible. Kelsen (1881–1973) advances it as a general theory and not as an interpretation of specific legal norms, although it is intended to offer a 'theory of interpretation'. It is designed so as to 'know and describe its subject'.

The theory makes possible the discovery of an answer to the basic question: 'What *is* the law?' It does not seek to answer the question: 'What *ought* the law to be?' Legal science should be fashioned, according to Kelsen, in terms which will reflect the unique nature of the phenomenon of law. This will involve the building of a framework of concepts having reference only to the law; the 'uncritical mixture of methodically-different disciplines which characterises much legal theory' is to be rejected. The appropriate methodology of investigation, which will be value-free, will require the interpretation of experience and 'the reduction of multiplicity to unity'; indeed for Kelsen, *all* knowledge reflected the endeavour to establish unity from chaos. In such an investigation, the concept of natural law would have no place. Kelsen viewed the claims of natural law as worthless, based on no more than speculative claims to immutability resting on 'Nature and Reason' – concepts which seemed to him to clothe with an objective character that which is non-existent and which contaminate the 'pure science' of law.

The 'purification' of the science of law and the removal of all subjective, evaluative criteria and elements of ideology, involve, first, a process of re-appraising the place of 'justice' in any definition of the law. Kelsen viewed the concept of justice as little more than the expression of an irrational ideal representing the value-preferences of an individual or a group. However indispensable the ideal of justice may be for the volition and activities of men, it is not subject to cognition. It may be considered 'just' for a general rule to be applied in practice in all those cases where circumstances demand that application. In this sense justice may be perceived 'in the maintenance of a positive order by conscientious application of general rules'. Let 'justice' be identified, therefore, with 'legality'. But the question of what constitutes justice cannot be answered with any scientific precision and is not, therefore, a fruitful subject for the investigation which is to characterise a 'pure theory' of law.

Not only should political and ideological value-laden judgments be expelled from an investigation of law, but all non-legal extraneous matters are to be considered as adulterants. Kelsen insisted on the total rejection of those elements of psychology, sociology and ethics which had found their way into jurisprudence. Such 'alien disciplines' had attracted the attention of jurists because they dealt with matters which might be perceived as having a close connection with the law. The connections of this type are to be neither ignored nor denied, but their uncritical use (which Kelsen referred to as 'methodological syncretism') had obscured the true nature of the science of law. If one were to admit into a precise study of positive law material relating, say, to the economic basis of society, the result would be an admixture which would defy attempts to make a fundamental analysis. The pure theory at which Kelsen aimed is, in his words, 'a science of law (jurisprudence), not legal politics'.

The appropriate materials for a study which will lead to a pure science of law are to be found in those 'norms' which have the character of *legal norms*, in that they make certain acts legal or illegal. The term 'norm' is used by Kelsen in a very precise sense so that it connotes a standard to which individuals should conform; it is the very meaning of an act by which a certain behaviour is commanded, permitted or authorised. Legal norms do not merely prescribe certain types of human behaviour, they attach to the contrary behaviour specific coercive acts as *sanctions*. Kelsen would argue, therefore, that our law does not merely state that dangerous driving is to avoided; it makes it an offence, under the Road Traffic Acts 1988 and 1991, attracting specified punishments. The element of coercion, which underpins a sanction, is, according to Kelsen, a vital constituent of the law as he envisages it. *Law is 'a coercive order of human behaviour'*. Sanctions are not merely of a psychological nature; when used by the law they are 'outward' in that they involve, *visibly*, a deprivation of the offender's freedom or property. It is its coercive nature which distinguishes law from all other social orders. The decisive criterion of the law is the presence of an element of force: it means that the act which is presented by the order as a direct consequence of socially detrimental facts ought to be carried out even against the will of the offender and, if he should resist, by physical force.

In Kelsen's terms, law is based on norms which stipulate sanctions; hence, law may be perceived as 'norms addressed to officials' (such as judges). These norms are prescriptive of conduct and may be interpreted in the following manner: if A, then B, that is, if the circumstances in question constitute A, then B should happen. Thus, if X is not in possession of an appropriate licence, and he imports controlled drugs, then a judge is required to apply sanctions in accordance with the Misuse of Drugs Act 1971. If Y, the owner of a pit bull terrier, allows the dog to be in a public place unmuzzled, a judge may apply the sanctions set out in the Dangerous Dogs Act 1991.

The *validity* of a given legal norm depends solely, according to Kelsen, on its having been authorised by another legal norm *of a higher rank*. An administrative order is valid if authorised by statute; the authorising statute is valid if it has been made in accordance with the provisions of a constitution which, in turn, is valid if it has been promulgated by the authority of an earlier constitution. But if, for example, the constitution in question is the first to be promulgated in a newly-founded state, then its validity may be considered in terms of what Kelsen describes as a 'basic norm' (Grundnorm). This is a norm *presupposed by legal thinking*. It must be presupposed because, in Kelsen's words, 'it cannot be "posited", that is to say, created by an authority whose competence would have to rest on a still higher norm'. The basic norm – the 'final postulate' – behind which one cannot go, may take a variety of forms; thus, it might be 'coercion of man against man should be exercised in the style and under the conditions determined by the state's first constitution'. A basic norm may be discovered in any legal order; it is viewed by Kelsen as the ultimate source for the validity of all those other norms belonging to the same legal order.

Within a given legal system it should be possible to discern a *hierarchy* composed of different levels of legal norms, at the apex of which is the Grundnorm, valid only because it is presupposed, and providing authority for all other norms within the system. Assume circumstances in which, under appropriate rules emanating from statute, and subsequent to his conviction by a court, X is imprisoned. The act of the prison officer who effects X's actual imprisonment derives its validity from the sentence ordered by the court following X's trial. The validity of the court's action is derived from an appropriate statute which, in turn, owes its authority to promulgation by the Queen in Parliament. Beyond that promulgation is the law and custom pertaining to the authority of Parliament. Beyond that is a *final, basic, norm*, relating to the unquestioning acceptance by the community of the overriding nature of Parliamentary pronouncements embodied within statute. In applying statute law in X's case, the judges are, in Kelsen's terms, 'concretising' the *general norms* controlling that case; the decision in X's particular case constitutes an *'individual norm'*. Where the administrative organs within a legal system apply general norms to a particular case so that an administrative decree results, the individual norms created constitute 'the law'.

Kelsen distinguishes the 'effectiveness' of a legal norm from its 'validity'. The term 'validity' implies that a legal norm should be *obeyed* and should be *applied* in given circumstances. 'Effectiveness' means that, in practice, the norm is actually obeyed and applied. In his revised version of the pure theory, Kelsen stated that a norm which is not obeyed by anyone anywhere, that is, which is not effective at least to some degree, cannot be regarded as a 'valid' norm. The implication is that, although a legal norm requires authorisation by a higher norm, a further condition of its validity is 'a minimum of effectiveness'. Hence, within a community, universal and total obedience to the basic norm is not essential; there must be within the community, however, a *sufficiency of adherence* to that basic norm, allowing it to be effective in practice. The 'principle of legitimacy' is restricted by 'the principle of effectiveness'. 'The efficacy of the total legal order is a necessary condition for the validity of every single norm of the order'.

The pure theory stresses the concept of law as possessing no moral connotation whatsoever; a decisive criterion in law is derived from the 'element of force' underlying sanctions. The apparatus of the law, its courts and other legal institutions, possess the capacity to protect any type of political structure. (Law may be thought of as a highly specific technique of social organisation.) Further, the law is all-embracing: in effect, there is no human behaviour which, as such, is excluded from being the content of a legal norm. From this, Kelsen suggests the identity of the state and the law. *The state is a political organisation expressing a legal order*; it is governed by law (a state not governed by law is, says Kelsen, 'unthinkable'). We may consider the state as *a totality of the norms within a hierarchy*; it is nothing other than 'the sum total of norms ordering compulsion' and is, therefore, co-extensive with the law. The state *is* the law, and the traditional dualism of 'law *v* state' can no longer be maintained.

The pure theory has been described as 'perhaps the most consistent expression of positivism in legal theory'. Its links with classical positivism and its exponents – Hume, Bentham and Austin – are clear. Rejection of natural law, concern for form and structure, a separating out from legal theory of the social and moral content of law, are obvious in Kelsen's analysis. The pure theory represents, according to Friedmann, 'a quest for pure knowledge in its most uncompromising form, for knowledge free from instinct, volition and desire'. Kelsen's task was to discover what he considered as the true essence of the law and, as a consequence, to reject all that which is clearly in flux or merely accidental. The result is a theory which carries the positivist analysis to an advanced stage and which treats the law, in Bodenheimer's phrase, 'as though it were contained in a hermetically-sealed container'. The pure theory attempts to see law as a systematic, unified concept; a legal order is presented in sparse terms as a *system* of normative relations whose unity stems from the *one reason* for the validity of norms – a *fundamental norm*. The value of the contribution of the pure theory to an understanding of law rests in its enunciation of the relation between the fundamental norm and other, lower norms within the society; it does not pronounce on the 'desirability' of the fundamental norm, for that is a task for the political scientist, not for the jurist.

Notes

Kelsen's *The Pure Theory of Law* has been translated and edited by Ebenstein. *The General Theory of Law and State* appears in a translation by Wedberg. Lauterpacht has written on Kelsen's 'Pure science of law', which appears in *Modern Theories of Law*, edited by Jennings. *Essays on Kelsen*, edited by Tur and Twining, is an examination of aspects of the pure theory. There are useful summaries of the pure theory, and extracts, in Harris, Chapter 6; Lloyd Chapter 5; Dias, Chapter 17; Riddell, Chapter 10; Davies and Holdcroft, Chapter 5; and Friedmann, Chapter 24.

Question 26

'An exercise in logic and not in life.'

Does this statement exemplify some of the main criticisms directed against the 'pure theory of law'?

Answer plan

The statement cited in the question was made by Laski (1893–1950), a prolific British writer on politics and jurisprudence, in 1925. It typifies, to a considerable extent, the kind of criticism commonly levelled against Kelsen's 'pure theory'. The search for an 'unadulterated' version of law produced, it is alleged, a theory which is arid, unreal and, therefore, far removed from the rich complexities of the law in practice. Other types of criticism should also be mentioned in the answer, for example, Kelsen's attitude to an examination of the place of justice in the law, his alleged confusion of duties and sanctions based on coercion, his analysis of international law in the light of the 'pure theory'. A skeleton plan could take the following form:

> Introduction – the essence of criticisms of Kelsen – results of his failure to examine law in its social setting – his attitude to a study of justice and rights – criticisms of the theory in relation to sanctions and obligations – problems of the Grundnorm – investigating law in terms of the pure theory – international law – Allen's criticism – conclusion, unacceptable narrowness of the theory's base.

Answer

The quotation comes from Laski's *Grammar of Politics* (1925), in which he suggests that, given its postulates, Kelsen's 'pure theory' of law is unanswerable, but that its substance is an exercise in logic, not in life. Many of the criticisms directed against the 'pure theory' do rest, indeed, on what is perceived as its aridity and separation from the realities of legal activity within the community. But there are other important criticisms, some of which are mentioned below, based on the implications of Kelsen's methodology of enquiry. The target of these criticisms is a theory which emerges from an attempt to view law *purely in terms of reason* and in a manner which excludes all ethical and political value-judgments. Law is seen essentially as a coercive order, based on a system of norms, the validity of which is derived from a basic norm.

A major criticism, encapsulated in Laski's comment, is that the theory chooses to disregard the *totality* of a society in which law plays a relatively restricted, albeit important, role. To attempt to abstract from a consideration of the law its surrounding social and political factors is, it is argued, virtually impossible, even if it were desirable. Law does not exist as an isolate: it is affected in considerable measure by the dynamic nature of the community of which it is a part. A perusal of any aspect of our common law and current legislation indicates the difficulties inherent in any attempt at investigating the law as a phenomenon 'in itself'. Thus, the law relating to theft may have little 'meaning' save as an expression of communal ethical attitudes to the ownership and possession of property. The European Communities Act 1972 expresses political and economic ideologies. The Children Act 1989 articulates deep and complex concepts of the community's social responsibilities. Remove discussion of the inner significance of legislation of this nature, and one is left merely with 'form' as an object of study – it has been given unwarranted primacy over 'meaning'.

An allied criticism is based on Kelsen's decision to ignore the concept of 'justice' and on his apparent lack of concern for the nature and significance of human rights. Kelsen seems to view 'justice' as a mere expression of an irrational idea. Because it is not subject to scientific cognition or investigation, it is not to be considered as having any role in the foundations of law. For Kelsen it involves little more than 'the conscientious application of appropriate general rules'. Justice as a measure of the validity of laws is rejected. Hence a concept which, for many communities and jurists, is seen as expressing the *end* of law, is dismissed by Kelsen because it appears to be beyond the pale of cognition. But because legal life as we know and experience it is often *consciously* based upon a desire to act in accordance with the tenets of justice, and because unjust behaviour is generally unacceptable within a community, Kelsen's doctrine gives the impression of ignoring the complex and deeply held *feelings* which characterise much legal activity. It is worth noting, too, that the history of the 20th century gives little reason to view with equanimity the advocacy and promulgation of a systematic interpretation of law from which the concept of justice has been banished.

The exclusion of 'justice' from the 'pure theory' has led some critics to question not only the resulting sterility of its findings, but the claim advanced by Kelsen to have 'explained' the *reality* of the law. It is suggested that, in dogmatic fashion, he has limited the data he wishes to explore to positive legal matters while ignoring other substantive, conceptual legal realities. The result is no more than a highly selective and incomplete investigation. The 'reality' of the theory is flawed by a misconceived approach to so called 'objective phenomena'.

The place of force ('coercion') in the 'pure theory' has evoked adverse comment. There is no explicit assertion in the theory that law is *only* force, but there is an inference that the effectiveness of law seems to be based solely on force or sanction. All law must possess 'an apparatus of compulsion', Kelsen argues, and the essence of law is in duty, not in right. One's legal duty is as the law commands, with coercion available for the enforcement of norms. But critics have suggested that this is a confusion of 'coercion' and 'obligation'. It is *because* a rule is considered by the community as obligatory that it is possible to attach to it some measure of coercion; the rule is not obligatory merely because there is coercion. The rules relating to individual, physical inviolability are considered by most communities to be of an obligatory nature, and, therefore, penalties are attached to their breach; the rules embodied in the Offences against the Person Act 1861, are not considered as obligatory merely because of the sanctions contained therein. Further, Kelsen is said to have ignored the discussions on communal attitudes to obligation, punishments, etc, which form the content of important work in the social sciences which has impinged on the workings of legal institutions: see, for example, ss 52–58 of the Powers of Criminal Courts (Sentencing) Act 2000 (drug treatment and testing orders). Kelsen's norms seem to be little more than formal, authoritarian commands enforced by those who happen to have a monopoly of force within the community. This has been criticised as a caricature of real life: laws are not obeyed, it is argued, merely because of threatened sanctions; some statutes impose duties without the threat of any sanction. Duties and sanctions require separate definitions because, in reality, they are not conterminous.

The concept of the Grundnorm (the 'basic norm'), which is central to the 'pure theory', is not without its critics. The basic norm ('presupposed in juristic thinking') is that which is said to give a unity to the legal system in that it tops the pyramid of norms and gives those norms their validity. This has been condemned as mere fiction, or as being little more than Austin's 'sovereign' in disguise, or as a mythical 'first cause', beyond which one ought not to venture in any investigation of law. A statement such as 'the first constitution must be obeyed' is criticised as self-contradictory. The reasons why the law *is* obeyed, argue some critics, are to be found in more than one so called 'fundamental reason', and certainly not in any fictitious basic norm, the very existence of which rarely figures in the conscious responses of citizens to their legal obligations. Further, if one considers the activities of the community's judges, the Grundnorm will not explain the many 'non-rule standards' which jurists such as Dworkin perceive as entering into decisions of the courts. Judges probably take into account, during the process of adjudication, much more than formal rules: they keep in mind wide principles and communal policies – matters which Kelsen seeks to exclude from an investigation and formulation of the essence of law.

The very search for a Grundnorm within a legal system cannot but be affected by the personal value-judgments of the investigator – so runs a common criticism of the methodology of Kelsen's seekers of the pure law. Further, it is very difficult to investigate the validity of Kelsen's test of 'a minimum of support' for a basic norm without enquiring into surrounding political and social facts – surely an unacceptable state of affairs for advocates of the 'pure theory'. If, for example, it is assumed that the basic norm of a community is 'belief in the divinity of the lawgiver', or in his 'charismatic lawmaking', it would be almost impossible to discover the level of support for that belief without enquiring into ways in which the lawmaker's subjects are affected in practice, and that would necessitate investigation of a variety of social matters of a 'non-legal' nature.

The problems raised by the existence of international law have been viewed by some critics as constituting a basic objection to the 'pure theory'. In Kelsen's view, international law can be interpreted correctly as a 'juridical order' which may be understood within the boundaries of a 'normative science of law'. But it appears that international law lacks a number of characteristics of a 'legal order' in Kelsen's sense. It has no developed apparatus of compulsion and, apparently, no Grundnorm. Kelsen's reply to this objection suggests an acceptance of war and reprisals as constituting the 'international sanction'. This, for many jurists, involves a negation of the spirit and essential purpose of the doctrine of international law. Further, it may be that a multiplicity of basic norms is required for the interpretation of the complex structure of the law of nations, but this would certainly offend the austere sense of parsimony which is characteristic of the 'pure theory'.

There are, then, many points in Kelsen's theory at which evidence emerges suggesting a lack of correspondence of its express and implied doctrines and legal life as we know it to be. The theory, it has been said, has no application to the everyday problems of the law; it solves none of the recurring difficulties which face legislators and judges. If the 'proper business' of a positivist jurist be with the actual operations of the law, then Kelsen might be considered as having contributed in small measure only to an understanding of those operations. Allen suggests that, in Kelsen's anxiety to keep perception of the law 'pure', he has raised investigation to such an inaccessible altitude that 'it has difficulty in drawing the breath of life'. Gény, writing before Kelsen, had warned against the 'palpable illusion' of attempting to erect a pure judicial science on the postulates of 'an inevitable and imperious logic', with the result that what is created is barren and without value. It is, perhaps, this criticism which Laski had in mind in his comment on Kelsen.

It is paradoxical that Kelsen, criticised for remoteness and a predilection for authoritarian jurisprudence, both of which are said to be evident in the 'pure theory', should have been, in his own life, a jurist who was intensely concerned with the practicalities of the law. He had rejected authoritarianism by choosing exile from his native Austria which was under totalitarian rule, and he made a fundamental contribution to the legal foundations of the United Nations in his commentaries on the basis of UN proposals for international security. His concern was to give to legal science a methodology which would enable the law – no matter what its form or origins might be – to be analysed and understood. The resulting edifice of theory seems to have been constructed, however, from postulates and perceptions which ignore the peculiar richness and complexities of developed legal systems; its base is now seen by some jurists as being unacceptably narrow. It may be that any attempt to create a rarified 'pure theory' which involves separating law from custom, tradition, communal conceptions of justice and morality, will succeed only in erecting a system of jurisprudential thought which, no matter how logical its methodology may be, is, in the event, at variance with the life of the law.

Notes

Criticisms of Kelsen's doctrines appear in Dias, Chapter 17, Lloyd, Chapter 5, Allen, Chapter 1, and Davies and Holdcroft, Chapter 5. Snyder's article, 'Hans Kelsen's pure theory of law' (1966) 12 Harvard LJ, is useful. Stone's 'Mystery and mystique of the basic norm' (1963) 26 MLR 34 analyses the theory of the Grundnorm. Moore, *Legal Norms and Legal Science*, provides a detailed examination of Kelsen's doctrine.

CHAPTER 7

HISTORICAL JURISPRUDENCE

Introduction

In this chapter, reference is made to the 'historical movement' in jurisprudence. The movement centres on the thesis that the study of existing structures of legal thought requires an understanding of its historical roots and its pattern of evolution. Current legal systems and jurisprudential concepts have developed over long periods of time; the common law jurisdictions, in particular, give evidence of a continuous process of evolution. It is in the records of the past that the keys to a comprehension of the present may be discovered. The questions in this chapter refer to Savigny (1799–1861) and Maine (1822–88). Savigny, a Prussian statesman and historian, sought for an understanding of law through an investigation of the individuality of national cultures, in particular, the ancient and enduring *Volksgeist* – the 'spirit of the people'. Maine, founder of the English school of historical jurisprudence, made an intensive study of ancient law which revealed to him the existence of evolutionary patterns of development. Both Savigny and Maine sought to use the lessons of history to assist in the analysis of jurisprudential problems of their own times.

Checklist

Ensure that you are acquainted with the following topics:

- *Volksgeist*
- codification of law
- Maine's 'static and progressive' societies
- status-to-contract theory
- customary law
- legal fictions

Question 27

'A cry against the rationalistic and cosmopolitan principles of the French Revolution, and a reactionary call for the recognition of law as the product of "internal, silently-operating forces".'

Do you agree with this comment on the work of Savigny in his role as founder of the German 'historical school' of jurisprudence?

Answer plan

Savigny shared with many of his country's thinkers opposition to the French Revolution and its philosophical foundations. His reaction was to stress the significance of authority, tradition and the 'creative force' of a people's 'common consciousness'. Law emerged, he claimed, from a people's 'special genius'. An answer to the question should note the essence of Savigny's teaching on the theme of the *Volksgeist* and should seek to show the background of his thesis within the setting of anti-revolutionary doctrine. The following skeleton plan is suggested:

> Introduction – context of French Revolution – Savigny's attitude to codification of law – law as product of the spirit of the people – significance of Roman legal doctrine – criticism of the *Volksgeist* theory – legislation according to Savigny – selectivity of his arguments – Savigny's hostility to revolutionary doctrine – his opposition to rationalism – conclusion, Allen's criticism in the light of the perversion of Savigny's theories.

Answer

An appraisal of the comment on Savigny (1799–1861) requires the posing and answering of two questions. First, how deeply was Savigny influenced by his perceptions of the significance of the French Revolution? Secondly, in what sense may one characterise as 'reactionary' (that is, backward looking and retrogressive) his belief that the essence of a system of law is a reflection of the *Volksgeist*, that is, the unsophisticated 'national spirit' of the group who created and developed it?

Savigny, a Prussian statesman, jurist and authority on the history of Roman law, lived in an era dominated by the effects of the French Revolution which destroyed the French feudal order. The revolutionaries believed that society's 'general will' would be guided by reason, its 'legislative will' would be guided by the *Code Civil*. Savigny shared with many other European jurists a deep hostility to revolutionary philosophy; liberty, equality, 'Supreme Reason', became anathema to him. Within Germany, a deep reaction set in: tradition, authority and the 'creativity' of a people's folklore and customs were stressed. 'Kindred consciousness of inward necessity' was invoked as the source and strength of a nation's legal system. Cosmopolitanism was rejected in favour of 'creative national character'. There is little doubt as to the basic anti-revolutionary character of Savigny's deliberate espousal of the 'virtues of the past' and his vision of ancient custom as a condition precedent of acceptable legislation.

Savigny opposed codification of the law for Germany. The time was not ripe, Germany had 'no calling' for the construction of a code, and, in any event, a code which was inorganic would merely fetter the development of the law and 'do violence to tradition'. His opposition to codification at that time became generalised in the theory he evolved, which would explain national law as flowing from, and reflecting, the age-old 'spirit of the people' – *the Volksgeist*. (This attitude was not shared by all jurists and philosophers. Hegel wrote, in his *Philosophy of Law*: 'No greater insult could be offered to a civilised people or to its lawyers ... than to deny them the ability to construct a legal system.')

The origin of the law was to be found, according to Savigny, in a study of certain principles. First, all law is formed originally by custom and popular feeling, that is, by 'silently operating forces' maturing over long periods of time. A people's common consciousness is 'externalised' in its customs and in the intrinsic coherence of its legal institutions. Law grows in organic, unconscious fashion. A people's laws embody 'popular genius'; their roots are to be found embedded in a people's spirit. Law resembles language; both evolve gradually from a people's characteristics; both flourish when a people flourishes; and both perish when a people loses its individuality. Laws have neither universal validity nor application: they apply only to a specific people. Law is not static; it develops organically according to the life of the people. Law emanates from no single lawgiver, but from a people's instinctive awareness of right and wrong; legislation, therefore, lacks the vitality of custom as a source of law.

Savigny turned to the ancient Roman law to provide material for a study of the needs of the German people in relation to law. He believed that 'what binds a people into one whole is the common conviction of the people, the kindred consciousness of an inward necessity, excluding all notion of an accidental or arbitrary origin'. The Romans, he suggested, were 'born jurists', and ancient Roman law could provide the legal doctrines appropriate to the needs of 19th century Germany. Critics see an inconsistency here: the *Volksgeist* theory should have concerned itself with ancient *Germanic* law, rather than Roman law. The same critics suggest that Savigny's insistence on the utilisation of Roman legal principles reflects a desire to embrace a far off authoritarian code which was seen as possessing eternal validity.

Savigny did not describe his concept of *Volk* (that is, 'a people') but said that it resembled a 'spiritual communion' of people living together, using a common language and creating a communal conscience and common traditions. This has been condemned as a loose description, incapable of proof and of little use in jurisprudential analysis. His concept of 'communal conscience' is difficult to comprehend. Where is 'communal conscience' when a nation is divided on some legal questions? (Consider, for example, current divisions within Britain's population on matters such as the need for common European law, or an intensification of retribution within sentencing policy.) How does one apply a people's 'feeling for right and wrong' to, say, a multicultural community? What of the important areas of law which have evolved from inter-communal political and legal conflict?

For some critics, the *Volksgeist* is mere fiction or 'reification' of some questionable abstractions. It is impossible to prove the validity of axioms Savigny formulated concerning a people's 'folk soul' and its alleged creativeness. Savigny, it is suggested, may not have wished to create a reactionary legal ideology, but, in the event, he did create a framework of concepts which was utilised to support in later eras those who actively desired authoritarian regimes based on mystical ideologies involving 'the people's will'.

Savigny's view of legislation as being of subsidiary importance to custom in the development of law is of significance. For him, the 'living law' does not result from a sovereign's command; rather, it does develop organically from the 'people's spirit'. Hence, legislation will be effective only when it is attuned to the voice and aspirations of the people and when it reflects national needs. Doubts within a community could be resolved by declaratory enactments. This view has been criticised. Vinogradoff shows that most customs arise from *local usage* and are rarely of national significance in their early stages. Legal history reveals, too, that formal legislation has often become necessary when custom has failed to respond to novel conditions. Allen is more emphatic: 'There are many customs which cannot be attributed to any conscious connections without metaphysical ingenuity which savours of pure invention.'

Other critics of Savigny pay attention to the highly selective historical data on which he draws. It seems that the conditions of his own era coloured indelibly his view of the past. In particular, his attitudes towards liberty and egalitarianism, conditioned by his reactions as a Prussian aristocrat to the political and social events of the French Revolution, may have prevented the adoption of the disinterested attitude which should characterise a scholar's work. The fact that he turned to the ancient Roman law for guidance, rather than to the well researched Roman jurisprudence of the Middle Ages, has been attributed to his personal predilection for the severe authoritarianism which seemed to him to typify Roman legal doctrine. The possibility that the *Corpus Juris* was no more than a reflection of the considered reactions of Roman lawyers and statesmen to everyday economic and social problems seems not to have entered into his commentaries on the 'eternal significance' of Roman legal doctrine.

Further evidence of undue selectivity emerges from Savigny's writings which suggest that the law grows *uniquely* 'within the *Volk*'. There was available to Savigny considerable historical research indicating that law does not always emerge from 'popular conscience, awareness of nationhood and common culture'. The ancient world, and Savigny's own times, had witnessed the transplanting of laws from one country to another. In his role of historian, Savigny should have been aware of the important part played in the development of a nation's law by the imposition of the will of alien conquerors. Consider, for example, the Norman conquest of England in 1066. Here the successful invaders were able to effect a transformation of the prevailing English legal order. A few centuries later, important developments of the land law were effected, but it cannot be said with accuracy that they emanated from 'the spirit of the English people'. The great statute, *Quia Emptores* 1290, which assisted in fixing the theory of estates, was in no sense a reflection of 'unconscious forces' moulding the shape of the legal order. *De Donis Conditionalibus* 1285, which had created the entailed estate, cannot be said to have emerged from the popular 'communal conscience'; rather was it a pragmatic reaction to problems arising from the descent of land. Savigny's *Volksgeist* is not to be discerned here.

Savigny seems to pay little attention to the lawmaking of judges. Those who, under the guise of unfolding and revealing the law effectively modify and extend it, are participating in the process of lawmaking as if they were legislators. 'Awareness of nationhood' is not easy to discern in activities of this nature. The *Volksgeist* is, clearly, not the unique source of law Savigny would have us believe.

We turn again to the statement embodied in the question and to the two problems which require consideration. First, to what extent was Savigny influenced in his jurisprudential thought by the phenomenon of the French Revolution? There can be little doubt as to the answer. Few jurists are willing or able to stand aside from consideration of the contemporary march of events. We have seen this in our own times, as evidenced in the writings of Radbruch, Friedmann, Hart and others. Savigny seems to have provided no exception to this generalisation. For him, the French Revolution was a cataclysm, threatening the very existence of the political, social and legal fabric of Europe. Revolution does breed reaction, and in Savigny's case the reaction took the form of a total rejection of the philosophical and political concepts associated with the revolutionary scholars of France. The result was, for Savigny, a flight to the 'comfortable and narrow certainties' of the ancient Roman law. The bastions offered by a remote system of legal thought would stand secure against the impact of revolutionary dogma. Out of the rock of the *Corpus Juris* would be fashioned a fortress within which German philosophical and legal doctrine would hold out against the alien principles of radical rationalism.

The second question, concerning the 'reactionary nature' of Savigny's thought is more complex. The anti-rational nature of *Volksgeist* theory is obvious: it elevates the role of the unconscious and the instinctive and seems to play down the role of reason in the growth and development of the law. Critics have suggested that Savigny generated a 'juristic pessimism' and effectively denigrated the efforts of mankind devoted to conquering its surroundings. The perception of ancient Roman law as a repository of panaceas which would cure the ills of the 19th century engenders an exaggerated reverence for a fictitious 'golden era' in the past and, in reactionary fashion, diverts attention from the necessary analysis of current events. There is indeed evidence of the reactionary nature of much of Savigny's juristic thought: it looks backwards, it invokes principles which are rarely amenable to rational interpretation, and it seeks solace in a fabricated mystique.

It would be wrong, however, to follow those critics who condemn Savigny totally as an unwholesome reactionary, addicted to the type of legal practices which flourished in the totalitarian regimes of the 20th century. Allen's suggestion that Savigny and his associates were 'National Socialists before the National Socialists' is, surely, unwarranted hyperbole. The fact that later generations of German politicians and jurists drew on some of Savigny's theories, and distorted them in order to provide justification for a racist tyranny, and that, in Friedmann's words, the sharp edge of state power was turned brutally against those who were perceived as aliens, polluting the party of the *Volk*, does not, in itself, justify total condemnation of Savigny as one who would have supported totalitarian excesses. It is highly probable that Savigny would have recognised as an evil the perversion of his doctrines under the Nazi regime. But it is almost certain that he could not have foreseen, and would not have approved, the uses to which the theory of the *Volksgeist* was put during the era of dictatorships.

Notes

Extracts from Savigny's *System of Modern Roman Law*, translated by Holloway, are given in Lloyd, Chapter 10. Friedmann, Chapter 18; Vinogradoff, Chapter 6; Bodenheimer, Chapter 5; and Allen, Chapters 1 and 2, provide criticisms of the *Volksgeist* theory. 'Sovereignty and the historical school of law', by Kantorowicz (1937) 53 LQR 334, is a useful survey of Savigny's contribution to jurisprudence.

Question 28

What do you consider to be Maine's singular contributions to jurisprudence?

Answer plan

Maine (1822–88) brought to the task of interpreting the history of law a very wide study of early societies, from which he constructed a theory of legal development which reflected the vision of inevitable progress prevalent in his day. The history of law is seen as portraying an upward movement made up from consecutive stages of development. Maine's contribution to jurisprudence rests, according to jurists such as Pospisil, in his systematic method of investigation. Others stress the acuity of his insight into ancient societies and their law. Two aspects of Maine's work are selected for discussion below: first, his view of legal ideas and institutions as possessing their own course of development; and, secondly, the concept of individual progress as resting on a move from fixed relationships based on individual status to relationships reflecting the free agreement of individuals. The following skeleton plan has been used:

> Introduction – Maine's significant contributions to jurisprudence – the three epochs constituting legal development – the importance of fictions, equity and legislation – from status to contract – criticisms of Maine – conclusion, the overall importance of Maine's work.

Answer

Jurist, historian and pioneer in the study of anthropology as applied to the evolution of legal ideas and institutions, Maine made a considerable contribution to the study of jurisprudence in the second half of the 19th century. Writing with unusual knowledge of the classical Roman tradition, primitive law, Biblical and Indian legal ideas (he had supervised the codification of Indian law as a member of the Governor-General's Council), he was able to produce a systematic account of the evolution of law. His principal work was *Ancient Law: Its Connection with the Earlier History of Society and Its Relation to Modern Ideas* (1861), in which he ranged widely over early law and embryonic legal systems. For Maine, history was no record of humanity's 'essential reasonableness'; rather, it did reveal the pervasive influence of emotions, deep instinctive reactions and habits. We select from his work two unique concepts: first, the view that legal history may be read as revealing an *evolutionary pattern* which affects in different measure 'static' and 'progressive' societies; and, secondly, the idea that within progressive societies there can be traced a movement in individual relationships marked by a change *'from status to contract'*.

The development of law is considered as involving three stages. The first stage emerges solely from the personal commands and judgments of *patriarchal rulers* – kings, for example – who propagate the notion that they are divinely inspired. 'The human king on earth is not a lawmaker but a judge.' Judgments precede rules; the judge exists before the lawmaker. Maine uses the Homeric term *Themistes* to describe the kings' judgments which are, essentially, separate, and are not connected by principles.

The epoch of kingly rule ends when royal power decays as a result of a weakening of belief in royal charisma and sacredness. Royal authority vanishes to a shadow and the *era of oligarchies* emerges. Elites of a political, military and religious nature appear, claiming a monopoly of control over the law and its institutions. The law in this era is based generally on customs upheld by judgments. In this second development period, which Maine refers to as 'the epoch of customary law', the ruling oligarchies claim to enjoy exclusive possession of the principles used in the settling of disputes. At this stage, law is largely unwritten; the interpreters of the law enjoy, therefore, monopolistic powers of explanation. This epoch does not endure; in particular, the spread of writing prepares the ground for a transition to a third era.

The third, sharply defined, epoch is dominated by *Codes*: this is, indeed, the 'era of the Codes', all of which, according to Maine, arose at similar points in the progress of Greece, Rome and parts of Western Asia. The Codes, such as the Roman Twelve Tables, promulgated in the fifth century BC, and Solon's Attic Code, which remained the basis of Athenian law until the end of that century, were, in some cases a mere statement of existing customs and, in other cases, sets of rules which declared the law as it ought to be. Maine saw as the principal advantage of codes the protection they claimed to offer against the results of debasement of national institutions. But the codes marked an end to spontaneity in legal development; henceforth, the law would be characterised by deliberate *purpose*. Changes in the law would be effected deliberately, often out of a conscious desire for improvements.

Having constructed a framework for systematising the interpretation of legal development, Maine introduced a remarkable concept of further progress being conditional on the very *nature* of a given society. He drew a distinction between 'stationary' and 'progressive' societies. The stationary societies (which were the rule) did not progress beyond the concept of law based on, and dominated by, a code. The progressive societies (which were the exception, and included most societies in Western Europe) tended to expand and refine the law and legal institutions. Maine believed that the stationary nature of most societies reflected a lack of desire on the part of their members to improve their legal institutions beyond the stage at which the law had been embodied in the permanence of a code. The result was an inflexible law which acted as a brake on legal development. By contrast, the progressive societies exhibited a dynamism which allowed them to engage actively and purposively in modification of the law, so that the gap between formal legal doctrines and the pressing needs of a developing society was narrowed.

The dynamic stage of legal development, confined to progressive societies, was characterised by the use of three agencies, *legal fictions, equity and legislation* (in that historical order). The term 'legal fiction' is used to refer to suppositions or assumptions of law that something which is, or may be, false is true, or that some fact exists when, in reality, it does not. Fictions are designed to assist in overcoming the rigidities of the law and advancing the ends of justice. Their use affects to conceal the fact that a legal rule has been altered or its operation modified, although the letter of the law remains unchanged. Maine gives as an example the Roman fiction of adoption which allowed vital family ties to be created in a wholly artificial manner.

The second mode of adapting the law to the requirements of a progressive society is the development of equity – a corpus of rules co-existing with the original law, founded on distinct principles and claiming an inherent 'sanctity' allowing it to supersede the original law. Equity involves open interference with original law, which separates it from legal fictions. It differs from legislation in that its principles are often expressed in terms of a 'higher authoritativeness'. Equity assists in the advance of society in that it softens the rigours of the law and is concerned with the spirit of the law rather than its letter. It suggests, too, according to Maine, a more advanced state of thought than that which created the legal fiction.

Legislation is the final 'ameliorating instrumentality' of the progressive societies in their process of legal development. It involves the enactments of a legislature (a parliamentary assembly, for example) which is, according to Maine, 'the assumed organ of the entire society'. It is important to note that, for Maine, the advance of civilisation presupposed legislation carried out by *formal bodies*; he was not favourably disposed towards 'judicial legislation' and thought that the very concept of judge-made law had serious weaknesses. Here is the ultimate stage in legal development within the progressive societies. The order of stages in legal development is not invariable, according to Maine, but he stressed that legislation, in its final and highest form of 'codification', marked a pinnacle of achievement.

Ancient Law includes a chapter entitled 'Law in primitive society', in which Maine produces a 'formula', which is considered here as encapsulating the second of his singular contributions to jurisprudence. 'The movement of progressive societies', he declares, 'has hitherto been a movement from status to contract'. Maine used the term 'status' to signify those personal conditions of an individual which are not the immediate or remote result of agreement. It is in this sense that Maine speaks of 'the status of a slave', or 'the status of the Roman female under tutelage'. He sees, in the history of some ancient societies, status as the fixed result of dominant family relationships. The Roman *pater familias* exercising *patria potestas*, wife, sons and daughters in a subordinate status, slaves serving the family but enjoying the lowest type of status – here are examples of 'family-determined status'. In time, the dynamism of the progressive society loosened the chains of familial status, and, in the words of De Jouvenel, 'the state breaks through into a world from which it was at first excluded, [and claims] as subject to its own jurisdiction those who had in former days been subjects of the father alone': Roman women were emancipated from tutelage, the *filius familias* was freed from his father's power, and even the slave might change his status through the process of manumission. New type of relationships begin to emerge from the free agreement of individuals. Slavery eventually disappears, serfdom is abolished, the free links, based on agreement between master and servant, burgeon into the employer-employee contract. In sum, one of the hallmarks of a progressive society is, according to Maine, an inexorable move by its people from legal relationships determined by a seemingly fixed status to the creation of conditions of relationship through free negotiations, leading to the free agreement of individuals.

Maine's jurisprudential concepts have attracted criticism. It is suggested that he may have over-simplified the early stages of society's development. The move from 'charismatic judgment' through 'autocratic interpretation' to 'code' is doubted by a number of anthropologists. Childe, for example, suggests that divisions based on the relative importance of hunting, agriculture and pastoralism may provide an important key to the understanding of legal development; he doubts the basis of Maine's interpretation, which he finds 'simplistic'. Further, recent investigation suggests that not all primitive peoples pass through the stages suggested by Maine: some may 'jump' a stage. It may be that there is no *universal* pattern of legal development as is pictured in *Ancient Law* and that the evolutionary movement described in its pages may be true for Europe and some parts of

India, but not for *all* societies. Additionally, Maine appears to imply a rigidity of thought among primitive peoples which has been challenged by some contemporary anthropologists who note the significance of the adaptive skills of the early societies.

Further criticism has centred on Maine's methodology of enquiry, dismissed by some jurists as totally inadequate for the tasks he set for himself. He is held to have extrapolated beyond his data, that is, to have assumed for societies in general the existence of patterns which characterised *unique groups* at specific stages in their development. The evidence for some of his generalisations has been held to be inadequate; it is noted, for example, that some of his illustrations derive from the evidence of epic poetry only. Allen suggests that the broad principle formulated by Maine 'needs larger corroboration than this'.

The 'status-to-contract' theory has also attracted critical comment. Friedmann observes that the development of feudalism seems to indicate a move from contract to status. He notes, too, that there are modern tendencies to replace individual bargaining by collective group agreements, and he points out the significance of the appearance of standardised contracts which result in the imposition of status-like conditions in the case of mortgages, lessor-lessee agreements and some insurance contracts. It has to be observed, however, that Maine spoke of the movement of progressive societies 'hitherto'.

Criticism of Maine should not be allowed to dim the overall significance of his work. He was writing in the era of pre-scientific anthropology – at a time when, for example, the very existence of the Palaeolithic (that is, Old Stone) Age was unknown. Frazer and Malinowski, who changed the direction of anthropological studies, were yet to come. It is, however, the *general pattern* of Maine's studies which constitutes his legacy for jurisprudence: his long range vision of the law as resulting from a continuous process of development, his view of law as an important aspect of general *social evolution,* his stress on the significance of the written word in the history of legal change, continue to play a role in the work of jurists who emphasise that the law does possess *a history of its own.*

Notes

Ancient Law, by Maine, appears in a number of editions. Comments on Maine's doctrines appear in Lloyd, Chapter 10; Dias, Chapter 18; and Friedmann, Chapter 18. Maine is criticised by Diamond in *Primitive Law*. There are interesting biographical details of Maine in *From Status to Contract: a Biography of Sir Henry Maine*, by Feaver, and *Sir Henry Maine: A Study in Victorian Jurisprudence*, by Cocks.

CHAPTER 8

THE SOCIOLOGICAL MOVEMENT IN JURISPRUDENCE

Introduction

Sociology studies the causes and effects of the participation of individuals in groups and structured organisations. It has attracted the attention of these jurists who see law as a reflection of human beliefs and behaviour and as a product of certain types of social organisation. Hence, there has emerged a body of jurists who have turned increasingly to a study of the data produced by sociologists. Three prominent sociologists and jurists are singled out here for attention: Jhering (1818–92), Weber (1864–1920), and Pound (1870–1964). The outlines of their contribution to the sociological movement in jurisprudence should be known.

Checklist

Ensure that you are acquainted with the following topics:

- law as purpose
- the theory of interests
- jural postulates
- law as social engineering
- norms for decision and conduct
- traditional and charismatic authority
- legal-rational authority

Question 29

'Law is the sum of the conditions of social life, in the widest sense of that term, as secured by the power of the state through the means of external compulsion.'

Show how Jhering's jurisprudential thought led him to this definition.

Answer plan

The 19th century German jurist, Jhering, viewed the essence of law in the relationship of man to the society in which he lived. Neither man nor his law can be understood save within the context of society. There is a profound purpose to society – the enabling of man to add to the very quality of his existence. This study of society – sociology – can throw light on the central problem of jurisprudence: 'What is the law?' An answer to the question involves an account of Jhering's views on 'purpose' and law in relation to 'social reality'. The following skeleton plan is suggested:

> Introduction – Jhering's views on law and the balancing of interests – law and purpose – individual and common interests – the levers of social motion – law and change – the state and coercion – conclusion, Jhering's definition of law considered.

Answer

Jhering (1818–92) achieved his reputation largely on the basis of his research into Roman law which culminated in the publication of *The Spirit of Roman Law* (1852). His later influential treatise, *Law as a Means to an End* (1877), was described by Friedmann as one of the most important events in the history of legal thought. In it, Jhering develops his theme of law as expressing *'purpose'*, and analyses the role of law in the protection and balancing of individual and social interests. It is from these concepts that Jhering derives the definition of law which is cited in the quotation above.

Jhering's early work in Roman law moved him towards an interpretation of law in terms of *purpose*. He analysed the Roman concept of 'possession' in very great detail and was able to construct a theory which explained the praetorian interdicts related to possession. Jhering emphasised the form of the interdicts in relation to their *purpose*. The Roman praetors had in mind the *need* to protect those in control of property; hence interdicted possession could be described as a 'reflection of purpose'. His studies of Roman law led him into total opposition to what he described as 'the jurisprudence of concepts'. The true significance of Roman law resided not in its logical refinement of concepts, but rather in its capacity (as illustrated by the case of interdicted possession) to provide a *basis* on which concepts might be moulded *so as to serve practical purposes*. Life, he said, did not exist for the sake of a study of concepts; to sacrifice the true interest of life to dialectic, and to turn jurisprudence into a sort of 'legal mathematics', was to act on mere illusion. The 'jurisprudence of concepts' was basically a misdirection of logical principle; it resulted in plausible abstractions which, in terms of the reality of life, were irrelevant.

Purpose, social reality and a jurisprudence which would reflect those principles emerged as the foundations of Jhering's approach to the law. *Purpose was all-important.* In his preface to *Law as a Means to an End*, he states that the fundamental idea of the text is to demonstrate that 'purpose is the creator of the entire law'. There is no legal rule which does not have its origin in some practical purpose, that is, in some practical motive. This he had demonstrated in his study of Roman lawmaking. The creating of legal rules resulted from an exercise of human will, and such an exercise was to be understood only in terms of a purpose. Human activity is undertaken in order that objectives might be attained. *Volition involves and reflects purpose.*

Enunciation of the principle of 'purpose' in relation to the law marked, for Jhering, a turning away from the doctrines of the German 'historical jurisprudence' movement to which he had been attached. Law could not be understood in terms of the product of Savigny's 'silently-operating forces of the people's spirit'; it did not well up from the springs of the nation's 'unconscious folk-soul'. On the contrary, it was to be interpreted as a *direct social response to perceived purpose*. Law emerged in order that problems might be solved and social needs met. It was purposive and existed for ends determined by society. *Outside society's problems and needs, law had no meaning, no rationale.*

Jhering asked what dictated the very purposes to be effected by law. His answer was: *interests dictate purpose*. A person's individual interests should be linked to the interests of others so that a social purpose might be enunciated and achieved. The linking of interests, the fusing of many sets of individual interests into a unity which reflected common, social purpose ('to effectuate every force in the service of humanity'), is one of the most important functions of the law. The demands of the individual are to be viewed within the context of society *as a whole*, and the social framework, in which law plays a prominent role, exists so as to ease the pursuit and attainment of social purpose.

For Jhering, the common interest of all was more important than particular individual interests. *'Every person exists for the world, and the world exists for everybody.'* Jhering refers to this aphorism as embodying the essence of culture and morality. It is the disproportion between man's needs and his purposes which necessitates his associating with others, so as to attain all those purposes to which he is, on his own, unequal. Nature 'refers' man to the outside world, to his fellows, from whom he may derive the assistance he requires. Common interest, which will emerge only from the very nature of social life, will require protection and it is the prime purpose of 'the protection of society' which must dominate the law, its ideology and institutions. Purpose, not abstract 'concepts', characterises the law within society.

Because of the superiority of the common interest, it is necessary that the conditions in which it will thrive shall be developed. The active encouragement of all those aspects of life which will intensify social cohesion is of great importance. This necessitates, on the part of the state, a recognition of the need to minimise the conflicts which may arise from the opposition of some individual and social interests. The reconciliation of those interests, in which the law will play a significant part, requires the utilisation of what Jhering refers to as 'the levers of social motion'. Those 'levers' are of two types: 'egoistic' and 'altruistic'. The 'egoistic levers' are reward and coercion. Reward is seen in terms of private gain. The threat of coercion is a vital element in law; Jhering sees the effectiveness of legal rules within society as depending on compulsion and force and this necessitates that the state shall possess an absolute monopoly of the right to exercise coercion. Without this element, rules of law will be 'like a fire which does not burn'. The 'altruistic levers', for example, feelings of duty, are of particular significance in the creation of social interest. Jhering suggests that the levers be utilised in a combination which will create and intensify the significance of 'social ends'. *The object of society – the very purpose for which it is brought into existence – is the securing of the satisfaction of the totality of human wants*. In that process, which involves coercion and the reconciliation of apparently-contradictory interests, the law will be of much importance.

Jhering categorises society's wants (the satisfaction of which is the purpose of the social structure) in an unusual fashion. These wants are termed 'extra-legal', 'mixed-legal', and 'purely legal'. The category of 'extra-legal wants' involves nature as the sole supplier. Food is an example: it is a basic requirement offered to man, but with the requirement of an effort from him. The 'mixed-legal' category refers to the conditions of social life, preservation of life, labour, trade, which are peculiar to humanity and which are generally independent of legal coercion. The third category, 'purely legal', refers to conditions *depending in their entirety upon legal commands*, for example, orders of the legal authorities requiring the payment of taxes and the settling of debts. Rewards, coercion, duty (the 'levers') have to be used by the state in providing the setting within which human wants may be satisfied. The satisfying of these wants necessitates a system determined by 'social purpose'. In brief, Jhering views the law, with its appropriate apparatus of coercion, as assisting in the attainment of those ends which characterise social activity and purpose.

The 'balancing' of individual and social interests so as to realise an appropriate equilibrium, which Jhering refers to as 'a realised partnership of the individual and society', is a necessary objective for society. It is the function of the law to act as a *mediator* in disputes which will stem from the opposition of interests. The mediating function of the law – its contribution to the creation of social harmony – has to be exercised, however, within the context of *changing social purposes and standards*. Hence, argues Jhering, the 'natural law', with its immutable, eternal standards, is of no use in this task. A law based on permanent and 'universally-valid' principle and content is, he says, no better than medical treatment which is administered in the same way for all patients. *Purpose is all*, and purpose is relative; the law must have the capacity to adapt to changing circumstances and to varying levels of individual and social needs.

Jhering's definition of law, to which we now turn, requires consideration in the light of his view of man, society and the law –

the essence of the sociological approach of jurisprudence. Bodenheimer suggests that the definition comprises 'a substantive and a formal element'. The essential features of the substantive element may be recapitulated. Law is to be perceived solely in terms of aims and purpose; to view it in the context of mere 'concepts' is to deny its true basis. The substantive aim of the law is 'social' and related entirely to the securing of the conditions of the life of society. Jhering interprets the phrase 'conditions of the life of society' as embracing much more than mere physical existence and self-preservation of its members; it includes all the goods and pleasures which give life its true value. Among these goods and pleasures are to be found honour, art and science, which give a savour to the individual's life. When Jhering speaks of the conditions of life 'in the widest sense of that term', he has in mind the quality of a society and the character of its individual members.

The values which underpin the social conditions of existence must be assured by the state's coercive powers – the 'means of external compulsion' mentioned in Jhering's definition. The means utilised by the state to achieve its purposes will vary according to social needs of a given period and according to the level of civilisation reached by the society in question. These means cannot be established by reference to so called 'immutable principles'. Hence, says Bodenheimer, the formal element of Jhering's definition involves the principle of 'power of constraint', that is, the coercion which will be applied by the state when it perceives social cohesion and standards to be in peril. Coercion, constraint will be employed to attain the state's overriding purposes. The law is to be comprehended only within an appreciation of this context.

In the final analysis, Jhering views law as a social, purposive phenomenon enabling man to add to the quality of his being. Individually, his powers of achievement are severely limited by his restricted capacities. In collaboration with his fellows he becomes a member of society – a unit possessing powers allowing him to achieve more for himself and enabling him to contribute to the welfare of the community in general. The law's purpose is to provide assistance in the creation and maintenance of the circumstances in which he adds to his capacities for self-realisation. A study of law within society is a study of rules and their purposes. The 'jurisprudence of concepts' is rejected: 'Life is not here to be a servant of concepts, but concepts are here to serve life.' In its place, we require legal study with a 'social bias', based upon an awareness of the *social nature* of law and its institutions.

Notes

Jhering's *Law as a Means to an End* appears in a translation by Hussik. Summaries of his theory are contained in Lloyd, Chapter 7; Bodenheimer, Chapter 6; Dias, Chapter 20; and Friedmann, Chapter 26 (which includes a criticism of Jhering's view of law as 'the protection of interests').

Question 30

What are the principal theoretical conclusions concerning the nature of law which Weber derived from his sociological investigations?

Answer plan

It has been said that few scholars had as powerful an influence on 20th century social sciences as Weber. A polymath who had mastered the disciplines of sociology, history, economics and jurisprudence, he stressed the need for objectivity in *all* areas of research and emphasised the importance of studying human actions in terms of the actors' *motives*. His studies in sociology and history, carried out in Germany, produced a theory of law in which typology (a study and interpretation of 'types') predominated. The types of law which form the basis of his classification should be outlined in the answer, and attention should be given to his general attitude to the *development* of the law. The following skeleton plan is used:

Introduction – Weber and the methodology of *'Verstehen'* – order and authority – types of legitimate authority – criticism of Weber's typology – rational and irrational systems – Weber's views on English law – conclusion, law and reciprocal relationships.

Answer

A theme which runs through the work of Weber (1864–1920) is the necessity for recognition of the human individual as the basic unit of any social enquiry. The motives of individuals who find themselves in situations such as legal disputes must be understood. Weber utilised a methodology of enquiry known as *Verstehen* ('to understand'), which concentrates on comprehending the *states of mind* of persons involved in events, and on the construction of *'ideal types'*, that is, generalised models of situations which could be applied to analogous cases. *Why* persons obey the law, *why* power is respected, *why* authority is accepted as legitimate, are matters of great interest to Weber.

Specifically, Weber was concerned for much of his working life with 'answering Marx', with refuting the doctrinaire finalities which had become associated with historical materialism. The Marxist search for a single, primal cause of social change was, in Weber's view, futile – there was much more to society than the relationships arising from the ownership of the means of production. Further, Weber argues, capitalism was not to be viewed, in Marxist terms, as a mere 'passing phase' in social development. The problems of law in relation to society in general, and capitalism in particular, could not be reduced to simplistic questions of class domination. A review of the history of law, and its recasting in terms of a typology, would, according to Weber, bring out and underline the deficiencies of Marx's interpretation of law in society.

Society and its law could be comprehended clearly if the significance of 'order' were investigated. Order requires norms and the power to enforce those norms. Weber perceived the phenomenon of power as the probability that a person within a social relationship will be able to carry out his will in spite of possible resistance, and regardless of the basis upon which the probability rests. (One is reminded of Bertrand Russell's statement that power is 'the production of intended effects'.) Power is needed if law is to be effective, but unrestricted power is the antithesis of law. It is 'legitimate authority' which must be accepted as underlying the exercise of power. A relationship based on legitimate authority exists only where the ruled accept the ruler as embodying the concept of 'power through authority'. Weber discerned three types of legitimate authority (or 'domination') in his investigation of the history of societies: the 'traditional', the 'charismatic', and the 'legal rational'. Each had its own appropriate type of law, reflecting qualities of the motivation governing the obedience of the ruled. But, as Weber pointed out, reality often shows a mixture of the three types.

'Traditional authority' was determined by ingrained habituation: legitimacy arose from the sanctity of age-old rules, decrees, regulations and powers. The ruled owed obedience, not to enacted rules, but rather to persons who occupied positions of authority by tradition, or who had been chosen by traditional rules. The law in societies characterised by this type of authority was not created openly; often, new rules were legitimised by their presentation as reaffirmations of ancient rules. Rule by elders, powerful patriarchies, seem to typify authority of this nature.

'Charismatic authority' ('*charisma*' means 'the Divine gift of grace') involves devotion to the perceived sanctity or heroism of an extraordinary person, and to the norms revealed or ordained by him. Heroes, prophets endowed with superhuman powers and qualities are examples. Authority of this nature often arises in revolutionary situations in which there is a sharp repudiation of the past; it is exercised often in the name of a group or party which claims an exceptional virtue or prescience. In such circumstances, a 'charismatic type' of law is enforced, but becomes difficult to maintain at a later stage when it comes into conflict with the demands of everyday routine structures.

The 'legal rational authority' requires from ruler and ruled a belief in the legality of enacted rules and in the right of those who enjoy authority under these rules to issue commands. Authority in this context is justified by the obvious 'rationality' of the rules promulgated. It is this type of authority and its appropriate pattern of law, which, according to Weber, may be seen as characteristic of contemporary capitalism. Thus, the general law within a capitalist society provides an ambience of certainty and predictability within which a law of contract, essential for this type of society, might grow and flourish. The law of Western societies is characterised, according to Weber, by strictly formal rules and procedures which command respect and obedience, not necessarily because of their content, but because they are *perceived* as fundamentally rational. They have been created and enforced by the state in conditions which are accepted by society as reflecting appropriate norms. The authority of the capitalist state rests fundamentally on the acceptance by society of the rules related to the exercise of power and the promulgation of 'rational' laws; those who obey the laws are obeying the legal ordinances, not those who execute or seek to interpret those ordinances.

Weber stressed the significance within the 'legal rational order' of acceptance by society of the principle that authority attaches 'to the office rather than to the person'. The authority of a particular prime minister, for example, derives from the office he holds, and obedience to him stems from ingrained attitudes to that office. The authoritative nature of decisions of the House of Lords stems from its place in the hierarchy of the courts rather than the personal reputations of the Lords of Appeal in Ordinary.

The 'legal rational order' provides a basis for Weber's definition of law. We may refer to a rule as 'law' if it is promulgated and is externally guaranteed by the probability that physical or psychological coercion to produce conformity or 'to avenge violation' will be applied by a group of persons holding themselves in readiness for that purpose. The law is viewed here in terms of *expectations and probabilities* acceptable to the individuals who make up society. Weber's attachment to the significance of *Verstehen*, of understanding the states of mind of members of society in relation to events in which they participate, is obvious here.

Weber's classification of law into three 'types' has been criticised by jurists such as Berman, who points out that no explanation is given of the similarities and differences among various historical legal orders. Weber provides no answer to the question of why charismatic law becomes 'routinised' in one society, but not in another. Nor does he explain the fact that the legal tradition in the West seems to be a combination of aspects of *all* three 'types' of law. Thus, within our own legal tradition, the position of the Monarchy, the conventions and prerogatives of Parliament, the phenomenon of Equity, may be viewed as containing principles derived from each of the three types of law.

Weber uses another typology to underline the importance of procedures within legal systems. He suggests a division of systems, based on 'rationality' and 'irrationality', and a subdivision reflecting the 'substantive' or 'formal' nature of procedures; this produces four categories: 'substantively irrational'; 'formally irrational'; 'substantively rational'; and 'formally rational'.

The essence of the 'substantively irrational' system is that cases are decided *entirely on their own merits*. There is no reference to general principles (which are rarely acknowledged). Those who dispense this form of justice make *ad hoc* decisions, taking into account ethical and political considerations. Intuition often controls decision. In the 'formally irrational' system, decisions tend to be made on the basis of *'tests' beyond the control of the human mind*. Intuitive pronouncement is replaced by reliance on some ordeal or oracle, from which an indication of guilt or innocence will emerge. The establishing of guilt will require more than a pronouncement by an individual invested with authority. There is an appeal to *judicium Dei* (the judgment of God). Ordeal by fire or water is interpreted as showing guilt or innocence, established by outside intervention. The fundamental irrationality of the system is clothed in apparent formality.

The 'substantively rational' system supposes *no separation of law from morality*. Theocratic systems provide an example – the Divine Word *is* the law. Rules and principles may be constructed and codified, but justice may be administered in the name of the Divinity; its sanctions may derive from an interpretation of the Revealed Word. Its procedures may be heavily dependent on traditional concepts of what should be done so as to restore a social balance which might have been broken, or so as to repair a breach in the ordained relationship between God and man.

The 'formally rational' system, exemplified in part by the codes of civil law based upon the classical Roman law, is characterised by *an apparently 'seamless web' of principles, rules and procedures*, which are intended to provide answers to all types of legal problem. The norms underlying such a system are perceived as rational and impersonal; the rules are formulated and applied by processes requiring logical generalisation. Rules are collected and often codified so that they appear as components of an internally-consistent system. The prime place occupied in the 'substantively rational' system by ethical considerations disappears when the principle of *logical consistency* achieves prominence.

Weber was particularly interested in the application of his typology to the characteristics of law in England, the first developed capitalist society. He suggests that, because of the importance of its political history in the formation of the legal system, England was, perhaps, an exception to the generalisation he had formulated. Capitalism had grown in England *before* full legal rationality had been established there. The common law was a mixture of substantive rationality (as evidenced, for example, by its concern for extra-legal matters such as 'the public good') and formal irrationality (such as the oaths taken by parties to a judicial hearing). He also perceived in English law some important characteristics of the 'charismatic epoch' of lawmaking, noting, for example, Blackstone's description of the judge as a sort of 'living oracle'. His general conclusion was that the capitalistic supremacy achieved by England over other nations arose in spite of its judicial system.

Weber's perspective of law is on a grand scale. Emanating from his concern with the individual participating in social processes and creating relationships, he interprets the evolution of the law in terms of those relationships within a system based on the legitimisation of authority. It is in the rationality of the law that its ultimate power may be perceived. (Perception of this relationship, and its implications for the jurisprudential interpretation of law, will be found at the basis of sociological legal theory.) Weber's answer to Marx is clear: a theory which seeks to explain law solely in terms of relationships founded upon the ownership of the means of production misses many of the complex features of law and society and must, therefore, be inadequate. A sociological interpretation of the law will be, above all else, many sided in concept and methodology.

Notes

Weber on Law in Economy and Society is published in an edition by Rheinstein. Lloyd, Chapter 7; Harris, Chapter 19; and Friedmann,

Chapter 19, expound Weber's theory of law. Berman offers a criticism of the theory in *Law and Revolution: The Foundation of the Western Legal Tradition*, in a chapter entitled 'Beyond Marx, beyond Weber'. Aron offers an extended treatment of Weber's basic thought, in his *Main Currents in Sociological Thought*.

Question 31

'Little remains of Pound's edifice of a theory of interests save an empty taxonomic shell; the critics have demolished everything else.' Do you agree?

Answer plan

Pound, an American jurist, former Dean of the Harvard Law School, and a leading figure in the American 'sociological jurisprudence movement', considered law as a social institution designed to satisfy society's wants. The 'theory of interests' involved a classification of 'demands, desires and expectations' which the law ought to recognise and secure. Intense criticism of the theory has resulted in a considerable decline in its significance. The answer should include a general exposition of the theory and an outline of the more important criticisms, particularly those centring on the inadequacy of Pound's 'jural postulates'. The following skeleton plan is suggested:

> Introduction – essence of the theory of interests – the balancing of individual and social interests – jural postulates – criticisms of the theory – conclusion, the shell of the theory acts as a reminder of the concept of law as a means to an end.

Answer

Pound (1870–1964) was concerned with the working of the law rather than its abstract content, and with its social purposes and institutions within the context of social progress. His attitude was essentially 'functional': 'law', as distinct from 'laws', was a system which provided the foundation for judicial and administrative action within an organised society. The theory of interests, the outlines of which are set out below, is based on a belief in the necessity of legal order which demands a classification, securing and protection, of a variety of *interests*. Pound's taxonomy of interests is his specific contribution to the objective of analysing social purposes. The criticism directed against the theory is noted below, together with the suggestion that most of the theory may be considered as effectively demolished.

One of the aims of Pound's jurisprudence is an understanding of the mechanisms appropriate to achieving a *balance* of the security of society and of each individual's life. The law must attempt to satisfy, reconcile and harmonise conflicting claims and demands so that the interests that weigh most in society are given an appropriate prominence. To this end, a process of 'balancing' is needed; it will involve reference to *rules* (precepts of a detailed nature), *principles* (starting points for legal reasoning), *conceptions* (the categorisation of causes and situations) and *standards* (markers of the limits of permissible conduct). The appropriate balancing process will reflect the aim of law, which Pound spoke of as 'social engineering', concerned with the ordering of human relations 'with a minimum of waste and friction'.

To secure for society 'the greatest number of interests with the least possible sacrifice of other interests' is a primary function of the law, according to Pound. He defines an interest as a demand or desire which human beings, individually or in groups, seek to satisfy and which must be taken into account in the ordering of social relations. The theory of interests recognises the existence of three types of interests, defines the limits within which they should be recognised and given effect by the law, and emphasises the need to secure them. From an inventory and classification of interests, decisions on their recognition, significance and modes of ensuring their security, will emerge the key task for jurists and legislators – the *balancing* of those interests.

Pound's taxonomy is complex and is based on a division of interests into three basic categories: *individual, social and public.* (These interests are not created by the law: the law recognises and classifies them.) *Individual interests* are interests of personality or interests in domestic relations or interests of substance. They involve claims and demands related to an individual's life, for example, personality (physical security, freedom of belief, etc), domestic relations (interests of parents, children, protection of marriage, etc) and substance (property, freedom of contract). *Social interests* are wider claims or desires of the group which constitutes the community. These include general security, security of social institutions, general moral standards, conservation of social resources, general progress and individual life (the very important claim of a person to live a full human life according to society's standards). *Public interests* relate to claims viewed from the standpoint of a politically-organised society. They include interests of the state considered as a 'juristic person' (its integrity and security), interests of the state in its role of guardian of social interests.

These interests must be balanced fairly and this can be achieved only by examining a conflict on the appropriate plane or level. One ought not, for example, to weigh an individual interest against a public interest. Further, the satisfaction of as many interests as possible might involve the testing of a claim to a 'new interest'. Pound's solution to the problem of recognising whether or not a claimed 'new interest' shall qualify for recognition is to consider that interest by reference to the *jural postulates* of a civilised society. The postulates encapsulate the underlying *values* of a society. Given these postulates, legislators may modify rules and make new ones so as to conform with general values.

Pound's 'jural postulates' may be stated in the form of assumptions. Men within a civilised society are entitled to assume: that others will commit no intentional aggression upon them; that they may control for beneficial purposes what they have discovered, created and acquired; that others will act in good faith and carry out promises; that others will act reasonably and prudently and will not impose, by want of care, unreasonable risk of injury; that others will restrain or keep within proper bounds, things harmful in their normal action outside the sphere of their use. Pound later added the following postulates: that men should be entitled to assume that the burdens incident to social life shall be borne by society; and that at least a standard human life shall be assured to every individual by way of immediate material satisfaction.

We may summarise the theory as follows: Pound views law functionally, as a necessary social institution created to assist in the satisfaction of human wants. The satisfaction of wants necessitates an analysis of interests so that they may be systematised and secured by society's legal institutions. Conflicts of interests will demand a process of balancing one against another on the same plane. Where conflict follows on a request to recognise a new interest, reference is to be made to the jural postulates which reflect society's (and the law's) values. These postulates are not immutable and will require revision from time to time.

Criticism of Pound's theory has been intense. It is claimed, in general terms, that his theory is not an integrated whole because he failed to synthesise his thought. It is not always possible to see the links between the instrumentalist outlook which dominates his view of law, and his insistence on the significance of values as the basis of the jural postulates. Critics suggest that Pound may have derived his 'purposes' of society from principles which are couched in a form of words making factual proof impossible, and that he made no actual advance in our understanding of the law. He has done no more than 'rationalise the actual'. His views are said to reflect the thinking peculiar to American society of his day and may be difficult to translate to another epoch. The theory has been said to be based too closely on the aim of 'making things work better' and to provide little more than a minimalist picture of social needs which is not entirely relevant to our day. His methodology, involving the articulation a taxonomy of interests, has been criticised as suffering from the 'reification' inherent in any attempt to classify in systematic form phenomena outside the range of the natural sciences, with the result that personal attitudes and subjective perspectives emerge as aspects of objective reality. These criticisms have certainly undermined the credibility of the theory of interests.

Specific criticism has been directed against the 'consensus model' of law adopted by Pound. This is condemned as founded on a view of society functioning through shared values and ideas, a view which, some critics suggest, is distorted. Pound, say the critics, has failed to take into account the deep conflict of values within our society and he has ignored the struggles for the dominance of interests which have characterised much of our recent history. A theory predicated on a model of a society which does not exist must be rejected as unreal.

Attention has been drawn, too, to the so-called 'inadequacies of analogy' as reflected in Pound's description of law, within the terms of the theory of interests, as 'social engineering' (a phrase which acquired unfortunate connotations, given the history of the totalitarian regimes in which it featured as an aim of the law). Engineering involves building according to a detailed plan on 'solid ground'. But the essence of law in our society is that it is, in general, unplanned; it involves ad hoc attempts to deal with situations which are often unforeseen, and there may be little 'solid ground' in a rapidly evolving community. Further, say the critics, 'engineering' involves the creation of 'agreed structures' according to agreed plans; this analogy is of no relevance to a consideration of law within a non-static society in which there is often dissent concerning legal ends and means.

The methodology employed by Pound in the taxonomy of interests is said to be inadequate, giving a spurious air of objectivity to essentially vague ideas, and often based on no more than his subjective reactions to events. The 'interests' are nebulous and it is not easy to see the basis of distinction drawn between 'public' and 'social' interests. Nor is it possible to discern the precise system of classification used in the theory. The result is, say the critics, a classification based on no obvious set of principles, so that what has emerged from Pound's analysis reads like 'a political tract issued by a liberal grouping'. The critics note that whether, for example, an interest is classified as 'individual' or 'social' must be a reflection of changing, relative, political concepts, and little more. Pound's commentary on the classification seems not to acknowledge limitations of this nature; he seems to have ignored repeated requests for the production of the data which he utilised in the production of the taxonomy of interests.

No real standards are provided, according to critics, for evaluating or weighing interests. In the event, 'weight' is likely to depend upon highly-subjective criteria. 'Balancing' – a concept which Pound favours – implies some objective 'measuring rod', but the word is used in a misleading sense since it suggests an absence of subjective ideals and sentiments which, in reality, will, almost certainly, affect the evaluation upon which the 'balancing' depends. Further, recognition of a 'new interest' cannot be divorced from aspects of social policy – itself a subjective matter. Thus, current controversies on the recognition of a 'right to privacy', or the 'right to a home', will reflect personal, often highly individualistic and political views.

Finally, the critics have launched a sustained assault on Pound's concept of the 'jural postulates'. Seen by some as derived from 'a cramped and myopic view', by others as an attempt to smuggle in by the back door the 'unchangeable verities' of the natural law, the postulates have been rejected as a mere reflection of the social mores of American society of the 1920s. Pound, it is said, has failed to perceive the *relative nature* of his postulates. His call for their continued revision does not face up to the problem inherent in their enunciation as the legal values of a 'civilised society' – itself a concept based on personal evaluation. Indeed, Stone has suggested that the postulates require 'a basic reworking' so that they may reflect social changes that have come about since the time of their initial formulation. One wonders whether Pound would have accepted some recent and fundamental legislative changes within the United States as being consistent with the values of the 'civilised society' he proclaimed.

The criticisms levelled at the theory of interests may have removed it from the mainstream of modern jurisprudential thought. The very concept of a taxonomy of interests ('overticketed, overdocketed') is considered as flawed. Little is left of the pretensions of the theory to have explained the significance of 'social effort' in creating a civilised society. But the general outlines of Pound's theory do serve as a continuing reminder of the approach to law as a 'means to an end' and as an enunciation of the socially important 'reconciling task' of law. In Friedmann's words, the theory does make inarticulate premises articulate, and serves to remind legislators and jurists of the need to consider the overall interests of the community when addressing matters relating to the purpose of the law within society.

Notes

The principles of Pound's theory of interests are discussed in Lloyd, Chapter 7; Friedmann, Chapter 25; and Dias, Chapter 20. 'Pound's Theory of Social Interests', by Patterson, appears in *Interpretations of Modern Legal Philosophies*, edited by Sayre. Pound writes on 'A survey of social interests' in (1943) 57 Harvard LR 1 and on 'The scope and purpose of sociological jurisprudence', in (1921) 25 Harvard LR 489. Pound's life and jurisprudential writings are discussed in Wigdor's *Roscoe Pound: Philosopher of Law*, and Hull's *Roscoe Pound and Karl Llewellyn*.

CHAPTER 9

MARXIST JURISPRUDENCE

Introduction

Marxist jurisprudence stems primarily from the writings of Marx (1818–83), Engels (1820–95) and Lenin (1870–1924), and involves the application of the philosophy of dialectical materialism to a consideration of the nature of society, state and law. The motivating force in history is seen as the class struggle, in which the law and jurisprudence are not neutral. The questions in this chapter concern Marx's analysis of law in the context of capitalist society, and the contributions of Pashukanis (1891–1937) and Renner (1870–1950), who challenged some of the orthodoxies in classical Marxist jurisprudence.

Checklist

Ensure that you are acquainted with the following topics:
- dialectical materialism
- historical materialism
- base and superstructure
- commodity-exchange theory
- class instrumentalism
- state and law
- withering away of the state

Question 32

Addressing the bourgeoisie in his *Communist Manifesto* (1848), Marx stated: 'Your jurisprudence is but the will of your class made into a law for all, a will whose essential character and direction are determined by the economic conditions of existence of your class.' Outline the theory behind Marx's statement and comment on its jurisprudential implications.

Answer plan

The *Communist Manifesto* is an analysis of the history of society in terms of the class struggle, and a 'call to arms'. Marx was concerned to show how law is an ideological weapon of the ruling class (the bourgeoisie) which is deployed by the state through the legal system so as to maintain class rule and oppress the working class. The question demands an explanation of the basis of Marx's theory of law which, in turn, involves a consideration of the 'base and superstructure' explanation of the state. The following skeleton plan is used:

> Introduction – Marx's world-outlook – materialist conception of history – laws of economic development – history as class struggle – base and superstructure – law and class instrumentalism – state and law – law in a classless society – conclusion, current rejection of Marx's jurisprudence.

Answer

The *Communist Manifesto* is an outline of principles and a call to action, a combination of the 'theory and practice of revolution' which Marx (1818–83) considered essential if society was to be transformed. 'Up till now', he had declared, 'philosophers have interpreted the world; the point, however, is to change it'. Marx had studied jurisprudence, philosophy and history at the universities of Bonn and Berlin and had been influenced profoundly by the teachings of Hegel which he adapted and transformed in the creation of his own world-outlook. Embedded in that outlook is a unique interpretation of law as reflecting economic relationships within society. The corpus of Marxist jurisprudence grew out of his general philosophy, and some of its essence is contained within the quotation from the *Manifesto*, addressed to the ruling class – the bourgeoisie – whose overthrow was, in Marx's view , necessary, inevitable and imminent.

Marx's jurisprudential thought is based on the doctrines which comprised his philosophical outlook: dialectical materialism, the laws of economic development and the materialist conception of history. Dialectical materialism is Marx's version of the basis of the 'laws of change'; it combines a materialist philosophy and the method of interpretation known as 'dialectics', which is a highly systematised mode of reasoning involving the examination and resolution of contradictions within phenomena. Marx's materialism embraces *all* phenomena, natural and social. Natural phenomena constitute a unity: everything is in motion and nothing exists (or can be understood) as an isolate. The bases of a system of law, its purposes and manifestations, have to be comprehended in terms of their relationships and changing nature. The Marxist jurist follows Marx in rejecting 'idealistic jurisprudence': ideas can have no meaning or significance outside a materialistic framework of analysis. Legal thought has to be interpreted in relation to the social fabric within which it was conceived and nurtured.

The laws of economic development reflect fundamental antagonisms ('contradictions') between those who own the instruments of production (the bourgeoisie) and those who own nothing save their labour power (the proletariat). The latter are exploited by the former; the mode of exploitation characterises the laws of economic development. Methodical exploitation sets in motion a struggle which can be resolved only by the expropriation of the bourgeoisie, together with the abolition of the legal system which has assisted in securing bourgeois class rule.

The materialist conception of history rejects the view of historical development as 'man's movement towards his spiritual destiny' or 'a struggle towards perfect freedom'. For Marx, history is a bleak record of the conflict of class against class, with the law 'taking sides'. The laws of historical development are inexorable in their operation. Society began with conditions in which a legal system was unnecessary because there was common ownership of property. Slave-owning society followed, with laws recognising and protecting the ownership of slaves. Medieval feudalism followed and, in turn, produced capitalism, with a developed legal system. Revolutionary activity will, according to Marx, produce from capitalist society the socialist, classless order in which a legal system will no longer be needed because, with the removal of economic contradictions, crime and other anti-social activities will disappear. Marx's fulminations against the bourgeoisie, recorded in the *Manifesto*, are intended to remind them of the transitory nature of their society and its legal system.

It is from the Marxist thesis of 'base and superstructure' that the significance of law emerges. The basis of a given social order is its economic foundation, which is characterised by relations of production. The relations are independent of men's will and are determined by the mode in which the factors of production (land, labour and capital) are organised and exploited by those who own the instruments of production (factories, mines, etc). The totality of these relations of production constitutes the economic structure of society. On this foundation, society erects a 'superstructure', which includes ideas, ideologies, theories, philosophies relating to religion, ethics, art, etc. Society requires, and, therefore, creates as part of the superstructure, legal rules and institutions, referred to, collectively, as 'the law'.

Legal ideology, according to Marx, owes little to so called 'eternal categories', 'innate ideas of justice' or 'immutable concepts of right'. It is an identifiable part of the social superstructure, built on the foundation of a certain mode of economic production and mirroring the antagonisms of a society characterised by class domination and suppression. The emergence and growth of the common law, rooted in the mores of an exploitative agricultural society, the growth of theories of natural law, are to be understood solely by reference to the framework of economic relationships in which they took root and flourished. It is the *relationships* engendered by society's economy which determine social consciousness and, therefore, the nature of legal ideology. In a passage in *A Contribution the the Critique of Political Economy* (1859), which has engendered much exegesis, Marx declares: 'It is not the consciousness of men that that determines their existence, but their social existence that determines their consciousness.' In Roemer's words: 'Law and politics implement what the economic structure requires, and the economic structure is, in turn, required by the underlying productive forces. Thus legal developments are determined two steps back by material economic developments.'

The doctrine of 'class instrumentalism', which exercised a significant influence on many European jurists of the mid-20th century, arises from investigation of the nature of superstructure and the concept of struggle. Ideas relating to the law – its content, theoretical basis, principles of legal institutions – must be viewed as aspects of the class interests jurists serve, consciously or unconsciously. Law, according to Marx, is an instrument of class domination, enabling the ruling class to control and suppress those groups which challenge its power. Behind the apparent scholarly and 'disinterested' jurisprudence which advocates 'human rights' or 'reason' or 'natural justice' is the veiled purpose of the *fundamental protection and preservation of fundamental class interests*. Jurisprudential ideas may be interpreted, therefore, not as 'phenomena in themselves', but as a rationale for the forging of 'ideological weapons' safeguarding those who hold power. It is this facet of law to which Marx is referring in the extract from the *Manifesto*. 'Behind your jurisprudence is your concern for the maintenance of your economic superiority. Your law is a mere expression, a rationalisation, of that concept.'

Also dependent on the theory of 'base and superstructure' is the Marxist concept of state and law, which is implicit in the extract from the *Manifesto*. The state, its apparatus and ideology, may be perceived as a part of the general superstructure of society and resting, therefore, on society's economic base. The state did not exist prior to the emergence of classes; its functions appear and are intensified as class divisions grow. In the era of bourgeois domination, to which Marx is referring in the passage cited in the question, the state is merely the 'executive committee' of the bourgeoisie, providing coercive power in a continuing class conflict of which it is aware. The structural form of the state reflects the prevalent mode of production. The feudal state, according to Marx, with its hierarchy of allegiances, mirrored aspects of the ownership of land. The modern state, with its emphasis on administration, is said to reflect large scale production systems. Today's state is interpreted by Marxist jurists as an organisation concerned primarily with the task of protecting a ruling class. The law provides assistance in manning the organisations of the state concerned with the protection and reinforcement of class rights, and jurisprudence performs its role of stabilising, legitimising, and otherwise justifying the existing economic structure.

Implicit in Marx's criticism of bourgeois law is his notion of 'change'. He gives no exemption to law, class or state from the workings of historical development. Following on the inevitable defeat of the bourgeoisie will come a radical transformation in the role of state and law. The new, victorious, socialist society will see a replacement of 'the government of persons' by 'the administration of things'. Mankind, in the new classless society will have no need of a state apparatus; there will be no classes and, therefore, no tasks for state organs of repression. Exploitation and poverty, the root causes of crime, will vanish, as will the jurisprudential ideology which sought to explain these phenomena as permanent aspects of social existence. In effect, the state will not be abolished, but will merely 'wither away'.

There is, therefore, the certainty that law will disappear from the classless society after a 'transitional period'. During that period, when society is shedding its old habits, new, temporary forms of law, designed to strengthen the powers of the new dominant class will be needed. Eventually the law will disappear and man will develop into a 'group creature' who no longer has a need for rules, codes and institutions of law.

Marxist jurisprudence now has few attractions for jurists. Its basic theses appear over-simplified, and its philosophy seems untenable in the face of actual historical development in our times. Marxist legal thought is seen to have been used to underpin authoritarian regimes in which justice and liberty were (according to our standards) non-existent. Vestiges of the system of thought originated by Marx may continue to be considered in discussions of the nature of the state and law, but it is unlikely that the school of classical Marxist legal ideology will long survive the disappearance of the states in which it was encouraged and in which it flourished as official dogma. Theories which proclaimed the withering away of the state under socialism, which foresaw the disappearance of crime and a replacement of the administration of people by the administration of things, now appear to have little credibility in the context of the harsh realities of state power which characterised the Marxist regimes and which were supported in the writings of Marxist jurists.

Notes

The principal works of Marx, including the *Communist Manifesto*, appear in a variety of editions, some annotated by contemporary scholars. Lloyd, Chapter 11; and Friedmann, Chapter 29, provide useful commentaries on Marxist jurisprudential thought. Collins' *Marxism and Law* gives a unified, comprehensive account of the

Marxist theory of law. Plamenatz, in *Marx's Philosophy of Man*, outlines aspects of Marxist jurisprudence. Roemer's *Free to Lose* gives an introduction to Marxist philosophy, presented in non-technical terms. *Marx and Engels on Law* is a valuable compilation of extracts from the writings of the fathers of classical Marxism. *Methodology of Law*, by Kerimov, is one of the final publications of Soviet jurisprudence on the eve of the collapse of the USSR; it outlines the nature of Marxist legal thought in the 1980s.

Question 33

Outline and evaluate the contributions of Pashukanis and Renner to jurisprudence.

Answer plan

Pashukanis, a Soviet jurist, professor of law and a Vice-Minister for Justice in the early days of the regime, produced an interpretation of law which was, in some respects, at variance with official, orthodox jurisprudence. In the light of his theory, he resisted the call for the creation of a 'proletarian law'. He disappeared in the purges of the 1930s, having been denounced as a 'wrecker'. The question requires an explanation of the 'commodity-exchange' theory from which Pashukanis derived his view of law. An estimate of his significance today is also required; this should take into account the apparent excesses of the legal system he helped to create. Renner, an Austrian jurist and statesman who became his country's President, was a critic of dogmatic Marxism which, he claimed, had failed to understand the way in which economic systems were developing. His calls for a revisionist approach went unheeded and he was denounced by the Soviet jurisprudential establishment in the same terms as those used in the ideological and political offensive against Pasukanis. The following skeleton plan is used:

> Introduction – Pashukanis' questioning of orthodox Marxist views of law – the political context of his writing – significance of the commodity-exchange theory – Pashukanis as a 'wrecker' – criticisms of the basis of his

legal thought – contribution of Pashukanis to jurisprudence seen as interesting but slight – Renner's challenge to dogmatic Marxism – stages of development in society and their implications – law and superstructure – conclusion, Renner's insistence on a new examination of Marxism and law.

Answer

It is paradoxical that Pashukanis (1891–1937), generally considered as one of the few outstanding contributors to Marxist jurisprudence in the 20th century, should now be known only for his deviation from orthodox Marxism as applied to law. His *Law and Marxism – a General Theory* (1924), was intended as a first draft of a Marxist critique of fundamental juridical concepts; in Marxist terminology, it was envisaged as 'an attempt to approximate the legal form to the commodity form'. Pashukanis proposed a re-thinking of the doctrine of law associated with earlier Marxists and a re-casting of some fundamental concepts of jurisprudence, particularly in relation to 'the withering away of the state'. The result was that he moved outside the mainstream of orthodox Marxist thought as interpreted by the official Soviet jurisprudential school, with predictable results.

The significance of political events during which Pashukanis prepared and published his theory should not be forgotten. The Russian Revolution was less than five years old, lawlessness was rife and the draconian legal system which was to characterise the Soviet State was already in embryonic form. By 1930, it had become obvious that world revolution – a basic dogma of Marxist official thought – was not imminent, and in 1936, a new constitution, which recognised the importance of obedience to the law of the state, was introduced. Pashukanis' work did not escape the attention of the Communist Party's vigilant theoreticians. They viewed it – correctly – as a deviation from orthodoxy and as an implied criticism of the role of law in the state. Pashukanis was denounced in the official press in 1937 and, later that year, was arrested as 'an enemy of the people'. He disappeared in a widespread purge of 'unreliable elements'.

Pashukanis writes as a convinced Marxist who accepts the basic thinking of Marx in relation to law. He accepts the doctrine of the class struggle, of class instrumentalism and of the role of law within society. The relations of production determine society's superstructure, including legal thought; 'right can never be higher than the economic structure of society'. But he gives a twist to these doctrines in *Law and Marxism* in an unusual emphasis on exchange, rather than production, within society. He calls for the rejection of a growing, popular call for a 'proletarian law' and stresses the significance of the doctrine of the withering away of the state – this at a time when the dominance of law and state was being deliberately intensified by the Party's theoreticians.

The commodity-exchange theory is at the basis of Pashukanis' thoughts on jurisprudence. Any theorising in law, he insists, demands deep historical enquiry. This will reveal that the real basis of all law is *the contractual relationship*. Fundamental to capitalism is exchange; goods produced are 'commodities' and are destined largely for exchange on the market. Law emerges when there is a perceived necessity to ensure the smooth running of systems based on trade and barter. The importance of contract as a legal expression of commodity exchange (the fundamental relationship within capitalism) grows and a legal structure emerges so as to resolve disputes and conflicts of interest.

Further, says Pashukanis, an analysis of law in the era of commodity exchange epitomised by capitalism reveals that 'the only law is bourgeois law'. The full logic of the very concepts of law and legal system can be asserted, therefore, only under capitalism (there would be, therefore, no post-capitalist law). The ideal of law comes to fruition at the same time as the ideal of the market, and this is no historical accident. Bourgeois economic doctrine and law are dominated by the concept of commodity-exchange. This had to be accepted by Marxists if they were to understand the historical nature of capitalism.

Calls for the establishment of a 'proletarian law' were rejected by Pashukanis as backward looking. He argues that the formal patterns of bourgeois commodity-exchange law continue during the transitional period leading to socialism, even though capitalist exploitation has ceased. Law will die out together with the state, and the withering away of categories of bourgeois law will involve the withering away of law *in its entirety*. The juridical factor will disappear from social relations. Lenin's view that there will remain for a time after the revolution not only vestiges of bourgeois law, but that the bourgeois state itself will continue – without the bourgeoisie – had to be remembered. The demand for a 'proletarian law' would delay the transition to socialism and was incorrect in the circumstances. The desirable objective was the withering away of the *entire legal form* as such.

The state will wither away, said Pashukanis, when commodity-exchange in *all* its forms has disappeared. State superstructure, including the law and morality associated with commodity-exchange, will *precede* the dissolution of the state. Law has attained its developmental peak under capitalism; its decline and disappearance will herald the end of the state.

The political implications of Pashukanis' thought were construed as 'objectively anti-Soviet'. His subsequent denunciation as a 'wrecker' was based on an interpretation of his doctrine as a mask for the activities of the state's enemies. At a time when the proletarian nature of the state was receiving official recognition in the constitution, he had chosen to deny the necessity for proletarian law; at the very moment when discipline and obedience to the law were urged as every citizen's duty, he was emphasising the temporary nature of the law; during a period of the strengthening of state power, he had decided to stress the withering away of the state. Law, which was being proclaimed as an instrument in the maintenance of 'revolutionary vigilance' was being explained by him in terms of commodity-exchange. Here, indeed, was the archetype of the 'intellectual wrecker of Soviet society', ignoring reality in favour of mere abstractions.

An evaluation of Pashukanis involves an examination of the doctrinal basis of his thought and his methodology. To a very large extent, his work stands or falls according to one's reactions to Marxist jurisprudence as an expression of revolutionary doctrine. There is considerable doubt today as to the logic and veracity of the reasoning behind the economic interpretation of history upon which Pashukanis relies. The doctrines of the withering away of the state and 'base and superstructure' now command little intellectual support and there seems to be a minimum of agreement on the worth of the 'laws of development of history' which Pashukanis uses to illustrate his theories.

Pashukanis' work has been dismissed as exemplifying the inadequacies of Marxist jurisprudence in general. Thus, the picture of societies dominated by legal structures based on the ideologies emanating from commodity-exchange is difficult to recognise in the records of economic and legal development. Commodity-exchange is merely one facet of the system of capitalism, and Pashukanis seems not to have noted the relationships arising from the *productive basis* of that system. It is not easy to see why a complex relationship involving producers and the market is to be analysed solely in terms of the final stages of commodity production and exchange. Pashukanis has been extraordinarily selective in his examination of the capitalist processes of production and exchange. The resultant legal theory is, of necessity, unbalanced.

Additionally, there appears to be a lack of empirical evidence to support the view of Pashukanis as to societies entirely dominated, in their economic and social development, by concepts of contract which embody ideas of commodity-exchange, and its significance. It is doubtful whether all primitive societies, with embryonic legal systems, utilised commodity-exchange transactions. It is suggested that Pashukanis was generalising from some few, highly specific views concerning early development within some parts of Europe. An overall, universal theory has been erected on a narrow, insubstantial foundation.

Claims that Pashukanis made a distinctive contribution to historical jurisprudence by his insistence on the recognition of pre-commodity-exchange and pre-capitalist societies as lacking legal structures are difficult to substantiate. There are many instances of the existence of complex legal structures within pre-capitalist society. Law *did* pre-date capitalist society in England, for example. Indeed, the very vocabulary of our contemporary land law remains marked indelibly with its feudal origins. The systems of tenure and estates, complex and far-reaching in their effect during the era of feudalism, testify to the existence of legal concepts and appropriate structures. *De Donis Conditionalibus* 1285, estates in fee tail, knight service, indicate a wide and growing network of relationships based on a law existing long before the industrial revolution and the emergence of capitalist society in England.

There is doubt, too, as to the truth of Pashukanis' assertion that communal morality is but a reflection of the commodity-exchange basis of society. There are strong arguments suggesting that morality exists and develops outside the framework of economic relationships. Thus, attitudes in Western society to those acts 'whose harm is plain, grave and universally unwelcome' have not undergone changes which coincide with new eras of economic development. Murder, theft, assault, have been condemned through the ages; the refinement in attitudes towards these offences does not suggest fundamental changes in moral perceptions determined by commodity-exchange relationships.

Pashukanis' forecasts of legal events derived from his theoretical analysis of capitalism and socialism have, in the event, been rendered false. No new and 'higher' morality emerged in the Marxist-controlled states; in none of those regimes was there ever any evidence of the withering away of the state; in no Marxist regime was there ever any inclination towards the replacement of the administration of persons by the administration of things. Judged by Lenin's own litmus test – 'the veracity of a theory can be tested only by action' – the lasting contribution of Pashukanis to jurisprudence is likely to be slight, save perhaps as a potent reminder of a system of legal thought placed at the service of a regime which could not tolerate any significant deviation from its proclaimed tenets of orthodoxy.

Renner (1870–1950), a prominent member of the Marxist-dominated Austrian Social Democratic party at the beginning of this century, was a lawyer whose jurisprudential writings were concerned with theories of property and social change. His scholarship and polemics were turned against the orthodox Marxists within his party and against Russian-style Marxism. After the end of the Second World War, Renner became Chancellor, and, later, President of Austria.

Renner's challenge to Marxist theory is of a radical nature. In 1916, he had argued that orthodox Marxists had failed to observe that the structure of capitalism had changed in fundamental fashion. They were wrong in assuming that legal institutions are determined *automatically* in their form and structure by the nature of economic substrata within society. His criticisms went to the very heart of an embryonic Marxist jurisprudence, prior to the 1917 revolution. Lenin perceived the nature of Renner's criticism as constituting an attack against the official Marxist theory of the state, and, in a secondary manner, against the tactics of the party which was preparing for the total destruction of the Russian autocracy and its legal organs.

In *The Institutions of Private Law and their Social Functions* (1919), Renner sought to show that the state's economic functions had grown in a manner which could not have been foreseen by Marx and his immediate circle. Marxists of the early 20th century seemed unwilling or unable to grasp and accept what had happened in the area of state economies. Renner noted that it was not merely a matter of observing and accepting as a fact some few examples of the nationalisation of factories. It was much more important to note that in some countries the entire private sector appeared to be dominated to a very considerable degree 'by willed and conscious regulation and direction'.

Renner's analysis of the situation took the form, common to Marxist analysis of his day, of investigating and enumerating the specific changes (the 'stages') in economic development. He suggested that *four stages* of development might be discerned in that pattern of development. *The first stage*, which he said had lasted over a decade (1878–90), was characterised by state intervention (and appropriate legal structures) on behalf of weak members of the community who lacked protection against the effects of intensified competition. *The second stage* was characterised by the growth of cartels (monopolistic organisations which restricted output so as to keep up prices). Renner spoke of this stage as 'the era of the organised economy of private enterprise'.

The third stage in Renner's analysis was characterised by the growth of 'the imperialist national economy'. In this stage of development, in which the state intervenes (through political and legal institutions) on behalf of the strong and powerful, there is a merger of state power and the more important institutions of the economy. In *the fourth stage*, he argued, the state economy predominates: the private sector's operations are largely determined by the state and laws which underpin the workings of the economic system. The type of capitalist society in which Marx lived had ceased to exist. *Laissez-faire* capitalism had been transformed, or was in the process of being transformed, into state capitalism.

Renner argued that his orthodox Marxist contemporaries were unable to sense the fact or nature of the fundamental economic transformation. They were blind to the problems arising from the need to create new types of legal structure. He stressed the significance of his belief that tensions between the forms and functions of legal institutions make for gradual changes in their functions. New laws emerge, but the process of tensions creating changes continues – as Marxist dialectic forecasts. Unless Marxists become aware of changes in society producing *a variety of tensions* which must be analysed, it will not be possible to create an appropriate jurisprudence for a new situation.

In a series of essays, Renner observed that Marxist colleagues within his party were slow to understand the significance of changes in the form and nature of *ownership*. Those who owned the instruments of production (factories, mines, railways) in a society dominated by state capitalism had increased their influence in capitalist-worker relationships within the law. The contract of employment was an example of the growth of inequalities, allowing one party to the contract to effectively dictate conditions of service to the other. Monopoly ownership had rendered contractual relationships much more oppressive than they had been. It was clearly a type of ownership which could threaten not only industrial relations, but the very nature of society. An appropriate jurisprudential analysis was needed which would take account of qualitative changes in the nature of 'social power through ownership'. Marxist jurists should acknowledge the significance of private *and* public types of ownership. The institutions involved in the creation and accumulation of wealth on a large scale should be owned in the name of the community; private ownership should apply only to consumer goods. Appropriate legislation would be enacted which would recognise this duality of ownership.

Essentially, Renner attempted to modify the rigid patterns of older, orthodox Marxism by arguing for an analysis in depth of existing society, to be followed by appropriate conclusions concerning the need for changes in the law. Law was not to be considered as mere superstructure (as Marx had argued); legal form is modified by function, in a continuing process of development. Capitalism in its dominant stage allows those who own the means of production to exercise a 'quasi-public' domination over those who sell their labour power through contracts of service. Renner argues that this has not been understood fully.

'Dreams and speculations', says Renner, are of little value in the struggle for the creation of 'a human society that acts in freedom and in full consciousness, that creates its norms in complete independence'. The regulations required by a socialist society in order to control relationships among citizens must be based scientifically on 'the way of experience'. The state of the future – and its laws – will be conditioned in part by the past. Marxist jurists must remember this and must accept, too, that the process of change leading towards a new social and legal order may demand a refurbishing – not a wholesale destruction – of existing institutions so as to prepare them for new tasks.

Renner ran foul of orthodox Marxism and for many years he was denounced as a 'renegade' and 'traitor to the working class'. His standing in political and jurisprudential circles was not assisted by his support for the Nazi-inspired unification of Germany and Austria in 1936. His place in jurisprudence now appear to rest, as in the case of Pashukanis, upon attempts to see the tenets of Marxism from a new perspective which allows for a fresh interpretation of social, economic and legal development.

Notes

Pashukanis' *Law and Marxism – a General Theory* appeared recently in a new translation by Einhorn, edited by Arthur; it contains an interesting biography and a critical assessment by the German jurist, Korsch. Lloyd, Chapter 11; and Dias, Chapter 19, discuss Pashukanis' contribution to jurisprudence. Schlesinger's *Soviet Legal Theory* includes an explanation of the commodity-exchange theory. *Pashukanis: Selected Writings on Marxism and Law*, edited by Beirne, provides useful background material. Articles on Pashukanis' legal thought include 'Pashukanis and Vyshinsky: a study in the development of Marxian legal theory', by Fuller ([1949] 47 Mich LR 1159). 'Pashukanis and the commodity form theory', by Swann in the International Journal of Sociology of Law ((1981) 9 International Journal of Sociology of Law), and 'Pashukanis and liberal jurisprudence', by Simonds (1985) 12 JLS 135. Extracts from Renner's writings appear in Lloyd, Chapter 11. His *Institutions of Private Law* was published in an English version in 1949.

CHAPTER 10

SCANDINAVIAN REALISM

Introduction

The school of Scandinavian realist jurisprudence is best known through the writings of its founder, Hägerström (1868–1939), Lundstedt (1882–1955), Olivecrona (1897–c 1980) and Ross (1899–c 1980). They were opposed to metaphysical speculation and were concerned with the general investigation of the 'fundamental facts' of legal systems. The nature of rights and duties was of particular interest to them. The questions in this chapter call for a knowledge of the general principles of the Scandinavian school, and of the jurisprudential thought associated with Olivecrona in particular.

Checklist

Ensure that you are acquainted with the following topics:
- mental constructs
- independent imperatives
- perception of rights and duties
- law as creating morality
- word-magic

Question 34

'It is not always easy to perceive the "realist" element in Scandinavian Legal Realism.'

Comment.

Answer plan

The essence of Scandinavian Realism is a reaction against 'pseudo-concepts' which are claimed to be merely 'shams'. Reality may be discovered by an analysis of facts. Assertions which cannot be proved, so called 'inherent qualities' of legal concepts, are worthless. Law creates our morality, not vice versa. The general principles of the Scandinavian approach require elucidation in the answer, together with a consideration of the criticism that, paradoxically, the Scandinavians have substituted their own 'non-realist' theory in place of the metaphysical speculation they attack. The following skeleton plan is suggested:

> Introduction – the Scandinavian reaction against metaphysics – Hägerström's views and criticism of his teaching – Olivecrona's views and criticism of them – teachings of Lundstedt and reactions to them – views of Ross and views of the critics – conclusion, problems of the Scandinavian approach.

Answer

The Scandinavian Legal Realist movement involves, essentially, a reaction against the 'chimera of metaphysics', its inadequacies and distortions, and a concentration on the 'facts' of legal life. It shares few features of the approach of the American Realist movement. The Scandinavians are less concerned than the Americans with the behavioural aspects of adjudication, preferring to raise questions concerning the *nature* of rights and duties. The 'realism' of the Scandinavians rests in a critique of metaphysics, whereas the American realists are concerned with a pragmatic approach to legal institutions. The Scandinavian realists, Hägerström, Lundstedt, Olivecrona and Ross, were trained philosophers; the American realists were, in general, jurists, judges and teachers of law. Outlines of the views of the leading members of the Scandinavian school are given below, together with criticisms of their basic approach to the law. Whether their jurisprudential thought may be correctly classified as 'realist' will be suggested as being open to doubt.

Initially, it is necessary to state the principal features of Scandinavian realism. First, metaphysics is rejected totally; it is interpreted as nothing more than a survival of mysticism, and a meaningless study, because its assertions and conclusions cannot be proved. 'What cannot be verified does not objectively exist.' Hence, objective values are non-existent; 'goodness', for example, is viewed as a mere emotional reaction of approval to certain types of stimulus; its 'objectivity and absoluteness' are illusory. 'Natural law' jurisprudence is unacceptable – it can be made to support almost any facet of legal theory: in Ross' words: 'natural law is like a harlot – at the disposal of everyone'. A scientific probe of the basis of legal concepts such as 'rights' and 'duties' generally reveals mere conceptualisations which possess no real or comprehensible meaning because they have no counterpart in the physical world. 'Justice' is a mere feeling engendered by habit and a prevalent ideology which suggests that the legal order is adequate. If, argue the Scandinavians, jurisprudence is to aspire to the status of a natural science, rooted in empiricism, it must act on the assumption that *there is no cognition other than empirical.*

Hägerström (1868–1939), founder of the Scandinavian school believed that metaphysical speculation distorts the 'true basis' of any appreciation of law. We tend to obey the law because of our psychological conditioning, not because of the law's 'inherent qualities'. 'Right' is a concept meaningless in itself: the 'right of ownership', he stated, has no empirical significance unless and until it is infringed and has become the subject matter of litigation. One cannot speak, therefore, of 'rights' in a context separated from remedies and enforcement procedures. Similarly, the concept of 'justice' (associated with rights) has, in itself, no meaning; it represents, says Hägerström, no more than a highly subjective evaluation which cannot be examined scientifically. The origins of terms such as 'right', 'justice', can be traced to the use of 'word-magic' in ancient, arcane ceremonies. The use of ritual is, according to the Scandinavians, common in the early days of the law, and words spoken in the form of incantation (as, for example, in the Roman ceremony of adoption) tend to give individuals feelings of *power*; hence their significance in law (which involves relationships founded on power).

It is difficult to perceive the 'realism' with which Hägerström claims to have replaced metaphysical interpretations of the law. The rejection of universal standards ('goodness', for example) stems from the questionable dogmas of logical positivism and its insistence on the 'verification' of all statements. (Logical positivism is itself a theory which has not been proved beyond doubt. Is it *ipso facto* merely an 'illusion'?) The view of 'justice' as meaningless seems somewhat exaggerated: its presence as a vital aspect in the functioning of legal institutions and its constituent features have been analysed repeatedly and there is broad general agreement on the desirability of many of them. The concept of word-magic is not always easy to support today: thus, the words, 'I now pronounce you man and wife', which conclude the authorised marriage ceremony, are perceived correctly by all those concerned as indicating a fundamental change in status and a modification of rights and duties, and are acted on accordingly. Far from possessing any connotation of 'magic', they are understood as a precise indicator of the existence of a new quality of relationship. There would seem to be little 'realism' in Hägerström's analysis; it is a highly speculative interpretation of some minor aspects of the real world, which does not, as a result, become more 'understandable'. The uncertainties of metaphysics have been exchanged for little more than the abstraction of the results of a so called 'realist investigation'.

Olivecrona (b 1897) pursued the same line of enquiry using the same methodology. Rights, he insisted, are subjective ideas existing only within the mind; there can be no objective 'right' or 'duty'. Psychology will explain the growth, power and persistence of concepts of this nature. The connection between moral standards and the law is of much interest to Olivecrona. He suggests that the promulgation of legal rules and the threat of sanctions are internalised in the form of 'imperative symbols' ('Thou shalt ...'), and when prohibited activities spring to the mind, they are imprinted with the symbols of communal disapproval. After the legal rules become dominant in an individual's psychology, their hold is increased by sanctions. It is the law, therefore, which creates our 'morality'.

Olivecrona produces no empirical evidence in support of his 'realist' theses; his generalisations concerning rights are based on little more than speculation. The suggestion that rights and duties are subjective phenomena, with no existence in the empirical world, would seem to be contradicted by the events which often follow on the promulgation of rights. A right is more than a mere psychological 'feeling of power': it is a phenomenon, the existence of which may be inferred from the events which surround its creation, its enforcement and its infringement. Thus, the mortgagor's 'right' to require the mortgagee to transfer the mortgage to a third party (under s 95 of the Law of Property Act 1925) is much more than a mere 'subjective feeling of power' enjoyed by the mortgagor. Further, Olivecrona's 'realism' applied to the question of law and morality produces its own problems. Is it possible to explain adequately in terms of 'law creating morality', the widespread abhorrence of murder, or the feelings within the community against racism, which preceded the Race Relations Act 1976? Olivecrona appears to be flying in the face of reality.

Lundstedt (1882–1955) argues that feelings of justice do not *direct* the law; on the contrary, they are *directed by* the law. Law expresses social and economic interests – all else is illusion. Concepts such as 'guilt' operate only within the individual conscience and have no objective meaning. If we say that D, the defendant, 'acted wrongfully', this is a mere circumlocution for the precise fact that he was adjudged to pay damages. To talk of D's 'violating his duties' is to make a mere value judgment; 'rights' and 'duties' derive solely from the rules of law. Law is the result of social pressures reflecting 'inescapable societal needs', that is, 'social interests'.

Here, again, is one set of allegedly-inadequate abstractions exchanged for another set of abstractions. Lundstedt's view of justice has been criticised as a travesty of what is understood, accepted and acted upon very widely. 'Violation of duties' is, arguably, a reference to a proven phenomenon, and much more than a 'value judgment'. 'Social interests', which Lundstedt perceives as the basis of law, is itself an abstract concept which involves the very type of value judgment against which he inveighs.

Ross (b 1899) also stresses 'justice' as an expression of emotional feelings. Indeed, to invoke 'justice' is, he says, the same as 'banging on the table'; it is an emotional expression, transforming one's demands into an absolute postulate. Further, he says, to know the legal rules which govern the functioning of legal institutions is to know everything about the existence and extent of the law. Primary rules, which may exist only in the minds of citizens, inform them of how they are obliged to behave; they are followed with regularity, and psychological pressures ensure that they are 'binding'. Secondary rules ('directives') specify sanctions and the conditions under which they will operate. Confidence in, acquiescence towards, and obedience to, the rules is also underlined by their 'predictability'.

Ross' assumptions and interpretations lack supporting evidence (yet he has spoken of the study of law as 'an empirical social science'). The hypothetical 'pressures' which are said to ensure the binding force of legal rules are pure conjecture and have not been investigated with the rigour generally used by psychologists in the investigation of theories of this nature. An absence of 'realist' methodology in Ross' work has been commented on by several critics.

The positive features of the Scandinavians' teachings ought not to be forgotten, however. The specialised vocabulary of the legal process ought not to be sacrosanct: words *can and do* obfuscate reality, verbal ambiguity may conceal contradiction, abstruseness may disguise error. Nor should any mystique attach to the functions of the law, as the Scandinavians point out. Yet it is difficult to ignore the unrealistic and sterile nature of much of their work. It has produced no useful answers to practical problems posed by jurists and lawyers and it has engendered no valuable discussion on the everyday activities of legal institutions. Its excessive concentration on semantic problems has not resulted in a more 'realistic' approach to the law. The forceful rejection of terms such as 'right', 'duty' and 'justice', and their dismissal as mere subjective feelings, have little relevance for those for whom the protection and security offered by the law reside in acknowledgement and acceptance of the ever present 'reality' of these concepts.

The dismissal of concepts of 'duty', etc, as incapable of factual verification, and, therefore, as 'nonsense' (itself a quasi-metaphysical term) may derive from the fallacy of considering words *solely* as parts of empiric, factual statements, whereas they can be used legitimately in a *normative context*. Indeed, the Norwegian jurist, Castberg, reminds Lundstedt and his colleagues that without notions such as 'duty' and 'norm', judicial thinking becomes not only difficult, but impossible. Further, the suggestion that law creates our moral standards involves an unwarranted rejection of the significance of the community's sensibilities which, in practice, often provide the driving force behind the making and modification of the law. On a number of counts, therefore, doubt may be expressed as to the Scandinavians having produced a body of jurisprudential thought which can be characterised as essentially 'realist' in the sense in which that term is generally understood by jurists.

Notes

The principal works of the Scandinavian Realists are: *Inquiries into the Nature of Law and Morals*, by Hägerström, translated by Broad, *Legal Thinking Revised*, by Lundstedt, *Law as Fact*, by Olivecrona, and *On Law and Justice*, by Ross. Summaries of the general approach of the Scandinavians appear in Harris, Chapter 8; Friedmann, Chapter 25; Dias, Chapter 21. Extracts from the principal works mentioned above appear in Lloyd, Chapter 9; and Davies and Holdcroft, Chapter 14. Hart's review of 'Scandinavian Legal Realism' [1959] CLJ 233, is of particular interest.

Question 35

Outline Olivecrona's interpretation of the meaning of 'rights', and rules of law as 'commands'.

Answer plan

Olivecrona follows the general pattern of legal enquiry characteristic of the school of Scandinavian Realism. Law emerges from normative rules based on social facts; it exists through the individual imagination and is concerned with rules which contain patterns of conduct often relating to the possible exercise of force. The term 'right', as generally used in jurisprudence, 'lacks semantic reference', but the subjective idea of 'rights' is a *fact* which must be recognised. The concept of 'command' in relation to law has, he argues, confused the task of understanding legal activities. He presents an analysis of rules in terms of 'independent imperatives'. The following skeleton plan is used:

Introduction – Olivecrona's basic outlook – essence of rights – perception of rights and duties – directive and informative functions of rights – problems of the term 'command' – independent imperatives – conclusion, rights with a factual context.

Answer

Olivecrona sets out his views on 'rights' and the meaning of 'rules of law' in *Law as Fact*, which was published in 1939, and revised in 1971. His general aim was to fit the complex phenomena covered by the word 'law' into 'the spatio-temporal world'. This involves a discussion of mental concepts of 'rights' and an application of the principles of realism to a study of the rules inherent in enacted law. Fundamental to his investigation and analysis is the philosophical outlook of the Scandinavian school of jurisprudence, which demands a total rejection of metaphysical speculation and a concentration on the 'real, objective facts' of legal life.

Hägerström, Olivecrona's mentor, had suggested that the reasons for the recognition of abstract conceptions of rights might be traced to historical and psychological sources; the former were to be found in ancient, arcane rituals, the latter were exemplified by the emotional 'power' experienced by an individual who believes that he has 'a just claim'. Olivecrona explores the psychological sources of 'rights', viewing the concept as a 'non-verifiable idea' which, however, could be explained in terms of the *fact* of those psychological feelings which move individuals to action. He considers the commonplace, paradoxical fact that individuals speak of 'rights' as though they exist, but rights cannot be shown to have 'existence'. The citizen is convinced that he possesses a variety of rights and duties – the right to vote and to receive his pension, the duty to repay loans and to refrain from stealing. He is *aware* that institutions exist for the purpose of adjudicating on disputes arising from an invasion of one's rights or a neglect of some duties. Yet, Olivecrona asks, where *are* the empirical realities of 'rights' and 'duties'?

Olivecrona examines and rejects the Benthamist relationship of 'rights' and 'duties'. Bentham had said that it is by creating duties, and by nothing else, that the law creates rights. When the law gives *you* a right it makes *me* liable to punishment if *I* do something which disturbs *you* in the exercise of that right. This, says Olivecrona, is based on a circular definition – the law creates rights by creating duties, but the duties are merely obligations to refrain from disturbing rights. The concept of 'right' has been presupposed in the concept of 'duty'.

Fundamental legal concepts, such as 'rights' and 'duties', belong, says Olivecrona, to the common hoard of concepts needed by people in their everyday contacts and transactions. When we buy, sell, hire, borrow, we require a conceptual understanding (no matter how vague) of what we are *doing*. We *expect* to receive what we have paid for; we are *aware* of the consequences of leaving a debt unpaid; we act on the basis of *expectations* and *awareness*. The mental constructs of 'right' and 'duty' are, in Olivecrona's view, 'vehicles for attaining practical ends', and they enable us to receive and convey information about events in which we are involved. We make personal interpretations of the changes effected in our position within society as the result of our obeying or disobeying rules. It is our *feelings* concerning what we may or may not do which constitute the basis of our perceived 'rights' and 'duties'.

A 'right' may be viewed in terms of 'feelings' and 'sensations of power'. The existence of, say, a document of title to property creates mental constructs ('feelings') or sensations of compulsion or restraint. 'When I am convinced of having a right, I am in some way more powerful than my opponent, even if he be actually stronger.' A 'right' has been perceived. The presence of these feelings may be explained as impressions passed, visually or auditively, to the mind and creating the illusion that we have power over some object. Illusion stems from emotional background. Under certain conditions, particularly in situations of conflict, the idea of possessing a right produces a feeling of strength. The subjective ideas of right cannot be excised from a consideration of 'law as fact'; their existence is a fact of psychological interpretation – but no more.

'Rights' as mental constructs may have, according to Olivecrona, two functions, directive and informative. The 'directive function' of a 'right' results from the part it plays in, say, commercial transactions when it directs human behaviour. It erects signposts needed to guide conduct. Responses to perceived 'rights' ('You have a right to this property and, therefore, I must react in a certain way') become part of general practices.

Eventually these practices may be backed by the power of the state. The 'informative function' of 'rights' is evident where, for example, a person is told: 'This house belongs to X.' It is not possible, argues Olivecrona, to explain *precisely* what this statement means without referring to the 'rights' of property. The use of the concept 'right' is needed to provide information as to the *nature* of X's title.

'Right' is, therefore, in Olivecrona's reasoning, little more than a useful mental construct. It exists as a 'fact' solely in terms of the 'feelings' its use engenders.

Olivecrona applies his non-metaphysical style of investigation to a study of the rules of law, which he perceives as essentially mental constructs. In general, he declares, it is possible to consider rules of law as 'ideas of imaginary actions'. To apply the rules of law involves using these imaginary actions as *mental models* for actual conduct when corresponding situations are seen to occur in real life.

Is a rule of law a 'command', in the accepted sense of that term? May we correctly interpret, for example, s 78(1) of the Criminal Justice Act 1991 ('Any person who assaults a court security officer acting in the execution of his duty shall be liable to ... a fine ... or imprisonment ... or to both') as a 'command' not to perform a specified act? Olivecrona is doubtful. A 'command', he claims, pre-supposes one *person* who commands, and another to whom the command is addressed. But the enormous quantity of rules in the law of a modern state cannot be said to represent the commands of any one human being; this is why such commands are ascribed to the state. Yet the state cannot be said to 'command'. The expression is a loose statement indicating, in reality, that the commands are given by persons 'active in the organisations' of the state. The command relating to refraining from assaulting a court security official emanates from the state, from Parliament, and not from any single individual. 'Command' cannot be used here, says Olivecrona, in its 'proper sense'.

It is possible to regard the rules of law as 'independent imperatives'. Although Olivecrona believes that the rules are not real 'commands', they are given in the imperative form ('Any person ... shall be liable ...'). (Legal language, he states, is 'directive', in that its purpose is 'to influence men's behaviour and direct them in certain ways.') It *shall* be an offence for a person to perform a proscribed act. But because a 'command' in the 'proper sense', according to Olivecrona, implies a *personal relationship*, we are not dealing with a 'true' command. A true command is given by X to Y in words or gestures with a perceived informational content intended to influence Y's will and his subsequent actions. The words, 'You will perform this action', or a gesture implying 'You will not continue the activity in which you are now engaged', constitute a command which is personal to X and Y. Nevertheless, the same type of words may be used to the same effect where there are no personal relations whatsoever between the individual who issues rules and those who receive and act upon them. Clearly, the Criminal Justice Act 1991 is not issued by any one person and is certainly not directed to any one individual. It is a generalised statement which functions independently of the context of 'personal command'. It functions as an 'independent imperative'.

It is not possible, argues Olivecrona, to make a *clear* distinction between a command and an independent imperative. He suggests that as the distance between the persons involved grows, so the command assumes the nature of an independent imperative. There is, for example, a difference in immediate perceptions of the 'personal relationship' existing between the motorist commanded in personal terms by a police officer to produce his driving licence, and the 'independent imperative' of the statute sanctioning the conduct of the police officer. It is our general habits of language which allow us to think in *identical terms* of *commands* and *imperatives*. The sight of a padlocked door (interpreted as 'Keep out'), of traffic lights (interpreted as 'Stop' and 'Go'), a perusal of an Act of Parliament, are transformed into the essential features of a command or an imperative.

Olivecrona gives an example of 'independent imperatives' by referring to the Ten Commandments, divinely revealed to Moses on Mount Sinai. The words of the Commandments are said by many persons to be the very commands of God, and have been accepted as such. But in reality, Olivecrona argues, they are a 'bundle of imperatives' carried down the centuries by oral tradition and in writing. They have the form of language characteristic of a command ('Thou shalt ...'); but they are 'nobody's words'. The rules of law, Olivecrona maintains, are of a similar character. Thus, in our day, the rules of law are generally independent imperatives that have passed through a series of formal procedures, for example, in Parliament, and have been promulgated. People 'feel' that they are bound by such rules. Olivecrona would insist that they have been 'conditioned' to think about the rules in a manner which *urges* them to comply with orders of a particular type and couched in a certain format. The power of the issuing authority is perceived at all levels of social existence: ceremonies, customs and habits of traditional reverence, interact so as to produce upon citizens the 'mental context' within which imperatives are accepted as 'objectively binding'.

The binding force of the 'independent imperatives' which constitute the law is, therefore, a 'reality' merely as an idea in the human mind. But in the external world, says Olivecrona, nothing can be found which corresponds to the idea of that binding force, of those imperatives. It must, nevertheless, be taken into account in an investigation of what makes the law. Olivecrona's conclusions are a direct consequence of his rejection of metaphysics: the features of the law are discernible, but only in 'factual circumstances'. Rights, rules of law, may be interpreted as concepts within a context of facts. Divorced from this context, they are without meaning and, therefore, without significance, in an investigation of the nature of law.

Notes

Lloyd, Chapter 9; and Davies and Holdcroft, Chapter 14, include extracts from Olivecrona's writings. Harris, Chapter 8; and Bodenheimer, Chapter 9, give the essential outlines of Olivecrona's thought. Articles by Olivecrona include 'Legal language and reality', in *Essays in Honour of Pound*, edited by Newman, and 'The imperative element in law' [1964] 18 Rutgers LR 774.

CHAPTER 11

AMERICAN REALISM

Introduction

The American Realist movement developed during the 1930s from the philosophical views associated with James and Dewey. Both rejected 'closed systems, pretended absolutes and origins' and turned towards 'facts, action and powers'. James insisted upon the study of 'factual reality'; Dewey called for an investigation of probabilities in law and reminded jurists that 'knowledge is successful practice'. The realists studied law on the basis of a rejection of 'myths and preconceived notions' and on the acceptance of recording accurately things as they are, as contrasted with things as they ought to be. A true science of law demands a study of law in action. 'Law is as law does.' The three jurists noted in this chapter, who contributed to the foundations and growth of American realism, are Holmes (1841–1935), Gray (1839–1915) and Cardozo (1870–1938).

Checklist

Ensure that you are acquainted with the following topics:

- legal certainty
- law as what the courts do
- integrative jurisprudence
- judicial hunches
- law as rules laid down by the judge

Question 36

'You see how the vague circumference of the notion of duty shrinks and at the same time grows more precise when we wash it with cynical acid and expel everything except the object of our study, the operations of the law': Holmes.

In what ways does this observation characterise Holmes' view of the 'path of the law'?

Answer plan

Holmes exerted very great influence as a jurist and a long serving member of the Supreme Court. He inspired the American Realist movement with a jurisprudential theory based on the need to 'think things, not words'. The examination of facts must dominate legal investigation. The object of a study of the law is 'prediction', that is, 'the prediction of the incidence of the public force through the instrumentality of the courts'. The study of the law's operations demands that the positive law be kept in focus and that it be investigated in a methodical, realistic fashion. The following skeleton plan is used:

Introduction – Holmes' emphasis on objective investigation – importance of removing extraneous factors from an investigation – law as more than mere logic – operations of the courts – criticisms of Holmes' approach – conclusion, significance for Holmes of pragmatism.

Answer

More than a century has passed since Holmes (1841–1935) published *The Path of the Law* (1897), which assisted in the provision of a theoretical basis for American Realism. Holmes, whose long career included 30 years as a member of the Supreme Court (an experience which contributed to his declared views on the significance of the judiciary in the American legal process), stressed that the essence of the 'realist' contribution to jurisprudence was to be found in the careful *examination and verification of factual data*. Concepts incapable of verification (such as 'the vague notion of duty') had to be scrapped. The jurist should be guided by what a contemporary of Holmes referred to as 'the humility of the experimental scientist' who wastes no time in worrying about the absence of 'ultimates'. In Holmes' early writings, such as *The Path of the Law*, there is emphasis on the need to identify problems and to investigate them by keeping one's observations uncontaminated by irrelevancies. The application of 'cynical acid' should remove extraneous factors, allowing the true form and proportions of problems to emerge. By studying the real operations of law, one would discover the facts which constituted 'the law'.

This quasi-scientific approach involved a deliberate exclusion from the pattern of study of 'every word of moral significance'. (It is not surprising to note that Holmes rejected 'the muddled metaphysic of the concept of natural law'.) This was not to suggest that society's moral standards were of no consequence. They were, however, rarely significant for an analysis of *operational* matters. Indeed, Holmes suggested, it might be advantageous for the jurist if he were to use only words which could carry legal ideas uncoloured by matters outside the law.

Holmes illustrated the importance of 'dissolving' extraneous irrelevance, by reference to the notion of 'legal duty'. We have filled the word 'duty' with a content drawn from morality. But when we wash away from the phrase 'legal duty' its moral overtones, we are left with 'duty' viewed in terms of the *consequences* for those who break the law. It is what the law *does* (as seen in sanctions, for example) that gives 'duty' its real meaning and significance. The law of contract provides further examples of confusion engendered by the use of 'moral phraseology'. The concept of 'irrefragable undertakings', with its high-sounding overtones of moral purpose, should be washed away from any study of the principles of contract as known to business men. Remove the irrelevancies and discover the realities of the contractual relationship: this is the guidance to be given to those who seek to discover the meaning of the law.

Holmes considers it necessary to expose as a fallacy, which has seriously affected investigation of the law, the notion that 'the only force at work in the development of the law is logic'. On the contrary, *the life of the law has been, not logic, but experience.* In a very broad sense, he argues, it may be true that the law is partly the result of some kind of logical development, but the danger is in a confusion among jurists relating to the *logical format* of a judicial decision and the inarticulate, unconscious attitudes of judges as to the relative worth and significance of competing claims. The language of logic, which may be used to provide the 'wrappings' of a judicial decision, may mask 'the very root and nerve' of unconscious determinants of legal judgments. To understand the precise reasons behind a judgment requires, in Holmes' colourful language, the use of an 'acid' of an investigation which will 'eat away' expressive formalities and the confusion of logic with legal principle, exposing at the heart of the problem a shifting array of preferences and values – often unacknowledged.

In *The Common Law* (1923), Holmes repeats and elaborates his injunction to jurists to discount the part supposedly played by logical reasoning in the courts' processes of adjudication. The rules by which men should be governed may owe something to formal modes of logical expression (such as the syllogism), but this must not be exaggerated. The role played by the perceived 'necessities of the time', prevalent political ideologies, intuitions concerning public policy, shared prejudices, cannot be over-emphasised in considering the basis of the law. Indeed, law may be seen as the embodiment of a nation's long development; it cannot be interpreted merely in terms of logic. Hence, it is important that lawyers and judges be well acquainted with the historical and social contexts of the law they administer. To be a master of the law, one must master the branches of knowledge that lie *next to it*. Anthropology, history, should not be neglected by the jurist, since 'In order to know what is, we must know what it has been, and what it tends to become'.

Holmes stated clearly what he understood by 'the law'. In his celebrated epigrammatic definition, which became one of the starting points of American 'functional' jurisprudence, he notes: *'The prophecies of what the courts will do in fact, and nothing more pretentious, are what I mean by the law.'* This is an application of the doctrine of 'washing away with cynical acid' the so called 'logical certainties', and the 'moral essence', of the law. Concentrate upon the law in action; the data produced will lend themselves to an interpretation of law *as reality*.

It has been objected repeatedly that Holmes' observation is, simply, incorrect. Cohen, in his analysis of 'definition in law', suggests that the real test of a definition is whether it is useful or useless. The words of a definition carry their own problems of ambiguity. 'What courts do' is a phrase heavy with a variety of meanings. Does it have equal application to *all* types of court? The magistrates' courts as well as the House of Lords? Is there a significant distinction between what courts *do* and what they *say*, given the fact that many jurists and lawyers tend to perceive most 'judicial behaviour' as verbal? It may be that the real value of Holmes' definition is in its power to draw attention to operations, to the functioning, of the courts. It is arguable, however, whether or not the definition advances our understanding of the *basis* of law. Goodhart criticised Holmes' formulation by suggesting that 'Law is what the courts do' can be no more satisfactory to the jurist than the statement, 'Medicine is what the doctor gives you'.

In an interesting extension of his argument concerning the perception of the essential features of law, Holmes suggested that if one wants to know the 'real law', and nothing else, one ought to consider it from the point of view of 'the bad man' who cares only for the material consequences which such knowledge enables him to predict. Do not, he urged, take into account the point of view of 'the good man', who may find reasons for his conduct in 'the vaguer sanctions of conscience'. The 'bad man' cares nothing for axioms or deductions; he wants to know what 'the Massachusetts or the English courts' are likely to do *in fact*. 'I am much of his mind', declares Holmes. It is the *consequence* of the mode of operations of the courts which is of importance; this constitutes, in reality, 'the law'. The events which follow on, say, failure to register a registrable land charge, under the Land Charges Act 1972, or the pickpocket's placing his hand into an empty pocket, intending to steal, as interpreted under the Criminal Attempts Act 1981, constitute parts of 'the law'.

Although Holmes draws attention to the importance of consequences of the courts' decisions, he is emphatic in his belief that the making of laws is the business, not of the courts, but of the legislative bodies within communities. He proclaims the urgency of recognising the principle that the people have the right to make, through their elected representatives, whatever legislation they feel to be necessary, given the needs of the community. Further, he reminds judges of their important duty of 'weighing considerations of social advantage'. The training of lawyers ought to lead them, and judges, 'habitually to consider more definitely and explicitly' the advantages to society of the rules they lay down. The workings of the legislature and the courts should not be seen in isolation from the societies from which they spring and from which alone they derive their significance.

To view the law in its true relationships, clearly and free from linguistic and moral overtones which distort the picture, forms the basis of the advice which Holmes offers to jurists who seek to understand the reality of the legal process. 'The common law is not a brooding omnipresence in the sky ... the United States is not subject to some mystic overlaw that it is bound to obey.' A *rational study* of law in action is possible and necessary. In investigating the work of the courts, one must keep in mind William James' insistence that adherence to the philosophy of Pragmatism involved 'looking towards last things, fruits, consequences'. Factual analysis of data from which 'cynical acid' has taken away layers of prejudice and invisible preconceptions is the key to the methodology required by jurists in their attempts to understand the path of the law.

It would be a mistake, however, to imagine that Holmes rejected the need for legal theory. The philosophy of Pragmatism, to which he adhered, is itself the product of a complicated process of applying principles to an interpretation of data. Holmes believed that 'we have too little theory in the law, rather than too much ... Read the works of the great German jurists and see how much more the world is governed today by Kant than by Bonaparte'. The 'path of the law' demands from those who seek to explore it a knowledge of legal theory, an awareness of historical development, and the continuous observation and analysis of the practical activities of the courts.

Notes

Holmes' *The Path of the Law* appears in several anthologies of jurisprudential texts; see, for example, *Philosophy of Law*, edited by Feinberg and Gross. *The Collected Legal Papers of Holmes*, edited by Laski, is a valuable anthology of Holmes' views on the essence of Realism. Lerner's *The Mind and Faith of Justice Holmes* provides an interesting picture of 'the Great Dissenter', as Holmes was called (particularly in view of his celebrated dissenting opinions in the Supreme Court). The most recent biography of Holmes, *Justice Oliver Wendell Holmes: Law and the Inner Self*, by White, contains a bibliographic essay. White suggests that understanding Holmes' life is crucial to understanding his work.

Question 37

Give a general account of the views of John Chipman Gray in relation to the nature of law.

Answer plan

Gray, Professor of Law at Harvard, was a close associate of Holmes and shared with him the approach to the nature of law which has been classified as 'realist'. He differentiated, in his principal work, *Nature and Sources of the Law* (1909) (which was based upon a series of lectures delivered at Columbia), between the 'sources of the law' and 'the law'. His basic thesis was that when judges settle what facts exist in a dispute, and lay down the rules by which they deduce legal consequences from those facts, those rules constitute the law. Gray's realist approach emerged fully in his assertion that a statute ought not to be considered 'law' unless and until it had been interpreted by the courts. The required answer should emphasise Gray's 'realism' in relation to the fundamental nature of the law. The following skeleton plan is used:

> Introduction – defining 'the law' precisely – a consideration of Austin's view of law – an examination of Savigny's theory of the *Volksgeist* – law as rules – judges and rules – the law does exist – conclusion, law as an explanation of our experiences.

Answer

Gray (1839–1915), an associate of Holmes and Professor of Law at Harvard, helped in the creation of the foundations of American Realism in his essay, *Some Definitions and Questions in Jurisprudence* (1892), and his textbook, *Nature and Sources of the Law* (1909). He defined jurisprudence as 'the science which deals with the principles on which the courts ought to decide cases', and expanded this later into a new definition: '...the statement and systematic arrangement of the rules followed by the courts and of the principles involved in those rules.' He wrote of 'particular jurisprudence', which analysed the law of a particular people, 'comparative jurisprudence', which involved a comparison of the laws of two or more peoples, and 'general jurisprudence' (which did not yet exist) as a comparison of all the world's legal systems. The real relationship of jurisprudence to law depended not upon *what* law is treated, but upon *how* law is treated. Gray brought to the development of realist jurisprudence the concept of law as that which is decided by *the judges*. Statute is merely a source of law until a court interprets it: the courts 'put life into the dead mouth of a statute'.

Gray seeks to define 'the law' comprehensively and precisely. The law of a state – or of any other organised body of individuals – comprises *'the rules which the courts, that is, the judicial organs of that body, lay down for the determination of rights and duties'*. Where the supreme tribunal in a country refuses to follow a given principle, then that principle is not 'law' in that country. Thus, where the House of Lords refuses to accept the principle that the term 'accommodation' as used in ss 58(1) and 60(1) of the Housing Act 1985, refers to 'settled' or 'permanent' accommodation, so that a person who leaves the accommodation is treated as 'intentionally homeless', that principle *ceases to be 'law' thereafter*: see *R v Brent LBC ex p Awua* (1995). Gray believes that, in the case of many definitions of law, 'some are absolutely meaningless, and in others a spark of truth is distorted by a mist of rhetoric'. Three theories seeking to explain the nature of the law are considered by Gray as deserving investigation and comment: each rejects the concept of the courts as the real authors of 'the law', and each views the courts as no more than 'mouthpieces which give the law expression'.

The first theory which Gray examines is derived from the views of Austin, who analysed the law in terms of 'commands of the Sovereign'. Positive laws are, according to Austin, created by state or Sovereign: they have been established by the monarch or supreme body, or by a subject individual or body exercising rights expressly or tacitly conferred by the monarch or supreme body. This concept of the law as comprising commands directly or indirectly imposed by the state may be considered as correct *only* if we accept the view that 'everything which the state does not forbid the judges to do, and which they in fact do, the state commands', even though, in reality, judges may not be animated by a desire to fulfil the state's wishes. In making a decision they may be activated by the consideration: 'What decision does *elegantia juris* or sound morals require?'

Gray differentiates '*a* law' and '*the* law'. '*A* law' is, in general, a statute made by the legislature: in this sense, the Care Standards Act 2000 is 'a law'. '*The* law is the entire system of rules applied by the courts within a state.' It is wrong to suggest that the law is merely an aggregate of single laws, each representing a command of the state. In suggesting that 'the law' proceeds invariably from the state, Austin was exaggerating; but he was correct in bringing out clearly 'that "the law" is at the mercy of the state'.

The second theory concerning the nature of the law, which Gray considers, is that associated with the 19th century Prussian jurist, Savigny, whose theory of the *Volksgeist* was applied to decisions of the courts which were seen as reflecting what existed in the 'common consciousness of the people'. It is this consciousness which 'lives and works in all individuals in common' and which begets the positive law. We can become acquainted with the *Volksgeist* 'as it manifests itself in external acts, as it appears in practice, manners and custom... Custom is the *sign* of positive law, not its foundation'. Gray is unable to accept this explanation of the nature of the law. He argues that the great bulk of the law is unknown to the individuals who constitute the community; law cannot be, therefore, 'the product of the common consciousness'. Gray illustrates his argument by noting that it is difficult, if not impossible, for jurists to interpret the American law concerning the right to recover compensation from a negligent neighbour as emanating in any real sense from the workings of the *Volksgeist*. Jurists who lend support to Savigny's theory are reminded by Gray that mass opinion may often be hostile to certain aspects of the law: thus, Roman law was introduced into Germany probably *against* the wishes of the majority of the German people.

Gray analyses, and rejects, Savigny's view of the significance of 'a separate class of legal experts' – the jurists and lawyers – who are said to 'represent the people' in the domain of thought pertaining to the law. This class is said to have 'the special task' of applying the demands of the 'common consciousness of the people' to problems involving detailed legislation. Gray insists that this interpretation of the functions of jurists and lawyers is incorrect; indeed, 'the notions of law, if they exist and are discoverable, which mostly they are not, of the persons among whom [jurists and lawyers] live, are the last things which they take into account'. Members of this class enunciate the opinions of the mass of the people no more and no less than do other trained classes of specialists within the community. (Could it be argued seriously today, for example, that Einstein and his fellow-physicists were interpreting the demands of the *Volksgeist* on the question of relativity?)

In his *Nature and Sources of Law*, Gray discusses a third theory, which suggests that the law is 'identical' with the rules as laid down by *the judges*. Rules are enunciated by the judges *because they are the law*; they are *not* the law merely because they are enunciated by the judges. According to this theory, judges *discover* the law, but they do not create it: the principles of law articulated in *Donoghue v Stevenson* (1932) ('Who in law is my neighbour?') were in no sense *created* by Lord Atkin and his colleagues, but were there, waiting to be 'discovered'.

The concept of law as pre-existent to its declaration by the courts is considered by Gray as being absurd. He asks rhetorically, but pertinently: 'What was the law on stoppage *in transitu* in the time of William the Conqueror?' Acceptance of the idea that at some time in the past, there was neither precedent nor statute, and, effectively no law on a particular matter, 'is certainly the view of reason and common sense alike'. Those who speak to the contrary and argue that law is there awaiting discovery seem only to demonstrate 'how strong a root legal fictions can strike into our mental processes'. (It is not always easy to deny, in our own day, that judges *do* create new law on some occasions. See, for example, the creation of the doctrine of equitable estoppel by Denning J (as he then was) in *Central London Property Trust Ltd v High Trees House Ltd* (1947).)

Gray urges total rejection of the 'judges-as-discoverers' theory. He asks why legal theory has struggled to gain acceptance of the concept of 'pre-existence of the law'. The answer is to be found, according to Gray, in an unwillingness to recognise the fact that, *with the consent of the state*, the courts have developed the practice of applying, in deciding difficult cases, rules which did not exist and which, therefore, could not have been known by the parties when the disputes in question arose. There is, says Gray, 'an unwillingness to face the certain fact that courts are constantly making *ex post facto* law'. The reality of the situation necessitates recognition of the function of a judge as not mainly to make declarations of the law, but 'to maintain the peace by deciding controversies'. He cites with approval the words of Bishop Hoadley, preaching in 1727 in the presence of George I: 'Whoever hath an absolute authority to interpret any written or spoken laws, it is he who is truly the lawgiver to all intents and purposes, and not the person who first wrote or spoke them.'

Where a judge is called upon to settle a dispute of a nature which has not been discussed previously by the courts, he has to attempt to make his decision on the basis of *principle*, not personal whim. He will lay down an appropriate rule, which proves acceptable in the circumstances. Future cases which turn upon similar or analogous facts will be decided, other things being equal, with that rule in mind. *That rule is the law*. But the parties to the original case were not aware, and, indeed, could not have known, of their rights and duties as set out in the decision. It is, says Gray, 'solemn juggling' to deny the reality of judge-made *ex post facto* law. (An interesting example may be seen in the judgment of the House of Lords in *White v White* (2000), in which a consideration of s 25 of the Matrimonial Causes Act 1973 has effectively 'created law' in relation to the division of matrimonial assets.)

Gray's jurisprudential writings were based largely on his interpretation of American law, and it is interesting to note how his concept of judge-made law may be applied to English common law principles. In *Jones v Secretary of State for Social Services* (1972), Lord Simon commented on the development of common law principles in a manner which is highly relevant to Gray's general arguments:

> In this country, it was long considered that judges were not makers of law but merely its discoverers and expounders. The theory was that every case was governed by a relevant rule of law, existing somewhere and discoverable somehow, provided sufficient learning and intellectual

rigour were brought to bear. But once such a rule had been discovered, frequently the pretence was tacitly dropped that the rule was pre-existing, for example, cases like *Shelley's Case* (1581), *Merryweather v Nixan* (1799) ... were (rightly) regarded as new departures in the law. Nevertheless, the theory, however unreal, had its value in limiting the sphere of lawmaking by the judiciary (inevitably at some disadvantage in assessing the potential repercussions of any decision, and increasingly so in a complex modern industrial society), and thus also in emphasising that central feature of our constitution, the sovereignty of Parliament. But the true, even if limited, nature of judicial lawmaking has been more widely acknowledged of recent years.

The concept of the judge as an *investigator* of 'the reasons why the law should be so or otherwise', in the style of a scientist investigating the laws of nature, is unacceptable to Gray. In a memorable passage in his *Nature and Sources of Law*, he examines the view that mistakes by judges assist in the eventual discovery of 'the truth', as is the case in the natural sciences. This, he claims, is based upon a false analogy. The difference between the judges and Sir Isaac Newton is this: a mistake by Newton in calculating the orbit of the earth 'will not send it spinning round the sun with an increased velocity'; but if the judges come to a decision which is wrong, it is, nonetheless, law. 'The planet can safely neglect Newton, but the inhabitants thereof have got to obey the assumed pernicious and immoral rules which the courts are laying down, or they will be handed over to the sheriff.'

The rules of conduct laid down by the courts of a country are, according to Gray, conterminous with the law of that country, 'and as the first change, so does the latter along with them'. Those who are given authority by the community to *interpret* its law and to enunciate what the law is, are, in truth (in Hoadley's words) 'the lawgivers'. There is no need to look beyond this fact in a search for the nature of law. Nothing will be gained in attempting to discover the sources and purposes of some mysterious entity called 'the law' and *then* to state that this law is expressed with precision in the rules used in the settlement of disputes by the courts. It is much better to call the rules themselves 'the law'.

The law is, then, no mere 'ideal': it does actually exist. 'It is not that which is in accordance with religion, or nature, or morality; it is not that which ought to be, *but that which is.*' The essence of law is derived from the existence of the state which is in being in order to protect and extend human interests, and that is to be achieved through the medium of individual rights and duties. If a state existed in which every citizen was totally aware of his rights and duties and those of all other citizens, the state would not require a judicial system; an administrative apparatus would suffice. This, however, is not a reflection of reality. The determination of rights and duties often requires judicial decision; this necessitates an integrated system of courts and judges. In these circumstances, judges will be expected to lay down rules 'according to which they decide legal consequences from facts'. *These rules are the law.*

Gray's outline of the nature of the law is a sparse, systematic account of law 'in the real world'. Concepts are no more than human artefacts, and the mode of investigation which will enrich jurisprudence requires, according to his approach, a 'reduction' of the problems to be examined to the essence of the evidence which is the basis of our beliefs. Gray cites with approval the principle attributed to the early empiricist, William of Ockham: 'Entities should not be multiplied beyond necessity.' Law will yield up the essence of its nature and sources through an examination of *what is*, and realist jurisprudence requires as a basis of its methodology the investigation only of those legal phenomena which will explain *our experiences* in the world.

Notes

Extracts from Gray's works are given in *The Nature and Process of Law: An Introduction to Legal Philosophy*, edited by Patricia Smith. His work is considered in *Jurisprudence – Its American Prophets*, by Reuschlein. In a review of Gray's *Nature and Sources of the Law*, by Vance ((1922) 32 Yale LJ 210), there is a suggestion that Gray may have failed to perceive the real dimensions of the problem he was investigating.

Question 38

What does Cardozo tell us about the nature of the judicial process?

Answer plan

Cardozo (1870–1938) was a very successful New York lawyer who became Chief Judge of the Court of Appeals for the State of New York in 1917. He was appointed to the Supreme Court in 1932, following the resignation of Justice Holmes, and served until 1938. He wrote widely on aspects of jurisprudence, basing his views on the realist approach of the 'integrative jurisprudence' school, whose members stressed the importance of viewing the aims and procedures of the law in relation to specific social conditions. A humanitarian and liberal, Cardozo's thinking concentrated in large measure on the tasks and responsibilities of the judge. The following answer plan is suggested:

> Introduction – Cardozo and integrative jurisprudence – the task of the judge – the significance of the will of the judge – precedent and its importance for the legal process – the essence of rational coherence in the law – criticisms of Cardozo – conclusion, Cardozo's contribution to our comprehension of the judicial process.

Answer

Cardozo (1870–1938) was a New York lawyer who was appointed to high judicial office in the Court of Appeals, prior to his elevation in 1932 to the Supreme Court. He produced a large number of essays on aspects of realist jurisprudence and became widely known as an analyst and interpreter of the American judicial process and, in particular, the role of the judge. He was one of a number of jurists who participated in the work of the 'integrative jurisprudence' school, founded by Hall, which had as its general outlook the utilisation of a 'realist' approach, based upon some findings of legal sociology. The basis of the 'integrated approach' was the search for 'adequacy' in legal philosophy. 'Adequacy' requires of jurisprudence 'ultimacy', 'comprehensiveness' and 'consistency'. An adequate legal philosophy will be constructed on simple ideas that are intellectually defensible; it will take account of all significant aspects of legal problems and will produce a coherent and consistent general theory. This approach characterised Cardozo's analysis of the processes of the courts and culminated in *The Nature of the Judicial Process* (1921), which was a record of a series of lectures delivered at Yale University.

Cardozo wrote of the judicial process as revealing to him the necessity for that process to show three approaches if it is to reflect not only 'the fugitive exigencies of the hour', but the necessity for the ordering of social life and its changing needs. The method of *philosophy* would allow the judge to utilise aspects of reasoning, such as those presented by the analogy. The method of *evolution* would allow the judge to recognise the importance of processes of development in the work in which he takes part and in the rules which he is expected to apply. The method of *tradition* would draw upon ideas of justice, morality and social welfare in the procedures resulting in a judicial decision. These methods are often to be discerned in the workings of the courts, and their integration into a unified approach to the problems arising from the functioning of the courts is to be encouraged. Such an approach becomes of unusual importance when the needs of society require from the judge 'the bending of symmetry, the ignoring of some aspects of history and the sacrifice of some customs', in the pursuit of justice.

The thinking of the judge affects the nature of the judicial process, often in a decisive manner. The need for his tasks to be guided by patterns of utility and morals which he may perceive in the life of the community is important. It is his task to declare the law on the basis of reason and judgment, and, where appropriate, in accordance with custom. A judgment is rarely made *in vacuo* and the judge's thinking should take into account the basic morality of 'right-minded men and women'; where this is ignored, the judge has contributed to a degeneration of the law into 'a jurisprudence of mere sentiment of feeling'. It is the nature of the judicial process that the communal support which feeds and sustains it demands recognition from the judges of the power of commonly-held attitudes towards justice, punishment and rehabilitation. Where a judge perceives that the customs of society are of unusual importance in a particular series of events, he must balance demands of custom against the specific problems of the case he is hearing. How the question of balance is to be determined necessitates the judge weighing up 'problems of experience and of life itself'.

The nature of the judicial process, Cardozo maintained, reflects the nature of the judge: his sympathies, conscious and unconscious, must not be forgotten in any analysis of his work. Cardozo's contemporary, Marshall CJ, insisted that judicial power is never exercised for the purpose of 'giving effect to the will of the judge'. In rejecting this point of view, Cardozo stressed that the nature of the judicial process could never be understood completely if the significance of 'the judicial will' were to be ignored. The Chief Justice's opinion, said Cardozo, 'has a lofty sound; it is well and finely said; but it can never be more than partly true'. A judge's consciously-held opinions and attitudes are affected by a subconscious element in his thought. In accepting this, Cardozo is aware of the problems this may create in the administration of justice. He advocates programmes of training for judges, designed to improve 'the judicial temperament' and urges that judges be made aware of the disproportionate effect of their likes and dislikes, so that the desirable neutrality of the judicial process be maintained and enhanced. He feels, in particular, that the judicial process demands, for its efficacy, judges who have been trained not only in the letter of the law, but in philosophy and social science, allowing them to see in the round the true nature of their work and the well-springs from which order and justice emerge.

Any investigation of the judicial process which ignores the significance of precedent in the growth of the law is vitiated from the outset. Cardozo acknowledges that stability in the law is one of the key determinants in the work of judges and lawyers. 'Existing rules and principles can give us our present location, our bearings, our latitude and longitude'; anything in legal procedures which suggests the presence of arbitrary whim in the rulings of the court is to be avoided. In general, there must be adherence to precedent if the law is to achieve stability and if it is to be seen by the community as based upon a principled approach. *Stare decisis* cannot be ignored as an everyday working rule. The importance of precedent in maintaining the sense of continuity which must be perceived as entering into the judicial process cannot be over-stated. At the back of precedents are 'the basic juridical conceptions which are the postulates of judicial reasoning, and farther back are the habits of life, the institutions of society, in which those conceptions had their origin and which, by a process of interaction, they have modified in turn'.

A slavish adherence to precedent is to be deplored. Cardozo gives his approval to a statement by Wheeler J, that it is essential to recognise that 'the rules of law which grew up in a remote generation may, in the fullness of experience, be found to serve another generation badly'. Where precedent provides no answer to a problem, or where it suggests an answer which is demonstrably out of keeping with the changed aspirations of the community and the declared intentions of the legislature, a judge must not hesitate to consider moving along new pathways, and this may demand, in turn, an extension, or even rejection, of an existing set of rules. Where the experiences of life indicate that precedent is out of step with widely-accepted perceptions of social life, then the law must move ahead in arguing for the acceptance of new perspectives.

The creative function of the judge in the processes of the courts is seen by Cardozo as of profound significance in any attempt to analyse the true nature of justice in the common law jurisdictions. Although stability remains a key element in the workings of the law, it must not be seen to be equated with a refusal to change with the times. *Balance is all*. Acceptance of and adherence to the principles of 'rational coherence' will assist in ensuring that the judicial process is seen as respecting the need for stability *and* the need to modify, change and reject in the interests of growth of the law. It is for the judge to recognise that at any given time, there will be within the community a group of jural principles, customs, rules, canons of behaviour and attitudes towards moral questions which may cohere so as to restrain his freedom to act as he wishes. He will consider the significance of prevailing attitudes and exercise a 'rational discretion' in matters affecting communal standards. The judge is never completely free in the performance of his judicial role, and he must accept the many pressures of convention, morality, habit and the inscrutable force of professional opinion, when contemplating decisions which may be perceived as introducing fundamental change.

'Where doubt enters in, there enters the judicial function.' Cardozo notes that study of the judicial process indicates that important moves in judicial attitudes often seem to be preceded by periods of 'sustained and intense doubt' as to the relevance of parts of the law. It is then, in this period of doubt, that the exercise of the judicial function assumes much importance. The judge is faced, on the one hand, with the need to preserve the workings of society and to do nothing to affect its stability, and, on the other hand, with the need to shift the frontiers of the law so as to recognise the inevitability of necessary change. How shall the judicial process operate? 'We go forward with our *logic*, with our *analogies*, our *philosophies*, until we reach a certain point.' At that point, the judge may have no trouble with the paths he is pursuing – they will seem to follow the same lines. But they then begin to diverge and it is for the judge to make his choices, conscious of the pressures upon him. His actions will be determined in large measure, says Cardozo, by history or custom or social utility or some other vital and compelling sentiment of justice '*or perhaps by a semi-intuitive apprehension of the pervading spirit of the law*'. The principles of 'rational coherence' will prevail where the desire for change is balanced by awareness of the dictates of reason. The judicial process is, in these circumstances, highly effective where the judge balances his philosophy, logic, sense of right, and all the rest, 'adding a little here and taking out a little there [so as to determine], as wisely as he can, which weight shall tip the scales'. Where exercise of the judicial process produces a result which is widely perceived as straining credulity or moving beyond the bounds of social acceptability, the various courts of appeal, and ultimately, the legislature, will act, on the basis of principle, to overturn and nullify the judgment. In general, says Cardozo, the nature of the judicial process will be taken as 'the expression of a principle of order to which men must conform in their conduct and relations as members of society ... and the judge, so far as freedom of choice is given to him, tends to a result that attaches legal obligation to the folkways, the norms, or standards of behaviour exemplified in the life about him'. In no sense is he 'a knight-errant, roaming at will in pursuit of his own ideal of beauty and goodness'. Service to the ideals of justice and the demands of social living must play a determining role in his judicial activities.

Cardozo refers repeatedly in his writings to the significance of *Riggs v Palmer* (1889). He discerns in the decision of the New York Court of Appeals an illustration of the 'directive force of a principle' in affecting the nature of the judicial process. In that case, a grandson who was named in his grandfather's will as his heir murdered the grandfather so that he might inherit swiftly. Could the murderer inherit under the will? Cardozo drew attention to two principles favouring the murderer. First, the principle of the binding force of a will disposing of the testator's estate in accordance with the law. Secondly, the principle that civil courts may not add to the pains and penalties of a crime. To follow these principles would, according to Cardozo, offend against the universal sentiment that no person should be allowed to derive an advantage from his own wrong. If we were to hold otherwise, that would be to support a dissolution of the bonds which link members of a family. It was held that the grandson could not take the legacy under the will. Cardozo suggested that attention be paid to the judgment of Earl J, who stated: 'No man may be permitted to profit from his own fraud ... no man may acquire property by his own crime. These maxims are dictated by public policy, they have their foundation in universal law administered in all civilised countries, and have nowhere been superseded by statute.' This ruling exemplifies for Cardozo the essential nature of the judicial process: principles direct a decision, law is seen as a means to a social end and the links between morality and law are deliberately recognised and strengthened. 'Justice reacted upon logic, sentiment upon reason, by guiding the choice to be made between one logic and another. Reason in its turn reacted upon sentiment by purging it of what is arbitrary, by checking it when it might otherwise have been extravagant, by relating it to method and order and coherence and tradition.'

Cardozo sums up his analysis of the nature of the judicial process thus: an analysis comes to this and little more – that logic, history, custom and utility, and the generally acceptable standards of right conduct are the forces which, singly or in combination, mould the law's progress. Which force shall be dominant in a given case will depend largely upon the comparative significance of the social interests that stand to be promoted or impaired. A vital matter is that law shall be uniform and impartial; nothing savouring of prejudice is to be allowed. Adherence to precedent becomes essential. 'There shall be symmetrical development, consistently with history or custom when history or custom has been the motive force, or the chief one, in giving shape to existing rules and with logic or philosophy when the motive power has been theirs.' But symmetrical development may be too expensive: uniformity is no longer a good when it has become uniformity of oppression. It then becomes necessary to balance the social interest served by symmetry against the social interest served by equity. The judge's duty is then to consider a departure from existing practice where he feels that this has become necessary. Stability and necessary change are the keys to interpreting the nature of the judicial process.

Criticisms of Cardozo have centred on the suggestion that he seems to have built his theories around observation and analysis of the work of the appeals courts. Frank, in his *Cardozo and the Upper Court Myth*, states that Cardozo rarely mentions the problem of the measure of discretion resting in trial judges and juries. The 'certainty' which Cardozo appears to find in the judicial process is often absent from the deliberations of jury members involved in matters relating to the significance of facts. It is suggested, further, that Cardozo has seen the workings of principles where none can be discerned, even on close analysis, and that the 'balancing' of stability and social desires for improvement is difficult to find in practice.

Cardozo's contribution to our knowledge of the judicial process may be said to rest on his having emphasised the social nature of the law and his belief that the judicial process cannot be interpreted as though it were an isolate, a 'thing-in-itself'. Law is nothing if not a means to an end, and the judicial process must respond continuously to that end if it is to flourish.

Notes

Cardozo's writings include: *The Nature of the Judicial Process, The Paradoxes of Legal Science, The Growth of the Law*. Posner's *Cardozo, A Study in Reputation*, analyses aspects of Cardozo's fundamental thought. Criticisms of Cardozo appear in Pollock's *Jurisprudence*.

CHAPTER 12

CONTEMPORARY AMERICAN JURISPRUDENCE

Introduction

The questions in this chapter concern jurists who typify certain strands of thought in contemporary American jurisprudence. Those selected are Rawls (b 1921), his pupil, Nozick (b 1938), Posner (b 1939) and Unger (b 1950). These jurists share no common platform: Rawls and Nozick have diametrically opposite views on matters such as the distribution of wealth; Dworkin seems to be a lone figure, rooted in the doctrines of no particular movement, but owing some patterns of analysis to the early Realist school; and Posner, a judge and jurist has fashioned a theory of 'pragmatic jurisprudence'. The representatives of the Critical Legal Studies movement such as Unger, appear to be mavericks, restating the doctrines of the ultra-left in novel fashion.

Checklist

Ensure that you are acquainted with the following topics:

- Rawls' 'original position' concept
- Rawls' two principles of justice
- primary social goods
- American Critical Legal Studies

- Nozick's 'minimal state'
- formalism and objectivism
- pragmatism

Question 39

'Rawls' theory of justice is a credible, radical alternative to the conception of justice based on classical utilitarianism.'

Is it?

Answer plan

Rawls is a contemporary philosopher who is interested particularly in questions of social justice. His theory is based on the necessity of perceiving questions of justice as more important than questions of happiness (which are central to utilitarianism); what is *right* is a matter of priority, whereas what is *good* is a secondary matter. The theory of justice associated with Rawls is, therefore, in contrast to the utilitarian concept. Essentials of the theory are based on a set of limitations which must be explained in an answer to the question. The following skeleton plan is used:

> Introduction – essence of Rawls' approach – the well ordered society – justice viewed in rational terms – social contract – 'original position' and the 'veil of ignorance' – primary social goods – principles of justice – priority of justice and liberty – credibility of the theory – conclusion, Rawls' theory as an alternative to utilitarianism.

Answer

The problem of what ought to be the principles of social justice – basic to ethics and jurisprudence – is subjected to a detailed analysis by Rawls in *A Theory of Justice* (1971). An elaborate, systematic argument emerges in which Rawls provided an alternative to earlier doctrines of justice as conceived by utilitarians such as Bentham, for whom a 'just system' required legal institutions directed at the creation of 'the greatest happiness for the greatest number'. Rawls' approach is epitomised in the statement: 'Justice is fairness.' His theory is, without doubt, a radical alternative to utilitarian justice; whether it is credible is less certain.

The society which Rawls uses for purposes of analysis is a more or less self-sufficient association of individuals who stand in a relationship one to the other and which is characterised by recognition of the binding nature of certain rules of conduct which are generally acted upon. Rawls assumes that this society wishes to decide a set of principles upon which to construct 'social justice'. The principles are to be used in assigning rights and duties and in defining the distribution of burdens and benefits considered appropriate for social cooperation. A well ordered society is seen as one which is designed to advance the good of its members and is regulated by 'a public conception of justice'. Each individual accepts the principles of justice and is aware of their general acceptance. Society's basic institutions seek to satisfy these principles. Essentially, a public conception of justice constitutes the 'fundamental charter' of society. Here, at once, is a concept at variance with the doctrine of classical utilitarianism

Rawls is concerned to show that the 'principles of justice' required for such a society would be precisely those that would be chosen by 'rational persons'. The circumstances in which the choice is made give Rawls' theory a highly unusual basis. He utilises the theory of 'the social contract' to suggest that principles of justice rest on *a compact* made by society's members. The realisation of these principles constitute the very *object*, the very *reason*, of the compact. We are to imagine, says Rawls, a hypothetical situation in which those who have entered the compact are deciding a fundamental charter for their society. The people involved are rational and free, and desirous of furthering their own interests. Their initial position is one based on equality – *'the original position'*.

If the principles of justice to be decided upon are to be objective and fair, then, says Rawls, those in the 'original position' must accept *limitations* and must step behind a 'veil of ignorance'. None of the participants knows (and, therefore, acts as though he does not know) any of his special circumstances. The veil eliminates any prejudices. One's place in society, class, position and intelligence are 'unknowns' for the purpose of this exercise. Since all participants in the inquiry accept this limitation, none will fashion principles deliberately so as to suit his own particular condition. The principles of justice which emerge will be the result of a 'fair' agreement. Rawls assumes, however, that those in the 'original position' will be capable of maintaining a 'sense of justice'. They will, apparently, without question, see justice as 'fairness'.

Rawls assumes, further, that those in the 'original position' will have no information as to the particular circumstances of their society, that is, they are presumed not to be aware of its level of culture and civilisation. Nor do they know the generation to which they belong, so that they must derive principles with which *they* are prepared to live. It is assumed, however, that they know the general facts about society and that they understand the basic principles of economics, politics and psychology. 'The veil' will ensure that they are not prejudiced by 'arbitrary contingencies'.

Because the participants intend to evolve their charter of justice on the basis of rationality, Rawls suggests that the communal structure which will be evolved as a result of the reflective equilibrium of the group, will be concerned with *the rational distribution of 'primary social goods'*. These are things which every rational person is presumed to want more of; they have a use whatever a person's rational life-plan may be; their distribution is always a matter of concern. The 'primary social goods' are rights and liberties, opportunities and powers, income and wealth. For every person, 'the good' is the satisfaction of rational desire; whatever one's ends, the primary goods are, in rational terms, the necessary means. (At a later stage, Rawls added 'the most important of the primary goods – self-respect'; this would include 'a person's sense of his own value, his secure conviction that his good, his plan or life is worth carrying out'.)

From Rawls' perception of the overall 'good' and his view of 'primary goods' comes his belief that there will emerge from the deliberations of those in the 'original position', two vital principles of justice. *The first principle will be a resounding affirmation of equality and fairness as basic to justice.* Each individual must have an equal right to the most extensive total system of equal, basic liberties compatible with a similar system of liberty for all (a principle similar to that which is basic to Mill's *On Liberty*). This involves a maximisation of liberty deliberately intended to furnish maximum freedom of speech and conscience. 'Liberty for all' may have to be restricted, but *only for the sake of liberty itself*, as where, for example, freedom of speech requires a system of public order regulations (see the Public Order Act 1986, for example). The maintenance of public order must be accepted as a necessary condition for each person to achieve his ends. Further, less-than-equal liberty may be justified but only where it is acceptable to those who have the lesser liberty; resulting inequalities in one liberty must be shown to have the effect of a greater overall protection of other liberties as a direct result of a restriction (the Road Traffic Act 1988 provides an example).

(Rawls argues that persons in the original position who, according to his hypothesis, will not know their true position in society will fear that when they return to the real world, they might be slaves deprived of all freedoms. Hence, they will seek to pronounce that slavery is incompatible with justice.)

The *second principle of justice* (as amended by Rawls after publication of his book in 1971) is as follows: *social and economic inequalities are to be arranged so that they will be to the greatest benefit of the least advantaged persons, consistent with a 'just savings principle', and are attached to offices and positions open to all under conditions of fairness and equality of opportunity.* Rawls recognises that those in the 'original position' will be aware of the facts of inequality and differences among individuals and will wish to ensure that these differences do not result in injustice. There is no suggestion that wealth and income ought to be divided equally; but any unequal division will be justifiable only if *all* persons are better off as a result, that is, the unequal division is to result to everyone's advantage. The 'just savings principle' involves justice operating not only among the members of society represented in the 'original position', but among those of succeeding generations also; savings involve a recognition of the responsibilities of one generation to the next.

Rawls is aware that there may be conflicts of principle. A resolution of such conflict may be effected, he suggests, by the application of 'principles of priority'. This concept is referred to as 'lexical', that is, the first principle must be satisfied *totally* before any consideration can be given to the second. (The term 'lexical' refers to a dictionary: the first letter is 'lexically first', so that no compensation at the level of subsequent letters can erase the negative effect ensuing from the substitution of another letter for the first.) The first priority rule is *the absolute priority of liberty*: one may restrict liberty *only* for the sake of liberty. The second priority rule is that *justice shall prevail over efficiency and welfare*. In a conflict of principles of liberty and social need, liberty has an unalterable priority, and must not be exchanged for other benefits. Concerns derived from 'maximisation of utility' must give way to the overriding necessity for liberty. To depart from the principle of equal liberty cannot be justified, therefore, by the promise of greater economic and social advantage, except, perhaps, where it is necessary to enhance the quality of civilisation 'so that in due course equal freedoms can be enjoyed by all'.

The credibility of Rawls' theory of justice has been questioned persistently. The 'original position' seems so hypothetical, so artificial, and so very difficult to visualise, that it is perceived by some jurists as weakening the basis of the theory. Is it possible to imagine persons from whom individual histories, environmental links, and values have been removed? Is what remains sufficient to constitute a 'rational person' from whom reasoning can be expected? Those in the 'original position' are not in possession of data appropriate to the task of working out principles of justice, say the critics. And if, as Rawls suggests, those 'behind the veil' must be presumed to know the principles of psychology, they will be aware of the results of speculating *in vacuo*.

It is not at all certain, continue the critics, that those in the 'original position' would come to the 'liberal-democratic' conclusions suggested by Rawls. Why would they necessarily prefer liberty to equality? Why would they not invoke a 'winner-takes-all' philosophy? Suppose that some of those in the 'original position' concluded, on the strength of their 'allowed knowledge', that there can be no true liberty save on the basis of economic sufficiency, or that material goods are of relatively small worth.

There is doubt, too, as to whether pure ratiocination 'behind the veil' would produce anything like Rawls' principles of justice. Has Rawls confused 'liberty' and 'liberties'? Is it that the logic of 'liberty as indivisible' has been overlooked? And would rational thought produce, inevitably, Rawls' catalogue of 'primary social goods'?

Dworkin, in *Sovereign Virtue: The Theory and Practice of Equality* (2000), finds the device of the original position implausible as the starting point for a philosophical interpretation of justice. It requires a more profound theory behind it which will attempt to explain *why* the original position possesses its particular features and *why* the principles chosen by people in that position should be categorised as 'principles of justice'.

It is certain that Rawls has produced a radical alternative to the rigidities of utilitarianism. The exponents of that philosophy were prepared to accept inequalities if the result would be the maximisation of the happiness of the greatest number. Rawls' principles constitute a rejection of this view. He sees liberty as a means to the promotion of society's good, but, unlike the utilitarians, he is not prepared to put it aside so as to 'increase' that good. Liberty, for Rawls, is a good *in itself* and may not be limited save in the few circumstances he mentions. This is indeed a radical alternative to the simplistic views of utilitarianism; whether it is 'credible', given the hypothetical circumstances postulated by Rawls as necessary for the emergence of principles of justice, must remain arguable.

Notes

Lloyd, Chapter 6; Dias, Chapter 22; Riddall, Chapter 12; and Harris, Chapter 20, contain outlines of Rawls' theory. A useful introduction to the fundamentals of Rawls' views is given in *Reading Rawls*, edited by Daniels. *John Rawls' Theory of Justice* by Blocker and Smith is a complete exposition of the theory. Wolff analyses the theory in *Understanding Rawls: A Reconstruction and Critique of A Theory of Justice*. Davies and Holdcroft, Chapter 9, explore Rawls' theory in detail. See, also, *Rawls and Rights*, by Martin, and *Modern Theories of Justice*, by Kohn (which considers criticisms of Rawls' theories). Ricoeur's *The Just* is a series of essays by a French jurist (translated by Pellaner) which include an analysis of Rawls' theory.

Question 40

'Nozick's theory of justice is really a political manifesto in the guise of jurisprudential fables.'

Outline the theory and comment on the criticism.

Answer plan

Nozick was a pupil of Rawls and rejected his teacher's insistence on the need for governmental intervention so as to achieve a redistribution of wealth. The concepts of individual libertarianism formed the basis of Nozick's view of society. Man's rights are of great importance, but their protection requires no more than the exercise by a 'minimal state' of 'night watchman functions'. Liberty and equality are not to be confused, and the right to property is inseparable from liberty. Nozick's appeal to politicians on the right of the political spectrum cannot be denied. An answer to the question involves an explanation of the 'minimal state' and a discussion of the 'fable' of its development. Nozick's attitudes to property and its distribution require comment. The following skeleton plan is suggested:

Introduction – Nozick's principal theses – right to acquisition and possession of property – creation of the 'minimal state' – distributive justice – Nozick's appeal to the political right wing – criticism of Nozick's 'poetic fantasies' – his 'taxation and forced labour equivalence' – conclusion, criticism of Nozick's 'parable of individuality'.

Answer

A 'just society', according to Nozick, is one based on *individualism*. The natural rights of the individual are to be considered inviolable, and each person may enjoy those rights subject only to certain moral 'side restraints' concerning the rights of others. The only type of state which is acceptable to those who believe in the virtues of liberalism is that which functions in a *minimal mode*; attempts by the state to redistribute wealth are generally unjustifiable and it is very doubtful whether liberty and equality are always compatible. These are the theses elaborated by Nozick in *Anarchy, State and Utopia* (1974). Ideas of this type have been used to underpin some political ideologies that have emerged in Western societies in recent years, but it is doubtful whether Nozick intended to produce a political manifesto as such. It is the *basis* and the *implications* of his ideas which have produced criticism from jurists and others.

Nozick assumes for purposes of his theory that persons exist as 'distinct entities'. Adopting and adapting Locke's fable of the 'state of freedom' which accompanied the 'state of nature' in which man originally existed, he draws attention to the 'law of nature' which allows no individual to act in ways which brought harm to another's life, liberty or possessions. We have our 'natural rights' – freedom from violence against the person, freedom to hold property and freedom to enforce our rights against those who violate these basic freedoms. The freedom to hold property is based on 'legitimate acquisition': *just initial acquisition*, by which an individual acquires the ownership of that which was previously unowned; *legitimate transfer*, for example, by gift, exchange; and *rectification of former unjust distribution*, as where a person has obtained property unjustly and it has been returned to its proper owner. *'Justice in holdings'* (in acquisition, transfer and rectification) constitutes the individual's natural right to possessions.

None of these rights may be interfered with in the absence of the individual's consent. A person's 'distinctiveness' ensures that he ought not to be treated as a means to an end; hence, the concept of one person's natural abilities being available for exploitation merely for the benefit of, say, those within society who lack some advantage, is unacceptable. There can be no justice where social 'goals' or 'end state' demand that one person may claim rights in another. No individual has a right to something the realisation of which requires the use of things, and activities, involving other individuals' rights and entitlements. 'There is no justified sacrifice of some of us for others.' We may have a right to life (that is, the right not to be deprived of it by others), but not to the means needed to sustain life.

If goal-based societies are to be rejected, what principle ought to be favoured in the search for justice? Nozick suggests the principle of 'historical entitlement'. In order to test the presence of justice within a society, it is necessary to ask whether that society emerged in 'just fashion', whether its workings infringe rights and whether property is acquired and held there on the basis of 'justice in holdings'. The touchstones are, according to Nozick, total respect for individual rights and the existence of moral 'side constraints', forbidding any actions which negate individual rights. The right to liberty, the right to property, are interdependent: take away one, and the other is rendered meaningless. (It is interesting to note that in 1830, Bentham had argued that property and law 'are born and must die together'.) An important expression of the individual's right to liberty is to be found in his right to acquire and keep property; indeed, says Nozick, an extension of private property may be interpreted as a growth of freedom.

What of the state in Nozick's theory? He approves only of the 'minimal state' which, he suggests, best realises the aspirations of many libertarian visionaries. 'The minimal state is inspiring as well as right.' He sees the 'minimal state' as expressing an 'invisible hand process' (the phraseology is that of Adam Smith, who used it to personify 'beneficent Providence'), which allows development of society without the violation of individual rights. Nozick uses his 'state of nature' fable to show how the 'minimal state' emerges. Initially, groups formed for themselves 'mutual protection associations' in which each member acted so as to defend all other members of the association. Eventually, there emerged 'protection agencies', paid for their services, acting as 'protection associations', and dealing with complaints by association members against one another. Conflicts among protection associations began, and one association emerged as the strongest and, therefore, dominant. Outside the protection associations were, of course, 'independents' who chose initially not to join. Finally, the dominant protection association agency took over control of all persons within its area of operations; the 'independents' received compensation for their loss of independence by being allowed to join the dominant association. The state was born. It has since developed in spontaneous fashion, its growth mirroring the self-interest of individuals.

The 'minimal state' is, in effect, no more than a 'night-watchman state': it operates only on a range of minimal activities. It will protect from force, fraud and theft; it will enforce contracts; it enjoys a monopoly of force; but it will not become involved in any form of economic redistribution. It has come into existence by morally permissible means and without violation of anyone's rights; it must operate so as to keep those rights inviolate. Nozick rejects any growth of the state beyond these narrow confines. That there ought to be a state is unquestioned, and to argue otherwise is to plunge into the errors of anarchy; but that there ought to be a 'supra-minimal state' is unacceptable, if liberty is to prevail.

Nozick's rejection of any form of state other than that of the 'night-watchman' type emerges in his attitude to 'distributive justice', that is, where poorer, weaker citizens are assisted through the fruits of taxation and redistribution of resources. This is unacceptable to Nozick. The 'difference principle', advocated by

Rawls, which allows an arrangement of economic and other advantages so as to assist those who are less well-off, is perceived as an unwarranted interference with the norms of distribution and a violation of individual liberties. Indeed, a state which acted in this way so as to effect a 'patterned distribution of wealth' is to be regarded as intrinsically immoral. The task is not to redistribute resources, but rather to protect persons' rights to what they already possess. If an individual has obtained his property by 'just initial acquisition', he is entitled to keep it and it may not be utilised by others through a process of redistribution, save by his agreement. Where each person's holdings are just, then the total set of holdings is just. The 'fair redistribution of resources' is, in Nozick's eyes, a mask for the violation of liberty.

In a celebrated aphorism, Nozick states that taxation of earnings of labour is on a par with forced labour. To take the earnings of, say, x hours of labour is like taking x hours from the person; it is like forcing that person to work x hours for the purposes of another, to ends not his own. The fact that others may intentionally intervene to threaten force to ensure that taxes are paid makes the tax system equivalent to forced labour. Those who create wealth have inviolable rights over its possession and utilisation. Redistribution on grounds of 'social justice', 'difference principles', 'welfare claims', is essentially unjust. Justice does not exist where processes involving redistribution of property or its fruits without consent are common.

Nozick's thesis, appearing at a period in American history during which legal, political and ethical argument seemed to be moving ineluctably in favour of an increased degree of state intervention, was unpopular among many jurists. On the agenda of public discussion were topics such as socialised medicine, free legal aid, improved welfare benefits and positive 'reverse discrimination' in favour of disadvantaged ethnic communities, all of which pointed to the need for intensified government intervention and a redistribution of social resources. Nozick's parable of the 'minimal state' and its social and legal consequences were highly unpopular. It was suggested by one lawyer that a subtitle for Nozick's book might be 'Forward to the 1770s', referring, presumably, to the period which saw the publication of Adam Smith's *Wealth of Nations*, with its emphasis on economic libertarianism. But it is not easy to accept the view that Nozick's writings constitute a political manifesto for the right wing. The fact that they may have given ideological comfort to those who espouse the politics of non-interventionism is no more proof of the 'political manifesto' charge than the purloining by the Nazis of extracts from the writing of Savigny is proof that he would have approved their political creed.

Objection has been taken to Nozick's theses on the ground of lack of supporting data; his views on the emergence of the state have been dismissed as 'little more than poetic fantasy'. There is no direct proof of the state's *evolution* as envisaged by Nozick. It may sound convincing, and it has a ring of authenticity, particularly in its insistence on 'survival' as being the aim of earlier societies. But there is little direct evidence in favour of the 'protective association' thesis. Indeed, no society has ever been created in the fashion envisaged by Nozick. Further, Nozick does not explain in convincing fashion the *derivation* of fundamental rights. Where and how did they originate? And why does his enumeration of fundamental rights exclude, say, the right to work, education and shelter? Why does he provide no catalogue of fundamental duties? Given the reciprocity and relationships without which our type of society would be doomed, would it not have been useful to postulate the duties arising 'naturally' from the right to have one's liberties respected?

Additionally, is it possible to keep a state in its 'minimal' form? Is it not mere wishful thinking to suggest that a 'night-watchman state' will not seek to grow as its tasks increase in scope and complexity? How will the 'minimal state' cope with problems of internal and external security save by a significant extension of its activities? Just as the state emerged, in Nozick's terms, by imposing restraints on the 'independents' outside the original 'protective associations', how will it be possible for a state to carry out its basic functions of 'night watchman' without infringing the rights of some individuals? Above all, how can the 'minimal state' be *controlled* by those on whose behalf it operates?

Nozick's 'discovery' of an equivalence of taxation and forced labour has been dismissed as a delusion. Thus, taxation can be avoided by a person's freely choosing not to undertake taxed employment; 'forced labour' arises from no free choice. Taxation may be viewed legitimately as a contribution to the welfare of others; forced labour is in no sense a contribution of this nature. Taxation is not an undignified violation of human rights; forced labour robs the individual of dignity and rights. Similarly, Nozick's claim that an extension of ownership of private property increases liberty may exemplify the error, pointed out by many contemporary jurists, of assuming that the conditions of freedom for *single* individuals can be defined *before* considering conditions of freedom for *all* individuals within a community. What is the nature of the 'freedom' enjoyed by a minority of individuals within a community which deprives the majority of its citizens of dignity?

It may be that Nozick's 'parable of individuality' rests on his refusal to accept that 'no man is an island entire of itself'. His concept of 'inviolable, individual rights' seems to ignore the social setting which is required to give substance to those rights. The relationship of rights and duties is indeed fundamental to our type of society. A perception of redistribution of social resources as invariably 'unjust' acts, it has been said, as a justification of a society without charity, philanthropy and compassion. The rejection of redistribution, in the form of welfare activities by the state, will, it is argued, rob sections of the community of the 'meaningful life' (which can be moulded in accordance with individual choice) to be found at the very heart of Nozick's philosophy. Nozick's elevation of individualism guided by the 'minimal state' is probably of limited value for an understanding of the complex web of rights, duties, relationships and reciprocity which we term 'society'.

Notes

Lloyd, Chapter 6; Riddall, Chapter 12; and Davies and Holdcroft, Chapter 11, discuss the concept of the 'minimal state'. Paul has edited a collection of essays entitled *Reading Nozick*. *Courts and Administrators: A Study in Jurisprudence*, by Detmold, contains criticisms of Nozick's theory of justice. Lessnoff's essay, 'Robert Nozick', in *The Political Classics*, edited by Forsyth and Keens-Soper, and Wolff's *Robert Nozick* explore implications of Nozick's philosophy.

Question 41

Discuss the significant features of Judge Richard Posner's 'pragmatic jurisprudence'.

Answer plan

Posner (b 1939) has been described as one of the most influential thinkers in contemporary American jurisprudence. A judge, law lecturer and writer on various aspects of jurisprudence, he has adapted aspects of philosophical pragmatism so as to fashion a new approach to the very pressing problems faced by contemporary jurists. He emphasises the need for very close links between philosophy and legal theorising and rejects the views of those who are occupied with an apparently fruitless search for absolutes and 'eternal verities' in the law. An answer will set out the essence of pragmatism and will show how Posner views the contribution of his jurisprudential thought to the general approach of legal realism. The following outline plan is used:

Introduction – Posner's views on the links between philosophy and jurisprudence – essence of philosophical pragmatism – pragmatism and the problems of the law – styles of reasoning – Posner's 'Pragmatic Manifesto' – some critical views of pragmatic jurisprudence – conclusion, what pragmatism has to offer law in our day.

Answer

Posner (b 1939), currently Chief Judge of the United States Court of Appeals for the Seventh Circuit, Senior Lecturer at Chicago University Law School and prolific writer on jurisprudence and its interdisciplinary aspects, has sought to popularise the theory associated with the pragmatic approach to questions of the law. Jurisprudence is perceived by him as 'the most fundamental general and theoretical plane of analysis of the social phenomenon called law'. The methodology of pragmatism can be utilised, he believes, in understanding that phenomenon so as to concentrate the minds of jurists and judges on the real purposes of the law.

If we are to build a jurisprudence appropriate for our day, attention must be given to the philosophical fundamentals of legal theory. A systematic philosophy is to be demanded from jurists, and a refusal to acknowledge what philosophy has to offer the law is tantamount to closing one's eyes to many of the intellectual achievements of the past and present. Posner gives his approval to Bertrand Russell's assertion that a man 'who has no tincture of philosophy' will pass his life 'imprisoned in the prejudices derived from common sense and from the habitual beliefs of his age or nation'. An examination of philosophical principles will reveal to jurists the virtues of pragmatism (Gr *pragma* = deed), derived from the concept that *'truth is no more than that which "works" consistently in human action'.*

Posner suggests that the views of the early pragmatists, such as Charles Peirce (1819–1914) and William James (1842–1910), be given a sympathetic hearing. Peirce believes that if we are to ascertain the precise meaning of an intellectual concept, we should consider 'what practical consequences might conceivably result from the truth of that concept; the sum of the consequences will constitute the entire meaning of the concept'. In short, Posner asserts, the 'real meaning' of a proposition in jurisprudential argument will be apparent in its logical or physical consequences. James states the pragmatic viewpoint thus: it is astonishing to note how many philosophical arguments and disputes collapse into insignificance as soon as they are subjected to the simple test of tracing a concrete consequence. 'The whole function of philosophy ought to be to find out what definite difference it will make to you and me, at definite instants of our life, if this or that world-formula be the true one.' The pragmatist, James states, must turn from abstraction and insufficiency, from verbal solutions, from bad *a priori* reasons, from fixed principles, closed systems, and pretended absolutes and origins. He must turn towards concreteness and adequacy, towards facts, action and power.

The application of principles of this nature to jurisprudential matters will produce, according to Posner, positive results. Law is to be perceived and understood, not as an idealist abstraction, but in more prosaic, and productive, terms as a servant of human needs. Those who are engaged in the administration and study of the law ought to have as their major concern, not only the origins of the law, but its goals; they should have in mind not the search for absolute principles, but exploration characterised by 'belief justified by social need'. In the field of contemporary jurisprudence, says Posner, there is 'too much emphasis oh authority, certitude, rhetoric and tradition, and too little on consequences and on social-scientific techniques for measuring consequences'. At present, the *consequences* of law are little known; the pragmatic outlook must accept the challenges raised by 'this dismal fact'.

Posner asks his readers to note carefully the significance of the absence from his writings of any remarks which could be construed as indicating the existence of any single canon of legal pragmatism. Commandments, touchstones, have no place in the pragmatic approach. The search for a single canon is inevitably jejune. An approach to the law which involves a search for 'what works' and, therefore, what is useful, will be more valuable than an attempt to discover immutable principles. Pragmatism is forward looking; it will not turn its back on the past, however, and, indeed, sees value in those links with the past which will assist in the comprehension of the present. Thus, the principle of *stare decisis*, fashioned in the past as the very basis of legal precedent, is not to be treated in the context of duty – it is to be considered as a matter of *policy*, hallowed by time, but in no sense to be characterised as a principle for all time. Hence, Dworkin's plea (set out in *Law's Empire*) that jurists ought to allow the past some special and unique power in judicial decisions, is unacceptable. A judge acting in the spirit of pragmatism would be foolish to ignore the past, but he will apply lessons from the past so that the rules which he intends to follow shall function well in the circumstances of the case with which he is faced.

The rejection of a search for final truth in jurisprudential thought is demanded repeatedly by Posner. Pragmatists view the law's 'certitudes' as, in many cases, mere masks for 'the common sense of social concerns'. However, no pragmatists will deny a place to common sense in the processes of juristic argument. They will caution, nevertheless, against forgetting that the very frames of reference used to denote 'questions of common sense' are not unchangeable. That which is cited as evidence of common sense in today's disputes may be scrapped later as dated dogma, to be forgotten as soon as possible. Hence, the premature closure of argument and debate on jurisprudential matters will be resented and resisted by pragmatists. So called 'received wisdom' on vital legal concepts such as 'consent', 'causation' and 'vicarious responsibility' must remain the basis of continuing debate. There can be no 'final word', according to pragmatists, on a living law. Consider, for example, the fundamental shift in public opinion, within a relatively short period of time, in relation to toleration of sexual activities which, within living memory, attracted dire penalties. Consider, too, the changes in the concept of 'the reasonable man', for purposes of the interpretation of the Homicide Act 1957, set out in the decision of the House of Lords in *R v Smith* (2000). Posner himself draws attention to the 'finality' in the law relating to abortion, which was confidently expected to follow the decision in *Roe v Wade* (1973) (which turned on the right to abortion); he notes that this remains a matter for intensive debate in contemporary American society.

To embrace pragmatism is to reject the spirit of dogmatism which Posner sees as blighting debate on legal theory. Dogmatism attends, for example, the wholesale import into jurisprudence of the methodology of formal scientific method. The pragmatist will not set aside the powerful tools of inquiry inherent in scientific method; indeed, he will 'seek to nudge lawyers into a closer acquaintance with science', but he will remember the limitations of scientific analysis in any interpretation of phenomena such as law. In a similar vein, he will welcome the light which can be shed on analysis of legal activity by the use of formal logic, but he will beware the dogmatic approach which ignores the untidy 'fuzziness' of the law in action in favour of the 'either-or' reasoning based on Aristotelian syllogisms. Where theories collide and produce a wide range of problems, the pragmatist will ask: 'What practical, palpable, observable difference will a resolution of this situation make for us?' Goals, purposes, objectives, and the practical, immediate demands of the law must be at the forefront of the pragmatic jurist's concerns.

Posner asks that the attention of jurists be directed to the problems created in jurisprudential argument arising from the growth of two extreme styles of reasoning. Legal reasoning 'from the top down' and 'from the bottom up' have polarised attitudes, particularly in relation to the interpretation of statute. The process of top-down reasoning is evident where judges invent or seek to adopt theories concerning the law in a given area and use the product of their reasoning so as to distinguish or extend decided cases in order that the decisions might be seen as complying with a fundamental theory. As new cases come before the courts, that theory will be utilised in authoritative fashion so that a line of continuity in reasoning is established. Bottom-up reasoning is apparent where the text of a statute is utilised so as to create groups of 'fundamental, indispensable principles of law' from which judges may deduce 'the correct outcome' of cases which they are considering. Posner claims that either method of reasoning may produce a 'formalistic approach' to adjudication, which is harmful because it is inflexible.

The pragmatist will not accept exclusive reliance on either pattern of legal reasoning. The courts have a duty to keep in mind the welfare of society as the final purpose of the law; the very process of adjudication should demand that its end be considered in instrumental terms. Reasoning is a means to an end, and the varieties of reasoning available to a judge ought to allow him to select procedures of statutory interpretation and modes of applying interpretation to factual issues which take into account the very essence of the particular events which are the subject of adjudication. Rules, and the reasoning processes which have led to their adoption, are not 'things in themselves': they have to be viewed as phenomena arising from social development at particular points in time. Posner asks that we do not forget the purpose of rules as 'means adapted to an end' – a basic aspect of the pragmatic approach to judicial decision making.

In his essay, 'A Pragmatist Manifesto', published in 1990, as a part of *The Problems of Jurisprudence*, Posner encapsulates the concerns of pragmatic jurisprudence in eight theses. These are preceded by a general review of the problems to which the pragmatist ought to give attention. The exaggerated 'legal formalism, which, he claims, has become the official jurisprudence of many lawyers, has to be countered by investigations which will proclaim the importance of reasoning in the judicial process. Decisions reflecting mere precedent in formalistic fashion do not advance perceptions of the law as a process capable of solving problems on the basis of social realities. Reasoning by analogy, associated with formalism, has to be seen as one of many methods of reasoning; pragmatists are aware of the limited power of the analogy and seek to explain the nature of the circumstances in which it might have little relevance in the making of an appropriate judicial decision. Further, problems have emerged from the continuing dichotomy of 'natural' and 'positive' law. Pragmatists declare that 'law is best approached in behaviourist terms': there is little value in describing law merely as a set of concepts based on positivist or natural law theories. To describe law in terms of 'activity' is to argue that the positivist-natural law approaches have outlived their usefulness. Judges make, but do not discover, law, and an analysis of their decision making *activities* will expose a complexity of *behaviour* which cannot be explained in simplistic terms.

The first thesis of the 'Pragmatic Manifesto' states that there is no such thing as 'legal reasoning'. Legal questions are answered by judges on the basis of a relatively simple logic and methods of practical reasoning used by 'everyday thinkers'. The emphasis of the law on attaining stability ensures that the complex methodologies of science and the scientific attitude 'are not at home in the law'. The second thesis emerges from the fact that the consequences of law are often unknown, so that feedback (an essential feature of scientific 'systems analysis') is impossible. Hence, the very justification of legal decisions, namely, the demonstration that a judicial decision has been proved 'correct', is often impossible.

A third thesis relates to 'difficult cases'. If 'objectivity' is taken to mean 'more than reasonable', then such cases can be decided objectively only on rare occasions. 'The more uniform the judiciary is, the more agreement there will be on the premises for decision, and, therefore, the fewer difficult cases there will be.' But premises for objective decision making will continue to emerge from the judiciary's many 'shared intuitions'. The fourth thesis states that important changes in the law often result from non-rational processes 'akin to conversion'. Indeed, persuasion which is not necessarily connected with the rational intellect may produce changes in the law as much as hard reality does. A fifth thesis states that law is to be viewed as 'an activity' rather than as a group of concepts. The sixth thesis states that there is no longer any useful sense in which we may say that the law is 'interpretive'. There are no logically correct interpretations of decision making, since interpretation is no longer to be considered as entirely a logical process.

A seventh thesis states that there are no 'overarching concepts of justice' that can be used meaningfully in judicial decision making. Finally, the law is to be viewed as functional, and not expressive or symbolic 'in aspiration or effect'. 'The law is not interested in the soul or even the mind.' The argument that law alters individuals' attitudes towards compliance with social norms, as distinct from modifying incentives, remains unproven.

These views do not deny the significance of the law, nor do they seek to belittle the importance of the place of the law in a civilised community. The pragmatist is merely demonstrating that law is to be seen in perspective and in terms which are essentially instrumental. Concepts of jurisprudential thought as seeking 'the truth' are of little interest to the pragmatist: his real interest is not in 'truth', but in 'belief justified by social need'. But although there may be no ultimate truths for which the pragmatist may search, there is 'knowledge' as a useful goal. The search for knowledge in jurisprudential inquiry is important and worthwhile. Posner notes that this will involve 'the continual testing and retesting' of so called 'acceptable truths' and this may necessitate 'the constant kicking over of sacred cows'. The pragmatist will welcome therefore, continuous inquiry with no bounds set and no intellectual quarter asked or given.

Above all, the pragmatist will resist the tendency, prevalent among many legal scholars, to look backward rather than forward. The search for 'essences' in the history of the law does not possess the significance or value to be attached to a study of an existing society in flux. This must be reflected, Posner argues, in the development of appropriate skills within jurisprudence. Skills of research, statistical analysis, knowledge of foreign legal institutions and an acquaintance with disciplines such as economics and philosophy should form an essential part of the overall requirements of the jurist.

Pragmatic jurisprudence has not proved popular. It has been pointed out by Posner's critics that there are fundamental objections to the claims of philosophical pragmatism. Russell described it as 'the lazy thinker's philosophy', in which rigorous thought is cast aside in favour of an eclectic approach. The philosopher, Bradley, has argued that, in general, pragmatists have tended to subordinate cognition to practice. Moore noted that pragmatists seem to have confused true beliefs and 'useful beliefs'. In any case, he argued, the canons of utility may change over time (as pragmatists tend to forget). Some American Marxist critics have observed, somewhat cynically, that Posner seems unaware of the fact that beliefs can, at one and the same time, be 'useful' yet false. Lawyers have questioned the implications of the pragmatists' concentration on the 'results and evaluation' of legislation in deciding whether it is 'good' or not. How may we 'evaluate' the general effect of the Children Act 1989? What analytical tools are needed for the process of deciding whether the goals of the Access to Justice Act 1999 have been attained? At what point in time ought the evaluation to be made?

Further, is there any general proof which may be advanced and tested in relation to the pragmatists' claim that their methods of inquiry have been more 'productive' than those associated, say, with jurists who write from a positivist point of view or those who use the concepts of the natural law in order to examine the general direction of the law? And may there not be an element of truth in the criticism that pragmatists have jettisoned one set of certainties and then taken on board another collection of certainties?

Posner's replies stress that pragmatists do not claim to have discovered 'superior truths' in jurisprudence. Indeed, he has stressed that pragmatism is concerned only that the law 'be more empirical, more realistic, more attuned to the real needs of real people' and this does involve a revision of attitudes and a search for new directions. Pragmatism offers the law the possibility of re-interpreting the objectives of 'official jurisprudence' in the light of social realities. It offers the opportunity of re-examining the methodologies of jurisprudential enquiry by presenting arguments which seek to prevent the premature closure of debate. It seeks to re-open controversy which is considered to have been resolved. It reminds the jurist that he is part of a wide community and asks him 'always to consider the possibility of adjusting categories of thought to fit the practices of the non-legal community'. All that a pragmatist can offer is a call for the rejection of the idea that law is rooted in permanent principles and grows through the logical transformation of those principles. 'In sum, it signals an attitude, an orientation, at times a change in direction ... That is something and maybe a lot.'

Notes

Posner has not written a textbook on pragmatic jurisprudence. In pragmatic style, he has preferred to publish collections of essays in which he explores the application of pragmatic principles to aspects of the law in action. Such collections appear in *Overcoming Law*, *The Problems of Jurisprudence* and *The Problematics of Moral and Legal Theory*. Criticisms of Posner's approach are given in 'The judicial universe of Judge Posner', by Bator, in (1985) University of Chicago L Rev 1146, and 'Posner's pragmatism', by Rakowski in (1991) 104 Harv L Rev 1681. A review of legal pragmatism, by Warner, is included in *A Companion to Philosophy of Law*, edited by Patterson. Singer's essay on 'Legal Realism now' ((1988) California L Rev 76) considers aspects of pragmatism: Singer argues that 'Truth and justice are both partly a matter of experimentation, of finding out what works and trying out different forms of life. The very process of discerning the truth is not passive'.

Question 42

What contribution has been made by Unger to the jurisprudence associated with the Critical Legal Studies (CLS) Movement ?

Answer plan

The CLS movement originated in the 1970s as a grouping of radical jurists who wished to see a total change in the direction of American jurists, away from formalism and in the direction of an acceptance of the 'truth' that 'law is politics by other means'. Unger, an academic and political activist, has made a distinctive contribution to the movement's jurisprudence through his theories of law concepts and rights. These matters should be given full treatment in the answer. Attention should be paid, too, to the nature of the criticism directed against Unger by those who see his work as undermining important aspects of traditional jurisprudence and legal life, particularly in relation to formalism and objectivism. A skeleton plan might take the following form:

Introduction – the CLS Movement – Unger's attitudes to
formalism and objectivism – the three concepts of law – a
new theory of rights – the problem of a 'post-liberal society
– the crisis in legal education – criticisms of Unger –
conclusion, the nature of Unger's radicalism.

Answer

The CLS Movement originated in 1970s around a group of
American legal scholars who were dissatisfied with the general
direction of American jurisprudence, which they saw as based on
'a studied neutrality of law and false formalism'. CLS members
were convinced that 'law is politics by other means', and that the
jurisprudence they sought to reject was little more than a
justification for the status quo; it was based upon a false picture of
consensus in society and ignored the contradictions at the very
heart of that society. The attachment of traditional jurists to so
called 'legal reasoning' reflected the inability of these jurists to
accept that such reasoning was 'mere manipulation of abstract
categories'. A new jurisprudence had to be created if American
society was to be saved from a post-liberal phase which boded ill
for the development of its people.

Unger (b 1950) lectured at Harvard, quitting his post for some
time in order to join the left wing political movement in Brazil
(where he had received his early education in law) as a
'community activist'. He believed that academics should be
involved in political activity at some stage in their lives. Unger's
work seems to have been affected by the South American
doctrines of 'liberation theology' and communitarianism, a social
philosophy based on the premise that 'communities and societies
legitimately define that which is virtuous'. His jurisprudential
thought is concentrated on the categories of thinking which are
necessary for the effecting of a total transformation of current legal
theory. He sees law as contributing to the struggle for a new
society, characterised by an enlightened communal solidarity. In
that society, equity and principles of solidarity will become major
sources of normative order rather than 'mere residual limitations
on formality'. In the new society, it will be the community, and not
the state, which will be at the heart of social purpose and

structure, and law 'will constitute the chief bond between culture and its organisation'.

Unger urges CLS members to intensify the intellectual struggle against the dominant role of 'formalism' in contemporary American jurisprudence. Formalism is exemplified by the 'law as science' tradition, in which law is perceived as a body of logically-connected homogeneous principles which need to be applied in a deductive manner, so as to solve legal problems. Formalism, declared Unger, 'characteristically invokes impersonal purposes, policies and principles, as an indispensable component of legal reasoning'. This approach is contrary to the general philosophy of CLS, which views formalism as having degenerated into a mere 'game of easy analogies'. Unger underlines what he sees as the fundamental flaw in formalistic reasoning. Thoughtful lawyers, he argues, have experienced the disquieting sense of being able to argue too well or too easily for too many conflicting solutions '... because everything can be defended, nothing can ... Analogy-mongering must be brought to an end'. Unger calls for a rejection of appeals to absolutes and the use of 'iron laws' of deduction in jurisprudential thought.

The struggle against formalism must be accompanied by a campaign against 'objectivism', defined by Unger as 'a belief that the authoritative legal materials – systems of cases, statutes and accepted legal ideas – embody and sustain a defensible scheme of human associations ... an intelligible moral order'. Assertions of this nature ignore the many antagonistic principles and counter-principles to be found in practice in the legal order. Objectivism tends to hide the instabilities of society as reflected in contemporary legal scholarship. Indeed, the attachment of many scholars to objectivism has resulted in a suppression of criticism intended to shed light on aspects of the conflicts which are inherent in legal institutions and the intellectual edifices which give them support. Unger's publications urge that CLS scholars give more attention to the dangers for jurisprudence arising from modes of thinking which result in an obfuscation of the very nature of the legal process.

It becomes necessary, Unger states, to make a fundamental analysis of law in its broadest sense. Three concepts of law are to be delineated and analysed: customary law, bureaucratic or regulatory law, and law as legal order. This necessitates the interpretation of law as 'a recurring mode of interaction among individuals and groups together with an acknowledgment by them that such patterns of interaction produce reciprocal expectations of conduct that ought to be satisfied'. What Unger has in mind is 'customary or interactional law', which has characteristics of regularity in behaviour, sentiments of obligation and entitlements, and standards of conduct, rather than rules which have been carefully formulated. This first concept of law is often inarticulate and rarely expressed in any formal style.

A second concept of law which Unger styles 'bureaucratic or regulatory' has a public and positive character, embodied in rules which are established and enforced by a government which can be identified. Law of this type arises where there are clear divisions between state and society and where some standards of conduct are formalised into explicit prescriptions and prohibitions addressed to categories of persons. The existence of centralised rulers and their staffs of specialists gives the law its 'bureaucratic' nature, which emphasises the fact that legal concepts and procedures have emerged, not spontaneously, but from the deliberate imposition by government of institutions and processes. A third concept of law 'as legal order' emerges only under very special circumstances. It may be described as autonomous, and reflects a societal structure of a complex nature in which there is wide awareness of the connections between norms of behaviour and rules seen as essential for the maintenance of those norms. Unger has reminded the CLS movement repeatedly of the necessity for an analysis of society which will reveal underlying patterns of behavioural norms.

It is in his formulation of a pattern of 'new rights for a new society' that Unger has made a distinctive contribution to CLS doctrine. Many CLS adherents campaigned against what was perceived as a 'fetishism' associated with the concentration of liberal lawyers and jurists on the struggle for the extension of civil rights. This was viewed as paralysing the will of those who ought to be campaigning for the radical action needed to transform society. 'Rights-talk' merely induced passivity in the face of 'the real struggle'. One CLS theoretician spoke thus: 'Exactly what people do not need is their rights ... It may be necessary to use the rights argument in the course of the political struggle to make gains. But the thing to be understood is the extent to which it is enervating to use it.' Unger did not accept this general approach. He noted that an application of his analysis of 'concepts of law' suggested that *in the existing stage of American society*, the concern of liberal jurists and activists with the rights movement was not to be ignored. A re-thinking of the place of formal rights within society is essential if communitarian principles are to be realised. To turn away from widely held and publicised popular concerns in any area of law is to ignore social realities.

Unger sought to re-think the concept of rights in its entirety. His investigations were characterised by seeking an answer to the question: what is the precise nature of the rights necessary if members of the community are to be empowered in the task of assisting the process of change? A new set of rights, new in concept, purpose and form was needed. They would in no sense be built upon the traditional, formalised definitions which had held sway in a jurisprudence which was no more than 'a legitimisation of an adversarial and atomistic conception of human relations'. Four types of rights ought to characterise the new society. *Immunity rights* were necessary to create 'the nearly absolute claim of the individual to security against the state, other organisations and other individuals'. Each individual is to be enabled to enjoy 'a proud and jealous independence'. In practice, immunity rights will operate so as to provide all citizens with basic levels of security and welfare, allowing and encouraging them to participate fully in the work of the democratic community.

Unger's second class of rights is highly unusual in concept and in relation to purpose: he classifies them as *destabilisation rights*. Rights of this nature are intended to represent citizens' 'claims to disrupt established institutions'. It is essential, Unger argues, that institutions be not allowed to ossify, and use of destabilisation rights will raise social awareness of the functioning of institutions to a high level. Further, citizens must be empowered to prevent any faction within society from gaining 'a privileged hold'. This can be achieved in part by allowing citizens the right to require disruption of social practices and institutions that have contributed to the very kind of crystallised plan of social hierarchy and division that the entire community wishes to avoid. The third class of rights is known as *market rights*. They entitle citizens to 'a conditional and provisional claim to divisible portions of social capital' and are, for example, those rights employed for economic exchange in society's trading centres; they appear to approximate to absolute property rights. *Solidarity rights* are the legal entitlements to 'life in the community' and involve effective social relations of trust, loyalty and communal responsibility.

A large part of Unger's writings is taken up with an expression of his deep concerns for the ways in which contemporary jurisprudence and the processes of the law seem to be moving society into a 'post-liberal' phase. Trends are appearing, in legal theory and practice, indicating an undermining of the rule of law and a strengthening of tendencies that discourage reliance on public and positive rules as bases of social order. It is possible to discern 'the overt intervention of government in areas previously regarded as beyond the proper reach of state action' and 'the gradual approximation of state and society, of the public and private sphere'. Welfare state developments and the burgeoning of corporationism exemplify the trends which alarm Unger, and which, he indicates, CLS theoreticians may have neglected.

Recent developments in the welfare state have resulted, according to Unger, in a rapid growth in the use of open-ended standards and general clauses in legislation, administration and adjudication. The codification of standards and their reduction to rules has further distorted legal reasoning by removing attention from the very nature of law. Rules and regulations are seen, mistakenly, not as aspects the law in action, but as law itself. The state loses any pretence of impartiality and becomes a tool of factional interest. The style of legal discourse falls to that of 'commonplace political argument'. Corporationism involves the state in losing the consciousness of its separation from society, so that there is growing evidence of society generating institutions rivalling the state in their power. The promise of liberal society of the concentration of all significant powers in government is vanishing.

Developments of this kind are to be deplored. Unger argues that society must seek to demonstrate the need for communitarian principles, must re-fashion the autonomy of the legal order and must fight for acceptance of the thesis that 'the overriding collective interest is the interest in maintaining a system of social relations in which men are bound to act, if not compassionately, then at least as if they had compassion for each other'. The message for jurists, lawyers and students of law, who sympathise in broad terms with the objectives of the CLS campaigns, is that deep thought needs to be given to a *comprehension* of changes in patterns of social thought and action. Awareness of the phenomenon of change and use of appropriate methodological tools of inquiry presented, above all, by an understanding of legal history, are the key to preparing lawyers and jurists for their participation in the work of CLS, and the transformation of society.

Criticism of legal education is of particular significance for Unger. A new jurisprudence will necessitate a new type of lawyer and this, in turn, will demand fundamental changes in legal education. Unger accepts the general CLS critique of legal education, as enunciated by his colleague, Gabel: 'Dominant groups maintain their social position through the creation of ideologies that have sufficient appeal to win over important segments of the lower and middle classes ... capture of the commanding heights of legal ideology becomes necessary.' Unger takes this analysis to a further stage and suggests that an investigation of the law studies curriculum often reveals a view that 'a mixture of low-level skills and high-grade sophisticated techniques of argumentative manipulation is all there is, and can be, to legal analysis'. He notes the influence of the law teacher, preaching 'an inward distance from a reality whose yoke, according to accepted wisdom, cannot be broken'. Students are distracted 'by enticing them into a hierarchy of smart alecks'.

Unger's remedy for this state of affairs is drastic. It is not a matter for changes in teaching techniques or for the adoption of novel psychological theories in the training of law teachers. Debates on the use of case studies, on the advantages of moots, computerised presentation of learning material in the law libraries and lecture rooms are missing the point. What is required is a fundamental debate on the very *purpose* of legal education and the study of jurisprudence. Above all, and as a necessary prelude to this debate is the need for law teachers and their students to forsake the classroom for a period and involve themselves in communal political activities which will make clear to them the real contradictions within society and its legal institutions.

Unger has a special message for law students who appear to downgrade the significance of 'the rule of law' in their work. He does acknowledge the danger inherent in the arguments of those who see the struggle for the rule of law as of primary significance in social advance and he provides a variety of examples of the ways in which these arguments can be used to defend or obscure existing injustice. But he cautions against forgetting the concept of the rule of law as a human accomplishment of enormous importance. It is for students to keep in mind a view of the rule of law as a means to an end, and to be critical of some perceptions of that 'end'.

CLS doctrines continue to attract the hostility of those who see in their propagation signs of a crumbling of the intellectual bastions of the free, ordered society. Unger has been accused of wilfully misunderstanding the very nature of formalism and objectivism which he condemns. Weinrib views formalism as a necessary element in 'postulating the coherence of judicial relationships'. What can be the objection, he asks, to a technique which attempts to elucidate 'the intelligibility of legal concepts and institutions [which are] crucial to understanding, the content of the law'? Why, in the name of a struggle against 'objectivism', is it necessary to downgrade the significance and value of studying case and precedent, as though acquaintance with systematic patterns of past thought were an evil in itself? Posner suggests, in answer to Unger, that 'legal formalism' may be a mere 'straw man' used by CLS theorists as an all-purpose term of abuse. Many jurists continue to believe that correct answers to legal problems can be, and are, found by reasoning from authoritative texts, enactments and decisions.

Berman, in his *Law and Revolution: The Formation of Western Legal Tradition*, denounces Unger for having contributed to the widespread cynicism about law, which has led to a contempt for its values, to be found now in all classes of the population. The revolt against formalism, in which Unger has played a significant role, has led to changes in the very meanings of some important legal words and phrases. 'Public policy' seems to have degenerated into meaning 'the will of the authorities in control of a state'; 'fairness' has become estranged from its historical roots and is now blown about by every wind of fashionable doctrine. Berman states, with Unger in mind: 'Cynicism about the law, and lawlessness will not be overcome by adhering to a so called realism which denies the autonomy, the integrity and the ongoingness of our legal tradition. In the words of Edmund Burke, those who do not look backward to their ancestry will not look forward to their posterity.'

Unger has responded to Berman's criticisms by asking that they be reduced to specific arguments which he will then answer in specific terms. In general, he has counter-argued by noting that the stance of CLS is principled and directed against the loose thinking which characterises much contemporary legal theorising, and is against an unwillingness to engage in open discussion on the ends of society, its legal systems and procedures, the manner in which it prepares students for the profession and, above all, the continuing failure to accept the need to examine the matter of rights in society within the context of means and ends. It is within those areas that Unger has made his contribution to the characteristic jurisprudence of CLS.

Notes

Kelman's *Guide to Critical Legal Studies*, and Boyle's introductory chapters to *American Critical Legal Studies* set out the the foundations of CLS jurisprudential argument. Unger's principal works are: *The Critical Legal Studies Movement*; *Law in Modern Society*; and *Knowledge and Politics*. Davies and Holdcroft provide extracts from Unger's works. The effect of Unger's work on CLS jurisprudence is discussed in *Rights and Unger's System of Rights*, by Eidenmuller, 'New rights for old', in Halpin's *Rights and Law*. 'Unger's philosophy: a critical legal study', by Ewald, appears in (1988) 97 Yale LJ 665.

CHAPTER 13

RIGHTS

Introduction

In this chapter, the questions concern problems arising from the concept of 'rights'. Some jurists have referred to jurisprudence as 'the science of rights', seeking to stress, presumably, the significance of human rights in any legal system and in any analysis of the purposes and functions of the law. The questions relate to Hohfeld (1879–1917), an American jurist who attempted to 'isolate' fundamental legal concepts so as to present them in a specific, unambiguous terminology, to Dworkin (b 1931) and his rights thesis, to the circumstances in which the overriding of individual rights might be justified, and to arguments concerning 'the right to euthanasia'.

Checklist

Ensure that you are acquainted with the following topics:
- jural relations
- basic, inalienable rights
- the overriding of rights
- opposites and correlatives
- Dworkin's 'principle of integrity'
- the controversy concerning euthanasia

Question 43

'In any closely-reasoned problem, whether legal or non-legal, chameleon-hued words are a peril both to clear thought and lucid expression': Hohfeld.

How does Hohfeld's analysis of rights attempt to deal with this difficulty?

Answer plan

Hohfeld believed that the assumption that all legal relations may be reduced to 'rights' and 'duties' was a hindrance to an understanding of the law. Other basic relations (the 'fundamental jural relations') existed and required discussion and elucidation. Simple diagrams will assist in an answer to the question. The 'fundamental unity and harmony in the law', with which Hohfeld was concerned, would emerge, he claimed, from an examination of the relations between basic concepts. The following skeleton plan is used:

Introduction – Hohfeld's concern for precision in the description of functions and relations – the four legal relations – jural relations – opposites and correlatives – diagrams – criticism of Hohfeld – conclusion, Pound's reminder as to the importance of Hohfeld's analysis.

Answer

The question of 'rights' is fundamental to jurisprudence: attempts to answer the question, 'What *is* a right?' fall within *analytical* jurisprudence; the question of what rights people possess or *ought* to possess is a matter for *normative* jurisprudence. Hohfeld (1879–1917) was concerned essentially with the analysis of rights. In his *Fundamental Legal Conceptions as Applied in Judicial Reasoning* (1919), he seeks to deal with the inadequate assumption that all legal relations can be reduced to 'rights' and 'duties' and he attempts to free the discussion of rights from verbal ambiguities.

Hohfeld seeks clarification of phrases, such as, 'X has a right'. The use of 'right' in the following examples is instructive. X, who loaned money to Y, has a *right* to be repaid. X, in his capacity as mortgagee, has a *right* of sale of the mortgaged property under s 101(1) of the Law of Property Act 1925. X, accused of an offence, has a *right* to be presumed innocent until found guilty. Here the term 'right' takes on a colour (rather like a chameleon) which may change according to context. Hohfeld attempts to split up the concepts embodied in the term 'right' (in its wider sense) and to give them precise meanings by grouping them into 'jural opposites' and 'jural correlatives'.

Hohfeld analyses, in terms of *functions and relationships*, the terms he refers to as 'the lowest common denominators of the law'. These are *right, duty, power, liability, privilege and immunity*. A consideration of their inter-relationships will help in lessening the effect of their ambiguities. Thus, the term 'right' involves four 'strictly fundamental legal relations' – 'right (or claim)', 'privilege', 'power' and 'immunity'. These terms are used by Hohfeld in a specialised sense that is often at variance with popular usage – as in expressions such as, 'He has a *right* to his point of view', 'It is a *privilege* to be taught by X', 'They seized *power* in 1917', 'This drug gives *immunity* against ...'.

By 'right', Hohfeld has in mind 'a claim': everyone is under a legal duty to allow A to perform some action, and A has a *claim* to enforce his right of performance. B has a 'claim right' in his capacity as landlord to receive a stipulated rent from C; he may enforce that right against those such as D, who seek to prevent its exercise. By 'privilege' is meant E's freedom to do, or refrain from doing, some act (E 'may' perform an act, if he so desires). F, in his capacity as landlord, may – but need not – grant leases; in general, no one has a claim on him should he decide to exercise, or not to exercise, his privilege. By 'power', Hohfeld means that G has freedom to perform some act which may alter his and others' legal rights and duties, whether or not G has a claim or privilege. An example is G's power to sell his property. By 'immunity', Hohfeld refers to the relation of H to I when I has no legal power to affect one or more of the existing legal relations of H.

Hohfeld proceeds to construct and analyse a scheme of 'jural relations' based on 'opposites' and 'correlatives'. The term 'jural opposites' may be illustrated by 'right and no-right', or 'immunity and liability'. In Hohfeld's scheme, no pair of opposites can co-exist in the same person: thus, if P has a privilege in relation to the sale of his house, he cannot have a duty in relation to the same subject matter at the same time. The 'jural opposites' are designated as 'right and no-right', 'privilege and duty', 'power and disability' and 'immunity and liability'.

The 'jural opposites' may be explained further. Should X have an enforceable claim to performance (action or forbearance) by Y, that is, a right, he is precluded from having a non-right in relation to Y concerning the same matter. Hohfeld speaks of non-right as a legal relationship involving a person on whose behalf society is not commanding some particular conduct or other. Where X has a privilege, for example, the right to sell or not to sell his property, that cannot co-exist with a duty (an act the opposite of which would constitute a legal wrong) to sell. Should X enjoy a power, that is, the freedom to alter legal relationships, he cannot be under a simultaneous disability which, in effect, forbids him to effect the alteration. Should X have an immunity as against Y, he cannot have a liability in relation to Y on the same matter at the same time. Hohfeld refers to 'disability' as the relationship of X to Y when, by no voluntary act of his own, can X extinguish one or more of the existing legal relations of Y. 'Liability' means, in his terms, 'the relation of X to Y where X may be brought into new legal relations by the voluntary act of Y'.

'Jural correlatives' may be illustrated by X's right against Y, whereby Y shall stay off X's land. The correlative of X's right is Y's duty not to enter. The correlative of X's privilege of entry on his land is Y's 'no-right' that X shall not enter. Where X enjoys a power, the correlative is a liability. Where X possesses an immunity, the correlative is a disability. Each 'pair' of correlatives must exist as a related unity; hence, if X has one of the pair, some other person (for example, Y) must have the other. The 'pair' is an expression of the relation of X to Y and of Y to X.

Jural opposites and correlatives may be summarised thus:

Opposites	right	privilege	power	immunity
	no-right	duty	disability	liability
Correlatives	right	privilege	power	immunity
	duty	no-right	liability	disability

Jural relations may be illustrated by the following diagram. Jural correlatives are connected by *vertical* arrows; opposites are connected by *diagonal* arrows; contradictories are connected by *horizontal* arrows. In the case of the correlatives, the diagram may be interpreted as indicating, for example, that a privilege in X implies the presence in Y of a no-right. In the case of the opposites, the diagram may be interpreted as showing, for example, that a duty in X implies the absence in X of a privilege.

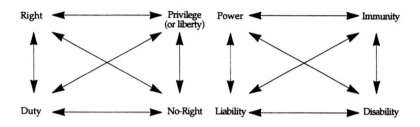

Hohfeld's aim of analysing rights so as to negate the influence of words that take colour from their context was generally applauded, but the resulting scheme did not meet with universal approval. Pound, for example, noting that Hohfeld's teacher was a celebrated exponent of Hegelian logic (which builds on 'opposites'), emphasises that the 'jural opposites' were often not 'opposites', but merely 'contrasts'. Hohfeld *contrasts* a power with the absence of a power, for example. He presupposes that there can be only *one* opposite and only *one* correlative and that there must exist an opposite and a correlative; but there may be several contrasts and sometimes *more than one* correlative. Further, says Pound, Hohfeld's scheme involves the discovery of opposites and correlatives whether or not they possess any legal significance; but, for example, a 'no-right' is not a legal concept of consequence.

Raz suggests that Hohfeld may have been in error in some matters. First, he appears to have considered all rights as *sets* of any number of the four elementary rights (right-claim, privilege, power and immunity). In fact, this is not so. To possess 'one right' may involve the possession of *other* rights, as where X possesses the fee simple in Blackacre, which gives him the right of possession, the right of alienation, the right to grant leases, etc. Ownership is, in practice, a 'bundle of rights'. Secondly, Raz comments on Hohfeld's apparent view of a right as involving a relationship between two persons, and no more. Yet this is incompatible with possession of a right *in rem* (against 'the world'). Nor, as Hohfeld appears to assume in his analysis, do all rights relate to persons only: X's right may be against a corporate body.

Criticism has arisen, too, from the attempted application of Hohfeld's analysis to the criminal law, where there are many examples of *duties* being imposed upon X, while no other specific individual has the correlative *right* relating to X's performance of his duties. Thus, a driver of a motor vehicle who drives while disqualified is in breach of a duty. But to whom is the duty owed? In whom is a correlative right vested? A general answer suggesting that the duty is owed to *every person* who may be a potential victim of the disqualified driver's conduct does not fit easily into Hohfeld's categories.

On another level, Hohfeld's analysis of rights has been criticised as no more than a mechanical exercise in logical analysis, involving an unusual terminology which has not found favour with jurists or practitioners. Hohfeld's expressed desire that judges and lawyers might be brought to a *use* of the terminology of his scheme has not come to pass. It may be that the very difficulty against which he warned – the chameleon-like quality of the vocabulary associated with 'rights' – clings to the terminology he has chosen to employ.

The positive features of Hohfeld's analysis should not be overlooked. His scheme has advanced our knowledge of concepts of 'rights' and 'duties', particularly through his specific comparisons. He has drawn attention to the legal circumstances which may flow from the existence or absence of defined rights, liabilities, etc. The practical effect of the analysis may be seen, for example, in the American Restatement of the Law of Property (1936), in which 'right', 'privilege', 'power', and 'immunity' are defined in Hohfeld's terms. Pound, in an article which is generally critical of Hohfeld, refers to the 'great service' he performed in bringing home to teachers, practitioners and judges the necessity to use caution in the employment of the conventional terms used in discussion concerning rights, and to realise that whatever we choose to call basic conceptions, they must be understood clearly. This is, to a large extent, what Hohfeld had in mind as the purpose of his analysis of rights in terms which would reduce significantly the deleterious effect of chameleon-hued words.

Notes

Hohfeld's analysis is reprinted in *Philosophy of Law*, edited by Feinberg and Gross. Lloyd, Chapter 6; Dias, Chapter 2; Harris,

Chapter 7; and Davies and Holdcroft, Chapter 8, contain accounts of the principles of the analysis. Radin's 'A restatement of Hohfeld' appears in (1938) 51 Harv L Rev. Halpin's *Rights and Law: Analysis and Theory* provides a detailed exposition and criticism of Hohfeld's views. Criticisms of Hohfeld are made in Pound's 'Fifty years of Jurisprudence' (1937) 50 Harv LR 557 and Raz's *The Concept of a Legal System*.

Question 44

How has Dworkin utilised his 'rights thesis' in his exploration of the concept of equality?

Answer plan

Dworkin (b 1931), an American jurist, holds chairs in Law and Philosophy at New York University, and Jurisprudence at University College, London. His writings in jurisprudence are concerned with the fundamental nature of rights and their significance in law and society. He is concerned, in particular, with the interface of jurisprudence and political ideas and has written extensively on current problems relating to abortion, euthanasia, civil rights and equality. His most recent major publication deals specifically with equality – 'the endangered species of political ideals'. The required answer should be based on a short account of his views relating to rights and his belief that equality and liberty are vital, substantial ideals, and are aspects of a single concept of the quality of social life. The following skeleton plan is suggested:

> Introduction – Dworkin's rejection of theories of positivism and natural rights – standards, principles, and significance of dignity of citizens of a community – entitlement to rights – problem of equality – possible conflict of liberty and equality – conclusion, affirmation of principle of integrity as basis of entitlement to rights.

Answer

Dworkin's jurisprudential writings seek to explore the essence of rights and to place them within a wider setting of social and political ideology. His work ranges beyond that generally associated with current American legal theory, in that he rejects the view of jurisprudence as a 'pure academic discipline' which should have little to say of immediate significance for political realities. For Dworkin, law and political ideology have close links: both co-exist as aspects of social aspirations and activities, and neither can be understood fully without reference to the other. Law in practice is for him 'an unfolding narrative' which can be interpreted only by comprehending its social setting. An analysis of rights, in particular, demands examination of their place within the wide culture, and very purpose, of social and political awareness.

In an examination of rights, Dworkin declares, little is to be gained from theories which suppose that rights have some special metaphysical character: the old theories of natural law that rely on this supposition are of no value. The doctrines of natural law, suggesting that lawyers tend to follow criteria that are not entirely factual when they ask whether propositions are 'true', or that law and justice are identical, in the sense that makes it impossible to consider an unjust proposition of law to be 'true', tell us nothing about the fundamentals of rights. The *a priori* reasoning associated with the natural law is unacceptable; if we wish to make an effective investigation of a legal structure and its validity, then empirical study is required.

Positivism offers no real alternative to natural law as the basis of an investigation of rights. Dworkin views it as reflecting a mere system of rules, applicable in an 'all-or-nothing' fashion. Further, the separation of law and morality, which characterises modern legal positivism seems to ignore the practice of the courts, in which questions of right are all-important, and, finally, the positivist claim that law is, in large and growing measure, judge-made, is at variance with the facts. These objections to the positivist assertion that the rationale of a system of rights is to be found within its doctrines are set out by Dworkin in the following terms.

If we examine rights in the setting of positivist theory, we are met with the assertion that law is rules, and that this is reflected in concepts of rights. Legal rules are applied automatically once appropriate conditions are met. 'Event A will bring in its train penalty B' Thus, s 16 of the Terrorism Act 2000 states clearly that a person commits an offence if he uses money or other property for the purposes of terrorism; the appropriate penalties are set out in s 22. The 'rules' of the statute dictate particular results, and, other things being equal, the statutory penalty will be inflicted on persons found guilty, under s 16. In a more specific sense of the term 'rules', the Civil Procedure Rules 1998 state that a person who makes a false statement of truth, or who causes such a statement to be made, without an honest belief in its truth, is guilty of contempt of court (r 32.14(1)). Given the requisite conditions, application of the rules then follows. But Dworkin rejects totally the claim that law consists in its entirety of rules of this nature. In making his generalised criticism of positivism, which fails to explain rights, he declares, that in making a basic attack on that doctrine, he will seek to show that the notion of a single fundamental test for law ('law as rules') misses the important role of those *standards* that are not rules.

The legal system, and the place of rights within it, requires an explanation involving not only the discrete rules and statutes enacted by its officials, but also consideration of the general principles of justice and fairness that these rules and statutes, taken together, presuppose by way of implicit justification. Thus, 'policy' is of great importance as an element of law: a policy is 'a kind of standard that sets out a goal to be reached, generally an improvement in some economic, political or social feature of the community'. Thus, the Pollution Prevention and Control Act 1998 has a clear social goal of 'preserving the coherence of our industrial pollution control systems'. To ignore communal aspirations and policies within the terms of a statute is to ignore the real meaning of law.

'Principle' is of great significance for Dworkin: from an understanding of its role stems a comprehension of the essence of law and the relationship of rights and justice. A principle is a standard that is to be observed, not because it will advance or secure an economic or political situation deemed desirable, but because it is 'a requirement of justice or fairness or some other dimension of morality'. Principles are fundamental to law; they have a dimension of weights so that it is for the courts to assess their weights in relation to a particular dispute, and to balance them. Thus, it may be necessary to balance the principle that a person may use his land as he wishes against the principle that no one may use his property in a way which inflicts injury on another. Rights may emerge from considerations of the weight of principles.

Existence of a firm dividing line between law and morality, which features in many statements of positivism, is rejected by Dworkin. A judge engaged in the task of adjudication may have to make moral judgments. The very process of balancing principles and policies may involve him in a consideration of the community's general attitudes to questions of right and wrong, which express commonly-held views on morality. Judgments ought not to vitiate social standards, and this involves, according to Dworkin, the important matter of 'law as integrity' and rights as expressing a 'community of principles'. The concept of 'law as integrity' asks the judge to assume, so far as this is possible, 'that the law is structured by a coherent set of principles about justice and fairness and procedural due process', and it asks him to enforce these in the fresh cases that come before him. For each statute that the judge is asked to enforce, he should construct some justification that 'fits and flows through that statute', and is consistent with other legislation in force.

The positivist contention that judges make law, and, therefore, have a duty to fashion rights, is not accepted by Dworkin. The judge has no occasion, he maintains, to utilise legal reasoning to produce new law (which is a task for the community's elected legislature). His task is to balance policies and principles so as to discover the correct solution to the problems emerging in a hearing. His task is to apply *principles* which may not be altered at his whim.

The law is to be interpreted as the embodiment of rights and responsibilities. Rights do not emanate from sources outside mankind. An individual's entitlement to rights in civil society depends on the practice and the justice of its institutions, political and legal. Existing political rights are enforced (but not created) by judicial decisions. Jurisprudence guides the community in its attempt to discover which rights a particular political theory assumes that citizens possess. It is within this context that questions of rights in relation to, say, freedom of speech, racial equality, have to be examined. The right of freedom of speech has emerged over the centuries as respect for human dignity has intensified. The framework of rights bolstering racial equality represents, in similar fashion, respect for fairness. Abstract rights stem from abstract principles; concrete rights are an expression of the weight of facts in relation to general principles. The courts do not fashion new rights; they tend to discover them within the existing law through an examination of an individual's entitlements under particular circumstances.

Dworkin's view of rights is predicated on his belief in the need for society to protect, through political and legal action, *the dignity of its members*. Some rights, which affect a person's individuality, should rarely be violated, even when it may appear that the welfare of society is in question. If rights make sense at all, then an invasion of a relatively important right is very serious indeed: an invasion of this nature necessitates treating a man as less than a man or as less worthy of concern than other men. 'The institution of "men's rights" rests on the conviction that this is a grave injustice ... and that it is worth paying the incremental cost in social policy or efficiency that is necessary so as to prevent it.' It is this aspect of Dworkin's rights thesis which underpins his treatment of the problem of equality in society.

In his recently-published examination of equality (*Sovereign Virtue: the Theory and Practice of Equality* (2000)), Dworkin argues that we must not turn our backs on equality, *no matter what the cost*. Our jurisprudence must propagate the argument that no government is legitimate 'that does not show equal concern for the fate of all those citizens over whom it claims dominion and from whom it claims allegiance'. Without equal concern for citizens, a government is little short of a tyranny. Equal concern for all is essential if we are to act so as to redeem our political virtue. This has little to do with ensuring that all persons have the same wealth, for Dworkin does not see equality in those terms. It has everything to do with 'equality of resources', of making available to all the resources of society, including the framework of rights which will ensure the triumph of 'ethical individualism'. Human lives must be successful, rather than wasted, and 'one person has a special and final responsibility for that success – the person whose life it is'. The principle of equality does not attach to a person's property and his property rights, but to the hope that his life shall come to something rather than being rendered ineffectual.

A government has the duty, according to Dworkin, of adopting laws and policies that will ensure that the fates of its citizens are, so far as this is capable of achievement, insensitive to who they otherwise are – in terms of gender, race, economic backgrounds. Further, governments must act through the courts and legislative institutions to ensure that the fates of citizens are sensitive to the choices they have made. Dworkin emphasises that he is interested in liberty in its 'negative sense', that is, in its relation to freedom of constraint; his general belief is that people's liberty over matters of fundamental personal concern ought not to be infringed. Nevertheless, he argues *against* the view that liberty is a fundamental value that must *never* be sacrificed to equality. In general, there should be no conflict between liberty and equality: equality is unlikely to exist in a society from which liberty is absent. But in a genuine contest between liberty and equality, liberty may have to lose out.

What are the circumstances in which rights to liberty might conflict with rights to equality? Dworkin suggests that this might arise where two conditions co-exist: first, that, 'on balance', the position of some group within the community could be improved by eliminating some existing liberty, and, secondly, that the principle of equal concern for the rights of that group requires that this step ought to be taken. Essentially, this will be a matter of balancing political and legal rights. As an illustration, Dworkin gives the example of a society in which private and state medical provision exist together. If the poorer citizens within that society would enjoy better medical care were private medicine to be abolished, then the principle of equal concern demands that this step be taken. To refuse to carry out this step implies, according to Dworkin, acceptance of the view that the lives of the poor are less important than the lives of others. The principle of liberty has little value except for the contribution it makes to the life of society; in a conflict of this nature, the principle of egalitarianism, which reflects concern for the rights of all, must prevail.

It is jurisprudential argument of this nature which has led Dworkin to emerge as a prominent supporter of policies of 'affirmative action' in the USA. Policies of this type (known also as 'reverse discrimination' or 'positive discrimination') have been defined by Katzner as 'a call to offset the effect of past acts of bias by skewing opportunities in the opposite directions'; they involve giving preferential treatment to disadvantaged groups so as to compensate for past discrimination. Dworkin sees legal-political action of this type as giving expression to his belief that there are circumstances in which the right to equality in resources (for example, the right to higher education) requires a fundamental reappraisal of the purposes of the liberty to which the community is committed.

The essence of Dworkin's teaching in this area of jurisprudence suggests that: *rights arise from the community's respect for the principle of integrity*. In his words: 'Integrity insists that each citizen must accept demands on him, and may make demands on others, that share and extend the moral dimensions of any explicit political decisions.' When the good citizen is faced with the question of deciding how he ought to treat his fellow citizen when interests collide, he must act so as fulfil the common scheme of justice 'to which they are committed just in virtue of citizenship'.

Notes

Dworkin's views on rights are set out in *Taking Rights Seriously* and *Law's Empire*. His examination of equality is contained in *Sovereign Virtue: the Theory and Practice of Equality*. Davies and Holdcroft, Chapter 10, sets out Dworkin's basic rights thesis; Harris, Chapter 4, summarises the reasoning behind the thesis. See, also, *Ronald Dworkin*, by Guest, and 'Professor Dworkin's theory of rights', by Raz in (1978) 26 Political Studies 123.

Question 45

Consider the circumstances in which the overriding of individual rights might be justifiable.

Answer plan

Arguments concerning 'inviolable rights' generally turn upon the belief that they are of an *absolute nature*, a belief which pre-supposes that there are no circumstances whatsoever in which an interference with those rights may be justified. Natural law jurists may suggest that a God-given right, by its very nature, is not subject to any violation. Other jurists take the view that circumstances are bound to arise in which it becomes necessary to override almost any rights, and this necessity is the basis for justification of the action. The answer should consider some of the circumstances in which legislators, judges and others might seek to justify an interference with human rights. The following skeleton answer is used:

> Introduction – inviolability of rights – substantial and procedural rights – restriction of rights in war and peace – competing rights – other conflict situations – attitude of Critical Legal Studies movement, and Rawls, to rights – ECHR 1950 – conclusion, problem of absolute rights.

Answer

The argument examined below rests on the assumption that there *are* circumstances in which it might be justifiable to override an individual's rights. The circumstances generally refer expressly or by implication to the existence of 'greater rights' to which individual rights have to be subordinated. There are arguments suggesting that there can never be such circumstances, that individual rights have a sanctity, a significance, a value-in-themselves which render them absolute and inviolable and that if one ignores the force of this argument, then the way is open to the wholesale disregard and destruction of those rights. To accept this argument, it has been suggested, is to close the debate before it begins. Thus, Finnis' enunciation of 'the right to life' as 'inviolable', which forms the basis of his contribution to the discussion on abortion, has been perceived as weakening the significance of that discussion. To pose the absolute nature of a matter under discussion is to render controversy difficult.

A right may be described, in Allen's phrase, as 'the legally guaranteed power to realise an interest'. Existence of the power is recognised under the law and its exercise is based on a guarantee by the law as to the acceptability of consequences. The rights of a human being may be *substantial* (right to life, liberty) or merely *procedural* (the right, in defined cases, to trial by jury, or to silence, resulting from exercise of the privilege against self-incrimination). Because rights are underpinned in practice by a guarantee bestowed by the law, it may be argued that, no matter what their nature (substantial or procedural), they can be negated if the guarantee ceases to apply. The repeal of a statute which allows certain rights to be exercised effectively ends those rights.

Possibly the most significant of the circumstances in which rights may be suspended or withdrawn arises during a period in which the security, or even the continued existence, of the community is perceived as under threat, as in time of war. Legislation such as the Emergency Powers (Defence) Acts 1939–40, and the subsequent Defence Regulations restricted some rights and imposed conditions considered appropriate for the defence of the realm during the Second World War (1939–45). The power of a government to detain individuals, with its clear effect upon rights is not easily controlled by the courts. *Liversidge v Anderson* (1942) (which concerned the detention of an individual believed to be 'of hostile origin or association') emphasises that 'the liberty of the subject is a liberty controlled by law, whether common law or statute. It is, in Burke's words, a regulated freedom. It is not an abstract or absolute freedom ... In the constitution of this country there are no guaranteed or absolute rights'.

Where the government believes that, in time of peace, the untrammelled exercise of certain rights would be disadvantageous to internal security, those rights may be limited or removed. Thus, the Official Secrets Acts 1911–89 limit the rights of certain classes of persons to freedom of speech. *Council of Civil Service Unions v Minister for the Civil Service* (1985) justified a restriction (since removed) upon the right to join a trade union of one's choice when the interests of national security could be interpreted as requiring this. Emergencies in time of peace, such as those arising in Northern Ireland, have produced restrictive legislation, that is, the Terrorism Act 2000, which proscribes certain named paramilitary organisations. The Diplock Courts, which removed the right to jury trial in some cases in Northern Ireland, and limitations upon the right of free expression, as evidenced by the decision of the House of Lords in *Brind v Secretary of State for the Home Department* (1991), exemplify the circumstances in which the overriding of a right might be considered justifiable.

Where individual rights are perceived as being in conflict with general 'communal rights', there may be little hesitation on the part of the government in overriding them. Some claims of the environment, for example, are held to be of greater significance than certain rights exercised by individuals. Thus, the Pollution Prevention and Control Act 1999 seeks to create an integrated system of pollution control which will restrict in very considerable measure the rights of individuals engaged in certain processes of production. Similarly, legislation aimed at restricting the right to sell tobacco in certain specified circumstances involves the overriding of some rights in the interests of other rights, perceived as having wider communal significance (for example, the health of minors).

In some cases, the courts will not hesitate to override the rights of one individual where they are weighed against the competing rights of another and found wanting. 'Judging the superiority of rights' may be seen clearly in the determination of some kinds of dispute relating to real property, as where X claims a right of way over B's land, or C sues to enforce a covenant entered into by D. The so called 'right of the adverse possessor', which arises from the general law of limitation of actions (see the Limitation Act 1980), may be considered by the court as overriding the claims of those who have 'slept on their rights'. The importance of land as a productive and scarce resource may be held to be of greater significance than the preservation of the rights of the 'paper owner'.

There are other 'conflict situations' – actual and potential – in which individual rights will bend and break before the overriding force of other rights. Thus, s 4(1) of the Public Order Act 1986 interferes with the exercise of freedom of speech where it results in threatening, abusive or insulting words causing individuals to fear that violence may be used against them. Indeed, the 'right to freedom of speech', if exercised by one person in a manner which robs another of his deserved reputation, may result in a tort. Bans on certain types of procession, on picketing a place of work under specified circumstances, exemplify the overriding of rights. The power of magistrates to bind over persons to keep the peace provides a further example of the suspension of some rights in the interests of a wider, communal right.

Statute and common law have created restrictions of the right to express one's views by the written word where questions of morality are thought to be involved. The Obscene Publications Acts 1959 and 1964, and the common law offence of blasphemy (see *R v Lemon* (1979)), have fettered the right of free expression. It is in the vexed area of 'law and morality' that calls for an extension of the overriding of rights continue to be made. Some jurists have interpreted Lord Devlin's contribution to the debate on the Wolfenden Report (1957) as suggesting that, in the wider interests of that community (its 'moral health', and indeed, its continued existence as a group united by a common standard of morality), some types of sexual behaviour ought not to be tolerated. Devlin seems to have challenged the notion of the expression of an individual right being tolerated when, by its very nature, it is destructive of the individual and of the 'seamless web' of morality necessary for communal existence. (It is questionable, however, whether arguments of this nature will continue to have much significance following the coming into force of the Human Rights Act 1998.)

In recent years, there has emerged in the USA a group of jurists who appear to be particularly concerned with the character and maintenance of individual rights. The Critical Legal Studies movement has engendered discussion on a variety of issues related to the question of the very existence of highly important individual rights. The neo-Marxist wing of the movement stresses 'the good of society' as an overriding principle which must outweigh the calls for the recognition of 'virtual individual rights'. Within the type of society which seems to be the desired objective of the movement's jurists, communal welfare will be the ultimate goal, and that can exist only when the rights of the individual are seen as subservient to his duties. ('Man has no rights, only duties', proclaimed jurists, such as Duguit, in the 19th century.) Outside that movement, the American jurist, Rawls, calls for a redistribution of wealth in the interests of society as a whole, which means that individual property rights may have to give way to the overriding interest of ridding society of economic and social inequalities.

Dworkin argues that individual rights can be 'political trumps' held by individuals. They arise 'when a collective goal is *not* a sufficient justification for denying them what they desire as individuals, to have or to do, or not a sufficient justification for imposing a loss or injury on them'. He would allow the restriction of rights in two cases only: first, to protect another and more important right; and, secondly, to prevent a state of affairs which might spell disaster for the community's general interests. The real significance of Dworkin's view may be in his belief that most rights are *not* inviolable and that the community's overriding of these rights can be justified in the light of the importance of overall communal goals, such as the preservation of equality.

It is of interest to observe that the European Convention on Human Rights (1950) appears to recognise the difficulties inherent in postulating absolute rights. Thus, it states: 'No one shall be required to perform forced or compulsory labour.' But this is stated to have no reference to 'any service exacted in case of an emergency or calamity threatening the life or well-being of the community'. The 'right to manifest one's religion or beliefs' is subject to 'the limitations prescribed by law' which 'are necessary in a democratic society in the interests of public safety ... or for the protection of the rights and freedoms of others'. From the content of the Convention, one may presume that the signatories accept that some rights (not to be subjected to torture, for example) are of an inviolable nature, but that others may be set aside in specified circumstances. (The Constitution of Japan, promulgated in 1946, and drawn up with the assistance of Western jurists, states: 'These fundamental rights guaranteed to the people by this Constitution shall be conferred upon the people of this and future generations as eternal *and inviolate* rights ... The right of the people to life, liberty and the pursuit of happiness shall, to the extent that it does not interfere with the public welfare, be the supreme consideration in legislation and in other governmental affairs.' Here, again, is the statement of inviolability followed by qualification.)

The Human Rights Act 1998, which has been in force since 2 October 2000, has focused attention on certain individual rights which are now accepted widely as being of a fundamental nature, but some of which, nevertheless, may be subject to the demands of the state in certain restricted circumstances. The Act, which 'seeks to give further effect to rights and freedoms under the European Convention', sets out in Sched 1 the Articles of the Convention. Some Convention rights pertaining to individuals are absolute and subject to no possibility of derogation: these include rights arising from the prohibition of torture, inhuman and degrading punishment, slavery and retroactive criminal offences. Some provisions allow a very limited derogation: for example, although under Protocol 6, Art 1, the death penalty is abolished, Art 2 allows such a penalty to be inflicted 'in respect of acts committed in time of war or imminent threat of war'. Section 14 of the 1998 Act allows derogation from the Act under certain circumstances, so that, effectively, the overriding of some 'fundamental human rights' is recognised in certain grave situations.

Individual rights recognised by governments as absolute, that is, inviolable, in *all* circumstances, seem, in practice, to be very rare – and this in spite of the contemporary movement in jurisprudence against relativism and in favour of the supreme importance of 'basic rights'. Radbruch, for example, has argued forcefully against the denial of human rights in arbitrary fashion; at a later period in his life, he argued against the denial in *any* circumstances of certain individual rights. Finnis stresses the validity of the claim to some rights for *all* persons in *all* circumstances. There remains, nevertheless, an abiding question as to the *purposes*, if any, for which a government may interfere justifiably with individual liberties. This question, fundamental to political science, is of much importance for legal theory also, because our legal institutions provide the means by which restrictions on rights are imposed and monitored. It is likely, therefore, that jurists will continue to investigate the legal aspects of the tensions which must arise from attempts to balance the recognition and protection of individual interests against some demands of the state.

Notes

Dworkin's *Taking Rights Seriously* is a valuable exposition of individual and communal rights. *Human Rights*, edited by

Kamenka, discusses problems of the inviolability of rights. 'Freedom of expression and its limits', by Feinberg, in *Philosophy of Law*, edited by Feinberg and Gross, considers the problem of the right to free expression. Part Five of De Smith's *Constitutional and Administrative Law* outlines the nature of civil rights and freedoms. *Civil Liberties: Cases and Materials*, edited by Bailey, includes useful source material relating to rights.

Question 46

Comment on some of the jurisprudential issues raised in recent years by debates on the so called 'right to euthanasia'.

Answer plan

Debates on 'rights at life's edges', relating to abortion and euthanasia, have intensified in recent years as extensive improvements in medical technology have come to public notice in the USA and Britain. A difficulty in answering a question of this nature is to avoid concentrating on purely religious or moral points of view to the exclusion of jurisprudential issues concerning 'rights'. The writings of Dworkin and Grisez include valuable summaries of the arguments surrounding euthanasia – the deliberate termination of a life of intense pain and incurable suffering in circumstances which would currently attract sanctions under the criminal law. The following skeleton plan is used:

> Introduction – definitions – situation in English law – Dworkin's thesis rights and human dignity – the case against euthanasia as presented by the Catholic jurist, Grisez – the problems of death with dignity – conclusion, the chance of agreement by both sides in the dispute.

Answer

Current debates on euthanasia tend to turn upon the recognition or rejection of *a right* to the termination of one's life where suffering has become intolerable. Supporters of euthanasia generally argue from the principle of human autonomy and its implications, while opponents emphasise the moral and legal dangers of interfering with 'life at its edges'. The central debate has been summarised in the writings of the American jurists, Dworkin, who lends general support to the legalisation of euthanasia (set out in his *Life's Dominion* (1993)) and Grisez, who rejects a right to euthanasia (as set out in the text, *Life and Death with Liberty and Justice* (1st edn, 1985)).

Active euthanasia involves the deliberate killing of one person by another, as, for example, where X, who carries out the killing, genuinely believes that Y, who is suffering from a grave, pitiable disease or defect, would be 'better off dead'. *Voluntary active euthanasia* involves Y, who is legally competent, giving his informed consent to being killed by X, or being assisted by X to take his own life, in conditions characterised by Y's very grave illness. *Involuntary euthanasia* involves the killing by X of Y, who is seriously ill, in circumstances where X does not consult Y, or overrides his (Y's) judgment.

The situation in English law in relation to so called 'mercy killing' seems clear. In *Airedale NHS Trust v Bland* (1993), Lord Goff stated:

> It is not lawful for a doctor to administer a drug to his patient to bring about his death, even though that course is prompted by a humanitarian desire to end his suffering, however great that suffering may be ... So to act is to cross the Rubicon which runs between, on the one hand, the care of the living patient and, on the other hand, euthanasia – actively causing his death to avoid or end his suffering. *Euthanasia is not lawful at common law.*

Dworkin's thesis, outlined in *Life's Dominion*, may be viewed as resting upon the closing peroration in his *Law's Empire* (1986), in which he speaks of the significance of the fraternal attitude which should unite the community even though it be divided on matters of interest and conviction. Aware of the very wide gulf which currently divides the pro- and anti-euthanasia jurists and other members of the community, he urges consideration of a measure of conciliation and unity, believing that the fundamental respect for human dignity which appears to characterise both sides of the argument may assist in bridging the gap. Dworkin's major concern is for *an extension of rights* which will recognise human autonomy and dignity.

Three main types of situation in which people may have to decide about their own, or some other person's, death are noted by Dworkin. The first type of situation involves a decision by a *conscious or competent* individual. The laws of almost all western countries generally prohibit the direct killing of a person (by a physician or other person) at that (conscious and competent) person's request. A physician who acts in this way is perceived by the law as having betrayed his unequivocal duty. The second type of situation involves a decision taken by a physician in relation to a person who is *unconscious and dying*. The person may be in a persistent vegetative state, that is, incapable of sensation or thought (see, for example, the *Airedale NHS* case, in which the House of Lords emphasised that continuing treatment was not in the patient's best interests). The third situation involves a patient who is *conscious but incompetent*, as in the case of a patient suffering from the dementia associated with Alzheimer's disease.

Dworkin suggests that decisions concerning death in these types of situation involve a consideration of three issues, the first of which is *autonomy*. A person's undoubted *right* to make important decisions for himself should be taken, it is argued, as including freedom to end his life when he wishes ('at least if his decision is not plainly irrational'). Where a person is unconscious, Dworkin suggests that we can respect his autonomy only by posing a question as to what he himself would have decided in relation to this situation before his competence disappeared (for example, by reference to a 'living will' which sets out his wishes as to what ought to be done in circumstances of this nature).

A second issue involves the argument concerning a person's *'best interests'*. Dworkin is aware that some persons may wish to remain alive for as long as possible, no matter in what condition they may live: a paternalistic view that they may be 'better off dead' suggests that they do not know their own interests. In some cases, however, as where a person is permanently unconscious, those responsible for him (including his immediate family) may feel genuinely that a termination of life would, in the specific circumstances, be preferable *in his interests* to a continued existence in conditions of severe distress.

The third issue is that of *the sanctity of life*. The argument that euthanasia and suicide are contrary to God's will, in that the termination of a life before its natural end runs contrary to the duties imposed by God's gift of life, is powerful. Its expression in jurisprudential terms suggests that there should be no right based upon the recognition and protection by the law of an act which seems contrary to God's commands. Dworkin's considered reply is based on a belief that the idea of the sanctity of human life 'has a secular as well as a religious interpretation'. Respect for the sanctity of human life can involve acceptance of the view that human beings must be allowed to end their lives *appropriately*, and, where possible, not in circumstances which are a denial of the values they have considered as characterising their lives. Attention ought to be given to the argument that persons ought to be allowed 'to die proudly when it is no longer possible to live proudly.' In considering juristic rights which might be involved in the deliberate ending of a life, Dworkin reminds us that the principal question posed by calls for the legislation of active euthanasia is how life's sanctity should be understood *and* respected. To make an individual sufferer die in a manner of which others approve, but which he believes to be an appalling contradiction of his own existence, 'is a devastating, odious form of tyranny'.

Dworkin gives particular attention to euthanasia in the context of the lives of those who have lost the very capacities which ought to be protected by the right to autonomy: he has in mind those who are living 'a life past reason'. Ought we to continue to recognise the right of a person to take a decision which is contrary to his interests so as to afford a measure of protection for capacities which he clearly lacks? How can we know the 'best interests' of a person who is in a permanent state of dementia? Have persons a right *not* to exist for long periods in degrading conditions which create or perpetuate indignity or which make them unconscious of that indignity? Our understanding of the significance of the kind of life a person has lived should bring us to an insistence that he must not be treated in a manner which 'in our community's vocabulary of respect, denies him dignity'.

Hence, Dworkin concludes, there must be engendered a right –
in the name of that freedom which is a cardinal requirement of
self-respect – for a person to be allowed to die in a way which we
think shows self-respect. Both sides in the euthanasia debate
accept the profound significance of concern for the sanctity of
human life; disagreement emerges from a consideration of how to
interpret that concern. The laws which the community makes must
express an understanding of *why* life is sacred and *why* rights and
freedom are of significance in 'life's dominion'.

Grisez, writing from the standpoint of neo-Thomist
jurisprudence, is an opponent of euthanasia. Fundamental to his
view is the teaching of the Catholic Church, re-stated in 1995 by
the Pope, in his Encyclical, *The Gospel of Life*: 'I confirm that
euthanasia is a grave violation of the law of God, since it is the
deliberate and morally unacceptable killing of a human being.'

In jurisprudential terms, Grisez denies the existence of rights
which allow or might allow the deliberate killing of persons at
their own request or for merciful motives.

Grisez notes the difficulty of defining 'death' in terms which
are acceptable to jurists and others who are concerned with the
question of euthanasia. Medical technology allows, for example,
the maintenance of 'vital functions' in persons who might
otherwise have been pronounced dead. A typical definition of
death, from the 1960s, is that given in *Black's Law Dictionary*:

> The cessation of life; defined by physicians as a total
> stoppage of the circulation of the blood, and a cessation of
> the animal and vital functions consequent thereon, such as
> respiration, pulsation, etc.

This would not now be acceptable to physicians. In English law,
death has not been defined in precise terms by statute. Some
English jurists have drawn attention to the value of the definition
given in the Kansas Statutes 1971: 'A person will be considered
medically and legally dead if, in the opinion of a physician, based
on ordinary standards of medical practice, there is the absence of
spontaneous brain function.'

The American Bar Association has used the following
definition in recent comments on the question of legalised

euthanasia: 'For all legal purposes, a human body with irreversible cessation of *total* brain function, according to usual and customary standards of medical practice, shall be considered dead.' Grisez emphasises the difficulties involved in defining precisely what is meant by euthanasia in the absence of a definition of death which is widely acceptable in legal institutions. Is death a 'process' or a 'single event'? Is the philosopher Wittgenstein 'correct' in assuming that death is not a part of life, but merely its limit? It is not easy to speak of a 'right to terminate life' when its very boundaries have not yet been marked with acceptable precision.

Grisez places emphasis on the significance of the jurisprudential principle of *justice* in relation to the arguments against euthanasia. If voluntary active euthanasia is to be legalised, then there would be a strong chance that 'persons who do not wish to be killed are likely to become unwilling victims', so that they might be denied the protection of the law of homicide which they now enjoy: that denial would constitute a grave injustice. Further, because physicians are not infallible, a wrong diagnosis could be made which constituted the sole significant factor in rendering a case 'hopeless', thus bringing it within the class of cases in which euthanasia is held desirable. And may not individual sufferers be easily pressured into consent, thus leading to a killing which is essentially unjust? Is it sufficient to rely on 'the good judgment and humanistic motives' of all concerned in order to ensure that justice will be done in the process of ending a life?

In his *Sanctity of Life* (1957), the jurist Glanville Williams suggested legislation to be based on the following clause: 'It shall be lawful for a physician after consultation with another physician, to accelerate by any merciful means the death of a patient who is seriously ill, unless it is proved that the act was not done in good faith with the consent of the patient and for the purpose of saving him from severe pain in an illness believed to be of an incurable and fatal character.' Such a formulation, argues Grisez, may not sound dangerous until it is recalled that what Williams is proposing is an amendment to the law which prohibits murder. 'Once this fact is taken into account, the danger is obvious.' How could the prosecution prove beyond reasonable doubt that the physicians did not act in good faith, or that they did not believe the illness to be incurable or fatal ?

Grisez suggests a careful consideration of the 'thin end of the wedge' argument, namely, that there can be no guarantee that the legislation of voluntary euthanasia will not move incrementally into a policy which legalises non-voluntary euthanasia. He notes the road travelled by the enthusiastic advocates (physicians and jurists) of eugenics in Germany who moved with ease from support of proposals in the 1920s for 'death with dignity' to the acceptance of arguments in favour of sterilisation and euthanasia for incurable mental defectives who were regarded as 'mere caricatures of real persons'. The road to eventual genocide was prepared at an early date. Grisez stresses the differences between euthanasia and genocide, but notes the way in which leading members of the German medical profession easily moved their stance, often with the support of prominent jurists.

The arguments of proponents of euthanasia expressed in the aphorism 'death with dignity' are analysed by Grisez in the light of the neo-Thomist view of man as entitled to dignity, and, therefore, to those rights which embody this entitlement, *because* he is made in the image of God. Dignity implies inherent worth: all persons have dignity and all are entitled to respect. But respect for dignity must involve a refusal to impose on non-competent sufferers a judgment of others that it would be better for them if they were dead. Further, dignity may be made manifest in one who is suffering by 'maintaining his uniqueness against the power of suffering and death' with a display of courage and patience. Grisez suggests that the work of hospices demonstrates in impressive fashion that 'there certainly can be dignity in dying without voluntary active euthanasia'. There is, he claims, no necessity for any person to die in misery, deprived of human dignity, . To see euthanasia as a solution to the problem of 'death with dignity' is to adopt a technically easy solution in a manner 'which least comports with the dignity of persons'. To provide 'appropriate and excellent care' for the dying is to respect their dignity in full measure.

In juristic terms, the plea from both sides in the debate involves a recognition of the equal dignity to be attached *through the medium of legal rights*, to all persons. The predicament of suffering is to be approached in a spirit of justice and understanding. Without a basis of justice, any attempt to deal with the problem of mortal suffering will, in the words of Grisez, expose people to the natural forces of the struggle of all to survive, 'a struggle in which the fittest to survive are those who survive, but the fittest to live with human dignity are more than others likely to die'. There is little difference between this view and that of Dworkin: there is probably a good chance of agreement on ends, but whether the gulf between their points of view concerning legal means can be bridged easily remains problematic.

Legal argument continues, fuelled by cases such as *Re A (Children)* (2000), in which the Court of Appeal considered, primarily, the lawfulness of a proposed surgical operation on conjoined twins which would result inevitably in the death of one of them. The Court decided that the operation would be lawful. The comments of Ward LJ sought to re-affirm the sanctity of life principle in circumstances in which the law, presented with an acute dilemma, 'had to allow an escape through choosing the lesser of two evils'. Some jurists, commenting on the decision, expressed concerns at what they perceived as a movement along the road to legalised euthanasia.

Elements of an important strand of judicial thought emerged in the discussions leading to the publication, in January 2000, of the Medical Treatment (Prevention of Euthanasia) Bill. Clause 1 stated: 'It shall be unlawful for any person responsible for the care of a patient to withdraw or withhold from the patient medical treatment or sustenance if his purpose or one of his purposes in doing so is to hasten or otherwise cause the death of the patient.' 'Medical treatment' was defined as 'any medical or surgical treatment, including the administration of drugs or the use of any mechanical or other apparatus for the provision or support of ventilation or of any other bodily function'. The Bill did not complete the necessary stages of passage through the Commons, but, again, concern was voiced in many quarters on judicial decisions which seemed, effectively, to support a right to end life, while opponents of the Bill felt that existing legal barriers against euthanasia were adequate.

Notes

The following short selection from the vast range of the literature on euthanasia is suggested as background reading: *To Die or Not to Die*, edited by Berger (1990); *The Human Body and the Law*, by Myers (1990); 'Against the right to die', by Velleman, in (1992) 7 Journal of Medicine and Philosophy; 'Involuntary euthanasia', by Robertson, in (1975) 27 Stanford L Rev; *The Morality of Killing: Sanctity of Life, Abortion and Euthanasia*, by Kohl; *Voluntary Euthanasia and the Common Law*, by Otlowski; 'Sex, death and the courts', in Dworkin's recently published *Sovereign Virtue: The Theory and Practice of Equality*, in which he poses and seeks to answer the question: 'May a "moral majority" limit the liberty of individual citizens on no better ground than that it disapproves of the personal choices they make?' The Journal of Medical Ethics carries regular articles on the medico-legal issues raised by discussions on euthanasia.

CHAPTER 14

LAW AND MORALITY

Introduction

In this chapter attention is drawn to the age-old question of the links between law and morality. Ought the law to reflect morality? Ought it to change as social morality changes? Ought the institutions of the law to be viewed as guardians of morality? The Wolfenden Report of 1957 precipitated an intensive debate on the law and sexual morality in which Hart and Devlin (a former judge of the Court of Appeal and the House of Lords) appeared as advocates of different attitudes to this problem. Fuller's allegory, the Case of the Speluncean Explorers (1949), explores the intertwining of law and morality.

Checklist

Ensure that you are acquainted with the following topics:

- the Wolfenden Report
- the 'seamless web of morality'
- inner morality of the law
- the 'right-thinking man'
- purposive jurisprudence

Question 47

In the discussion which followed the publication of the Wolfenden Report (1957), Devlin posed as a fundamental question: 'What is the connection between crime and sin and to what extent, if at all, should the criminal law of England concern itself with the enforcement of morals and punish sin or morality as such?'

How did Devlin answer this question, and what reactions did his answer elicit from Hart?

Answer plan

In the controversy which followed publication of the Wolfenden Report (1957), Devlin (1905–92) spoke for those who rejected its findings. His personal ground of opposition was the failure of the Report to justify the philosophy upon which it appeared to be based. In support of his opposition, he raised the fundamental problem of the relationship of crime, morality and the law. Hart (1907–92) sought to support the recommendations of the Report and in so doing attempted to expose some of Devlin's arguments as fallacious. The answer ought to concentrate on the essential features of Devlin's three questions and his answers, together with an outline of Hart's stand on the law-morality link as he perceives it. The following skeleton plan is used:

Introduction – background to the controversy – Devlin's interrogatories and answers – Hart's counter-arguments – summary of the debate – conclusion, the unresolved questions concerning the social significance of morality.

Answer

The *Wolfenden Report on Homosexual Offences and Prostitution* (1957) suggested the decriminalisation of specific homosexual acts between consenting adults in private, and stressed the significance of two particular principles. First: that the function of the criminal law, in the area with which the Report had been concerned, was to preserve public order and decency, to protect the public from that which was injurious or offensive and to safeguard the vulnerable against corruption and exploitation. Secondly: that there must remain a realm of private morality which is not the law's business (but to say this was not to condone in any way private immorality). Devlin criticised the thinking behind the Report; Hart supported the general proposals of the Report and sought to attack the principles from which Devlin argued.

There are, said Devlin, certain moral principles which our society does require to be observed; their breach can be considered as an offence against society *as a whole*. The law does not punish *all* immorality; it does not condone *any* immorality. It is always necessary to investigate the links between sin and the purpose and tasks of the criminal law. Devlin put three questions. The *first* asked whether a society had the right to pass judgment at all on matters of morals, and whether there ought to be a public morality, or whether morals should always be a matter for private judgment. The *second* question asked whether, if society has a right to pass a judgment, it may use the law to enforce it. The *third* question asked whether the weapon of the law should be used in all cases or only in some, and, if only in some, what principles should be kept in mind.

Devlin answered the first question with a resounding 'Yes'. The Report took for granted the existence of a public morality. If the bonds of that morality are relaxed too far, then members of society will drift apart. These bonds are a part of the 'price of society' and, because mankind has a need of society, the price must be paid.

The second question produced an uncompromising answer. A society *is* entitled to use the law in order to preserve its morality in precisely the same way that it uses the law to safeguard anything else considered essential to its existence. It is not possible, says Devlin, to set any theoretical limits to the government's power to legislate against immorality. A society has an undeniable right to legislate against internal and external dangers – the law of treason provides an example. The loosening of communal bonds may be a preliminary to total social disintegration and, therefore, a society should take steps to preserve its moral code.

The third question involves the circumstances in which a government ought to act in the event of a threatened disintegration of its moral basis. How may the moral judgments of society be ascertained? Devlin suggests that reference be made to the judgment of 'the right-minded man' (not to be confused with 'the reasonable man'). He may be thought of as 'the man in the jury box'. Let *his* judgment prevail and, for the purposes of the law, let immorality be thought of as what 'every right-minded man' considers to be immoral.

At this stage of his argument, Devlin refers to certain 'elastic principles' to be kept in mind by a legislature. First, there ought to be toleration of the maximum individual freedom consistent with society's integrity. Secondly, only that which lies 'beyond the limits of tolerance' ought to be punished; these limits will be reached when an activity creates disgust among 'right-minded persons'. Not everything can be tolerated, and general, widespread disgust marks the point at which tolerance must be questioned. It should be remembered, too, that the limits of tolerance may shift from generation to generation. Thirdly, privacy must be respected and this needs to be balanced against the need to enforce the law. Finally, the law is concerned with minima, not maxima; society should set its standards above those of the law.

Hart reacted by questioning the basis of Devlin's axioms. He was concerned in particular with Devlin's implicit 'legal moralism' – the attempt to prevent and prohibit conduct because it is perceived as immoral, even though it harms no person. Hart objected to Devlin's stress on 'intolerance, indignation and disgust' as marking the boundaries for tolerance. Hart reminds legislators that the popular limits of tolerance shift; they are not static over long periods of time. Devlin's concept of morality as a 'seamless web' which will collapse unless the community's vetoes are enforced by law is not accepted by Hart. He denies that breaches of morality will necessarily affect the integrity of society as a whole. Devlin's analogy which was drawn between the suppression of treason and the suppression of sexual immorality was 'quite absurd'. It was 'grotesque' to suggest that homosexual activity could lead to the destruction of society. To offend against one aspect of society's moral code is not necessarily to jeopardise its entire structure. Devlin ignores, according to Hart, the fact that there cannot be, logically, a sphere of 'private treason', but there is, undoubtedly, a sphere of 'private morality and immorality'.

Hart is moved to argue, further, that legal punishment which may follow on sexual misdemeanour may provide disproportionate personal misery. This must not be disregarded. Indeed, he claims, blackmail and other evil consequences of criminal punishment may outweigh the harm caused by the practices classified as sexual offences.

Hart's argument continues with a caution to legislators. Devlin's criterion for the 'immorality' of a sexual practice is, apparently, the disgust it produces in the mind of 'the right-thinking man'. Given this criterion, the legislator must ask himself certain questions. What is the *nature* of the general morality embraced by 'the right-thinking man'? Is it based in any way on ignorance, superstition or misunderstanding? Does that morality engender the misconception that deviants from its codes are in some other ways dangerous to society? Is the weight of the misery attendant on punishment for homosexual offences well understood? (It should be remembered that Hart was writing before the Sexual Offences Act 1967.) Hart concludes with a warning against 'populism' as an arbiter of how we should live. There is, he suggests, a danger of 'populism' in Devlin's reliance on the feelings of 'the right-minded man'; it should be resisted.

To summarise: Devlin sees the preservation of morality as vital to society's well-being; morality is very much more than mere integument, it expresses essential aspects of the bonds which serve to unify society; the law has an important, inescapable, role to fulfil in safeguarding society from attempts to shatter its shared morality. Hart does not accept Devlin's fundamental assumption that morality in its entirety forms a unique 'seamless web'; deviants from a conventional sexual morality are not necessarily antagonistic in other ways to society as a whole and its demands; there is always the danger of entrenching irrational and harmful prejudices in the guise of a legal stance designed to safeguard 'basic patterns' of morality. Devlin turns his attention on society as a whole; Hart, on the individual. Devlin accentuates, therefore, the significance of a shared public morality and its maintenance; Hart underlines (as did the Wolfenden Report) the important distinction between public and private behaviour, public and private areas of morality, and reminds legislators that there is a private area which ought not to be the concern of the law.

The debate has not ended. Its preoccupations are revived particularly on those occasions upon which legislators make proposals relating to basic changes in the law in areas concerned with sexual behaviour. The debate which preceded the passing of the Sexual Offences Act 1967 (the provisions of which reflected the recommendations of the Wolfenden Report) was a reminder of the intensity of feeling which surrounds this area of the criminal law. Devlin's supporters continue to insist that 'the suppression of vice is as much the law's business as the suppression of subversive activities'. They are reminded by their opponents of Spinoza's warning, some three centuries ago, that: 'He alone knows what the law can do who sees clearly what it cannot do ... He who tries to fix and determine everything by law will inflame rather than correct the vices of the world.' Hart's supporters repeat his view that: 'To use coercion to maintain the moral status quo at any given point in history would be artificially to arrest the process which gives social institutions their value.' They are warned by opponents of Holmes' reminder that a sound body of law must correspond with the community's actual feelings and demands. They are urged to remember that legal and moral rules 'are in a symbiotic relationship – people learn what is moral by observing what other people tend to enforce'.

Essentially, the debate turned on the *social significance of sexual morality* and, in particular, on the importance for society of private reactions to a generally-accepted code of moral behaviour. But some jurists saw the debate as drawing attention to a deeper question for general jurisprudence, namely, how far legality ought to be considered simply in terms of *restraint*. Is it to be 'the whip of the animal trainer or the voice of conscience'? The path from the authoritarian 'must' to the autonomous 'ought' is tortuous. It is suggested that for some jurists, the principal value of the debate might reside in its insistent reminder that the concept of law as a means to an end demands continuous examination of that end; for others, there is the reminder of the continuing separation of law and morality: in Korkunov's words – 'The distinction between morals and law can be formulated very simply. Morality furnishes the criterion for the proper evaluation of our interests; law marks out the limits within which they ought to be confined. To analyse out a criterion for the evolution of our interests is the function of morality; to settle the principles of the reciprocal delimitation of one's own and other peoples' interests is the function of the law.'

Notes

The key texts in this area are Devlin's *The Enforcement of Morals*, Hart's *Immorality and Treason* and *Law, Liberty and Morality*. The Wolfenden Report (Cmnd 1957) contains the precise recommendations which were discussed in the subsequent debate on law and morality. Riddall, Chapter 14, summarises the debate on enforcement of morality. Mitchell's *Law, Morality and Religion in a Secular Society* treats in detail some of the questions posed by Hart and Devlin. Lee's *Law and Morals* is a useful summary of the fundamental questions; it contains a bibliography relating to the problems. Shiner's essay, 'Law and morality', in *A Companion to Philosophy of Law*, edited by Patterson, asks whether 'morality' is a jurisprudentially neutral term. Grey's *The Legal Enforcement of Morality* examines the legislature's 'right' to enforce morality by law.

Question 48

How does Fuller's allegory of the Case of the Speluncean Explorers reflect his general approach to the relationship between law and morality?

Answer plan

Fuller (1902–78) is a representative of the school of legal thought known as 'purposive jurisprudence' which sees the activities of the courts as reflecting the very purposes of the law, which turn upon the subjecting of human conduct to the control of 'rules'. Law and morality are intertwined and, according to Fuller, a law which is totally divorced from morality ceases to be law. The facts of the Case of the Speluncean Explorers – an allegory based upon a fictitious hearing, set in the mythical future – should be given in some detail, and Fuller's use of the judgments in the case should be noted as expressions of his views of the law–morality relationship. The following skeleton plan is suggested:

> Introduction – Fuller and the 'morality of law' – facts of the Case of the Speluncean Explorers – the judgments – how the allegory underlines Fuller's general thesis relating law and morality – conclusion, the allegory as representing a contribution to the thinking of jurists who see the need to search for a rapprochement between positivism and natural law.

Answer

The jurisprudence associated with Fuller (1902–78) is based upon his perception of the law as 'purposive'. Interpretation of the law and the legal process indicates his view that 'a court is not an inert mirror reflecting current mores, but an active participant in the enterprise of articulating the implications of shared purposes'. The essence of law is to be found in its *purpose*, which is the bringing of human conduct within the governance of rules. This involves a full recognition of the significant interaction of the positive law and the community's general moral perceptions. The history of jurisprudence shows a widening rift between legal positivism and the natural law doctrine, which Fuller seeks to heal. Positivist doctrine fails to give any coherent meaning to the moral obligation of fidelity to law, and the basic postulate of the positivist school of thought, namely, that law and morality must be strictly separated, 'seems to deny the possibility of any bridge between the obligation to obey law and other moral obligations'. The great tradition of the natural law has produced a literature which contains 'much foolishness and much that is unacceptable to modern tastes'. The positivist-natural law argument needs, initially, clarification.

Fuller argues that the meaning of morality requires consideration. He attempts to distinguish 'the morality of aspiration' and 'the morality of duty'. The former is concerned with 'the desired norm of human conduct, independent of human activity'; the latter involves the standards followed by human beings in social relations in particular circumstances. Fulfilment of the morality of aspiration necessitates a legal system which will assist in this task by the recognition and maintenance of social order. The morality of duty will involve the creation of acceptable codes of conduct which the law will seek to enforce. Further, law itself must have its own morality, and this necessitates, for example, that the law's principles shall have general applicability, that standards of action shall be stated with clarity, that impossible standards shall not be imposed, and that the law shall be 'efficacious', in that it should demonstrate consistency between prescribed norms and actions of the agencies concerned in enforcing them.

Fuller frequently adopts the principle of 'teaching through allegory'. An allegory is a story with multiple layers of meaning: underneath the primary surface story will be found a secondary layer of more profound meaning. Essentially, the allegory seeks to teach a lesson by illustration. In the Case of the Speluncean Explorers, which appeared in 1949 in the Harvard Law Review, Fuller's lesson is that the law's basic integrity is to be found within the very processes which are utilised 'in the attainment of its proclaimed goals'. The case is set in a mythical future, the year 4300. Fuller did not choose the date at random: he estimated that in 1949, when he produced the allegory, 'the centuries which separate us from the year 4300 are roughly equal to those that have passed since the Age of Pericles'. The case is heard in the

Court of General Instances of the County of Stowfield in the Commonwealth of Newgarth, which has a charter of government drawn up originally by the survivors of a past catastrophe ('the Great Spiral'). The case is based upon a statute which states in specific terms: 'Whoever shall unlawfully take the life of another shall be punished by death.'

The facts of the case are, in outline, as follows. Four defendants and Whetmore (W) are members of the Speluncean Society, which encourages the exploration of caves. In 4299, they were trapped within a cavern which they were exploring. On their eventual release, it became apparent that some 23 days after their entry into the cave, the defendants had killed and eaten W. In evidence, it was indicated that W had suggested that the group's survival would be impossible without nutriment, and that this would necessitate the eating of the flesh of a member of the group. W also suggested the casting of lots in order to determine who was to be killed. W later withdrew from the arrangement, declaring that, after reflection, he found the arrangement frightful and odious. He was accused by the defendants of a breach of faith, and they proceeded to cast dice which W was carrying in his pocket. W declared that he had no objection to one of the defendants casting the dice on his (W's) behalf. The throw of the dice went against W, who was killed, after which the defendants ate his flesh.

After the defendants had been rescued from the cave, they were indicted for the murder of W. All were found guilty and were sentenced to death by hanging. Following the discharge of the jury, its members joined in communicating with the state's Chief Executive and requesting that the death sentences be commuted to imprisonment for a period of six months. Similar action was taken by the trial judge. The defendants brought a petition of error to the Supreme Court of Newgarth. The court issued its opinions in the year 4300.

The Chief Justice, Truepenny CJ, stated that, in his opinion, there were no errors in the trial court. Jury and judge had followed the only course open to them under the law; that course was fair and wise. The language of the relevant statute was well known and it permitted of no exceptions applicable to this case. But sympathies 'may incline us to make allowances for the tragic situation in which the defendants found themselves'. In such a case, the principle of executive clemency seemed 'admirably suited to mitigate the rigours of the law'. The Chief Justice then proposed that his colleagues should join him in following the example of the trial judge and jury by joining in their communication to the Chief Executive, asking for clemency. He presumed that some form of clemency would be shown to the defendants and, if this were done, then justice would have been accomplished without impairing either the spirit or the letter of the statute and without offering any encouragement for the disregard of the law.

Judge Foster expressed shock at hearing the Chief Justice proposing an expedient 'at once so sordid and obvious'. To assert that the law which the court upholds and expounds has led to a conclusion which is shameful and from which escape can be contemplated only by appealing to 'a dispensation resting within the personal whim of the Chief Executive', is tantamount to an admission that the law of the Commonwealth no longer pretends to incorporate justice. He did not believe that the law compelled the 'monstrous conclusion' that the defendants were murderers. On the contrary, that law declares them to be innocent of any crime. First, the positive law of Newgarth was inapplicable to the case; the case was governed by 'the law of nature'. Positive law is predicated on the possibility of men's co-existence within society, and when a situation occurs in which that co-existence becomes impossible, then the force of the positive law disappears. The defendants had been as remote from the legal order as if they had been a thousand miles away; indeed, even in a physical sense, they were separated from the courts. They were existing, trapped in a cave, in a 'state of nature', not in a 'state of civil society', and they had drawn up their own 'charter of government' appropriate to their very unusual circumstances. The usual conditions of human existence did not exist for the defendants. We think of human life as an absolute value, not to be sacrificed under any circumstances, but absolute values of this kind had no application to the desperate situation in which the defendants and W found themselves.

Foster J argued, further, that although the defendants may indeed have violated the *letter* of the statute, they had not violated its *spirit*. The propositions of the positive law whether in statute or precedent, had to be interpreted reasonably in the light of their evident purpose. The question of self-defence had to be taken into account. One of the main objects of criminal legislation is that of deterring men from crime; but if it were declared to be the law that a killing in self-defence is murder, then such a rule would have no deterrent effect. A man whose life is threatened will seek to repel the aggressor no matter what the law may say. This reasoning may be applied to the case under consideration. He therefore concluded that, assuming that the defendants had acted in self-defence (in protection of their lives), then, on any aspect under which this case may be viewed, the defendants are innocent of the crime of murdering W and the convictions should be set aside.

Tatting J declared himself unable to accept any of the arguments put forward on either side, and he was unable to resolve the doubts that beset him about the law of the case. The arguments of Foster J were shot through with contradictions and fallacies. Why had the defendants been 'in a state of nature'? At what point did that occur? By what authority could the court resolve itself into a Court of Nature? Whence comes the court's authority to apply the law of nature? With reference to the argument that the defendants did not violate the provisions of the statute, and that reasoning could lead the court into accepting the excuse of self-defence, only *one* of the purposes of the criminal law is to deter; the difficulty is that other purposes are also ascribed to the criminal law. What of the question of retribution? 'Assuming that we must interpret a statute in the light of its purpose, what are we to do when it has many purposes or when its purposes are disputed?' He was repelled by a feeling that the arguments of Foster J were intellectually unsound and approached 'mere rationalisation'. He was struck by the absurdity of directing that the defendants be put to death when their lives had been saved at the cost of the 10 heroic workers who had attempted to effect their rescue from the cave. It would have been wiser not to indict the defendants. He then announced, with regret, that he was withdrawing from the decision of the case.

Keen J declared that, in the discharge of his duties as a judge, it was not his function to address directions to the Chief Executive, nor to take into account what he may or may not do in reaching his decision, which must be controlled in its entirety by the law of the Commonwealth. Nor was it his concern as to whether what

the defendants had done was 'wicked', 'good', 'right' or 'wrong'.
His own conceptions of morality were not relevant; what was
relevant was the law of the land. There is an obligation on the
judiciary to enforce faithfully the written law and to interpret it in
accordance with its plain meaning; this principle was at the very
heart of the legal and governmental order which had to be upheld.
It was doubtful whether the statute had a 'purpose' in the
ordinary sense of that term, other than to reflect the deeply-held
human conviction that murder is wrong and that something must
be done to those who commit it. Where was the gap in the statute?
Neither he nor Foster could know what the 'purpose' of the
statute was.

Keen J proceeded to acknowledge that hard decisions were
never popular, but that hard cases 'may even have a certain moral
value by bringing home to the people their own responsibilities
toward the law that is ultimately their creation', and by reminding
them that there is no principle of personal grace that can relieve
the mistakes of their representatives. He felt deeply that his
colleagues might be insufficiently aware of the conceptions of
judicial office advocated by Foster J. The convictions should be
affirmed.

Handy J expressed his amazement at 'the tortured
ratiocinations to which this simple case had given rise'. He
wondered at his colleagues' ability to throw an obscuring curtain
of legalisms about every issue presented to them for decision. He
warned his colleagues of the danger of the judiciary losing its
contact with the common man. Judges would do their jobs best if
they were to treat forms and abstract concepts as instruments,
selecting from among the available forms those best suited to
reach 'the proper result'. Where wedges are driven between the
mass of the people and those who direct their legal life, then
society will be ruined. The case had aroused enormous public
interest and a poll of readers of one newspaper had revealed that
90 per cent expressed a belief that the defendants ought to be
pardoned or let off with a kind of token punishment. This made it
obvious, not only what had to be done, but what was necessary to
preserve a reasonable and decent accord between the judiciary
and public opinion. He was aware that what he was advocating
would be met with the argument that the safeguards of the legal
process would go for naught, 'if a mass opinion formed outside

this framework is allowed to have any influence on our decision'. But he warned against the danger of his colleagues becoming lost in the patterns of their own thought and forgetting that those patterns often cast not the slightest shadow on the outside world. Finally, it should be noted that the jury had found the facts (as stated), but found, further, that *if on those facts*, the defendants were guilty of murder, then they found the defendants so guilty. The jury seemed to have been allowed to dodge its usual responsibilities. He concluded that the defendants were innocent of the crime charged; conviction and sentence ought to be set aside.

Tatting J made a further statement in which he declared that after hearing the opinions of other members of the court, he felt greatly strengthened in his conviction that he ought not to participate in the decision of the case.

The Supreme Court being equally divided, the conviction and sentence of the Court of General Instances was *affirmed*. Execution of the sentences by the Public Executioner was fixed for the morning of 2 April 4300.

Fuller is seeking, through the allegory, to urge consideration of the *purposes* for which the law exists. The varying natures of the judgments in the Supreme Court are used to illustrate a variety of approaches to law. The opinion of the Chief Justice seems to be based upon a belief in the significance of executive clemency in appeals against conviction and sentence. Foster J (who accepts aspects of Fuller's own views) draws attention to the importance of the spirit of the law rather than the letter. Tatting J evades responsibility by declaring his inability to reach a decision. Keen J follows the philosophy of positivism in separating matters of law and morality. Handy J advocates a decision which he believes to be administratively convenient and popular.

Through the decision of Foster J, Fuller affirms his belief in the need for an intertwining of law, morality and reason in deciding legal questions. Each strand of the process is necessary. Positivism provides a distorted view of law, which is seen as a 'one-way projection of authority' – the law is set out and it is the duty of the citizen to obey its letter. The wide pretensions of natural law theory are often seen as having little relevance for the contemporary world. Fuller seeks to draw these conflicting views together by arguing for a law with its own inner morality, which would proclaim the virtues of a comprehensible, promulgated law, based on the recognition of the demands of morality. The process of reasoning would be evident in the work of the courts. Some of the problems of the type evident in the judgments of the Case of the Speluncean Explorers might be solved with relative ease.

Fuller's own postscript to the case is of particular significance. The case, he notes, was constructed for the sole purpose of bringing into a common focus certain divergent philosophies of law and government, philosophies which have been with us since the days of the ancient Greeks. Even after we have sought solutions to the problems raised in earlier times, the debates will continue. 'If there is any element of prediction in the case, it does not go beyond a suggestion that the questions involved are among the permanent questions of the human race.'

Notes

The Case of the Speluncean Explorers appears in (1949) 62 Harvard L Rev 616. Extracts are given in Lloyd's *Introduction to Jurisprudence*. Fuller's philosophy of law is set out in *The Morality of Law* and *The Anatomy of Law*. Duxbury's *Patterns of American Jurisprudence* contains an analysis of Fuller's purposive jurisprudence. The reality upon which Fuller's allegory is founded appears in *R v Dudley and Stephens* (1884); the speech of Lord Coleridge CJ is of particular interest. *Cannibalism and the Common Law*, by Simpson, explores problems raised by the case and forms a valuable commentary on Fuller's allegory.

CHAPTER 15

FEMINIST JURISPRUDENCE

Introduction

This final chapter is built upon two questions which concern the new movement in legal theory known as feminist jurisprudence. The movement is essentially radical and is concerned with an analysis of law from the perspective of women. Its exponents believe that contemporary formal jurisprudence is flawed because it has been created almost exclusively by men, with the result that the point of view of women – 'silenced, misrepresented, disadvantaged and subordinated' – has been ignored or falsified. Feminist jurists seek a re-interpretation of legal theory from a new perspective which involves, primarily, a rejection of theory which reflects the values of patriarchy organised in a hierarchical structure, in which the subordination of women to men is taken to be part of an unalterable scheme of things.

Checklist

Make sure that you understand the following topics:

- patriarchal society
- gendered language
- principle of empowerment
- radical feminism

Question 49

What is meant by 'patriarchy' in the context of feminine jurisprudence?

Answer plan

The ideological struggle against patriarchy marks out the objective, arguments and methodology of feminist jurisprudence. Patriarchy is the social structure characterised by male domination, having an ideology which seeks to justify this arrangement and a legal theory which interprets the law from a standpoint characterised by a belief, explicit or implicit, in fundamental inequalities. It involves, essentially, the systematic subordination of women to men. The required answer should seek to define appropriate concepts and explain the reasons for the feminist movement's hostility to much contemporary jurisprudence. The following skeleton plan is used:

> Introduction – definition of patriarchy – male dominance taken for granted – the negative aspects of patriarchy – patriarchy reflected in the literature of libertarianism – gendered patterns of legal language – conclusion, necessity to challenge patriarchy in a variety of ways.

Answer

'The rejection of patriarchy is the one point on which all feminists agree', writes Patricia Smith, a leading theoretician of the school of feminist jurisprudence, a movement which seeks to erect a new philosophy of law on principles which involve the disappearance of patriarchal domination and the oppression and injustice said to be associated with it. An analysis of patriarchy, an examination of its history, its ideological content and, above all, its effect on contemporary jurisprudence and law in action, form the core of the ideology of the feminist jurisprudence movement. The recognition and the rejection of patriarchy are viewed by feminist jurists as having revolutionary implications for society in general and for contemporary jurisprudence in particular.

Patriarchy is defined by Janet Rifkin in her authoritative essay, *Toward a Theory of Law and Patriarchy* (1980): 'By patriarchy, I mean any kind of group organisation in which males hold dominant power and determine what part females shall and shall not play, and in which capabilities assigned to women are relegated generally to the mystical and aesthetic and excluded from the practical and political realms, these realms being regarded as separate and mutually exclusive.' The term 'patriarchy' was used in earlier times to refer to a system of society ruled by men, with descent through the male line; it is used today in a much wider sense, with specific reference not only to a society which is built on male domination, but also to the ideologies which seek to justify and stabilise this domination.

Law is not neutral in the patriarchal society: it exists upon the basis of acceptance (conscious or unconscious) of the systematic subordination of women, and its assumptions 'uncritically assume a traditional male standard of what is normal': P Smith. The legal ideology which underpins patriarchy is little more than 'a medium for making male dominance both invisible and legitimate by adopting the male point of view in law at the same time as it enforces that view on society': Mackinnon. Jurisprudential theory and legal institutions within a patriarchy provide a justification for the authority of men and symbolise the norm, which accepts that men and women must not be regarded as equal because this is 'demonstrably not so', and, therefore, women must be subordinate to men. Dominant legal ideologies within a patriarchy, the profoundly unequal role assigned to women in the administration of justice, testify to a legal process which is designed to ensure that the fact of male domination is seen as beneficial, natural and entirely inevitable: so runs the critique of patriarchy which is associated with feminist jurisprudence.

The key role of jurisprudence and legal processes within the patriarchy makes necessary a continuous, principled attack on contemporary male-dominated legal theory. Jurisprudence which is clearly seen to reflect injustice and discrimination will not survive for long: this view sets the agenda for feminist jurisprudence as a movement. It becomes essential for an explanation of the causes and effects of patriarchy that its underlying beliefs be understood and exposed, particularly in relation to legal scholarship and social practice. Mackinnon notes the significance of legal mediation in the patriarchal structure: 'Through legal mediation, male dominance is made to seem a feature of life, not a one-sided construct imposed by force for the advantage of a dominant group ... Coercion legitimated becomes consent ...' To challenge the seemingly 'natural and eternal values' proclaimed by the legal apologists for patriarchy can be the beginnings of loosening the grip on society of institutionalised discrimination and oppression; this involves attaining an understanding of the key features of the typical apologia for the institution of patriarchy.

A primary feature of patriarchy is belief in the general inequality of woman in relation to man. Biological and anthropological data are interpreted so as to suggest that there is a fundamental, ineradicable measure of sex inequality which has to be recognised by society and its legislators through social arrangements and legal theories. Laws protecting women, regulations establishing hierarchies embodying the 'fact' of male dominance, must be devised. Subordination is not equated with inferiority: it involves an acceptance of a natural, unalterable 'fact of existence'. The patriarchy, argue feminist jurists, cultivates sedulously the ideology of 'subordination as necessary protection'. To attempt to combat these views is to reject what nature has ordained; the propagation of points of view which question the meanings attached to the concept of inequality necessitates flying in the face of destiny. To query the basis of discrimination, in, say, employment law, is to misunderstand 'the true nature' of men and women.

Wide acceptance of the veracity of the concept of inequality has led to the emergence within patriarchies of an ideology concerning women which reflects a wide gap between patriarchal descriptions of human nature (often underwritten by jurisprudential theory) and the true nature of women. 'Feminists,' says Patricia Smith, 'take women's humanity seriously, and jurisprudence does not because the law does not.' The Aristotelian concept of woman as 'misbegotten male', Tennyson's line, 'Woman is the lesser man', indicate patterns of thought which are alleged by feminist jurists to have surfaced in contemporary family law in relation to adoption, parental responsibility and some procedures associated with divorce. Custom and law have coalesced, it is claimed, so as to characterise men in one way and women in another, essentially inferior, way, with the result that mythology and misunderstanding concerning women are rationalised and legitimised by the patriarchal law and its institutions.

An interesting illustration of the attitudes of patriarchy in relation to social hierarchy and the law may be found in Filmer's text on absolutism, *Patriarcha*, published in 1679–80. Filmer interpreted the state as a patriarchal society under the King. Subjugation of the wife and children to the father is seen in terms of a 'divine institution'. Haslett, who edited the 1949 version of

Filmer's work, noted that the patriarchal family has been considered by many politicians and jurists as an archetype of social hierarchy; law has acted as a tool of patriarchy, he avers, with one of its tasks involving the justification of subordination of women as part of 'the natural order'. The implications of patriarchal ideology are so deeply embedded in our culture and institutions that 'male domination and patriarchal values have yet to be relegated to historical obscurity'.

It is the all-pervading nature of the ideology of patriarchy which presents feminist jurisprudence with an unusually difficult task. A sociologist associated with the movement, Dorothy Smith, writing on women's exclusion from man's culture, states:

> The universe of ideas, images and themes – the symbolic modes which are the general currency of thought – have been either produced by men or controlled by them. In so far as women's work and experience has been entered into, it has been on terms decided by men and because it has been approved by men.

The power of patriarchal ideology is so strong, say the feminist jurists, that it has permeated our culture at all levels: jurisprudence, political theory, social and economic thought, were predicated over the centuries on an acceptance of customs, principles and rationalisations which delegated different roles to men and women on the ground that nature had defined the essence of those roles. The tortuous path leading to women's political emancipation in the West was often blocked by appeals to legal precedents relying on 'cultural patterns' and a 'natural order' which enshrined a presumption of inequality. It was very difficult, and often impossible, to seek to envisage human society in terms other than those which embodied the idea of subordination of one sex as 'natural'. No manifestation of social culture – education or artistic endeavour – was entirely free from this ideology of inequality.

Not surprisingly, according to feminist jurists and political activists, revolutionary circles which might have been expected to denounce patriarchy, were themselves affected by the negative aspects of its thought. Many early feminist jurists and social reformers were disappointed in the solutions proposed by leading

Marxist jurists and political leaders for the problems arising from the phenomenon of women's exploitation which had become embedded in law. Lenin's statement in 1916 on the emancipation of women called for 'the participation of women in general productive labour ... the women will occupy the same position as men'. This declaration was viewed by feminists as not moving beyond the limited horizons of patriarchy and as suggesting a solution to women's problems exclusively in terms of male-created norms. The inability of Marxist jurists to perceive the effects of patriarchy 'across and within classes' (a phenomenon analysed by Sargent in *Women and Revolution*) seems to have alienated many feminist jurists from the jurisprudential theories of Marxist scholars. The later experiences of women under Marxist regimes seemed to validate the perceptions by feminist jurists of 'socialist equality' as a patriarchal ruse aimed at the intensification of the degree of exploitation of women by the state.

Little is to be gained by women in the important task of understanding patriarchy from a study of the literature which has been considered as embodying the principles of libertarianism – so runs an argument associated with feminist jurisprudence. Almost invariably, it is argued, the texts have been written by men from a perspective which excludes a correct understanding of the nature of women's role in society. All too often, the problems arising from subordination and institutionalised discrimination in the patriarchy are either not perceived or are studiously ignored. In *Women in Western Political Thought* (1979), Susan Okin considers the American Declaration of Independence and the Constitution. These celebrated statements of freedom have been phrased, she argues, in universal terms, but in the event they have been interpreted judicially on many occasions in the light of patriarchal ideology so that, objectively, women are excluded. 'All men are created equal' – here is a 'self-evident truth' proclaimed by the Founding Fathers. They would have been 'amused and sceptical', suggests Okin, had they been reminded that women, too, were to be considered 'equal'. In a similar vein, Okin states that there has grown up a tradition under which resounding rhetoric concerning freedom, rights, equality, often tends to exclude women explicitly or implicitly.

The pervasive nature of patriarchal thought has been examined by some jurists who have discerned a distinctive trend towards the use of 'a gendered pattern of legal language'. Lucinda Finley, in *Breaking Women's Silence in Law* (1989), reminds legal theorists that the language of the law has been defined, shaped and interpreted largely by men, so that it reflects the legal reasoning and systems of thought associated with patriarchy and its legal ideology. 'Law is a patriarchal form of reasoning, as is the philosophy of liberalism of which law (or at least post-Enlightenment Anglo-American law) is part.' Privileged males have set legal norms reflecting 'male realities'; they have expressed those norms within the framework of patriarchal Western liberalism in a linguistic framework which mirrors their background, culture and aspirations. The language of the law seeks to be 'objective', to abstract 'legal situations' from their social contexts, and to put matters in terms which relate to men 'and to which men can relate'. Recent modifications of statutory definitions of the offence of rape, in English and American law, have been described as exemplifying the limitations of patriarchal ideology which appears impervious to the growing concerns of women. Finley urges that in any consideration of legal change involving women, attention be given to the voice of reason *and* the voice of emotion. This may necessitate deliberate changes in the nature of legal discourse and the language in which it is generally couched. New modes of communicating, reasoning, evaluating, are required if the restrictive influence of patriarchal thinking and gendered language are to disappear from law. A re-examination of the terminology of the law, with the objective of removing ambiguities, erasing the traces of discriminatory attitudes, and allowing for the introduction of experiences, in the form of linguistic innovation, should be considered if legal language is to embrace the real needs of men and women who have been 'disempowered or silenced ... by the traditional [legal] discourse'.

In *The Emergence of Feminist Jurisprudence* (1986), Ann Scales argues that the carrying out of an important task is overdue, namely, the exposure of a legal language which is often used deliberately so as to express and uphold patriarchal ideology. The apparatus of formal linguistic analysis is irrelevant to this task: what is required is analysis from a feminist perspective, that is, an investigation by women of the *purpose* of language used in legal discourse within the context of contemporary patriarchal society.

Feminist jurisprudence interprets patriarchal society in unequivocal terms: it is fundamentally a society based upon a hierarchy which utilises the paradigm of law as a symbol of the authority and dominance of the male. It must be challenged in ways which necessitate a thorough examination of its origins, institutions and ideologies (particularly in relation to jurisprudence). The weakening of patriarchy will be, according to the tenets of feminist jurisprudence, a pre-requisite for the fabrication of a 'new jurisprudence' and legal institutions which will be needed for the introduction and maintenance of 'the good society' in which discrimination in social and legal practices will have disappeared.

Notes

The concept of patriarchy is discussed in *Justice Engendered* (1987), by Martha Minow; *Jurisprudence and Gender* (1988), by Robin West; and *Reconstructing Sexual Equality* (1987), by Christine Littleton. Frug's *Postmodern Legal Feminism* (1992) provides material for an understanding of the social context for theories of patriarchy.

Question 50

What are the general principles of feminist jurisprudence?

Answer plan

The feminist jurisprudence movement, which has emerged during the past 30 years, has as its aim an ideological revolution designed to overturn the intellectual basis of support for existing male-dominated political and legal structures. The rejection of patriarchal jurisprudence should be followed by a new legal theory which has been fashioned primarily by women and which recognises the need for a 'good society' in which all individuals will be able to realise 'the basic potentials of personhood'. The movement's principles include a new methodology of jurisprudential investigation. Different schools of feminist jurisprudence have appeared. The following skeleton plan is used:

Introduction – aim of abolition of patriarchy – new systems of thinking about the law – changing the institutions of the law – campaigning for empowerment – new methodology of investigation – schools of feminist jurisprudence – conclusion, moving to 'the good society'.

Answer

The feminist jurisprudence movement seems to have originated in the 1970s in the USA as a group within the Critical Legal Studies movement which was centered on the law faculty within Harvard University. It was concerned in its formative years with discussions on ways in which law might serve the American women's liberation movement. At a later date, it had written its own agenda and moved rapidly to a fundamental re-thinking of the contribution made by orthodox jurisprudence to the maintenance of a society which appeared to accept the subordination of women as a manifestation of the 'immutable laws of nature'. The movement has emerged from its earlier years, furnished with a systematic, radical approach to the analysis and transformation of a legal order which, consciously or unconsciously, perpetuates and justifies the domination of women by men. A jurisprudence based upon 'an alternative vision' is needed urgently.

A primary principle of feminist jurisprudence is acceptance of the objective of the abolition of patriarchal society, in which the dominant schools of jurisprudence ignore or reject the concept of the real equality of men and women. Feminist jurisprudence is, according to its jurists and historians, the only school of legal theory which seeks to produce an analysis and critique of legal ideology and processes as a manifestation of patriarchy. 'The virtual abolition of patriarchy is', according to Patricia Smith (see *Feminist Jurisprudence* (1993)), 'the political precondition of a truly ungendered jurisprudence'. She speaks of 'a supposedly universal jurisprudence, which is, in fact, masquerading as the objective analysis of neutral legal principles ... Much feminist jurisprudence and law are not neutral or universal, but biased in favour of the dominant culture, at the expense of all others'.

Entirely new perspectives in jurisprudence have become essential. Feminist jurisprudence aims to challenge public discourse on legal topics which is conducted almost entirely by male jurists who think and write from the perspective of men, a perspective which, in the words of Lorenne Clark, reflects 'a dominance which is assumed and asserted to be "natural", a dominance of those who are naturally stronger, freer from the grinding necessities of biological reality'. Women must re-examine their assumptions about their nature and their relationships within society; they must adopt a fundamentally different approach to the problems created by a law which assists in fostering concepts of inequality. New insights should follow on from new thinking and new perspectives. When the place of law in society is examined from the point of view of women who have experienced its inadequacies, new capacities for understanding will emerge.

The sharpening of insight will demand from women new systems of thinking about the law. Feminist jurisprudence places emphasis on the patterns of thought needed to comprehend the schematic structure of the law. New perspectives demand a recognition of relationships within structures. It is no longer sufficient to investigate concepts of inequality, or sex discrimination within employment, as 'things-in-themselves': their history, their development as features of patriarchal ideology must be made the object of research if a rounded, radical jurisprudential analysis is to be created.

Acceptance of the significance of the role of law within a patriarchy would constitute, according to Patricia Smith, 'a cultural revolution'. In such a revolution, 'what changes is what people think', and this is epitomised in radical changes in individual assumptions concerning 'normal' or 'natural' phenomena. Feminist jurisprudence accepts as a principle the radical implications of approaching investigation of the law from a new standpoint. Once one's 'world view' (in relation to society) is transformed, this is likely to lead to a re-organisation of patterns of thought so that objective reality is seen, with acuity, through a new lens. Industrial law, family law, for example, should yield new vistas, indicate novel interpretations, when analysed in the context of new doctrine.

Since feminist jurisprudence is, according to many adherents, a *'philosophy of action'*, intended to assist in the transformation of society, it must be concerned with the principle of changing the very institutions and policies of the law so as to reflect 'human needs without patriarchal bias'. Feminist jurists do not confine their activities to the university campus and the lecture circuit. Several important campaigns for change have been inspired or led by activists within the movement. In recent years, Ruth Ginsberg (now a member of the Supreme Court of the USA) planned a campaign which resulted in the courts allowing women to administer estates. Catherine Mackinnon assisted in the drafting of a statute which sought to outlaw practices related to the commercial exploitation of pornography (which she defines as 'a systematic practice of exploitation and subordination based on sex that differentially harms women'). (Andrea Dworkin's *Against the Male Flood* (1985) gives details of the draft anti-pornography law and its fate. She comments incisively: 'Women have had to prove human status before having any claim to equality. But equality has been impossible to achieve, perhaps because, really, women have not been able to prove human status. The burden of proof is on the victim.')

The principle of campaigning for empowerment has been adopted by some sections of the feminist movement. It is enunciated and analysed by Ann Scales in her essay, *The Emergence of Feminist Jurisprudence* (1986). The 'empowerment model' involves action by the legislature or court which is intended to deal with inequalities at a *structural or cultural level*. Legal judgments ought to be made *deliberately* with a view to ending manifestations of male domination. Should the presentation of a bill in the legislature, or the essence of a dispute being heard by the court, reveal that the underlying issue turns upon domination or subordination, steps should be taken so as to empower the subordinated group (for example, women). In this way, the power of the patriarchy is confronted and vitiated.

A very important feature of feminist jurisprudence is its search for an appropriate methodology of jurisprudential investigation. Jurisprudence in patriarchal society has produced methodologies of research which, because they are built upon the flawed concept of 'natural inequality', are incapable of utilisation by those seeking new perspectives. For a phenomenon to be accessible to investigation, it does not suffice that it be merely perceived; there must be in existence a theory which is prepared to accommodate it. This, it is claimed, is the weakness of patriarchal ideology and the strength of the methodology of feminist jurisprudence.

The methodology which appears to be common to the schools of feminist thought in relation to legal theory does not seek to reject the tested methods of scientific investigation: the collection and systematisation of data, the use of induction and deduction, the formulation and continuous testing of hypotheses are fundamental to the work of feminist jurisprudence. There must be, however, a high degree of concentration upon the examination of the validity of commonly-accepted ideas in law. A leading feminist jurist has suggested that the movement might take to heart the words of Einstein, in his 1916 essay on the physicist, Mach:

> Concepts which have proved useful for ordering things assume easily so great an authority for us, that we forget their terrestrial origin and accept them as unalterable facts. They then become labelled as 'conceptual necessaries', *a priori* givens, etc. The road of scientific progress is frequently blocked for long periods by such errors. It is therefore not just an idle game to exercise our ability to analyse familiar concepts, and to demonstrate the conditions on which their justification and usefulness depend, and the way in which, in special cases, they developed.

In *Feminist Legal Methods* (1990), Kathleen Bartlett suggests that legal inquiry be conducted in terms of 'the organisation of the apprehension of truth: it determines what counts as evidence and defines what is taken as verification'. Three specific methods can be employed by feminist scholars. First, 'asking the woman question'. This method of investigating problems is intended to reveal how the essence of law may be modified in ways which result in a submerging of women's perspectives. The 'gender implications' of apparently neutral and objective rules must be identified, and questions must be asked repeatedly about the possible effects of legislation upon women. It is worth considering in this context the Children Act 1989, the Child Support Acts 1991,

1995 and the Child Support, Pensions and Social Security Act 2000.

A second method relates to so called 'feminist practical reasoning'. This aims to take into account women's alleged 'sensitivity to situation and context' and to draw upon women's powers of abstraction. It has been suggested, for example, that research into the effects of the law of provocation might have been qualitatively improved had women been asked to contribute to discussions on this area of the law from their own specific experiences.

A third method involves 'consciousness-raising'. This technique offers a means of testing the validity of accepted legal principles when viewed 'through the lens of experience' as where, for example, legislation relating to domestic violence or desertion is considered.

A number of schools of feminist jurisprudence have emerged, each stressing specific *principles of inquiry* and *modes of investigation*. *Liberal feminism* emphasises the need for a concentration of activity on equal rights and opportunities and the heightening of constitutional rights. The principle of this school of thought is the extension of rights by building upon a stratum of rights which have been won. Whatever formal barriers are preventing the full participation of women in all aspects of society must be removed so that equal opportunity for all might prevail. The task demands a long, arduous programme, but there is no other way to the attainment of full equality. *Radical feminism* concentrates on women *as a class*, as contrasted with the individual woman who is the concern of liberal feminist ideology. Women's specific problems as workers must be emphasised and an unremitting struggle against the legal ideology which seeks to minimise the effect of these problems must be waged.

Cultural feminism stresses the importance of changing legal and social conditions so as to give equal weight to 'woman's moral voice'. Relationships between mother and child and concepts of equality within the family group must be stressed in appropriate ideological controversies. *Post-modern feminism* denies the value of any theory of equality which seeks to portray women as 'a group'; the differing psychological needs of women must be reflected in legal ideology and legal rules. In Patricia Smith's words: 'For postmodern feminists, there is no "single solution" and no "single oppression of women", but only solutions tailored to 'the concrete experience of actual people.'

Marxist jurisprudential feminism seeks to apply the Marxist canons of interpretation of history to women's problems. These are to be analysed as part of the wider group of problems arising from women's economic position as workers. Women's problems will disappear only when class divisions have disappeared. Opposition within the feminist jurisprudence movement to alliances with Marxist jurisprudence groups has been strong and is summarised by Elizabeth Grosz in her essay *Marxism and Feminism* (1991): 'The political and institutional power of Marxism is such that any feminism can only be tolerated in so far as it accepts Marxism's fundamental premises and modes of thinking. This amounts to a form of subjugation that can never provide the space for developing theories and practices independently.'

The goal of feminist jurisprudence is 'the good society' which is characterised by an absence of discrimination and inequalities and the presence of institutions and ideologies which proclaim the worth and dignity of all men and women. Movement towards that goal involves an unremitting struggle based upon an interpretation of law from entirely new perspectives: this is the task of those committed to creating and utilising the principles of a feminist jurisprudence. If law stands for justice, argues Patricia Smith, it must be justice for all; but the fact is that law has been notoriously bad in providing justice for persons outside the dominant culture. The principles of feminist jurisprudence have been fashioned, and must be applied, in the name of 'legal outsiders'.

Notes

A Reader in Feminist Knowledge (1994), edited by Sneja Gunew, provides a background to feminist thought. Professor Patricia Smith's anthology of classic essays in this area, *Feminist Jurisprudence* (1993), is of much interest. Her short essay, 'Feminist jurisprudence', in *A Companion to Philosophy of Law*, edited by Patterson (1999), is a useful introduction to the subject area. Professor Frances Olsen's *Feminist Legal Theory* (1984) examines a variety of topics which are fundamental to the feminist perception of law and its place in society. *Justice and Gender,* by Rhode (1997), comments on aspects of the workings of the judicial system in relation to women in society. Hilaire Barnett's *Sourcebook on Feminist Jurisprudence* (1997) provides valuable background information. Iris Marion Young's *Justice and the Politics of Difference* (1990) explores arguments of a jurisprudential nature concerning the oppression of women.

Index

A

Adler,	89, 92
Affirmative action,	301
Allegory,	321
Allen,	151, 183, 303
American jurisprudence, contemporary,	259–88, 296–301
Dworkin,	296–301
Nozick,	265–71
Posner,	272–79
Rawls,	259–65
Unger,	280–88
American realism,	239–58
Cardozo,	252–58
Gray,	245–51
Holmes,	239–44
Analogy, use of,	17, 148, 207, 282
A priori thinking,	103, 296
Aquinas,	68–72
law, divisions of,	70–71
natural law, essence of,	71
neo-Scholasticism and,	92, 93
neo-Thomism and,	88
Aristotle,	28–33
government, on,	32
law, on,	29, 31–33
logic,	15
Arnold,	1, 2
Austin,	146–58, 246–47
criticisms of,	152–58, 246–47
law as command,	52, 147–49, 246
laws, types of,	148
psychology, and,	146–52
sanctions, on,	149
sovereignty, on,	150
Ayer,	141

B

Base and superstructure theory,	214, 215
Beccaria,	118
Bentham,	118–23, 131
criminal law, on,	120
felicific calculus, on,	119
jurisprudence, on,	141
punishment, on,	118–22
utilitarianism, and,	118–19
Berman,	200, 287–88

C

Cardozo,	252–58
judicial process, on,	253–57
precedent, and,	255
Carnap,	141
Categorical imperative,	75, 104–05
Childe,	188
Cicero,	33–39
duty, on,	38
law, essence of,	37–38
natural law,	36–37
philosophy, and,	34, 36
state, on,	35–36
Class instrumentalism,	214–15, 219
Commands, law as,	148–49, 234–38, 246
Communitarianism and law,	281–82, 285
Comte,	142
Critical Legal Studies,	282–84, 287, 305, 339

D

Dabin,	89, 90
Death, definitions of,	312–13
Definition, problems of,	8–13, 242

Printed in the United Kingdom
by Lightning Source UK Ltd.
123682UK00001BA/16-24/A

Q & A SERIES
JURISPRUDENCE

THIRD EDITION

Cavendish
Publishing
Limited

London • Sydney

TITLES IN THE Q&A SERIES

'A' LEVEL LAW

BUSINESS LAW

CIVIL LIBERTIES

COMMERCIAL LAW

COMPANY LAW

CONFLICT OF LAWS

CONSTITUTIONAL & ADMINISTRATIVE LAW

CONTRACT LAW

CRIMINAL LAW

EMPLOYMENT LAW

ENGLISH LEGAL SYSTEM

EQUITY & TRUSTS

EUROPEAN UNION LAW

EVIDENCE

FAMILY LAW

INTELLECTUAL PROPERTY LAW

INTERNATIONAL TRADE LAW

JURISPRUDENCE

LAND LAW

PUBLIC INTERNATIONAL LAW

REVENUE LAW

SUCCESSION, WILLS & PROBATE

TORTS LAW